FEARFUL SPIRITS, REASONED FOLLIES

FEARFUL SPIRITS, REASONED FOLLIES

THE BOUNDARIES OF SUPERSTITION IN LATE MEDIEVAL EUROPE

MICHAEL D. BAILEY

CORNELL UNIVERSITY PRESS

Ithaca and London

First published 2013 by Cornell University Press

Printed in the United States of America

Library of Congress Cataloging-in-Publication Data

Bailey, Michael David, 1971–
    Fearful spirits, reasoned follies: the boundaries of superstition in late medieval Europe / Michael D. Bailey.
        p. cm.
    Includes bibliographical references and index.
    ISBN 978-0-8014-5144-7 (cloth: alk. paper)
    1. Superstition—Europe—History. 2. Superstition—Religious aspects—Catholic Church—History.
    3. Civilization, Medieval. I. Title.
    GR135.B35   2013
    398'.41094—dc23   2012033791

Cornell University Press strives to use environmentally responsible suppliers and materials to the fullest extent possible in the publishing of its books. Such materials include vegetable-based, low-VOC inks and acid-free papers that are recycled, totally chlorine-free, or partly composed of nonwood fibers. For further information, visit our website at www.cornellpress.cornell.edu.

Cloth printing   10 9 8 7 6 5 4 3 2 1

To the memory of my aunt

❦ CONTENTS

❧ ACKNOWLEDGMENTS

Books are curious things. Who can say exactly where their histories begin? The idea for this book should have been obvious. I first encountered late medieval debates about superstition while researching emerging ideas of witchcraft in the fifteenth century. As other scholars have noted, and as I argue here, concern over superstition fed into concern over witchcraft. My next project was staring me in the face. But I was tired of witchcraft and magic and the theologians who codified and condemned them, so I looked away.

That didn't last long.

In the fall of 2003, soon after my book on witchcraft had appeared, I began a fellowship year at the University of Pennsylvania, which holds among its special collections the only manuscript copy in North America of the important early fifteenth-century treatise *On Superstitions*, written by the Heidelberg theologian Nikolaus of Jauer. So I am, rather romantically, going to extend the roots of this book back to 1877, when the indefatigable collector of ecclesiastical and inquisitorial texts Henry Charles Lea acquired that codex for his personal library, later donated by his children to the university. For as I sat in the Rare Book & Manuscript Reading Room atop Penn's Van Pelt Library, working my way through that treatise and other material on medieval superstition, I decided that there was indeed another book I wanted to write.

For financial support, crucial time to read and think, and stimulating environments in which to do so, I thank the University of Pennsylvania and its Humanities Forum, where this project began in earnest, and the University of Wisconsin–Madison and its Institute for Research in the Humanities, where I did most of the writing. In between, the Alexander von Humboldt Foundation supported essential research in Europe, and the Monumenta Germaniae Historica welcomed me (again) into its halls and its wonderful library. The manuscript research for this book was conducted mainly amid the riches of the Bayerische Staatsbibliothek. For those occasions when I needed to look beyond Munich, I am grateful to librarians at the Staats- und Stadtbibliothek in Augsburg, Staatsbibliothek in Berlin, Sächsische Landesbibliothek—Staats- und Universitätsbibliothek in Dresden, Bibliothèque nationale de France in Paris, Stadtbibliothek in Trier, and Biblioteka Uniwersytecka in Wrocław. In the United States, I have drawn on special collections at Cornell University, the University of Pennsylvania, and the University of Wisconsin–Madison, as well as the Vatican Film Library at Saint Louis University. The general collections and interlibrary loan services of Penn, Wisconsin, and the Parks Library at Iowa State University have been invaluable.

Over the years, I have presented ideas and arguments related to this project, and gained valuable feedback, at the Akademia Świętokrzyska in Kielce, the German Historical Institute in Paris, the Newberry Library in Chicago, and the Universities of Essex, Iowa, Konstanz, Lausanne, Mannheim, Pennsylvania, and Wisconsin. My thanks go to the audiences and especially the organizers of all those talks, seminars, and symposia. In particular, the communities of fellows at Penn's Humanities Forum (class of 2003–4) and Wisconsin's Institute for Research in the Humanities (class of 2010–11) contributed tremendously to my ideas and their expression. At Iowa State University, the Center for Excellence in Arts and Humanities provided funding that allowed for productive summer work, and the history department and College of Liberal Arts and Sciences allowed me several research leaves to make use of the resources listed above.

Also at Iowa State, Kevin Amidon, Jana Byars, Sara Gregg, David Hollander, Jeff Houghtby, John Monroe, Leonard Sadosky, and Matthew Stanley all talked through ideas with me or commented on work in various forms. At Wisconsin, Susan Friedman helped me think more clearly about modernity. Daniel Hobbins, at the University of Notre Dame, generously read a draft chapter, as well as taught me an enormous amount about late medieval intellectual culture through his own scholarship. Jimmy Mixson, at the University of Alabama, and I have been conspiring to figure out the fifteenth century for well over a decade now. Louisa Burnham, Jennifer Kolpacoff Deane, and Samantha Kelly have been helping me be a better historian for even longer. In Europe, Krzysztof Bracha, Sabine von Heusinger, Georg Modestin, Martine Ostorero, and Kathrin Utz Tremp have shown me great hospitality, collegiality, and friendship. At assorted conferences and symposia (as well as bars, cafés, and dining tables) Willem de Blécourt, David Collins, Tamar Herzig, Gábor Klaniczay, Ann Matter, Erik Midelfort, William Monter, Michael Ryan, Maryse Simon, Walter Stephens, Laura Stokes, Julien Véronèse, and Rita Voltmer have all contributed ideas or inspiration to this project. Christian Lohmer, Alexander Patschovsky, and Herbert Schneider made the Monumenta and Munich a more inviting place. Barbara and Charles Bowlus provided an excellent place to live, as well as their own good company for much of my time in Munich/Oberschleißheim. Lillian Lee and Jon Kleinberg put a roof over my head for a quick but valuable trip to Ithaca, NY. I thank them all.

My debt to Richard Kieckhefer and Edward Peters, my masters in the field of medieval magic, is immense. Regarding superstition, Euan Cameron's *Enchanted Europe*, which appeared as I was writing, provided me broad shoulders on which to stand. Robert Lerner gets credit for long ago handing me a copy of an article he had written about Werner of Friedberg, introducing me to a remarkably rich and multilayered case of late medieval superstition to which I have been returning every since. Richard and Robert both read full drafts of this book, which improved greatly because of their comments. I was delighted that Laura Smoller, my master in all things astrological, read the entire manuscript for Cornell University Press. Her insights and suggestions proved invaluable. My thanks go also to the other, anonymous, Press reader, who reinforced a number of Laura's points and made many good points of her/his own. Finally, at the Press I must thank Peter Potter, who saw the book through from initial idea to final product, and all the other members of the editorial and production staff who made the final product what it is.

My aunt Ambriel Carpenter, who gave me the Saint Joseph the Realtor kit discussed in the prologue, died just as I was completing the final draft of this book. She would have been pleased to find her gift mentioned in its opening.

✿ Note on Names and Titles

Most of the men who figure prominently in this book belonged to an international intellectual culture. They typically wrote in Latin, which was the lingua franca of their professional lives. Nevertheless, I have generally given their names in what I deem to be an appropriate vernacular form, such as Nicolau Eymerich for the Catalan inquisitor, Nicole Oresme for the Parisian scholar, and Nikolaus of Dinkelsbühl for the Viennese theologian. This is a debatable business, since borders both political and linguistic were different in the fourteenth and fifteenth centuries, and some of these men spent most of their working lives in regions other than those in which they were born. Poles may well object that in this book Mikołaj of Jawor is called Nikolaus of Jauer, but at the time Jauer was in a relatively Germanized area of Silesia, and in any event Nikolaus was educated in Prague and then taught in Heidelberg. Likewise the Dutch may question why Hendrik of Gorinchem is here Heinrich of Gorkum, but he spent his career in Cologne. Whenever a standard English version of a name exists, however, I use that: hence Thomas Aquinas and William of Auvergne (rather than Tommaso or Guillaume). Likewise with place names: Strassburg rather than Strasbourg, because it was in all ways a German city in the late medieval period, yet Cologne instead of Köln, because the former is standard in English. I have also translated all titles into English, except when no clear equivalent exists for a Latin term, or in rare cases when a Latin title has become relatively standard in English, such as the canon *Episcopi*.

✍ ABBREVIATIONS

Major fourteenth- and fifteenth-century texts addressing superstition are cited by author and short title, with full bibliographical information appearing in the appendix. Other abbreviations are as follows:

AHR	*American Historical Review*
BSB	Bayerische Staatsbibliothek
CCCM	Corpus Christianorum Continuatio Mediaevalis
CCSL	Corpus Christianorum Series Latina
CLHM	Cahiers Lausannois d'Histoire Médiévale
CSEL	Corpus Scriptorum Ecclesiasticorum Latinorum
EETS	Early English Text Society
MGH	Monumenta Germaniae Historica
ML	Micrologus' Library
MRW	*Magic, Ritual, and Witchcraft*
OC	Jean Gerson, *Oeuvres complètes*, ed. P. Glorieux, 10 vols. (Paris, 1960–73)
PL	Patrologiae Cursus Completus Series Latina
Quellen	*Quellen und Untersuchungen zur Geschichte des Hexenwahns und der Hexenverfolgung im Mittelalter*, ed. Joseph Hansen (1901; reprint, Hildesheim, 1963)

Prologue

It is difficult to fix the boundaries of superstition. A Frenchman traveling in Italy finds nearly everything superstitious, and is not far wrong.

—Voltaire, *Philosophical Dictionary*

Irreverence/is a greater oaf than Superstition.

—W. H. Auden, "Moon Landing"

For an icon of numinous power, it was humble enough. The figure of Saint Joseph was barely three inches long. Its simple, white, stamped-plastic form fit easily in my palm. Yet it promised to draw down the grace of an almighty deity and sway the will of my fellow human beings so that I could achieve a desired goal. Specifically, if I buried the statue in my front yard, Joseph, patron saint of homes and home life, would exert his celestial influence to help me sell my house.

Like almost everything else in the modern Western world, Joseph's power has been packaged and marketed. The small figure I held in my hand came as part of a kit, one of several varieties of Saint Joseph home-selling aids readily found in religious retail outlets or on the Internet. As with any modern gadget, it included an information sheet containing basic operating instructions. According to this, the rite to invoke Joseph's heavenly assistance consisted of a single essential element: burial of his figurine in the yard of the house that one wanted to sell. Then came numerous possible variations. Some people chose to bury the statue upside down, while some buried it right-side up. Some interred Joseph facing away from the house, others toward it. Some preferred to place him near the curb, so that his power could attract prospective buyers, while others thought he should be situated near the for-sale sign, presumably so that he might empower it in some way. While certain people covered him with only a thin layer of soil, others planted him six inches or more into the earth. I did not have to face such fearsome choices myself, for I had no house to sell at that time and no intention of using Joseph for his packaged purpose. I had instead received the statue as a gift and something of a gag. My work involved researching late medieval superstitions, and here was the modern merchandising of a seemingly superstitious rite. In fact, as I considered the mechanistic ways in which the small statue could be used, as well as the somewhat caution-ary tone of the instructions, I was struck by how much they resonated with practices and concerns I knew from centuries past.

Superstitions surround us in the modern world. We knock on wood and avoid black cats, carry lucky rabbits' feet and read our horoscopes. Or at least we know people who do these things. While statues of Joseph are undoubt-edly employed mainly, if not exclusively, by people who revere him as a saint, superstitious acts are in no way limited to tradition-minded Catholics or even to religiously inclined people in general. Embedded in the floor just inside the main entrance of the student union at the profoundly secular state university where I work (a university "of science and technology" no less) is a large zodiac relief. Entering and leaving the building, most students and more than a few faculty members deliberately divert their course around the inlay, the tradition being that those who tread on it will fail their next exam or suffer some equivalent calamity. Many schools have such supersti-tions. Freshmen at the University of Michigan are not supposed to step on a large brass "M" set in a central campus plaza lest they fail their first college exam. Princeton undergraduates avoid leaving campus through the main FitzRandolph gate, the legend being that they will not graduate with their class if they do so. Visitors to Harvard Yard may rub the foot of the John Harvard statue there in order to attract good luck, while a statue of Abraham Lincoln at the University of Wisconsin–Madison is not only rubbed for luck but is said to rise from its seat in the presence of a virgin. Surveys have found that even in the late twentieth and early twenty-first centuries nearly 70 percent of U.S. college students manifest some kind of superstitious be-lief or practice, especially pertaining to luck on exams, dating, sports, and so forth.[1] For most who perform them, these are very casual rituals, done more from an automatic observance of tradition or simply as a source of fun rather than from any deep belief in their efficacy, and no university officials appear

---

1. George Gmelch and Richard Felson, "Can a Lucky Charm Get You through Organic Chem-istry?" *Psychology Today,* December 1980, 75–78; Jerry M. Lewis and Timothy J. Gallagher, "The Salience of Friday the 13th for College Studies," *College Student Journal* 32 (2001): 216–22.

to object to them. Yet some modern authorities working in the natural and social sciences can and do regard superstitions as dangerous and corrupting. In their contention that adherence to such acts engenders erroneous perceptions of cause and effect and prevents people from understanding how the world really works, they are not altogether unlike a long line of medieval authorities who regularly castigated superstitious behavior and the people who engaged in it.

I might, therefore, have begun this book with almost any example of modern superstition, but the rite of Saint Joseph the Realtor is particularly apt. This is not so much because it is a religious or a Catholic rite per se, but because the marketers of the little statue felt compelled to establish certain boundaries as clearly as they could, articulating at some length how to use their product in a proper, non-"magical" manner. After carefully listing all the variant forms of the burial rite, the instruction sheet that accompanied my Joseph statue then sternly warned me that none of these details were particularly important or meaningful. What mattered would be my faith in the saint himself. The power that would help me sell my house did not lie in a buried bit of plastic or in any ritual I might perform with it, but would flow from God on account of my devotion to his saint. If I did not understand the real nature of this operation, the directions continued, then whatever I might do with my Joseph statue would only be so much "hocus-pocus," "magic," and "superstition." As I read these warnings, I could not help but note how similar they sounded to some of the injunctions found in detailed medieval treatises on superstition written by theologians, canon lawyers, and other religious and intellectual authorities more than half a millennium ago.

While medieval conceptions of superstition could be quite different from those one might typically encounter today, continuities still exist, as Saint Joseph's statue and its instructional packaging both exemplify. Medieval Christians frequently employed devotional objects in rites intended to invoke or supplicate divine help or protection, just as some modern believers now do when confronting a flat real estate market. And medieval authorities frequently expressed concern about incorrect beliefs and improper understanding of what constituted real, effective action, just as psychologists and scientists do now when they bemoan popular credence in superstitions generally. Of course, significant changes have occurred over the centuries, especially with respect to the consequences of superstitious beliefs or behaviors. Today superstition is generally seen as something silly or inefficacious. My statue's instruction sheet told me how I should properly comprehend the rite it urged me to perform, but it did not threaten any serious repercussions if I proceeded improperly, beyond the implication that Saint Joseph would not then intercede with the Almighty to help me get a good selling price. For medieval authorities, a lapse into superstition could be a much more dangerous transgression. A rite intended as a pious devotion but incorrectly understood or enacted could desecrate a sacred object. Worse still, rather than simply proving impotent, the rite might inadvertently invoke diabolical power instead of divine grace, thereby opening the door to (tacit) heresy, demon worship, and apostasy. The consequences of what we might consider "scientific" misconceptions—errors in understanding or manipulating natural forces in the physical world—could also be more serious than simple inefficacy, for the physical and spiritual worlds were generally held to be much more tightly interwoven in those days.

Acknowledging these important differences, I nevertheless want to stress a fact about human nature that was perhaps more clearly evident in the medieval era but that remains true in our own, namely that how people understand metaphysical forces—divine and also demonic power, miracles and magic—and the manner in which they believe that these forces operate in the physical world, interacting with and potentially surpassing the forces of nature and the laws of science, affects their lives and shapes their actions in ways grand and transcendental but also common and quotidian. Examining such beliefs and actions is vital to understanding any culture, past or present, and their change over time is a crucial element in history. Indeed, many conceptions of modern Western culture and the very concept of Western "modernity" deployed by many academic disciplines often rest on the perceived historical development that the German sociologist Max Weber termed the "disenchantment of the world," that is, the gradual stripping away of all putatively "magical" or "superstitious" elements from religion and the eventual triumph of "scientific" rationalism as the primary means to understand the operations of the material world.

Scholars have spilled gallons of ink debating what exactly disenchantment entails and when exactly it may have occurred. The very prevalence of such debates about modernity's disenchanted state, however, sometimes lends credence to the simplistic and simply incorrect notion that modern culture has completely severed itself from its magically besotted past through some grand moment of sudden and absolute transformation—the Reformation, the Scientific Revolution, and the Enlightenment are the watersheds most frequently suggested. Moreover, the notion can fester that the magical beliefs and superstitions of the premodern world represent unfathomably ancient traditions that endured essentially unchanged and unaffected by the dynamics of history until some singular instance of disenchantment swept them away. That, too, is undeniably wrong. Beliefs and actions labeled as superstitious have shifted continually, and sometimes dramatically, over time, as have the levels of concern that such superstitions have evoked.

In Europe beginning in the late medieval period debate about the nature and consequences of superstitious beliefs and practices raged particularly fiercely. By categorizing and controlling superstition, church authorities sought to promote what they regarded as proper religious devotion, but also to regulate legitimate scientific inquiry, appropriate medical practices, methods of prognostication and prediction, and correct understanding of both the spiritual and the physical worlds. Discussing superstition required them to address fundamental questions about the operation of divine power in the world, the scope of demonic malevolence, and the existence and potency of a multitude of entirely natural forces potentially infusing material creation. They vigorously contested whether and how humans might access and manipulate such power through words, ritual actions, specially crafted objects, and natural substances. All these issues continued to figure significantly in the intellectual discourse of the Protestant Reformation, Catholic counterreform, Scientific Revolution, and Enlightenment. By focusing our attention prior to any of those putative great moments of historical disenchantment, however, we can disentangle the issues surrounding superstition, the debates they engendered, and the developments they underwent from potentially distracting discussions of "progress" and "modernity" (although inevitably the specter of modernity will hover over this entire book, and will be addressed at length in the final chapter). My purpose here is to explore late medieval conceptions of and concerns about superstition in their own context, and in all their complexity, regarding them as important and illuminating in their own right, while still recalling that medieval developments in these areas helped set the stage for much of the reform, revolution, and self-proclaimed enlightenment to come.

As L. P. Hartley famously wrote in his novel *The Go-Between*, "the past is a foreign country: they do things differently there." Yet the past is also inescapably the country to which we all trace our ancestry. In a period of European history often regarded as a "late" medieval era teetering on the brink of some kind of early modernity, issues of superstition that we might now regard as foolish or frivolous could be debated with great seriousness and fearful consequence. The beliefs and practices of that foreign world, however, are not absolutely severed from our own. The story of late medieval superstitions, the beliefs they encoded and the fears they elicited, and how these changed or remained stable in the face of other historical developments is part of the story of how Europe, and Western culture writ large, moved slowly toward what is now perceived as its modern condition: in some sense defined by a rejection of magic and the supernatural but never completely disenchanted, in which certain people may still firmly believe that burying a statue of Saint Joseph can help them sell a house, but also in which they remain careful to distinguish that act, in their own understanding, from any kind of improper or foolish superstition.

Introduction

The Meanings of Medieval Superstition

> The attitude of the late medieval mind towards super-
> stition, that is witchcraft and magic, is quite vacilla-
> tory and fluid. The age is not quite as helplessly given
> to all this witchcraft madness as one is tempted to
> conclude given its general credulity and lack of
> critical thinking.
>
> —Johan Huizinga, *The Autumn of the Middle Ages*

At the dawn of the fifteenth century, a boy living in the central Rhineland near the episcopal city of Speyer had hurt his finger. His mother wanted to know whether she might use a certain blessing (*segen*, in the German vernacular) to help relieve his suffering. A local cleric said no, apparently deeming this practice to be erroneous and illicit. In the nearby town of Landau, however, the woman found another clergyman who knew of such "superstitious blessings" (*benediciones supersticiosas*, as rendered in the Latin record of his case), generally approved of them, and had even used them successfully to heal himself on one occasion.[1] At the very end of the fifteenth century or early in the next, near the city of Pamplona in what was then the small, Pyrenees-straddling kingdom of Navarre, people turned to their local clergy in times of drought, begging them to hold a procession in honor of the apostle Peter, perform a Mass to specially consecrate a statue of the saint, and then immerse it in holy water in order to bring rain. Other clergy, however, wondered if by this action they sank into the sin of idolatry or superstition.[2] In 1349 a renegade Aragonese prince supposedly relied on

---

1. Werner of Friedberg, *Revocatio* (in German), 198r; Werner, *Responsiones* (in Latin), 280.
2. Martin of Arles, *De superstitionibus*, 3r: "Utrum in hoc commitatur aliquod peccatum secundum idolatrie, superstitionis, vel alterius huiusmodi?"

astrologers to determine the optimal moment to wage war on his brother the king and ended up dead on the battlefield, a victim of false and superstitious divination. In the early 1400s in London, an educated physician crafted an astrological image out of gold and used it to treat his patients. Similar astral talismans were employed by university medical faculties in both Paris and Montpellier, but were decried as superstitions by other, equally highly placed academics. Also in Paris, in the mid-fourteenth century, the future king Charles V assembled an enormous library of astrological texts, to the consternation of at least some of his courtiers, who feared the superstitious potential of this art. Earlier at the French court, suspicions had flourished that another king, Philip V (d. 1322), had been bewitched by his mother-in-law, who used love potions to keep him enamored with her daughter and so under her control. Many in the court of the later monarch Charles VI (d. 1422), who suffered prolonged bouts of madness, were certain that he was the victim of some sorcery, perhaps at the hands of Valentina Visconti, the seductive Italian wife of a powerful French duke. While some sought to cure the king by magical rites, others feared that those attempts veered into superstition every bit as vile as the sorcery that caused the original affliction. Similarly, in Avignon a hundred years earlier the austere and energetic (some might say cold and combative) pope John XXII (reigned 1316–34) accused the bishop of his hometown of Cahors of trying to murder him through sorcery, and issued many pronouncements against the "superstitious pestilence" of demonic magic and divination.[3]

All of these incidents, which will receive more attention in later chapters, were discussed in the fourteenth and fifteenth centuries by writers addressing the topic of superstition. That charged and accusatory term could mean many things in medieval Europe, and the examples above illustrate some of the range it could encompass, particularly in the late Middle Ages. Superstitious beliefs and practices were evident at all social levels, from laity to clergy and from commoner to king. Not just uneducated peasants but also university professors could succumb to superstition (although typically in different ways). The spectrum of broad categories in which superstitious actions might manifest, or into which superstitious beliefs or behaviors might be grouped, extended from magical rites and religious ritual to natural philosophy and medicine. Moreover, superstition might provoke quite varied reactions and elicit very different levels of concern depending on where it manifested and who perceived it to exist. Medieval clerical authorities in

---

3. *Quellen*, 2–8.

particular (and most intellectual authorities in the Middle Ages were, by virtue of the ecclesiastical domination of education, clerics of some kind) often regarded superstition with great consternation, recognizing in many superstitious actions the terrible danger that they might, or inevitably would, invoke the power of demons and bind their perhaps unwitting practitioners to the forces of hell.

Even amid such terrible concerns, however, there was room for mirth. The great father of the early church Augustine of Hippo, for example, had declared in his endlessly influential discussion of superstition from *On Christian Doctrine* (*De doctrina Christiana*) that superstitious arts would entangled humans with demons "as if by a pact of faithless and deceitful friendship," and so "must be utterly repudiated and shunned by a Christian."[4] He also, however, derided the countless "utterly inane observances" to which many people pointlessly adhered, and he allowed himself to chuckle at the Roman statesman Cato's quip that while many people took it as some kind of omen if they found that mice had gnawed on their shoes in the night, the real portent would be if shoes were found to have gnawed on the mice.[5] More than a millennium after Augustine's death in 430, the zealous German witch-hunter Heinrich Kramer described how witches could seem to snatch men's penises right off their bodies, storing them in large chests or even stashing them in birds' nests. Most contemporary fifteenth-century theorists of witchcraft agreed that demonic power could destroy fertility and sexual functioning, and could also create deceptive illusions. The bit about penises in trees, however, probably derived from bawdy Italian humor. Male genitalia had been associated with birds at least since Boccaccio's description of a father who discovered his daughter asleep with her lover, still grasping his "nightingale" in her hand. It seems that Kramer did not get the joke.[6]

Apparent dichotomies abound in the arena of medieval superstition: high and low culture, the spiritual and the scientific, the serious and the frivolous. These complexities are often glossed over, however, by the common perception of the medieval period as a pervasively and somehow uniformly superstitious age. My primary contention in this book is that the debate

---

4. Augustine, *De doctrina Christiana* 2.23(36), ed. Joseph Martin, CCSL 32 (Turnhout, 1962): "Omnes igitur artes huiusmodi uel nugatoriae uel noxiae superstitionis ex quadam pestifera societate hominum et daemonum quasi pacta infidelis et dolosae amicitiae constituta penitus sunt repudianda et fugienda christiano."

5. Ibid., 2.20(31).

6. Walter Stephens, *Demon Lovers: Witchcraft, Sex, and the Crisis of Belief* (Chicago, 2002), 303–4; Boccaccio, *Decameron* 5.4.

over superstition that raged in the late Middle Ages was considerably more multifaceted and nuanced than common perceptions admit or even than much previous scholarship has generally acknowledged. In fact, a driving force behind that debate was the mercurial nature of superstition and the variability of meaning that the term and the underlying notion could convey. Put simply, superstition meant different things to different people, and many kinds of thought or action could be deemed superstitious, sometimes to quite different effect. This variability of meaning went largely unacknowledged by contemporary writers and critics, who typically sought to present themselves as being completely certain and stable in their understanding of the topic, but it shaped the contours of their thought in critical ways. In this book I trace several strands of that thought, exploring the various meanings of superstition and the major ways in which mainly clerical authorities used the term over the course of the fourteenth and fifteenth centuries in order to bring greater clarity to their debate as it unfolded and to cast some new light on the important developments that conceptions and concerns about superstition underwent in this period.

The broad outlines of the story told here will be familiar to experts. The fourteenth and fifteenth centuries witnessed rising concern about magical and superstitious practices across Western Christendom on the part of theologians and magistrates, as well as popes, princes, and preachers.[7] Some of this concern had to do with academic authorities' efforts to define a category of "natural magic" that drew on hidden forces in the material world and to prescribe the limits of its legitimate use. Much more anxiety, however, stemmed from their conviction that most magic, especially what they eventually framed as diabolical witchcraft, involved some kind of interaction with demons and functioned only because of their malevolent power. Many scholars have noted a heightened fear of the devil in late medieval Europe and increased anxieties about demons as active and menacing figures in all areas of life.[8] Authorities also worried about the difficulties they faced in "discerning spirits"; that is, correctly identifying demonic activity, mainly in cases of possession, as opposed to divine inspiration and

---

7. For an overview, see Michael D. Bailey, *Magic and Superstition in Europe: A Concise History from Antiquity to the Present* (Lanham, Md., 2007), 107–40.

8. Jeffrey Burton Russell, *Lucifer: The Devil in the Middle Ages* (Ithaca, N.Y., 1984), 274–301; Peter Dinzelbacher, *Angst im Mittelalter: Teufels-, Todes- und Gotteserfahrung; Mentalitätsgeschichte und Ikonographie* (Paderborn, 1996), 100–132; Robert Muchembled, *A History of the Devil from the Middle Ages to the Present*, trans. Jean Birrell (Cambridge, 2003), 21–27; Alain Boureau, *Satan the Heretic: The Birth of Demonology in the Medieval West*, trans. Teresa Lavender Fagan (Chicago, 2006).

rapture.[9] Here concern extended to the realm of sometimes quite extravagant mysticism but also to a range of common devotional behaviors, often piously intended but which might nevertheless be perceived as excessive or inappropriate.

Superstition figured in all these areas of contention and debate. It was, in fact, among the most versatile, broadly applicable terms that Christian authorities used to establish boundaries between licit and illicit action, as well as between proper and improper belief. Studying superstition, therefore, affords us a valuable overview of a substantial range of late medieval thought and culture, and allows us to see the similarities and in many cases interconnections between different areas. For example, many scholars, including myself, have linked the idea of diabolical witchcraft developing in the fifteenth century to notions of a distinctly elite, learned form of demonic magic known as necromancy.[10] Others have drawn connections between necromancy and astrology, alchemy, or other elite magical practices. Aside from general surveys of all medieval magic, however, only rarely are all these areas of concern and condemnation treated together.[11] Nevertheless, a clearly connected rhetoric of superstition weaves through them all in the works of late medieval writers. By following that connecting thread, we will gain both a fuller perspective and deeper insights. The devil here (so to speak) will be in the details. Rather than entirely overturning existing narratives, I want to expose the complexities and sometimes even competing trajectories of thought and concern that ultimately drove those narratives and the important historical changes they encompass.

Undeniably the most powerful and enduring overall narrative in the history of European magic and superstition would be the progression from an "enchanted" premodern period rife with superstitious thinking to a supposedly "disenchanted" modernity governed by scientific reason. That paradigm weighs particularly heavily on studies of the late medieval and early modern centuries, when various aspects of this great transition are mainly supposed to have occurred. Nevertheless, an important trend in "magical"

---

9. Nancy Caciola, *Discerning Spirits: Divine and Demonic Possession in the Middle Ages* (Ithaca, N.Y., 2003); Dyan Elliott, *Proving Woman: Female Spirituality and Inquisitional Culture in the Later Middle Ages* (Princeton, N.J., 2004).

10. Michael D. Bailey, "From Sorcery to Witchcraft: Clerical Conceptions of Magic in the Later Middle Ages," *Speculum* 76 (2001): 960–90; Bailey, *Battling Demons: Witchcraft, Heresy, and Reform in the Late Middle Ages* (University Park, Pa., 2003), esp. 32–46.

11. Richard Kieckhefer, *Magic in the Middle Ages* (Cambridge, 1989); Jean-Patrice Boudet, *Entre science et nigromance: Astrologie, divination et magie dans l'Occident médiéval (XIIe–XVe siècle)* (Paris, 2006).

scholarship now argues against any simple decline of magic or eradication of superstition by a steadily advancing tide of modern rationality. Instead such scholarship points to more nuanced transformations in levels of serious belief in supernatural or occult forces, consternation over their potential consequences, and condemnations of their use. These transformations need not be linear or progressive in the sense of inevitably moving toward what is generally considered to be the modern condition. As one historian of these developments has insightfully noted, it may be more useful to think of oscillating "cycles of desacralization and resacralization, disenchantment and re-enchantment."[12] But even that valuable schema sets historical developments in modern terms. To better understand these processes in the past, we must pay attention to the actual language past authorities most regularly used to define the boundaries between what we then chart as the sacral or the secular, the magical or the disenchanted.

Even the notion of oscillation rarely does justice to the complexity of actual historical change. This is especially true with a topic so inherently convoluted as late medieval authorities' attempts to define superstition across all levels of their society. Johan Huizinga, whose classic *Autumn of the Middle Ages* (1919) still sets much of the tone for discussions of this period, regarded a variable, "vacillatory" attitude toward superstition to be a basic characteristic of the era.[13] Focusing, in this regard, on the dismal reality of Europe's developing witch hunts, he was surprised less by the credulity of the "late medieval mind" than by its occasional demonstrations of critical skepticism. His judgment on this score, however, was hardly fair. Superstition evoked such complicated and at times variable reactions from late medieval thinkers (we will avoid positing a single late medieval "mind") because superstition itself was such a broad and mutable category, yet one in which they were convinced they needed to draw certain clear and coherent boundaries, so that through their conception of superstition they could impose order on the broad range of debatable beliefs and practices to which the label of superstition could apply. In the late Middle Ages, and for several centuries thereafter, any serious deliberation about superstitious beliefs or practices inevitably touched on a host of complex and fundamental questions, either explicitly or implicitly: about the nature of divine power and

---

12. Alexandra Walsham, "The Reformation and 'the Disenchantment of the World' Reassessed," *Historical Journal* 51 (2008): 497–528, at 527.

13. Huizinga, *The Autumn of the Middle Ages*, trans. Rodney J. Payton and Ulrich Mammitzsch (Chicago, 1996), 287; John Van Engen, *Sisters and Brothers of the Common Life: The Devotio Moderna and the World of the Later Middle Ages* (Philadelphia, 2008), 8, discusses Huizinga's enduring influence.

the extent of its operation in the world, the degree to which the opposing power of the devil and his demons might infect seemingly innocent acts or even pious rituals, and how all these spiritual forces interacted with the natural operations of the physical universe as it was understood by the best science of the day.

As Huizinga perceptively recognized, therefore, superstition can help reveal something of the essential spirit of a complex and dynamic age. For many readers, the discussions and debates involving superstition that I chart in the following pages may seem at times shockingly credulous (as they once did to Huizinga himself) and at other times reassuringly rational. My hope is to render the credulity comprehensible and at the same time to complicate the rationality so that it can be understood as what it was: not some precocious eruption of "modern" skepticism but one aspect of the varied (and variable) attitudes that authorities in the Middle Ages could exhibit regarding superstition. Certainly all those who penned lengthy treatises about superstition considered it to be a critical issue that needed to be understood in all its complexity, and so should we. For while the developments that I trace in this book will never quite coalesce into one absolutely clear and unidirectional historical trajectory, they nevertheless presage many later conceptions of magic, ritual, religion, and even science (themselves never simple or singular concepts) that have shaped how the world is understood down to the present day.

The Scope of This Book

Superstition was not a new concept in late medieval Europe. Christian thinkers and writers had wrestled with it since the earliest days of the church. Particularly important were the foundational writings of the early church fathers and then those by the great scholastic authorities of the thirteenth century, mainly Thomas Aquinas and his near-contemporary William of Auvergne. These men provided the basic definitions and the overall intellectual framework in which all Christian authorities who dealt with superstition in the fourteenth and fifteenth centuries operated, and so in my first chapter I chart this long tradition, with a particular eye toward how it was used in the period of my central concern. What distinguishes the later Middle Ages from earlier periods is the heightened level of attention given to superstition and the urgency with which authorities addressed the matter in very practical ways. Rather than muse only on definitions and abstract categories, they increasingly singled out specific instances of questionable practice or belief, whether they addressed them in brief, focused tracts or in more expansive treatises.[14] This outpouring of writing affords us the opportunity to hear multiple voices in the debate over superstition and to peer somewhat through the veil of learned discourse and perceive at least the outlines of actual practices that authorities condemned as superstitious, or on occasion defended against such charges (although this can be quite problematic, as I will address in the final section of this introduction).

Concern over superstition began to swell in the fourteenth century at a number of courtly centers in western Europe: in Burgundy and Catalonia, in England and Avignon, but especially at the French court and the great university in Paris, which was the most important and influential intellectual center in northern Europe at the time. Avignon and Paris will be the two poles around which my initial consideration will orbit. Early in the century at the papal seat in Avignon, Pope John XXII, a canon lawyer by training, had issued several fundamental proclamations against demonic magic, and these were taken up in the second half of the century by the Catalan Dominican Nicolau Eymerich, himself a two-time resident of Avignon while in exile from his native Aragon, who wrote what became the standard guidebook for church inquisitors for the remainder of the Middle Ages and beyond. These two men represent a strain of concern focusing on elite magical practices that sometimes explicitly involved the invocation of demons and was always suspected of doing so. It was this entanglement with the forces of darkness that rendered these practices superstitious and even heretical, for as the great Saint Augustine had written, "All arts of this kind of worthless and harmful superstition" arose ultimately from "a pestiferous fellowship of humans and demons."[15] Running alongside this current of "religious" condemnation was a more "scientific" critique that also employed superstition to demarcate licit from illicit acts. In addition to condemning demonic conjuration, Nicolau Eymerich also attacked what he regarded as serious errors in astrology, astral magic, and divination, as well as alchemy. The most important debates about astrology in the later 1300s, however, took place at the University of Paris. Here powerful intellects like Nicole Oresme and Heinrich of Langenstein sought to define the limits of appropriate astral science, labeling improper and erroneous uses of astrology as superstitious. Although they acknowledged that demonic malevolence might also infect these sorts of practices,

---

14. On new intellectual approaches and modes of expression, see Daniel Hobbins, *Authorship and Publicity before Print: Jean Gerson and the Transformation of Late Medieval Learning* (Philadelphia, 2009), esp. 56–60.

15. Augustine, *De doctrina Christiana* 2.23(36).

their main criteria for labeling an action superstitious or defending it against such a charge was whether it derived from an incorrect understanding of natural forces and natural philosophy. Setting these two trends in contrast to one another will be the work of my second chapter.

A mainly scientific approach at least to potential superstition in the arena of astrology would continue in Paris into the fifteenth century, exemplified by the astrological writings of the theologian and ultimately cardinal of the church Pierre d'Ailly. The period around 1400 would also prove to be an important turning point, however. Whether they dealt with demonic sorcery or sidereal divination, most authorities throughout the preceding century had focused their attention on the clearly elite practices of learned astrology or complex ritual magic, which found their natural home in court and university settings and were often practiced by educated clerics.[16] In the fifteenth century, however, authorities increasingly extended their considerations of superstition to include common practices as well—the simple spells, blessings, or appropriated bits of ecclesiastical ritual that ordinary laypeople used in the course of their daily lives, or the countless casual omens or divinatory signs that they observed. Such rites and observances had, of course, always existed and had always been castigated to some degree. Again Augustine had derided people who foolishly thought that if they sneezed while putting on their shoes in the morning it meant that some misfortune would befall them that day, or that they could cure hiccups if they held their left thumb in their right hand.[17] Now, however, authorities attacked common practices with greater seriousness and vehemence. A pivotal figure here is Jean Gerson, the influential chancellor of the University of Paris (and Pierre d'Ailly's erstwhile pupil), who wrote the first of what became a string of important tracts against magical and superstitious practices, *On Errors concerning the Magic Art* (*De erroribus circa artem magicam*), in 1402. He continued to discuss erroneous astrology, astral magic, and other vices among the educated clerical elite, but he also warned about superstitious errors among the average laity and especially among simple, uneducated women—an ominous development given the rise of concern over witchcraft in subsequent years. Unlike his master d'Ailly, Gerson also returned to emphasizing the threat of demonic power in most forms of superstition.

16. Kieckhefer, *Magic in the Middle Ages*, 153–56, describes a "clerical underworld" of necromancy; Edward Peters, *The Magician, the Witch, and the Law* (Philadelphia, 1978), 9–11, 112–35, discusses a courtly demimonde of magic.

17. Augustine, *De doctrina Christiana* 2.20(30–31).

In addition to this shift in focus and points of emphasis, concern over superstition also shifted geographically in the fifteenth century. After Gerson (and shaped by his influence), the majority of treatises on superstition in the early to mid-1400s came from lands within the German Empire (again an ominous foreshadowing of the later geographies of witch-hunting). Here in the space of a few decades a number of authorities, mainly theologians at central Europe's several relatively new universities, produced a series of works, many still dealing with errors in astrology and other elite superstitions but also dissecting common practices and, like Gerson, dwelling at length on the threat of demons.[18] As critics of superstition increasingly addressed common rites and practices, with all their vagaries and frequently muddled elements, however, they encountered a morass. The rigid rationales that they had developed for distinguishing licit from illicit action—often debatable even when applied to the more "scientific" superstitions of the learned elites—now proved profoundly inadequate. I refer to this as a "dilemma of discernment," and I argue that it drove many authorities to focus more on the identity and character of those who engaged in suspected superstitions (whether they were educated or not, moral or not, male or not) rather than the often inscrutable details of their practices. This, too, presaged the emerging notion of the diabolical (and typically female) witch, sinful as much in her very person as in any harmful magical actions she might perform.

Historians of late medieval witchcraft have long noted a connection between early-to-mid-fifteenth-century treatises on superstition and mid-to-late-fifteenth-century treatises on witchcraft.[19] But the relationship was complex, and the progression, as with most developments relating to conceptions of superstition, was not altogether straightforward. All witchcraft as conceived by late medieval authorities was automatically superstitious, since it necessarily entailed a pact with demons, but by no means did every superstitious spell or rite entail witchcraft. Even the most aggressive witch-hunters

---

18. For earlier discussions of these writers, see Lynn Thorndike, *A History of Magic and Experimental Science,* 8 vols. (New York, 1923–58), 4:274–307; Françoise Bonney, "Autour de Jean Gerson: Opinions de théologiens sur les superstitions et la sorcellerie au début du XVe siècle," *Le Moyen Âge* 77 (1971): 85–98; Jan R. Veenstra, *Magic and Divination at the Courts of Burgundy and France: Text and Context of Laurens Pignon's "Contra les devineurs" (1411)* (Leiden, 1998), 143–53; Michael D. Bailey, "Concern over Superstition in Late Medieval Europe," in *The Religion of Fools? Superstition Past and Present,* ed. S. A. Smith and Alan Knight (Oxford, 2008), 115–33.

19. Werner Tschacher, *Der Formicarius des Johannes Nider von 1437/38: Studien zu den Anfängen der europäischen Hexenverfolgungen im Spätmittelalter* (Aachen, 2000), 269–91; Edward Peters, "The Medieval Church and State on Superstition, Magic and Witchcraft: From Augustine to the Sixteenth Century," in *Witchcraft and Magic in Europe: The Middle Ages,* ed. Bengt Ankarloo and Stuart Clark (Philadelphia, 2002), 173–245, at 228–29.

could be surprisingly blasé about other, now-lesser forms of superstition, and many demonologists now positively recommended a number of common charms and rites that flirted dangerously with superstition for protection against the greater threat of diabolical witchcraft.

The rise of witchcraft in the mid- to late-fifteenth century did not eliminate debate about other varieties of superstitious practice, but it did change their parameters. In a way, therefore, witchcraft forms a natural conclusion to a consideration of specifically "late medieval" superstition. Also at this time south of the Alps (where this book will not much tread), currents of "Renaissance magic" inflected by Neoplatonism and Hermeticism were emerging, at least among some humanist elites. Here too, superstition was a central issue, but once again significant new elements were injected into long-standing debates. And in the sixteenth century, of course, the Reformation dramatically affected debates about superstition, preserving many elements of "medieval" concerns, to be sure, but recasting them into interconfessional struggles over the appropriateness of different forms of rite and religion.[20]

Despite these notable developments grouped loosely around the year 1500, many scholars now emphasize the porous nature of the traditional medieval/early modern divide, particularly in the history of magic.[21] Regarding the history of superstition, Euan Cameron's monumental study, *Enchanted Europe,* moves fluidly from the thirteenth to the eighteenth century (while still maintaining that the Reformation, and reformed Protestant theology in particular, significantly changed the nature of debate). I should state for the record that, while I obviously think there are valid reasons for bracketing off the pre-1500 "medieval" period for particular study in terms of superstition, I largely agree with Cameron's approach, both his focus on an intellectual and mainly theological history of superstition and his general chronological parameters.[22] I hope that my more detailed focus on the fourteenth and fifteenth centuries will complement and usefully refine some aspects of the broader sweep that he presents. I do, however, also want to engage somewhat with broader issues myself, and in particularly to press these beyond what Cameron, who stops resolutely in the Enlightenment, addresses.

The questions with which late medieval authorities had engaged through the issue of superstition—about the scope and nature of divine and demonic

---

20. Euan Cameron, *Enchanted Europe: Superstition, Reason, and Religion 1250–1750* (Oxford, 2010), 141–239, provides an excellent overview of superstition in these contexts.
21. Michael D. Bailey, "The Age of Magicians: Periodization in the History of European Magic," *MRW* 3 (2008): 1–28.
22. See Bailey, *Magic and Superstition*, esp. 109, in this regard.

action in the world, the meaning and effect of ritual action, and the possible ways humans could understand and employ purely natural forces in the universe—undeniably continued to drive many of the great debates of the Reformation, Scientific Revolution, and Enlightenment. Therefore, although my purpose is to explore the contested boundaries of superstition specifically in the late Middle Ages, I cannot entirely end my account at the close of the fifteenth century. In my last chapter, I will survey postmedieval continuities and transformations. I will also finally address directly the issues of disenchantment and modernity, which I largely avoid in the rest of the book. This approach reflects one of my basic convictions as a historian, namely that the past is best understood on its own terms, insofar as this is possible, and not in light of preconceived modern theories. I also recognize, however, that historians inevitably frame the past in terms of the present. The only other possibility would be to embrace absolute antiquarianism. Moreover, it is undeniable that the idea of medieval superstition has played a major role in theoretical discourses framing modernity; indeed, this may be the most important meaning attached to medieval superstition in the modern period. Thus, as part of my conclusion I will seek to relate the richer, more nuanced understanding of medieval superstition that emerges in this book to some present theories of modernity, including some that seek to undermine the entire notion of "the modern." I do so not because I think these modern theories will sharpen our understanding of medieval superstition, but because I think a fuller understanding of medieval superstition may clarify and enhance some of our conceptions about the modern world—conceptions that ideas of superstition and "the medieval" have helped create.

Terminology in Context

"Superstition" in the Middle Ages did not refer to any one specific or permanently fixed body of practices. It was instead a label that, across the centuries, religious or intellectual authorities used to identify various actions and beliefs as improper or illicit. "Superstition" was always a term of censure, although the intensity of condemnation could vary and its targets could change over time. It is important, therefore, to understand the terminology that medieval writers employed when debating superstition, how basic meanings changed or remained stable over many years, and how the implications of certain words could sometimes shift significantly beneath a veneer of stable meaning. It is also necessary to clarify how I will approach terminology in this book.

The origins of superstition extend deep into antiquity. Pagan Roman authors, not medieval Christian ones, coined the Latin term *superstitio*, while the ancient Greeks had a similar concept, *deisidaimonia*, which meant something like an incorrect understanding or excessive fear of *daimones*, powerful spiritual entities inferior to the gods but well above humanity.[23] In Latin, the great orator and moralist Cicero may have originated the noun "superstition" in the first century BCE, but the Romans already had an adjective for "superstitious" (*superstitiosus*) at least two centuries before that. Its earliest meaning seems to have been associated with divination, particularly private and therefore potentially threatening divination, as opposed to public divinatory rites performed as part of the Roman state religion. Nevertheless, "superstitious" in its original sense does not appear to have been uniformly negative. Some sources present the term in neutral or even positive ways; a superstitious person could simply be someone who closely and carefully observed certain rites.[24] Negative connotations would prevail, however. Probably under the influence of Greek concepts of *deisidaimonia*, when Cicero began using the noun *superstitio* he very clearly meant excessively fearful and unwarranted rites and observances. A superstitious person was now someone who frantically offered prayers and sacrifices all day long.[25] Roman usage also always maintained a sense that superstition was unofficial, foreign, and therefore potentially politically threatening. After all, the power of the Roman state depended on proper and undistracted devotion to the public rites of officially sanctioned cults.[26]

Roman writers began castigating Christians as superstitious shortly after 100 CE, or roughly when Roman officials began to recognize Christianity as distinct from Judaism.[27] They saw in the teachings of this new breakaway sect a system of unofficial clandestine devotion, certainly foreign and definitely drawing believers away from the official cults of the empire. Christian apologists, in their turn, quickly seized on the notion of superstition, appropriating it for their own uses and turning it back against the Romans

---

23. Dale B. Martin, *Inventing Superstition: From the Hippocratics to the Christians* (Cambridge, Mass., 2004).

24. On Roman usages, see L. F. Janssen, "'Superstitio' and the Persecution of the Christians," *Vigiliae Christianae* 33 (1979): 131–59; Michele R. Salzman, "'Superstitio' in the Codex Theodosianus and the Persecution of the Pagans," *Vigiliae Christianae* 41 (1987): 172–88; Dieter Harmening, *Superstitio: Überlieferungs- und theoriegeschichtliche Untersuchungen zur kirchlich-theologischen Aberglaubensliteratur des Mittelatlers* (Berlin, 1979), 14–25.

25. Cicero, *De natura deorum* 2.28, ed. Arthur Stanley Pease, 2 vols. (Cambridge, Mass., 1955–58).

26. Harmening, *Superstitio*, 23–25; Janssen, "Superstitio," 142 and 150; Martin, *Inventing Superstition*, 26 and 30–31.

27. Martin, *Inventing Superstition*, 2–3.

and paganism in general. Christianity came to conceive of all pagan deities and *daimones* simply as "demons"—evil spirits cast out of heaven by the Christian God and now worshipped in false guises by the assorted cults of antiquity. Following this logic, all non-Christian religion could be castigated as erroneous and illegitimate. It was, in short, superstitious, and Christian writers soon designated (somewhat gleefully, one imagines) all pagan rites as *superstitio romana* or *superstitio gentilium*.[28]

At the end of the fourth century, Augustine of Hippo crafted the most important and enduring Christian definition of superstition. In the second book of *On Christian Doctrine*, written around 396, he stated that "superstition is anything instituted by men having to do with crafting or worshipping idols, or worshipping a created thing or any part of a created thing as if it were God, or consultations and pacts concerning prognostications agreed on and entered into with demons."[29] Among the forms of superstitious practice he listed were the magic arts (*artes magicae*), the divinations of soothsayers and augurs, and various amulets and healing rites "that medical science condemns." He also included many predictions made by astrologers and those who attempted to forecast a person's character or course of life from a natal horoscope.[30] Certainly Augustine's most important legacy regarding later Christian conceptions of superstition was the link he drew between superstitious rites and the power of demons. We have already seen how, in this same text, he declared that superstition was rooted in "a pestiferous fellowship of humans and demons."[31] We have also seen, however, that he could mock certain superstitious beliefs held by simple folk as being more foolish than fearful, just as pagan intellectuals had done in the Roman world.

The better part of a millennium after Augustine, the thirteenth-century Dominican theologian Thomas Aquinas considered the meaning of superstition and provided another definition that would prove fundamental for authorities in the late medieval period. Like the great bishop of Hippo, he drew on ancient Roman definitions to ground the essential meaning of superstition in notions of erroneous devotions and excessive observances, but he argued that, because the Christian God was infinitely good and worthy of

---

28. Salzman, "Superstitio," 175; Harmening, *Superstitio*, 33–36.

29. Augustine, *De doctrina Christiana* 2.20(30): "Superstitiosum est, quicquid institutum est ab hominibus ad facienda et colenda idola pertinens uel ad colendam sicut deum creaturam partemue ullam creaturae uel ad consultationes et pacta quaedam significationum cum daemonibus placita atque foederata."

30. Ibid., 2.21(32).

31. Ibid., 2.23(36). See n. 4 above.

unceasing worship, the only excess possible in a Christian context would be the incorrect performance of some religious observance. "Therefore superstition is a vice opposed to religion according to excess, not because it gives more worship to God than true religion, but because it gives worship either to that which it ought not, or in some manner which it ought not."[32] In the ominous phrase of worship given to that which it ought not be, Christian authorities could again easily read the presence of demons.

Whenever late medieval writers discussed the abstract meaning of superstition, they typically clung tightly to the definitions provided by Augustine and Aquinas. The Heidelberg theologian Nikolaus of Jauer cited both men in his widely circulated treatise On Superstitions (De superstitionibus) of 1405, as did another anonymous treatise of the same title written sometime in the first half of the fifteenth century probably in southern Germany, while the theologians Johannes of Wünschelburg, Denys the Carthusian, and Johannes Schwarz all relied on Aquinas in their works.[33] The English Dominican Alexander Carpenter cited both Augustine and Aquinas, and sought to clarify them for his readers, distilling three basic varieties of superstition from the definitions of these great authorities. The first two were, in fact, the Thomistic categories of worship offered to God but in an improper fashion, or worship offered to something that did not deserve it, namely some created thing. Last, Carpenter made explicit the danger only implied by Thomas by creating a third category that closely echoed some of Augustine's language; a practice became superstitious "when through such worship demons are consulted through some pact, either tacit or express, made with them."[34]

While basic Christian definitions of superstition proved durable, usage could change dramatically over time. That a clerical author in the fifteenth century cited Augustine's definition of superstition verbatim does not mean that he was concerned about exactly the same sort of superstitious practices as the bishop of Hippo in the fifth century. Terms acquired different connotations over the years, and sometimes these could alter their meanings profoundly. One of the clearest examples of such a shift occurred in the late

---

32. Aquinas, *Summa theologiae* 2.2.92.1, in *Summa theologiae: Latin Text and English Translation*, 60 vols. (New York, 1964–81): "Sic igitur superstitio est vitium religioni oppositum secundum excessum, non quia plus exhibeat in cultum divinum quam vera religio, sed quia exhibet cultum divinum vel cui non debet, vel eo modo quo non debet." (I have modified the English translation somewhat.)

33. Nikolaus of Jauer, *De superstitionibus*, 49r–v; anonymous, *De superstitionibus* (M), 16v–17r; Johannes of Wünschelburg, *De superstitionibus*, 231r; Denys the Carthusian, *Contra vitia superstitionum*, 599; Johannes Schwarz, *De divinationibus*, 315r–v.

34. Alexander Carpenter, *Destructorium viciorum* 6.43: "Et tertia quando per talem cultum consuluntur demones per aliqua pacta cum eis inita tacita vel expressa."

medieval period with the emergence of the notion of diabolical witchcraft. Most basically, the Latin word for "witch," *maleficus* or the feminine *malefica*, meant evildoer or criminal. It had for centuries also commonly designated someone who performed harmful spells or magical rites (*maleficia*). Then in the fifteenth century, *maleficus/a* acquired another, more fearful connotation, still designating a person who performed *maleficia*, but no longer as an individual evildoer. Now a "witch" operated as a member of a perverse and malevolent society that gathered in secret to worship the devil, desecrate the sacraments, murder and cannibalize infants, and engage in sexual depravities with each other and with attendant demons.[35] This stereotype of corporate evil and conspiratorial threat would furnish one (although not the only) basic framework for the conceptualization and condemnation of witchcraft for centuries to come.[36] Sometimes later writers would be attentive to the fact that they employed the word *maleficus* differently than earlier authorities had done, and sometimes they would pass over such distinctions in silence.

"Necromancy" was another important term associated with superstition that had changed its meaning rather fundamentally over the course of time. *Necromantia* was a Latin word derived from Greek, literally meaning divination by means of the dead (as *hydromantia* meant divination by water and *pyromantia* meant divination by fire). Christian authorities, however, generally maintained that no mere human rites could summon back the spirit of a deceased person from its divinely appointed station in the afterlife. Those shades that did appear in response to necromantic rites were deemed to be demons instead. By the later medieval period the term "necromancy" had expanded to encompass any kind of ritual demonic conjuration and designated a whole category of elite, learned magic.[37] The fifteenth-century theologian Johannes Nider discussed these shifting connotations explicitly in his influential moral treatise, the *Anthill* (*Formicarius*), explaining that "they are properly called necromancers who claim that by superstitious rites they can raise the dead from the earth in order to speak about hidden things. . . . But in accommodation of common use they are called necromancers who, through

---

35. See such general accounts as Bailey, *Magic and Superstition*, 143–52; Brian P. Levack, *The Witch-Hunt in Early Modern Europe*, 3rd ed. (London, 2006), 4–12.

36. On the interplay of multiple stereotypes, see Richard Kieckhefer, "Mythologies of Witchcraft in the Fifteenth Century," *MRW* 1 (2006): 79–108.

37. Fundamental here are Kieckhefer, *Magic in the Middle Ages*, 151–75; and Richard Kieckhefer, *Forbidden Rites: A Necromancer's Manual of the Fifteenth Century* (University Park, Pa., 1998). Boudet, *Entre science et nigromance*, also provides a detailed account, although he argues that the term should be rendered "nigromancy" in deference to a typical medieval corruption of the spelling. On this, see n. 39 below.

pacts with demons and putting their faith in certain ceremonies, predict the future, or who discover certain secrets through the revelation of demons, or who harm those around them through malevolent sorcery."[38] Many late medieval critics of superstition noted the original etymology of "necromancy" before going on to use it in the common sense of ritual demonic conjuration, mainly, it would seem, because this allowed them to show off some pretend knowledge of Greek. Ironically, though, they actually revealed the limits of their linguistic skills, for they typically used the standard late medieval corruption of *nigromantia* instead of *necromantia*. This led them to assert the garbled proposition that *"nigro* [rather than *necro*] means 'dead' in Greek."[39]

While sometimes, as with necromancy, writers took the time to explain their usages, more often they either recited basic definitions from earlier authorities or they simply let standard terminology stand on its own, assuming their audience would know what it meant. Yet this terminology also blended together to some degree. "Magical art" (*ars magica*) was a frequently given category of superstition, but not all "magic" was necessarily superstitious. Moreover, some authorities writing in detail about demonic conjuration seldom or never used the term "superstitious," being more concerned, for their immediate purposes, to describe such operations as idolatry, or heresy, or simply as an abomination. Yet all authorities recognized that entanglement with demons was one of the basic conditions of superstition. Discussions about astrology often presented particularly dense terminological minefields. Authoritative definitions held that astrology (*astrologia*) differed from the pure science of astronomy (*astronomia*), and moreover that astrology itself was "partly natural [scientific] and partly superstitious."[40] Yet some authorities used "astrology" and "astronomy" interchangeably, even in works addressing precise distinctions between natural, licit science and illicit superstition. Astrologers could legitimately make certain predictions based on their observations of the heavens, but when prediction veered into

---

38. Johannes Nider, *Formicarius* 5.4, pp. 352–53: "Necromantici proprie hi dicuntur, qui de terra superstitiosis ritibus mortuos se posse suscitare ad loquendum occulta ostentant. . . . Ex accommodatione tamen usus necromanctici dicuntur, qui per pacta demonum per fidem ceremoniis futura predicunt, aut occulta reuelatione demonum aliqua manifestant, aut qui maleficiis proximos laedunt."

39. "Nigro in grece mortuus." See anonymous, *De superstitionibus* M, 54r; Carpenter, *Destructorium viciorum* 6.51; Jakob of Paradise, *De potestate demonum*, 263v; Schwarz, *De divinationibus*, 298r, 316r. In many cases, the error stemmed from writers copying corrupt texts of Isidore of Seville's *Etymologies*, which gave the standard derivation (*Etymologiarum sive originum libri XX* 8.9.11, ed. W. M. Lindsay, 2 vols. [1911; repr., Oxford, 1971]); e.g. anonymous, *De superstitionibus, magia, sortilegiis, etc.*, 297r.

40. Isidore of Seville, *Etymologiarum libri XX* 1.27.1.

"divination" (crossing another uncertain and contested terminological boundary), then their practices became superstitious.

Throughout this book, I will try to clarify contemporary usages of terminology whenever possible, first summarizing the long, authoritative Christian tradition that preceded the late Middle Ages, and then focusing on fourteenth- and fifteenth-century debates. The historical reality, however, is that the precise meanings of *superstitio* itself and many of its attendant terms were always somewhat mercurial and elusive, even for the authorities who addressed them systematically. Seeking to draw clear boundaries in one area, they often reverted to generalities in another. This, too, I want to capture. When making generalizations myself, I will try to use terms more or less as I judge that most late medieval writers dealing with the same subject would have used them, including the uncertainties inherent in their usages. Blessing might shift into curse (*execratio*), prayer might mutate into spell or incantation (*incantatio*), various forms of prediction teetered precariously on the brink of divination. Authorities mostly agreed on basic definitions, but they might still disagree on any number of specific categorizations. This was an essential element of their debate.

Religion, Science, and Magic

Problems similar to those that affect specific terminology also manifest in the broad categories of religion, science, and magic, all of which relate to and help shape the meaning of superstition, as indeed superstition does for them. From certain perspectives, these three categories are patently distinct, while from others they can blur into one another, sometimes in uncomfortable ways. Moreover, their relationship can be quite different depending on when in the course of their histories one chooses to look. Modern scholarship has frequently set religion, science, and magic in fruitful tension with one another, and I will not rehearse such discussions here.[41] I do, however, need to make a few comments about how each category related to superstition in medieval Europe.

Describing superstition as a deviation from prescribed religious norms, in an era when Christian doctrine dominated almost every aspect of life, can often be quite accurate. Saint Augustine himself noted that "true religion" in the sense of binding (*religans*) oneself to God meant freeing oneself from all superstition, and subsequent medieval writers often defined superstition

---

41. Michael D. Bailey, "The Meanings of Magic," *MRW* 1 (2006): 1–23, esp. 2–4.

as "false religion."[42] Nevertheless, the notion of superstition as incorrect or improper religion, while evocative and literally true, can also prove somewhat misleading. In the modern Western world, many people consider the essence of religion to lie in internal faith, not external ritual acts. In the Middle Ages, however, *religio*—that which bound humanity to the divine—referred not just to proper beliefs and spiritual convictions but to the careful performance of prescribed rites.[43] Medieval notions of superstition as false religion therefore focused on the incorrect enactment of rites and rituals far more than what certain modern understandings of religion and hence religious error might suggest.[44]

Modern conceptions may obscure medieval distinctions in other ways as well, especially when medieval critics of superstition come to discuss acts that modern readers might consider science rather than religion. Even some experts on medieval superstition have argued that if superstition meant primarily a "perversion of religion" in the Middle Ages, that meaning fell away during the Enlightenment of the seventeenth and eighteenth centuries, and subsequently superstition came to mean primarily a "perversion of [scientific] reason."[45] It is certainly fair to maintain that the Enlightenment helped distance the spiritual world from the physical and separate religious belief from the realm of scientific rationality, such that ultimately some enlightened thinkers came to consider organized religion itself to be an irrational superstition. These developments, however, were never as complete as Enlightenment propaganda or subsequent notions of an entirely disenchanted and secularized Western "modernity" might assert.[46] More to the point, such modern distinctions cannot simply be reversed and then applied to the Middle Ages. Medieval thinkers too regarded superstition as a "defect of reason," although they grounded their notion of reason firmly in Christian dogma, so that they understood an irrational act to be one that did not conform to proper religion.[47]

---

42. Augustine, *De vera religione* 55.111, ed. K.-D. Daur, CCSL 32 (Turnhout, 1962); Harmening, *Superstitio*, 34.

43. Jonathan Z. Smith, "Religion, Religions, Religious," in *Critical Terms for Religious Studies*, ed. Mark C. Taylor (Chicago, 1998), 269–84, here 269–70.

44. Harmening, *Superstitio*, 34.

45. Ibid., 5, 259.

46. Thomas Ahnert, *Religion and the Origins of the German Enlightenment: Faith and the Reform of Learning in the Thought of Christian Thomasius* (Rochester, N.Y., 2006); S. J. Barnett, *The Enlightenment and Religion: The Myths of Modernity* (Manchester, 2003).

47. Anonymous, *De superstitionibus* (M), 16v: "Notandum quod vicium opponitum religioni consistit in hoc quod inclinat ad actus deformes recte rationi circa diuinum cultum."

Just as religion was "rational," so science was inevitably "religious" in the Middle Ages. The operations of the physical universe were ordained by God and reflected divine order. Hence all legitimate knowledge (*scientia*) about nature conformed to and helped reveal religious truths, and the misapplication of such knowledge was a serious moral matter. Here too authorities deployed the concept of superstition in an effort to draw distinct boundaries in what could often be fairly confusing terrain. Their focus fell principally on the complicated art of astrology. All authorities agreed that the heavens exerted certain natural effects on the earth. One need only note the heat of the sun or the pull of the moon on the tides to accept this fact. Calculating more complicated astral effects and drawing detailed predictions from such calculations, however, could easily exceed the capacity of human reason and lead to superstition. Worse still, in the eyes of many authorities the claims of some astrologers appeared to contradict divine precepts about the ordering and operation of the universe, or even the divine promise of human free will. Worst of all, demons might intrude into any erroneous operations, offering false knowledge or producing unnatural effects.

This fluid overlap of religion and science leads to a third troublesome category through which to think about superstition: magic. Medieval writers frequently labeled practices as superstitious that were or could also be regarded (in either a medieval or a modern sense) as magical—anything from common healing spells, protective amulets, or simple forms of divination to distinctly learned varieties of astrology or the ritual invocation of astral forces or spiritual powers. It is tempting, therefore, to use the word "magic" as a convenient stand-in for superstition. Again, however, complications arise. First, magic is itself a difficult and contested category, often understood quite differently in varying contexts and certainly in different historical periods, and use of the term inevitably obscures as much as it illuminates unless it is defined very precisely each time it is deployed.[48] Second, while medieval intellectual authorities had a general term for magic—the Latin *magia,* or more frequently *ars magica* (magical art)—and while they generally deemed magic to be superstitious, they almost never discussed superstition exclusively in terms of "magic."[49] Rather,

---

48. See Bailey, "Meanings of Magic," esp. 5–13; on medieval usages, Kieckhefer, *Magic in the Middle Ages,* 8–17; Richard Kieckhefer, "The Specific Rationality of Medieval Magic," *AHR* 99 (1994): 813–36.

49. The great exception is Gerson's influential *De erroribus circa artem magicam,* 77, which refers specifically to the "pernicious superstitions of magicians" ("de superstitionibus pestiferis magicorum").

they tended to refer to specific kinds of "magical art": astrological divination, demonic conjuration, and so forth, which they listed alongside other superstitious practices.

Ultimately, we cannot understand the medieval meanings of superstition simply or straightforwardly through the categories of magic, science, or religion because superstition itself was often the means by which medieval authorities defined the boundaries of those categories, distinguishing licit from illicit knowledge, belief, and behavior. Charges of superstition arose, or at least concerns were evoked, primarily when medieval people sought to employ spiritual forces (either demonic or divine) or natural powers to achieve some practical end, whether to gain knowledge, secure success, heal or protect from harm, or strike out at their enemies. There were, of course, countless legitimate ways in which they could do these things. To be labeled superstitious meant that someone in a position to judge worried that they had slipped across a critical but ephemeral boundary into improper action or erroneous understanding.

Medieval authorities frequently (although not universally) regarded the potential consequences of such slippage into superstition to be very dire. The great gap between their time and ours in terms of all three corners of the great triad of religion, science, and magic pertains perhaps less to the essential nature of these concepts (although important variances exist there too) than to the seriousness with which we regard what are now commonly considered superstitious errors in any of them. If I misspeak the words of a prayer, no priest or minister now thunders that I may have invoked the forces of hell instead of heaven, especially if I have pious intent in my heart. If I try to predict some event based on a false understanding of astrophysics or to cure a fever with some homey folk remedy, my prediction will probably be wrong and my cure may not work, but my actions will not have transgressed what is viewed as the divine order of the universe. Most intellectual authorities in the modern Western world, and certainly most legal authorities, no longer believe in the real efficacy of magic themselves and so no longer care if people dabble in magical practices (so long as no other criminal actions are involved). They may bemoan the wasted time and resources that go into what they consider misguided efforts, but they no longer advocate that such people be subject to serious punishments.[50] In all such cases, the situation in late medieval Europe could be dramatically different.

---

50. Stuart A. Vyse, *Believing in Magic: The Psychology of Superstition* (New York, 1997), 23, 209–11.

The "Reality" of Medieval Superstition

One final point needs to be made about what "superstition" meant in medieval Europe, and what it will mean in this book. There is little cause to doubt that across Western Christendom, and at all levels of society, people uttered blessings or curses and performed ritual acts to ward off danger or attract good fortune. They gathered special roots and herbs, and they sought to infuse power into any number of natural or crafted items. They read meaning into the course of the stars as well as all kinds of terrestrial omens and portents.[51] For all their apparent pervasiveness, however, specific practices actually employed in the late Middle Ages that might raise the alarm of superstition are not altogether easy to access. The physical items used either in simple rites or complex rituals have left some archaeological record, but removed from their original contexts these isolated objects are often difficult to interpret.[52] A surprising number of textual amulets have survived from the Middle Ages. These consist of scraps of paper or parchment covered with formulaic passages of various lengths and then worn or carried to achieve certain effects.[53] In some cases the writing may directly indicate how the amulets were used. Most of the written records of medieval superstition that we have, however, come from a relatively small literate elite who sought not to preserve such practices for posterity but to accuse, correct, and condemn.

For specifically elite practices, we can sometimes compare the derisive descriptions of condemnatory accounts and legal proscriptions to records left by actual practitioners. Clerical necromancers and specialists in astral magic, for example, participated in a learned, literate culture. Inquisitorial and other authorities knew the books these men used in their rites—the *Table of Solomon* and *Sworn Book of Honorius* ("known to necromancers as the *Thesaurus of Necromancy*"), or the famous astral text known as *Picatrix*, for example—and often pursued these texts with as much vehemence as they did the magicians themselves.[54] Many such books no longer exist,

---

51. Jean Verdon, *Les superstitions au Moyen Âge* (Paris, 2008), offers the fullest survey, but little historical analysis. Likewise Stephen Wilson, *The Magical Universe: Everyday Ritual and Magic in Pre-Modern Europe* (London, 2000), treats common beliefs and practices as almost entirely ahistorical.

52. Although he focuses on a later period, see Brian Hoggard, "The Archeology of Counter-Witchcraft and Popular Magic," in *Beyond the Witch Trials: Witchcraft and Magic in Enlightenment Europe*, ed. Owen Davies and Willem de Blécourt (Manchester, 2004), 167–86.

53. Don C. Skemer, *Binding Words: Textual Amulets in the Middle Ages* (University Park, Pa., 2006).

54. Nicolau Eymerich, *Directorium inquisitorum* 2.43.1, p. 338. Also anonymous, *De divinacionibus*, 182v; Nicolas Jacquier, *Flagellum haereticorum fascinariorum* 14, p. 101; Felix Hemmerli, *Tractatus exorcismorum*, 107v–108r; Johannes Hartlieb, *Buch aller verbotenen Künste*, 34, 48.

having been either consigned to the flames or simply lost over the course of time. Yet many do survive, often in the less-well-cataloged corners of medieval manuscript collections, and scholars have increasingly turned to them, rather than just the texts condemning them, to augment our understanding of elite magical practices.[55] In the main, condemnations seem in keeping with magicians' own descriptions of their practices. Necromancers, for example, regularly stood accused of performing horrible bloody rites in honor of demons. To take only one extreme and clearly politically motivated charge, no less a figure than Pope Boniface VIII was accused (posthumously) by agents of the French king Philip IV, against whom Boniface had struggled mightily in life, of summoning demons by burning human blood dried into a powder like some gruesome incense, as well as offering them goats' blood, and of immolating white roosters, doves, and (assumedly black) jackdaws in their honor.[56] Yet rites described in necromantic texts themselves could be even more gruesome. One spell required that a sorcerer bite out the heart of a dove with his own teeth, then use the blood to draw a figure on parchment made from the flesh of a female cat that had been in heat when it was skinned, all in order to compel a woman's love.[57] Similar (although far less gory) correspondences can be found between opponents' and practitioners' descriptions of elite astrological rites or medicinal practices. We can construct a fairly confident picture, therefore, of what elite practices that attracted charges of superstition "really" involved.

For common practices, matters are much more slippery. As alert as late medieval critics of superstition appear to have been to the world around them, they inevitably saw the superstitions of their day in the light of centuries of Christian discourse on this topic to which they were heirs. One expert has remarked that they regarded superstition as a basically "a-historical phenomenon," while another has commented on the "literary-traditional character" of their writings as they endeavored to situate any contemporary practices they observed within authoritative categories established in

---

55. See Kieckhefer, *Forbidden Rites*; essays in Claire Fanger, ed., *Conjuring Spirits: Texts and Traditions of Medieval Ritual Magic* (University Park, Pa., 1998); and Fanger, ed., *Invoking Angels: Theurgic Ideas and Practices, Thirteenth to Sixteenth Centuries* (University Park, Pa., 2012); also Benedek Láng, *Unlocked Books: Manuscripts of Learned Magic in the Medieval Libraries of Central Europe* (University Park, Pa., 2008).

56. Jean Coste, ed., *Boniface VIII en procès: Articles d'accusation et dépositions des témoins (1303–1311)* (Rome, 1995), 420–21.

57. Kieckhefer, *Forbidden Rites*, 82.

the (sometimes quite distant) past.[58] At the same time, another scholar has asserted—rightly, in my view—that approaching medieval condemnations of superstition only as a self-perpetuating literary tradition is surely "too pessimistic" about the possibility of discerning real practices, as well as changing contexts and circumstances, in our sources.[59] When addressing superstition in any general way, late medieval writers almost always fell back on the terms and categories of earlier authorities. As I have already discussed, however, they surely adapted established terminology to reflect contemporary developments. Moreover, seeing that some terms did fall out of regular use over the centuries, one could also reasonably argue that certain categories remained in use precisely because they continued to reflect real practices with at least some degree of accuracy.

All too often, especially when discussing common superstitious practices, late medieval critics stuck to generalities, describing broad types of practice (always in traditional terminology) but never giving specific examples. At times, however, they also presented glimpses into what look like real rites that they may have directly observed or even used themselves. I began this chapter, for example, by mentioning an educated cleric in the German Rhineland who knew certain "superstitious blessings" and even admitted to using one himself. This was a verbal formula in the German vernacular that invoked Christ to heal an injury: "Christ was born, Christ was lost, Christ was found again; may he bless these wounds in the name of the Father and of the Son and of the Holy Spirit."[60] Yet even in such cases of seemingly clear reportage there is room for some skepticism. Late medieval authorities not only knew the long tradition of Christian writers addressing superstition, but they read each others' works as well. Fifty years after the "Christ was born" incantation was recorded in the Rhineland, a Swiss author in Zurich addressed both it and the 1405 ruling of the theological faculty at the University of Heidelberg that condemned it, and two centuries later it was still being discussed, for a Lutheran pastor in the Bavarian city of Augsburg mentioned it in a treatise

---

58. Karin Baumann, *Aberglaube für Laien: Zur Programmatik und Überlieferung spätmittelalterlicher Superstitionenkritik*, 2 vols. (Würzburg, 1989), 1:274; Harmening, *Superstitio*, 72.

59. Bernadette Filotas, *Pagan Survivals, Superstitions and Popular Cultures in Early Medieval Pastoral Literature* (Toronto, 2005), 46; likewise Baumann, *Aberglaube für Laien*, 1:483–84, recognizes the degree to which late medieval writers reflected contemporary practices and concerns, despite her judgment about their ahistorical approach.

60. Werner of Friedberg, *Revocatio*, 198r: "Christus wart geboren, Christus wart verloren, Christus wart wider funden, deer gesegen dise wunden in namen des vatters und des sunes und des hailigen geistes."

on sorcery and witchcraft that he wrote in 1628.[61] Should we glean from this that the blessing itself continued in common use for over two hundred years, or had it long since become a purely literary artifact? Similarly in 1423, the Vienna theologian Nikolaus of Dinkelsbühl included a vernacular charm in his treatise *On the Commandments of the Decalogue* (*De preceptis decalogi*): "Until God welcome, new moon, gracious lord, increase my wealth." Another treatise circulating in southern German lands at roughly the same time then repeated the formula.[62] Does this mean that the charm was common across this region, or simply that one writer copied the account of another?[63] In one of his works the early fifteenth-century Dominican Johannes Nider described a rite intended to cause rain by stirring a pail of water with a broom handle, and in another he described a spell to stop hail by invoking the three nails of Christ's crucifixion. Fifty years later, the Dominican Heinrich Kramer also included these rites in his infamous treatise on witchcraft and witch-hunting, the *Hammer of Witches* (*Malleus maleficarum*). We know that Kramer had read Nider and often cited him explicitly as a source of information, but in these cases he did not. Medieval writers typically cited haphazardly, but it is also entirely possible that such rites were fairly common, such that Kramer could have witnessed or heard reports about them himself and so felt no need to attribute his account to an earlier author.[64]

These uncertainties of usage all arise from the fact that late medieval theologians and other intellectual authorities writing about superstition worked in a tightly bound and self-referential tradition. Could we, then, escape some of these problems by looking at other kinds of sources? The vernacular literature of this period, for example, often treats the same issues that churchmen would deem superstitions. Some do so at length, such as

---

61. Hemmerli, *Tractatus exorcismorum*; Bernhard Albrecht, *Magia: Das ist Christlicher Bericht von der Zauberey und Hexerey*, cited in Peter A. Morton, "Lutheran Naturalism, Popular Magic, and the Devil," in *The Devil in Society in Premodern Europe*, ed. Richard Raiswell and Peter Dendle (Toronto, 2012), 409–35, at 410.

62. Nikolaus of Dinkelsbühl, *De preceptis decalogi*, 29v: "Bis got wilkum newer mon holder her mach mir myns geltes mer"; anonymous, *De superstitionibus* (M), 49r: "Bis got wilkomen nawer moᶜn de hulder hirre meer nur meyn guth."

63. Jacob Grimm assumed this charm represented authentic German folklore (see *Teutonic Mythology*, trans. James Stevens Stalleybrass, 4 vols. [London, 1882–88], 2:704), and his opinion shaped later German scholarship, such as G. Hertel, "Abergläubische Gebräuche aus dem Mittelalter," *Zeitschrift des Vereins für Volkskunde* 11 (1901): 272–79, at 279; thence into the *Handwörterbuch des deutschen Aberglaubens*, ed. Hans Bächtold-Stäubli, with Eduard Hoffmann-Krayer, 10 vols. (1929–42; repr., Berlin, 2000) 6:535. Grimm's only source, however, was Nikolaus of Dinkelsbühl.

64. On rain, Johannes Nider, *Preceptorium divine legis* 1.11.16(v); Heinrich Kramer, *Malleus maleficarum* 2.1.11, 1:458. On hail, Nider, *Formicarius* 5.4, p. 358; Kramer, *Malleus maleficarum* 2.2.7, 1:550.

Dives and Pauper in English, but perhaps most remarkably the *Distaff Gospels* (*Évangiles des quenouilles*), an anonymous work written in Old French, probably in the mid-fifteenth century in Flanders.[65] Its (male) author purports to have met secretly with six women over the course of several days and to have recorded their "gospels," which amount to a multitude of popular beliefs and practices supposedly common among women. The *Distaff Gospels* are a piece of courtly literature, however, and their author was likely familiar with more "academic" critiques of superstition also circulating through French-speaking courts at this time.[66] His basic attitude did not differ from that of most schoolmen; within his text the character of the author openly derided and condemned much of what he heard, albeit in a more satirical, less serious vein than was the case with most clerical writers. In addition to a somewhat different perspective, the *Distaff Gospels* provide a treasure trove of specific practices to compare against the typically more generic tradition of clerical writings. Of course, details taken from a literary account can no more readily be related to "reality" than those drawn from a theological treatise. Moreover, the very wealth of detail in the *Gospels* presents another problem. Some of the practices they describe resemble those discussed in other works, but many are unique, at least in terms of surviving medieval evidence. In order to conjecture about the relation of the *Gospels* to actual practices, their modern editor had to leave the Middle Ages entirely and build an argument based on their similarity to peasant rites and behaviors recorded more systematically by folklorists in the nineteenth century.[67]

Where does this leave us, in terms of identifying "real" practices within late medieval authorities' accounts of superstition? Our authors worked within a long tradition that they regarded as enormously authoritative, but they did not bow entirely to tradition and reworked established categories in often subtle ways that can be difficult to detect. They also read and freely borrowed from one another. Yet unless we choose to be entirely skeptical of their many declarations of direct experience with certain practices, they also frequently drew on their own observations. The modern editor of the *Distaff Gospels* has called their author an early folklorist, and if our clerical writers

---

65. On the *Évangiles*, see Madeleine Jeay, *Savoir faire: Une analyse des croyances des "Évangiles des quenouilles" (XVe siècle)* (Montreal, 1982); also Jelle Koopmans, "Archéologies des *Évangiles des quenouilles*," in *Autour des quenouilles: La parole des femmes (1450–1600)*, ed. Jean-François Courouau, Philippe Gardy, and Jelle Koopmans (Turnhout, 2010), 13–29, for textual history.

66. For example, the account of superstition in the French courtier Philippe Mézières's *Le songe du vieil pelerin*, ed. G. W. Coopland, 2 vols. (Cambridge, 1969), 1:590–619, derives from the academic Nicole Oresme's *Livre de divinacions* and *Contra judiciarios astronomos* (discussed in chapter 2).

67. Jeay, *Savoir faire*, 20–22.

were not exactly objective anthropologists, nevertheless they clearly had some interest in understanding the "popular culture" of their day.[68] That culture was in no way foreign to them, and they themselves might have employed some of the very same spells and rites as ordinary laypeople (although by definition they would not have considered any practice of which they approved to be superstitious). Neither can we ignore how authorities' repeated pronouncements about superstition, transmitted to the laity via homilies, sermons, advice and correction given during confession, and other mechanisms, may have helped shape common practices.[69] Nevertheless what primarily concerns us here, and what I mainly mean by "medieval superstition," is not so much the specific practices that may or may not have really existed in the past but rather how authorities perceived, depicted, and deployed that concept. Their often shifting and contentious accounts allow us to perceive only dimly and at some remove how things "really were" among Western Christendom's rank and file, but they present much more directly what Christian authorities thought their world looked like and the dangerous beliefs and practices that they feared were threatening to engulf it.

While medieval authorities widely accepted that real harm could arise from superstition, they did not uniformly agree on when that harm might arise, what form it might take, or even what practices should be categorized as superstitious. Many authorities demonstrated deep suspicion in all areas, but some were relatively skeptical, and despite their desire for certainty they did not always shy away from admitting the limits of their understanding. For Huizinga, their sometimes "vacillatory" attitudes characterized the inherently erratic tendencies of a waning age. In fact, the complexities and at times convolutions of their thought arose from the seriousness with which they took the issue. Their concerns can serve as evidence not of decay but of the dynamism that characterized this period, and of the vibrant multiplicity that some now see as the real essence of late medieval Christianity.[70]

---

68. Ibid., 11; cf. Carlo Ginzburg, "The Inquisitor as Anthropologist," in Ginzburg, *Clues, Myths, and the Historical Method*, trans. John and Anne Tedeschi (Baltimore, 1989), 156–64.

69. Harmening, *Superstitio*, 72–73, argues strongly that antisuperstition material should not be read to reflect historical "reality" (*Wirklichkeit*), but also notes how rhetoric could "provoke reality"; see also Dieter Harmening, "'Magische Volkskultur': Ethnographischer Befund oder literarisches Konstrukt? Quellenkritische Probleme zwischen historischer Anthropologie und Volkskunde," *Mediaevalia Historica Bohemica* 7 (2000): 55–90.

70. John Van Engen, "Multiple Options: The World of the Fifteenth-Century Church," *Church History* 77 (2008): 257–84.

Discourse and debate about superstition reveals important elements of this dynamic age, changing and struggling to understand that change but not yet ready to abandon traditional structures of belief and knowledge in any wholesale fashion. In this sense, in fact, the authorities who addressed the issue of superstition in the fourteenth and fifteenth centuries can offer a kind of clarity not found in later periods, because, unlike the religious reformers and scientific revolutionaries to come, they did not feel the need to tie their critique of superstition to any profound break with the past or to any powerful rhetoric of newness and advancing modernity. Neither have subsequent historical developments imposed this framework on them. Through their writings, we can see how debate about this important issue developed in one particular period, how conceptions of superstition and concerns about the threat it posed changed by virtue of their own dynamics, and how they advanced along complex and multifarious routes toward the future.

✒ CHAPTER 1

The Weight of Tradition

> During that period . . . we were seduced and we
> seduced others, deceived and deceiving in various
> lustful desires, both openly through what they call
> the liberal arts and secretly by a false show of religion,
> here proud, there superstitious, everywhere vain.
>
> —Augustine, *Confessions*

The theologians and other intellectual authori-
ties who wrote about superstition in the fourteenth and fifteenth centuries
generally had their eyes fixed much more on past tradition than on the future into which they were moving. So it is with that tradition that we must
begin to chart their movement, surveying how Christian views of superstition developed from the time of the church fathers to the flowering of high
medieval scholasticism in the thirteenth century. It is worth noting again
that late medieval writers were never absolutely beholden to past authority
on this subject. They readily modified earlier definitions and categorizations,
sometimes overtly but more often tacitly. Yet there can be no denying that
they all knew and felt the heavy weight of tradition, and their own work
cannot be properly understood if separated from it. What follows here will
not be a thorough study or even, frankly, a complete survey of patristic and
earlier medieval writing on superstition—that would require a book in its
own right, if not several.[1] Instead we will focus here on those earlier figures

---

1. Dieter Harmening, *Superstitio: Überlieferungs- und theoriegeschichtliche Untersuchungen zur kirchlich-theologischen Aberglaubensliteratur des Mittelalters* (Berlin, 1979), covers through the thirteenth century; Bernadette Filotas, *Pagan Survivals, Superstitions and Popular Cultures in Early Medieval Pastoral Literature* (Toronto, 2005), focuses on the sixth through tenth centuries.

who exerted the most profound influence on late medieval writers. A few other figures, less directly influential in later centuries, will also be included in order to flesh out the tradition. Late medieval writers addressing superstition were, in fact, so circumscribed in their acknowledged influences that to restrict ourselves exclusively to the sources they regularly cited would have us jumping from Augustine in the fifth century to Isidore of Seville in the seventh to William of Auvergne and Thomas Aquinas in the thirteenth. While remaining quite selective, in this chapter I will nevertheless seek to provide at least some skein of connecting material between those great names, and to describe how a tradition that seemed monolithic in the late medieval period actually underwent important changes over the course of centuries.

One small source amply demonstrates the attention intellectual authorities of the late Middle Ages paid to the past when considering the issue of superstition. Brief, fragmentary, and anonymous, the text is found in a fifteenth-century manuscript originally in the possession of, and we may provisionally assume produced by, the Augustinian Hermits in Munich. Consisting almost entirely of quotations from patristic and early medieval sources, this pastiche could have originated almost anytime after the ninth century (when the last source it quotes was likely written). Its unique and fragmentary nature, however, suggests that the fifteenth-century copy is probably the original composition. The catalog of the Bavarian State Library, where it now resides, labels it a *Tract on Superstitions, Magic, Sorceries, etc. (Tractatus de superstitionibus, magia, sortilegiis, etc.)*, but this designation is not found in the manuscript itself. Lacking any title, it begins abruptly "Item: from the first book of *On Christian Doctrine*," and proceeds to quote extensively from Augustine's work—although not, in fact, from book 1 of his *On Christian Doctrine (De doctrina Christiana)* but rather his fundamental definition of superstition found in book 2 of that work.[2] Other texts quoted at length are Augustine's *On the Divination of Demons (De divinatione daemonum)* and sections on magic and divination from Isidore's *Etymologies*. Also included is an important decree of church law, the canon *Episcopi* (so-called after its first word, "bishops"), well known to scholars of witchcraft for its description of certain women's superstitious belief that they journeyed at night in service to the goddess Diana, an image that powerfully influenced fifteenth-century notions of witches flying to diabolical sabbaths.

---

2. Anonymous, *De superstitionibus, magia, sortilegiis, etc.*, 294v. In addition to quoting much of *De doctrina Christiana* 2.20(30), the text also includes material from ibid., 2.23(35) and 2.23(36).

Episcopi dates most likely from the late ninth century. Its earliest known iteration appears in a legal collection assembled around 906 by the canonist Regino of Prüm.[3] This makes it by far the youngest text included in this fifteenth-century pastiche. Medieval authorities, however, believed that the canon originated at the Council of Ancyra (modern Ankara), held in 314, which is how the scribe labeled it here, so he would have thought it to be his oldest text, predating Augustine by almost a century.[4] With virtually no original commentary inserted between its excerpts from ancient sources, and completely lacking an introduction or conclusion (it remains obviously unfinished), the compilation's purpose is obscure. The most likely explanation for its composition is that a scribe either took upon himself or was instructed to assemble early authoritative material on superstition. Such a primer would have been an obvious way for a late medieval cleric to get quickly up to speed on the most fundamental, authoritative discussions of superstition from the early Christian era.

If only this anonymous clerical compiler had known the real date of the canon *Episcopi*, we might be able to extrapolate from his selection of texts some kind of perceived periodization: a grouping of sources stretching from the patristic era to the beginning of the tenth century. Instead, however, it would have been Isidore of Seville, in the seventh century, whom our scribe would have thought to be his chronological outlier (if he thought about the chronology of his sources at all—he certainly did not place them in any such order). Yet there are valid grounds for us to impose this periodization anyway onto medieval thinking about superstition, although it is not one that any medieval thinker would consciously have recognized. Already in the second and third centuries CE, church authorities began redefining Roman notions of *superstitio* to fit a Christian framework, and by this maneuver they effectively categorized all pagan religion as superstitious. They continued to think of superstition mainly in terms of paganism long after Rome fell and Christianity achieved dominance in western Europe, as late as the tenth century and even into the very early eleventh.[5] Between the eleventh and the thirteenth centuries, however, superstition was reconceived again, thanks to a major intellectual revival that took place in western Europe, giving rise to much more systematic natural philosophy and also more developed demonology than had been known for centuries, into which ideas of superstition

---

3. Text of the canon in *Quellen*, 38–39. It will be discussed at greater length later in this chapter.

4. "Item ex concilio anquirensi . . .": anonymous, *De superstitionibus, magia, sortilegiis, etc.*, 296v.

5. See Michael D. Bailey, *Magic and Superstition in Europe: A Concise History from Antiquity to the Present* (Lanham, Md., 2007), 43–75; Jean Verdon, *Les superstitions au Moyen Âge* (Paris, 2008), 15–100.

had to be fit. This broad periodization and the conceptual shift it entails will provide the backbone of this chapter and essential background for understanding how authors of the late medieval period appropriated earlier sources and how they approached the perceived superstitions of their own time.

The Superstition of the Pagans

As we have already seen, the term *superstitio* arose in antiquity. It carried multiple and complicated meanings, but in general, since Roman paganism did not assert a strictly dichotomous moral system of absolutely good deities opposed by absolutely wicked demons, superstition for the Romans entailed less the complete opposite of proper *religio* and more an excess of devotion or observance. They also applied the term to unofficial or foreign cults that they deemed to entail dangerous or "unreasonable" practices. For Roman authorities, early Christianity fulfilled all the conditions of a superstition. Of course, Christian writers rejected such charges against their faith. They turned them back against the Romans, and against all pagans (a word whose meaning they also bent to their purposes to mean anyone who was neither Christian nor Jew), proclaiming all the deities of the ancient world to be false and all the devotions honoring them to be erroneous. In the process they upended some fundamental features of ancient metaphysics. This revolution was, in fact, not exclusively Christian in the making. Christianity's monotheism grew out of Judaism's, of course. Also certain late-antique pagan philosophers who conceived of fully benevolent deities or even a single deity governing the entirety of creation struggled with the implications of rites directed to other lesser and more ambivalent creatures, just as Christian thinkers would.[6] Ultimately, however, Christianity raised such issues more aggressively and more successfully than any previous intellectual system. The Christian universe became a sharply bifurcated one. On one side stood Christ and his angels while on the other massed all the dark forces of perdition. Moreover, thanks to Christianity's sweeping universalism, all human beings were implicated in these divisions, whether they accepted them or not. Roman cults, and those of all other ancient peoples, were not simply empty and meaningless; as conceived by Christian authorities, they were instead directed toward fallen Christian angels. All the deities and *daimones* of the ancient world became

---

6. Dale B. Martin, *Inventing Superstition: From the Hippocratics to the Christians* (Cambridge, Mass., 2004), 187–206; Kyle A. Fraser, "The Contested Boundaries of 'Magic' and 'Religion' in Late Pagan Monotheism," *MRW* 4 (2009): 131–51.

for the Christian polemicists who pronounced against them irrevocably evil demons.[7] Since these entities were entirely malevolent and bent on harming humankind, any sort of worship or veneration shown to them automatically became excessive, unreasonable, and superstitious. This transformation, beginning very early in the Christian era, was far from sudden, but its ultimate success was nearly absolute.

"Therefore, my dear friends," wrote the apostle Paul to the early Christian community in Corinth, "flee from the worship of idols." He went on to explain why. "What pagans sacrifice, they sacrifice to demons and not to God. I do not want you to be partners with demons."[8] In the second century, the apologist Justin Martyr urged faithful Christians to reject all false "opinions of the ancients" and not to be swayed by the "superstitious people" who continued to profess them.[9] In the third century, the theologian and church father Origen, defending Christianity against the Greek philosopher Celsus, established *daimones* as entirely evil demons, thereby cementing the notion that all paganism was inevitably superstitious.[10] Of course, Christian pronouncements did not necessarily matter much to non-Christians until the new faith assumed a powerful place in the Roman world, which would not happen until the fourth century, in the wake of the emperor Constantine's declaration of official toleration in 313. Even during the fourth century, however, newly ascendant Christianity, basking in imperial support, coexisted with respectable and entrenched pagan systems. In this period, it seems that many authorities recognized the beneficial mutability of the term "superstition." Because *superstitio* implied improper rites or devotions, but did not invariably designate any specific set of observances, Roman officials could interpret statutes and rulings against *superstitio* as applying to either Christian or pagan practices as their own particular local contexts (and one would assume their own consciences) dictated.[11]

Around the turn of the fourth century and into the early fifth, the time for such ambiguities came to an end. By imperial decree in 380 Christianity

---

7. See Valerie I. J. Flint, "The Demonisation of Magic and Sorcery in Late Antiquity: Christian Redefinitions of Pagan Religions," in *Witchcraft and Magic in Europe: Ancient Greece and Rome*, ed. Bengt Ankarloo and Stuart Clark (Philadelphia, 1999), 277–348.

8. 1 Corinthians 10:14 and 10:20, translation from the New Revised Standard Version.

9. Justin Martyr, *Apology* 1.2, translation from Justin Martyr, *The First and Second Apologies*, trans. and ed. Leslie William Barnard (Mahwah, N.J., 1997), 23.

10. Discussed extensively in Martin, *Inventing Superstition*, 160–86, esp. 177–80, although Martin does not think Origen realized how fundamentally he was altering the meaning of *deisidaimonia/superstitio* (ibid., 188).

11. Michele R. Salzman, "'Superstitio' in the Codex Theodosianus and the Persecution of the Pagans," *Vigiliae Christianae* 41 (1987): 172–88, at 176–80.

became not just a tolerated cult within the empire but the official state religion, and by the early 390s pagan temples were being closed and their rites effectively banned. Patently Christian understandings of superstition began to dominate law codes, until finally the Theodosian Code, issued in 438 but compiling laws from the late fourth and early fifth centuries, declared in no uncertain terms that *superstitio* was to be understood in contrast to proper *religio*, here invariably meaning proper Christianity. It repeatedly labeled pagan rites as inherently superstitious, as it did heretical forms of Christianity itself.[12] Also at this time lived the greatest of the Latin fathers of the church, Augustine of Hippo. He first addressed magical and superstitious rites almost immediately after his famous conversion experience in 386 in an early treatise *Against the Academics* (*Contra academicos*), and he would continue to do so in a series of fundamental works until his death in 430.

As in many other areas of Christian thought, so too with superstition, Augustine established the basic framework in which all subsequent medieval authorities operated.[13] Although Christianity was clearly in ascendancy during his lifetime, the bishop of Hippo had been born into a world of vibrant paganism, and his thinking about superstition very much emerged from that context. Although he would become a supreme critic of superstition, he was himself no stranger to superstitious magical practices, particularly early in his life (to which this chapter's epigraph alludes). By his own account, as a young man in Carthage he had once turned to a diviner, a man named Albicerius, to locate (of all things) a lost spoon, and he later rejected the services of a soothsayer (a *haruspex*, who would have foretold the future by examining the entrails of an animal) while he was seeking to win a competition in rhetoric.[14] Recalling his reaction to this offer many years later in his *Confessions*, Augustine lamented the fact that he had rejected the magical aid not out of any deep Christian piety but merely because he found the animal sacrifices that the sorcerer would have performed as part of his rites distasteful. No such qualms, he noted, prevented him from frequently consulting astrologers.[15]

---

12. *Codex Theodosianus* 16.10, "De paganis, sacrificiis et templis," in Theodor Mommsen and Paul M. Meyer, eds., *Theodosiani libri XVI cum Constitutionibus Sirmondianis et Leges novellae ad Theodosianum pertinentes*, 2 vols. (Berlin, 1905); cf. 16.5, "De haereticis."

13. See Thomas Linsenmann, *Die Magie bei Thomas von Aquin* (Berlin, 2000), 31–98; Fritz Graf, "Augustine and Magic," in *The Metamorphosis of Magic from Late Antiquity to the Early Modern Period*, ed. Jan N. Bremmer and Jan R. Veenstra (Leuven, 2002), 87–103.

14. Augustine, *Contra academicos* 1.6(17), ed. W. M. Green, CCSL 29 (Turnhout, 1970); Augustine, *Confessionum libri XIII* 4.2(3), ed. Lucas Verheijen, CCSL 27 (Turnhout, 1981).

15. Augustine, *Confessionum libri XIII* 4.3(4). See Linsenmann, *Magie*, 74–79, on Augustine's early familiarity with astrology.

Later in his life, of course, Augustine came to regard such activities as the antithesis of true Christian religion. Ironically, his own conversion experience, at least as described in the *Confessions*, relied on a form of "sorcery," the *sortes bibliae*, in which a book of the Bible was opened at random and the first passage lit upon was read as having predictive or instructive power. He would have rejected any accusation that his own action was superstitious, however, because he believed himself to be following a divine command to "take up and read."[16] In general, later Christian authorities carved out an allowable space for *sortes bibliae*, in no small part because of Augustine's example, although even in light of this precedent some steadfastly condemned the "vain examination of psalms or gospels or other scripture" to discern anything about the future.[17] Concerning most practices that might be regarded as magical or divinatory, however, the bishop of Hippo saw no room for equivocation. In the aptly titled *On True Religion* (*De vera religione*) he noted that binding (*religans*) one's soul to God meant abandoning all superstition, and in *On Christian Doctrine*, he stated that all those who truly entered the church cut themselves off from superstition by this act.[18] Further on in that work, he presented his fundamental definition of superstition, already discussed in the introduction above, and as examples of superstitious rites he held up many of the magical and divinatory practices with which he had flirted in his youth.

> Such are the efforts of the magic arts, which the poets are more accustomed to mention than to teach. Of this same sort, but like an officially licensed falsehood, are the books of soothsayers and augurs. To this category also belong all amulets and healing charms that medical science condemns, whether they involve enchantments, or certain marks called "characters," or certain things hung or fastened [on the body], or even performed somehow, not for tempering the body, but in order to make certain signs, either secret or manifest.[19]

---

16. Augustine, *Confessionum libri XIII* 8.12(29).

17. Alexander Carpenter, *Destructorium viciorum* 6.54, pointed explicitly to Augustine as an example of tolerable *sortes*; anonymous, *De superstitionibus* (E), 175v, decried all "vanam inspectionem psalmorum ewangeliorum et aliarum scripturarum futura prenoscitare."

18. Augustine, *De vera religione* 55(111), ed. K.-D. Daur, CCSL 32 (Turnhout, 1962); Augustine, *De doctrina Christiana* 2.6(7), ed. Joseph Martin, CCSL 32 (Turnhout, 1962).

19. Augustine, *De doctrina Christiana* 2.20(30): "Qualia sunt molimina magicarum artium, quae quidem commemorare potius quam docere adsolent poetae. Ex quo genere sunt, sed quasi licentiore uanitate, haruspicum et augurum libri. Ad hoc genus pertinent omnes etiam ligaturae atque remedia, quae medicorum quoque disciplina condemnat, siue in praecantationibus siue in quibusdam notis, quos caracteres uocant, siue in quibusdam rebus suspendendis atque inligandis uel etiam saltandis quodammodo, non ad temperationem corporum, sed ad quasdam significationes aut occultas aut etiam manifestas."

Actions or items functioning as "signs" (*significationes*) rather than producing direct effects themselves came to hold an important place in Christian conceptions of superstition because signs were forms of communication that needed to be directed toward some intelligence, and suspicious authorities readily assumed that those intelligences were demonic. Just prior to the passage quoted above, Augustine had defined the essence of superstition as pertaining to "consultations and pacts" with demons.

As we have already seen, however, the bishop of Hippo noted that superstition also extended to countless "utterly inane" beliefs and practices.[20] For example, he derided people who thought that if they sneezed when putting on their shoes in the morning or if they stumbled when first leaving their houses, they would suffer some misfortune that day. His most famous example, often repeated in late medieval texts, concerned timorous folk who were convinced that if they and a friend passed on different sides of any sizable stone or other object in the roadway while walking together, or if a small child or even a dog ran between them, their friendship would dissolve. To ward off this evil fate, these people often struck the offending intruder. Augustine wryly observed that this otherwise senseless superstition could in fact cause its practitioners some real misfortune. A stone or stump could be counted on to remain passive when attacked, and even young boys would likely suffer a blow from their elders rather than retaliate, but a kicked dog was liable to bite back and "quickly send the one who strikes it from this worthless remedy to a real physician."[21]

Despite his willingness to deride some superstitions as ridiculous and comical, about most of them Augustine was earnest indeed. He devoted his longest discussion not to the inane errors of the foolish but to what he regarded as the dangerously erroneous practice of certain educated men, warning that astrologers who attempted various forms of astral divination "must not be excluded from this type of pernicious superstition."[22] While basic astrological knowledge and study of heavenly motion constituted a learned science, pressing beyond the natural limits of such knowledge led into superstitious error. One of his most effective (and enduring) arguments against

---

20. Introduction, n. 5.

21. Augustine, *De doctrina Christiana* 2.20(31): "Namque a uano remedio cito ille [canis] interdum percussorem suum ad uerum medicum mittit." Repeated in Denys the Carthusian, *Contra vitia superstitionum*, 625–26; Jakob of Paradise, *De potestate demonum*, 261r; Martin of Arles, *De superstitionibus*, 19r; Ulrich of Pottenstein, *Dekalog-Auslegung*, 75.

22. Augustine, *De doctrina Christiana* 2.21(32): "Neque illi ab hoc genere perniciosae superstitionis segregandi sunt, qui genethliaci propter natalium dierum considerationes, nunc autem uulgo mathematici uocantur." His full section on astrological superstition runs 2.21(32)–2.22(34).

natal horoscopes, a major element of such divinatory practice, was to point out the manifest differences between many twins, especially the biblical pair Jacob and Esau, who could not have been more different from one another. If, as astrologers argued to justify their predictions, the stars really imprinted much of human nature at birth, how could those born under the same stars be so different? Some astrologers countered that, because of the tremendous speed at which heavenly bodies moved, while they might appear stable from the vantage point of earth, they could actually assume significantly different positions, and so impart different effects, even in the few moments separating the births of twins. This, however, allowed Augustine to explode their entire claim to practice a "scientific" art. How could they maintain, he retorted, that they grounded their predictions in careful observation and calculation of astral motion if they also asserted that movements entirely unobservable from earth could produce such dramatically variable consequences?[23]

The greatest danger that superstitious practices presented for Augustine, however, was that they could, and likely would, involve demons. His writings marked a culmination of the trend prevalent throughout early Christian writings connecting superstition to demonic forces. He warned of the likelihood that, when making astrological predictions or engaging in other erroneous rites, human beings would entangle themselves in the snares of demons, and he sternly concluded that most forms of superstition stemmed from "a pestiferous fellowship of human beings and demons, as if by a pact of faithless and deceitful friendship."[24] The notion of superstition entailing some kind of demonic pact would reverberate through Christian thought for centuries. So would Augustine's fundamental discussion of demonic power and abilities in his *On the Divination of Demons*. Composed in the first decade of the fifth century, this short treatise was Augustine's response to questions arising in the wake of the Christian destruction of the pagan temple of Serapis in Alexandria in 391. A temple priest had supposedly prophesied the coming destruction, and this raised the question of whether the demons whom Christian critics were certain this priest must have consulted could truly know the future. Augustine replied that demons possessed keen senses and could move at tremendous speed from one end of the earth to the other, thus acquiring knowledge beyond human ken. Also, because of their immortal existence, they had far greater experience than any human in interpreting the course of events. No wonder, then, that with such knowledge

---

23. Ibid., 2.22(33–34).
24. Ibid., 2.20(30), 2.22(34), and quoted passage at 2.23(36).

and experience they could frequently predict future events quite accurately, but they could not actually know the future per se. Only God, and through him his prophets, possessed true foreknowledge in that sense. Demons also frequently made a show of "foreseeing" actions that they themselves then caused to occur, and here Augustine offered a short excursus on how they, with their airy, supple bodies, could affect many things in nature and even powerfully influence, although not absolutely control, human beings in order to make their own predictions come true.[25]

In his greatest work, City of God (De civitate dei), written in the final decades of his life, Augustine reiterated and expanded most of these points. He dedicated the entire fifth book of that long work to astrology, so problematic precisely because it was so respectable in many ways and grounded in such a rich and ancient intellectual tradition. Again he sought to undermine the "scientific" status of many kinds of astrological prediction by pointing out the quandary of twins, born at almost the same moment and so assumedly shaped by the same or very similar natural astral energies, but often very different in their characters and fates. More basically, he pointed to the vast multitude of beings—humans, animals, and even plants—born or otherwise generated at any given moment, which nevertheless possessed very different traits and could be expected to come to very different ends. Another major argument against excessive, hence superstitious, astrological predictions was that attributing too much determinative force over human actions to celestial influences would infringe on free will. Here Augustine found himself defending the power that Christians ascribed to God, arguing that divine foreknowledge of all human ends did not mitigate free will in the same way that the claims of some astrologers did. He again asserted that almost always when astrologers made accurate predictions, which they "wondrously" managed to do quite often, their knowledge derived from some "secret inspiration" by wicked spirits.[26]

Augustine discussed the nature of demonic spirits and their power in books 8 and 9 of City of God, and he treated the involvement of demons in various magical arts in book 10. Against pagan philosophers who argued that such spirits could be neutral or even benevolent mediators between human beings and the gods (daimones in the older sense), he maintained that demons

---

25. Augustine, De divinatione daemonum 3(7), 5(9), 6(10), ed. Iosephus Zycha, CSEL 41 (Vienna, 1900).

26. Augustine, De civitate dei 5.2–9, ed. Bernard Dombart and Alphonse Kalb, CCSL 47–48 (Turnhout, 1955), quote at 5.7: ". . . occulto instinctu fieri spirituum non bonorum."

were utterly evil and malicious toward humans.[27] In particular he challenged the assertion by the Neoplatonist philosopher Porphyry and others that there were two forms of powerful spiritual rites: those drawing on evil spirits (*goetia*, usually translated as witchcraft or sorcery) and those drawing on good spirits (theurgy).[28] For Augustine, all such rites, even if seemingly positive in effect, were superstitious and condemnable because they drew on the power of demons. But even in this negative art, the omnipotence of the Christian God shone through, as he only allowed demons to act in response to such rites in order to tempt and test the faithful.[29]

Augustine did more than just repeat and extend many of his fundamental points about superstition in *City of God*. Since that entire work functioned as a rejection of paganism and an assertion of the superiority of Christianity, Augustine also delved into, and rejected, pagan understandings of superstition, replacing them with superior (in his depiction) Christian ones. Numerous Greek and Roman philosophers and rhetoricians decried what they regarded as erroneous beliefs and foolish rites—superstition—that had accrued around the various cults of pagan antiquity. While criticizing the dross, however, men such as Cicero, Seneca, and Varro sought to preserve the core of pagan religion. Augustine's more incisive solution was, naturally, to depict the entire system as fundamentally flawed. Superstition did not cluster around pagan rites merely through excess; rather all pagan rites were erroneous in their essence.[30] In that maneuver he supplanted pagan antiquity's notion that a practice could be superstitious by virtue of degree with Christianity's basic assertion that superstition lay in the inherent nature of certain rites. Unlike pagan philosophers, Christian authorities could not seek to moderate superstitious practices; they must endeavor to eradicate them.

A century after Augustine of Hippo, Caesarius of Arles, sometimes known as the "Augustine of Gaul," carried on the church's struggle against pagan superstition.[31] As bishop of Arles in the early sixth century, he composed numerous sermons, several of which criticized the continued superstition that he believed existed in his day. Although his direct influence faded in the later

---

27. Esp. ibid., 8.22, 9.13.

28. Ibid., 10.9–10.

29. Ibid., 10.21.

30. Ibid., 4.30–31, also 6.9–10 on Roman writers' attempts to distinguish "mythical" or "fabulous" rites from "natural" ones.

31. See Guillaume Konda, *Le discernement et la malice des pratiques superstitieuses d'après les sermons de S. Césaire d'Arles* (Rome, 1970).

Middle Ages, he was one of the most important early medieval writers to address this topic.[32] His own reliance on previous authorities, such as Augustine, has caused some modern scholars to question whether he or those who wrote in his wake actually reflected any real, enduring practices in their descriptions of superstition.[33] Some have also noted that for all his vitriol when addressing superstitious practices, they actually figure in only a few of his numerous sermons, implying that they were perhaps not really much present in the sixth-century bishopric of Arles.[34] Since we are ultimately more concerned with perceptions about superstitions than with potential realities, however, these debates are less crucial for us. Caesarius remains one of the best sources to illustrate how religious authorities thought about superstition, to whatever degree they did think about them, in the very early medieval period.

More than Augustine, who frequently dealt in broad categories and focused on underlying elements of superstition such as the nature of demonic power, Caesarius in his sermons provides a clearer sense of what early medieval authorities conceived specific superstitious practices to be. He criticized those who observed omens, based on anything from the flights of birds to the frequency of human sneezing.[35] He also frequently condemned seers and soothsayers, although he typically used various terms for diviners (*aruspex*, *caraius*, *divinus*, *sortilegus*) in combination with other terms for enchanters or sorcerers (*incantator* or *praecantator*, *maleficus*) to label practitioners of any kind of magical rite, so we often cannot be certain whether he meant to attack forms of divination specifically or superstitious magical arts more generally.[36] He clearly reviled both and perhaps saw no need to distinguish consistently between the two. As a worried pastor, he frequently warned his flock against any reliance on charms and amulets for healing or protection.[37] He does not seem to have conceived of these last practices, at least, as always necessarily pagan, for he described people sometimes learning such charms from priests or monks, and he inveighed against protective amulets inscribed with Christian prayers and other holy words. Nevertheless, he continued to

32. Harmening, *Superstitio*, 50; Filotas, *Pagan Survivals*, 1; Valerie I. J. Flint, *The Rise of Magic in Early Medieval Europe* (Princeton, N.J., 1991), 42–43.

33. Yitzhak Hen, *Culture and Religion in Merovingian Gaul, A.D. 481–751* (Leiden, 1995), 162–67; but to the contrary, see Filotas, *Pagan Survivals*, 45–46.

34. Hen, *Culture and Religion*, 163; Konda, *Discernement*, 14.

35. Caesarius of Arles, *Sermones* 12.4 and 54.1, ed. Germain Morin, CCSL 103–4 (Turnhout, 1953).

36. Ibid., 13.3, 50.1, 54.1, 70.1, 189.2, 229.4. On his use of terms, see William E. Klingshirn, *Caesarius of Arles: The Making of a Christian Community in Late Antique Gaul* (Cambridge, 1994), 219.

37. Caesarius, *Sermones* 1.12, 13.5, 19.4, 50.1–2, 204.3.

describe most forms of superstition as remnants of paganism or at least as stemming from pagan roots. When discussing what he presented as patently pagan healing rites he repeatedly asserted to his listeners that they would be far better served if they would simply come to church when they were ill, to pray and partake in the sacraments.[38] Regarding a particularly dark area of health care, Caesarius sternly rebuked those women and men who employed herbs, charms, potions, or rites either to help them conceive children against God's will or even more terribly to impede conception or abort fetuses already gestating in the womb.[39]

One can easily imagine Christians in sixth-century Arles engaging in traditional healing or other similar practices without reverting to any kind of real paganism, and some scholars contend that, despite some heated clerical rhetoric, truly vibrant pagan practices had already died out in this era.[40] Nevertheless, such rites seemed to stem from the pagan past, and Caesarius maintained that all who used them "became pagans" (although in employing this language, he himself may well have recognized that he meant something rather different from the paganism of Augustine's era).[41] While he assumed that most blatant remnants of pre-Christian culture had been eradicated, he nevertheless repeatedly instructed his clergy to watch for any evidence of people continuing to worship at pagan shrines or performing devotions at pagan holy sites, particularly certain trees and springs.[42] They were also to remain vigilant for any signs of enduring reverence for pagan holy days, such as people refusing to work on Thursday, in honor of Jupiter, even though they might readily work on Sunday, in violation of Christian precepts.[43] Caesarius also worried that certain elaborate forms of pagan worship still persisted. He condemned people participating in rites in which they dressed as animals, or in which men dressed as women, or honored the sun or the new moon.[44] Such seemingly overt pagan rites may or may not really have taken place in Christian Arles in the sixth century, and if they existed then the degree to which they represented vibrant and enduring paganism as opposed to simple traditionalism now deployed in an essentially Christian context can be questioned. Regardless of such considerations, however, Caesarius's

---

38. Ibid., 13.3, 19.5, 50.1, 52.5, 184.5.

39. Ibid., 1.12, 51.4, 52.4.

40. Esp. Hen, *Culture and Religion*, 154–206.

41. Caesarius, *Sermones* 50.1. On possible slippage of meanings, see C. S. Watkins, *History and the Supernatural in Medieval England* (Cambridge, 2007), 80 and 98.

42. Caesarius, *Sermones* 1.12, 13.5, 33.4, 53.1, 54.5, 229.4.

43. Ibid., 52.2.

44. Ibid., 13.5, 52.2, 192.2, 193.1, 193.4.

focus on them illustrates how paganism continued to frame concern over superstition in this period.

Roughly half a century after the bishop of Arles composed his sermons, Archbishop Martin of Braga (in modern Portugal) addressed superstition in a short treatise *On the Correction of Rustics* (*De correctione rusticorum,* or *Pro castigatione rusticorum*).[45] He wrote this work in the early to mid-570s, shortly after presiding over the Second Council of Braga. That council had ordered bishops across northwest Iberia to better instruct their flocks, both laity and clergy, in the faith. Thus it had broached a number of issues related to superstition. It stipulated, for example, that clergy should not perform incantations or craft amulets, seemingly echoing Caesarius's concern that churchmen were sometimes implicated in superstitious practices. It also forbade the clergy to perform masses over graves and the laity to leave offerings of food at tombs, as this seemed too reminiscent of pagan ancestor worship. Above all, Christians were not to observe any "pagan customs" such as divination or sorcery, nor should they participate in "heathen" astrology.[46]

Martin wrote his treatise at the request of a fellow bishop to expand on these and other points raised at the council. In format, he modeled the work heavily on Augustine's *On Instructing the Unlearned* (*De catechizandis rudibus*), although Augustine actually dealt very little with superstitious practices in that work. In terms of content, Martin appears to have been influenced by Caesarius of Arles's sermons.[47] We can therefore certainly question Martin's accuracy in terms of depicting practices actually present in late sixth-century Iberia, but he unquestionably indicates a continuing clerical mind-set regarding superstition. His short treatise seems to have filled a great need at the time, for in the words of one modern scholar it "spread like wildfire" both within Iberia and beyond.[48] Martin's most basic point, made in the very outset of the treatise, was that the superstitions he would discuss were essentially pagan practices, and that they entailed the worship of demons.[49] These superstitions took many forms, most of them already familiar to us from Augustine and Caesarius. People continued

---

45. The first is its traditional title, while the second is more literally accurate, coming from its opening sentence. I have used the edition in *Martini episcopi Bracarensis opera omnia,* ed. Claude W. Barlow (New Haven, Conn., 1950), 159–81. See also Martin of Braga, *Pro castigatione rusticorum,* ed. and trans. Gennaro Lopez (Rome, 1998).

46. *Concilios Visigóticos e Hispano-Romanos,* ed. José Vives, with Tomás Marín Martínez and Gonzalo Martínez Díez (Barcelona, 1963), 100–103.

47. See Barlow's introduction to his edition, *Martini episcopi Bracarensis opera omnia,* 163–64.

48. Flint, *Rise of Magic,* 44.

49. Martin of Braga, *De correctione rusticorum* 1.

(supposedly) to venerate pagan holy sites: rocks and trees, springs and cross-roads. They relied on augury and other forms of divination, and paid attention to all manner of omens and signs. They continued to observe a pagan calendar, such as, for example, by seeking to marry on Fridays, the day of the goddess Venus.[50] Whether the residue of paganism really continued to lie so heavily on lands that had long since been Christianized, at least nominally, we may again wonder. That Christian authorities in this period continued to describe superstition primarily in terms of the remnants of paganism is indisputable.

Martin, writing in late sixth-century Braga, leads somewhat naturally to another great Iberian authority, Isidore, who served as archbishop of Seville in the early decades of the seventh century (he died in 636). His great work, the *Etymologies* (*Etymologiae*), set out, as its title suggests, to examine the meanings and origins of words. In fact, it became a virtual encyclopedia of classical and early Christian knowledge. His main discussion of superstitious and magical practices comes in book 8 of the *Etymologies*, dealing with "the church and sects" (*De ecclesia et sectis*). Here he defined superstition in mainly Ciceronian fashion as "superfluous and excessive observance," and in a separate section he would quote Cicero directly that superstitious people were those who prayed and offered sacrifices constantly and excessively.[51] His main value to later medieval authors, however, owed to the extensive catalog he compiled of varieties of magical and divinatory practices. He provided, for example, the classical definition of necromancy as divination by summoning the spirits of the dead, while also implying the distinctly Christian notion that it actually involved the invocation of demons. Geomancers, aeromancers, pyromancers, and hydromancers worked with the four elements of earth, air, fire, and water (with hydromancers specifically calling up the "shades of demons" to appear in pools or water-filled basins). Enchanters (*incantatores*) employed words and verbal rites. Soothsayers (*haruspices*) observed what "days and hours" were propitious for various activities and undertakings as well as reading the future in the spilled entrails of animals, while augurs offered predictions based on the flights of birds. Astrologers, in turn, "augured" according to the movements of the stars. And the list goes on.[52]

---

50. Ibid., 16.

51. Isidore of Seville, *Etymologiarum sive originum libri XX* 8.3.6, ed. W. M. Lindsay, 2 vols. (1911; repr., Oxford, 1971): "Superstitio dicta eo quod sit superflua aut superinstituta." Ibid., 10.244: "Superstitiosis ait Cicero (Nat. Deor. 2, 72) appelatos qui totos dies precabantur et immolabant, ut sibi sui liberi superstites essent."

52. Ibid., 8.9.11–22.

At the conclusion of his magical catalog, Isidore encapsulated how all Christians should regard such practices. He never, in this long list, used the word *superstitio*, nor did he in his final summation. He clearly signaled that concept to readers familiar with the larger Christian tradition, however, as he reiterated almost verbatim Augustine's conclusion to his discussion of superstition in *On Christian Doctrine*. "In all these things," wrote the bishop of Seville, "is the art of demons, arising from a certain pestiferous fellowship of humans and evil angels."[53] He did use the term "superstition" directly in another influential summation that would be repeated by almost every subsequent Christian authority, in which he distinguished astronomy from its close cousin astrology. Astronomy, which according to Isidore had first been developed by the ancient Egyptians, dealt with studying "the revolution of the heavens, the rising, setting, and motion of the stars." It was an entirely legitimate science. The early Chaldeans, on the other hand, had inaugurated the practice of astrology when they began to observe the movement of the stars in order to draw horoscopes and make other predictions. As has already been mentioned, medieval science held that all heavenly bodies exerted some natural influence over terrestrial ones, and so therefore virtually all medieval authorities asserted that a certain degree of prediction was possible based on observations and calculations of astral motion. Isidore influentially opined that, whereas astronomy was an entirely legitimate science, "astrology is partly natural and partly superstitious," indicating a nebulous boundary that would trouble authorities for centuries to come.[54]

After Isidore, in the later seventh and eighth centuries, influential individual authors tend to fade from the story of Christian consideration of superstition. A plethora of law codes and church canons, however, continued to address superstitious practices. One convenient example is the brief (often cryptically so), anonymous list of thirty condemned superstitions appended to the canons of the Council of Leptinnes (modern Estinnes, in Hainault, Belgium) around 743.[55] The practices this document condemned seem not to have varied much from those of previous centuries. It censured pagan-seeming worship or rites at graves or over the dead (nos. 1–2); rites before trees, stones, or springs, and of course rites directed overtly to pagan deities (nos. 6–8, 11); the observance of pagan feasts, holy days, or festivals

---

53. Ibid., 8.9.31: "In quibus omnibus ars daemonum est ex quadam pestifera societate hominum et angelorum malorum exorta."

54. Ibid., 3.27.1: "Astrologia vero partim naturalis, partim superstitiosa est."

55. *Indiculus superstitionum et paganiarum*, in Alfred Boretius, ed., *MGH Leges 2, Capitularia regum Francorum 1* (Hanover, 1883), 223; Filotas, *Pagan Survivals*, gives a good sense of other source material.

(nos. 2, 20, 24); the use of amulets or incantations (nos. 10, 12); and the use of augury or divination (nos. 13–14). It also condemned the construction of "little houses" (*casulae*) as sanctuaries for pagan worship (no. 4). While many of the seemingly more overtly pagan practices denounced in this and other early medieval sources found little resonance in late medieval writing on superstition, a curious parallel to this last proscription can be found in one text from the early fifteenth century. In addressing the issue of demonic power in a scholastic debate, the theologian Johannes of Frankfurt condemned people who constructed "little houses" (*domuncule vel casule*) in fields, where they would expect to receive visions.[56] We can only speculate about what this fragmentary similarity really means: a singular instance of an early medieval decree still influencing a late medieval academic; a trace of an ancient practice that had actually endured over many centuries, at least in the Low Countries and middle Rhineland; or merely a coincidence.

Skipping ahead several hundred years from this mid-eighth-century list of superstitions, and passing (just barely) the millennial mark of the year 1000, we come to one final significant early medieval source. Around the year 1010, Bishop Burchard of Worms compiled his *Decretum*, a collection of church canons and codes.[57] He dealt with magic in book 10 of this work, while in book 19, entitled "The Corrector" or "The Physician" (*Corrector sive medicus*) and often circulated separately, he presented a long list of superstitious beliefs and practices.[58] His coverage is extensive, but his content is not astonishing. He defined superstition from Augustine, and he listed various categories of magic drawn from both the bishop of Hippo and Isidore of Seville.[59] He also quoted Augustine to explain how demons could predict the future and how they might infect divinatory rites, and he roundly condemned any consultation of magicians or diviners.[60] He noted that Christians who engaged in superstition were "worse than pagans," but he also admitted that clerics, and not just the laity, might succumb

---

56. Johannes of Frankfurt, *Quaestio*, 77.

57. See Greta Austin, *Shaping Church Law around the Year 1000: The "Decretum" of Burchard of Worms* (Farnham, U.K., 2009).

58. Burchard, *Decretorum libri viginti*, PL 140 (Paris, 1880), cols. 537–1058. For citations from book 10, in which chapters are typically quite short, I give only book and chapter numbers. For citations from book 19 chap. 5, which is very long, I also give section numbers from the edition in Hermann Joseph Schmitz, *Die Bussbücher und das kanonische Bussverfahren: Nach handschriftlichen Quellen dargestellt*, 2 vols. (1898; repr., Graz, 1958), and column numbers from PL in parentheses.

59. Burchard, *Decretum* 10.41–42.

60. On demonic divination: ibid., 10.45–46. Condemnations: 10.3–8, 10.23, 10.28, 19.5.60 (col. 960).

to such error.[61] He castigated the use of ligatures (items bound to a sick person's body) and other amulets, the observance of omens, the belief that incantations or other rites could affect the weather or arouse love or hatred between people, and the use of rites or potions to cause infertility, impotence, or abortions.[62] He also condemned what might appear to be mainly natural healing practices, forbidding (in what would become a standard element of medieval canon law) people to use any kind of incantation other than the sanctioned formulas of the Apostles' Creed or Lord's Prayer when gathering medicinal herbs.[63] As authorities had for centuries, Burchard clearly viewed most such practices as remnants of paganism. Also like earlier authors, he cataloged such superstitious practices alongside what appear in his descriptions to be more overtly pagan rites, such as worshipping at certain stones, trees, or crossroads, performing traditional funerary rituals instead of strictly Christian ones over the dead, and continuing to observe non-Christian feasts and festivals.[64]

Again we confront the vexing issue of whether these sources accurately reflected any real contemporary practices or just reiterated previously established categories. Northern Germanic authors like the one who produced the anonymous list of superstitions in 743 drew heavily from sources that were not only centuries old but which were themselves produced in a very different cultural context, that of southern Gaul and Iberia.[65] Yet some scholars warn, with validity, that while we must guard against using such material too credulously, we must equally guard against reading it too skeptically. Burchard of Worms, in particular, has been held up as a reliable witness who "almost certainly reflect[s] practices prevalent in the Rhineland of the eleventh century."[66] There is little reason to doubt that people in the Rhineland around the year 1000 performed healing rites of some kind, practiced various forms

---

61. On superstition being worse than paganism: ibid., 10.10. On clerical superstition: 10.30, 10.33, 10.48.

62. On ligatures and amulets: ibid., 10.18, 10.23, 19.5.63 (col. 961), 19.5.69 (cols. 961–62), 19.5.92 (col. 964). On omens: 10.13, 19.5.149 (cols. 970–71). On weather magic: 10.8, 10.28, 19.5.68 (col. 961), 19.5.194 (col. 976). On love or hatred: 19.5.69 (cols. 961–62), 19.5.172–73 (col. 974), 19.5.176 (col. 974). On fertility: 19.5.159 (col. 972), 19.5.186 (col. 975).

63. Ibid., 10.20, 19.5.65 (col. 961).

64. On springs, stones, trees, etc.: ibid., 10.2, 10.10, 10.21, 10.32, 19.5.66 (col. 961). On funerary rites: 10.34, 19.5.59 (col. 960), 19.5.91 (col. 964), 19.5.96–97 (cols. 964–65). On observance of feasts, festivals, and *kalends*: 10.15–17, 10.36–39, 19.5.62 (col. 960), 19.5.99 (col. 965), 19.5.104 (col. 965), 19.5.153 (col. 971).

65. Ian N. Wood, "Pagan Religions and Superstitions East of the Rhine from the Fifth to the Ninth Century," in *After Empire: Towards an Ethnology of Europe's Barbarians*, ed. G. Ausenda (Woodbridge, U.K., 1995), 253–68, esp. 254.

66. Filotas, *Pagan Survivals*, 56.

of divination, observed omens, and engaged in other activities that aroused real concern about superstition among authorities. Whether these practices still bore the strong imprint of paganism, as Burchard feared, is much more debatable. Unless we want to assume complete duplicity on the part of medieval writers, however, we must grant that Burchard generally thought of them as pagan. Also clear is that this way of thinking about superstition, still so evident in his *Decretum*, would begin to fade soon thereafter. Authorities addressing superstition in the high Middle Ages (conventionally the eleventh through thirteenth centuries) might occasionally bandy about the label of paganism, but their actual descriptions would not paint superstitious actions as pagan with anywhere near the vehemence evident in most early medieval sources. They were, simply put, writing in a very different time, possibly in terms of the practices they actually saw in the world around them, but certainly in terms of their own approach to the topic under debate.

While much of Burchard's framing of superstition would not carry forward, in one area he marks a trend that continued powerfully into the later medieval period, reaching a kind of crescendo in the fifteenth century, namely the strong association of superstition with women.[67] Medieval clerical writers were never especially well disposed toward women. They drew from an intellectual tradition in which all classical authority proclaimed that women were less intelligent than men, and all Christian authority declared that women were more sinful and prone to demonic deception and temptation. That women would be more inclined to superstition than men was, therefore, all but self-evident. Yet many early writers did not address superstition in any strongly gendered way. The canons and regulations that Burchard collected, however, perhaps because of their practical legal nature, specifically targeted women again and again. One version of the *Corrector* even makes a point of noting, before a long list of practices associated with women (not all of them superstitious), that "while the preceding questions are common to both women and men, the following pertain particularly to women."[68]

Burchard included in his collection one text (in two slightly different versions, no less) that would have particularly severe ramifications for women

---

67. See Martha Rampton, "Burchard of Worms and Female Magical Ritual," in *Medieval and Early Modern Ritual: Formalized Behavior in Europe, China and Japan*, ed. Joëlle Rollo-Koster (Leiden, 2002), 7–34.

68. Burchard, *Decretum* 19.5.152(α) (col. 971). Women are specifically mentioned in relation to superstition in *Decretum* 10.1, 10.8, 10.14, 10.24, 10.29, 10.35, 19.5.69–70 (cols. 961–62), 19.5.90 (cols. 963–64), 19.5.96 (cols. 964–65), 19.5.153 (col. 971), 19.5.159 (col. 972), 19.5.168 (col. 973), 19.5.170–73 (cols. 973–74), 19.5.175–77 (col. 974), 19.5.179–81(cols. 974–75), 19.5.185–86 (col. 975), 19.5.193–94 (col. 976).

through the centuries: the canon *Episcopi*.[69] This document recounted the delusion of "certain wicked women" who believed that they journeyed at night in the train of the goddess Diana, whom they served as their mistress. The canon asserted that there was no reality to this belief, and that these foolish women had been "seduced by the illusions and phantasms of demons." In the fifteenth century, this image of women traveling through the night to participate in demonic assemblies would become an important, although often contested, element of the emerging concept of the witches' sabbath.[70] By that time, however, the overtones of paganism associated with the canon had grown very muted indeed. Fifteenth-century sources might still assert that these delirious women believed that they went with Diana, or the Germanic goddess Holda, or other similar mythological figures, but these names were simply ciphers for demons in the minds of clerical authorities. Any thought that such assemblies represented an enduring pagan tradition had largely vanished. What remained was demonic malevolence and the perennial threat it represented.

Scholastic Superstitions

Beginning in the eleventh century, Christian authorities' treatment of superstition, and especially of the demonic elements they so often associated with superstitious practices, underwent an important change. While in late antiquity the church fathers had debated the nature of demons and *daimones* with pagan philosophers and other educated elites, in the course of the early medieval centuries, demonically inspired superstitions, still strongly linked to paganism, had become the purview of the uneducated laity and the less well-trained members of the clergy. There were, simply put, no more educated pagans with whom the church needed to contend. In the high medieval period, however, some learned men again began to practice demonic rites, superstitious in the eyes of others. They were not pagans working with an erroneous concept of demons' basic nature or inherent malevolence, but Christian clergy who understood only too well the dark forces with which they entangled themselves. In the mid-eleventh century, the scholar Anselm of Besate wrote his *Rhetorimachia*, a work that, as the title suggests, focused

---

69. Ibid., 10.1, and 19.5.90 (cols. 963–64).

70. See Werner Tschacher, "Der Flug durch die Luft zwischen Illusionstheorie und Realitätsbeweis: Studien zum sog. Kanon Episcopi und zum Hexenflug," *Zeitschrift der Savigny-Stiftung für Rechtsgeschichte* 116, Kan. Abt. 85 (1999): 225–76; Martine Ostorero, *Le diable au sabbat: Littérature démonologique et sorcellerie (1440–1460)*, ML 38 (Florence, 2011), 580–617.

on the learned art of rhetoric.[71] To demonstrate accusatory modes of argument and persuasion, he indicted his own cousin, Rotiland, for practicing demonic magic. In one particularly detailed account, he related how Rotiland took a young boy outside the city walls (assumedly those of Parma, where Anselm had studied), buried him up to his waist, lit fires that burned with acrid smoke, and performed a complex demonic conjuration, all as part of an elaborate love spell to make women swoon for him. His cousin, Anselm asserted, had learned this art from a book of demonic magic in his possession. Later, Anselm also related how Rotiland acquired some of his craft from a Saracen physician, and how he performed other horrible rites with such gruesome instruments as the severed hand of a corpse.[72]

The charges that Anselm brought against his cousin were quite literally rhetorical—we cannot be certain that Rotiland really practiced such horrific rites or even that he existed at all.[73] Real or not, however, he represents an early depiction of a figure that would become increasingly familiar to educated authorities addressing magic and superstition: the learned clerical necromancer who performed superstitious but nevertheless powerfully effective and deliberately demonic rites. In the twelfth century, the English clergyman John of Salisbury reported that he had been forced to participate in a form of demonic divination while only a boy. A priest from whom he was learning Latin made John and another pupil observe as he performed certain rites and called on demons (so John was certain because of the revulsion the unknown names that the priest uttered inspired in him) in order to conjure images in a polished basin or even in the boys' own fingernails, which had been anointed with oil. The rationale was that young boys would be more sensitive to any illusory images that might appear, but in fact the effort was not terribly successful, as John saw nothing at all and the other boy perceived only "cloudy figures."[74] In the thirteenth century, the Cistercian Caesarius of Heisterbach wrote in his Dialogue on Miracles (Dialogus miraculorum) about a certain knight, Henry of Falkenstein, who doubted the existence of demons. The skeptical knight sought out a cleric named Philip who was famous for

71. Beth S. Bennett, "The Significance of the *Rhetorimachia* of Anselm de Besate in the History of Rhetoric," *Rhetorica* 5.3 (1987): 231–50.

72. Karl Manitius, "Magie und Rhetorik bei Anselm von Besate," *Deutsches Archiv für Erforschung des Mittelalters* 12 (1956): 52–72; see also Edward Peters, *The Magician, the Witch, and the Law* (Philadelphia, 1978), 21–28.

73. Peters, *Magician*, 23, 32.

74. John of Salisbury, *Policraticus I–IV* 2.28, ed. K. S. B. Keats-Rohan, CCCM 118 (Turnhout, 1993), 167–68.

his skill at necromancy and asked him to summon a demonic spirit as evidence. Philip was only too happy to oblige, and, taking Henry to a remote crossroads at midday, conjured up various demons and ultimately the devil himself in such terrifying forms that all the color drained from Henry's face and he retained that stricken look for the rest of his life.[75] Such stories, true or not in their particulars, illustrate authorities' increasing familiarity with the "clerical underworld" of necromancy emerging in the high Middle Ages.[76] Although the term "necromancy" was of course centuries old, the form of elite magic to which it now referred, consciously and explicitly demonic, represented a new aspect of superstition.

Concerns about superstitious practices among the common laity persisted, too, and authorities worried about any number of potential foolish errors that endured or might arise among ordinary Christians. In fact, as the pastoral infrastructure of the church grew more elaborate and sophisticated in these centuries, opportunities for clerical authorities to observe and censure common practices increased.[77] In a remarkable example from the mid-1200s, the French inquisitor Stephen of Bourbon encountered a cult near Lyon dedicated to the veneration of a dog, the "holy greyhound" Guinefort. He immediately condemned the cult as superstitious and worked to extirpate it.[78] In this he acted more as a preacher and pastoral minister than as an inquisitor prosecuting erroneous belief, although in fact these two roles could blend easily together. Ever since the sermons of Caesarius of Arles and indeed the catechetical efforts of Saint Augustine himself, Christian ministers had sought to instruct their flocks in proper beliefs and instill correct devotional practices by warning of the dangers of superstitious rites. During the high medieval centuries, the Western church developed mechanisms of both legalistic control and pastoral care to a tremendous degree. Through figures such as Stephen, and through the issue of superstition, we can see how these developments reinforced one another. Behind them we can also discern a new degree of education and clerical training. At whatever level men such as Anselm of Besate, John of Salisbury, Caesarius of Heisterbach, and Stephen of Bourbon encountered superstition, and however they responded to it,

---

75. Caesarius of Heisterbach, *Dialogus miraculorum* 5.2, ed. Joseph Strange, 2 vols. (1851; repr., Ridgewood, N.J., 1966), 1:276–78.

76. Richard Kieckhefer, *Magic in the Middle Ages* (Cambridge, 1989), 153–56.

77. Jean-Claude Schmitt, "Les 'superstitions,'" in *Histoire de la France religieuse*, vol. 1, *Des dieux de la Gaule à la papauté d'Avignon*, ed. Jacques Le Goff (Paris, 1988), 417–551, at 497–502.

78. Jean-Claude Schmitt, *The Holy Greyhound: Guinefort, Healer of Children since the Thirteenth Century*, trans. Martin Thom (Cambridge, 1983).

what they had in common was their intellectual background and formation. They were scholastics, educated in the new schools and ultimately the first universities that arose in western Europe in the eleventh and twelfth centuries, and they were steeped in the new intellectual method of scholasticism that developed in those schools.

Scholasticism can imply many things, but here we need touch on only a couple of salient elements: a powerful systematization of thought, and an imperative to harmonize Christian doctrine with ancient, predominantly Aristotelian philosophy then being recovered in the medieval West. In terms of understanding and defining superstition, intellectual authorities began to develop more systematic forms of demonology. As critical a concern as demons had always been to Christian writers since the earliest days of the church, not until the late thirteenth or even early fourteenth century, some modern scholars would argue, did a truly coherent system of demonology develop.[79] The study of natural philosophy was also advancing in the schools, and by the mid-fourteenth century a notion of natural magic had emerged that profoundly shaped how scholastics conceptualized certain forms of superstitious practice. Moreover, no matter what kind of superstition educated authors addressed in their writings, they almost always had some direct familiarity with elite forms of magical practice—mainly astral magic, astrological divination, and necromancy—since these either made inroads into the official curriculum of the schools where these men had trained or existed in a shadowy world that ringed them.[80]

Canon law provides a good example of the scholastic impulse toward systematization. As we have seen, superstition had long been a topic of church canons and early canonical collections, such as that of Burchard of Worms. In the first half of the twelfth century, however, at the law school of Bologna, the systematization of canon law reached a new level of sophistication with the legal scholar Gratian's monumental *Decretum*, which he composed, in good scholastic fashion, to harmonize the multitude of legal rulings that had accrued within the church over the centuries.[81] This work provided the basis of ecclesiastical law for the remainder of the Middle Ages (and for the

79. Alain Boureau, *Satan the Heretic: The Birth of Demonology in the Medieval West*, trans. Teresa Lavender Fagan (Chicago, 2006), 3–4, 8–9.

80. Kieckhefer, *Magic in the Middle Ages*, 117–19; Peters, *Magician*, 63–67; Charles Burnett, "Talismans: Magic as Science? Necromancy among the Seven Liberal Arts," in Burnett, *Magic and Divination in the Middle Ages: Texts and Techniques in the Islamic and Christian Worlds* (Aldershot, U.K., 1996), 1–15.

81. On the work's actual composition, see Anders Winroth, *The Making of Gratian's Decretum* (Cambridge, 2000).

Catholic Church deep into the modern period as well). Gratian organized part of his vast compilation into "cases" (*causae*), and he dealt with sorcery, divination, and superstition primarily in *causa* 26, which then became an authoritative source for later jurists and legal scholars.[82] Law, however, tends to be a very conservative field, with legal codes focusing more on past rulings than present innovation (the law in practice can, of course, be much more dynamic). The underlying case of *causa* 26 was that of a priest who practiced sorcery and divination, refusing to stop even when his bishop censured him. Possibly Gratian intended this example to speak to the contemporary context of distinctly elite, learned clerical magic. As we have seen with Burchard of Worms, however, church law had forbidden clergy to engage in magical practices for centuries, and simple parish priests were often suspected of succumbing to common superstitions just as their parishioners did. All the material Gratian collected in *causa* 26 was very traditional. He defined sorcery (*sortilegium*) from Isidore, and on superstition he quoted Augustine's long definition from *On Christian Doctrine* in full. He outlined all the standard forms of magic and divination from both Augustine and Isidore: aeromancy, hydromancy, augury, astrology, and so forth. Drawing on Augustine's *On the Divination of Demons* he explained how demons could predict the future and contribute to divination. In the long fifth "question" of *causa* 26 he gathered over a dozen early legal rulings against such practices, including the canon *Episcopi*, which he attributed to the fourth-century Council of Ancyra, as had earlier legal authorities. For the real developments in high medieval thought on superstition, we must look beyond the law.

In addition to the schools, scholastics also brought their concerns over superstition into the various ecclesiastical and secular courts of Europe, whose growing bureaucracies they staffed in this era. A good example here is the English cleric and courtier John of Salisbury. He was born in the second decade of the twelfth century in what is now Old Sarum, the original site of Salisbury (the cathedral, and so the city around it, transferred to its current location in 1220). Educated at Paris, he served for a long time in the archiepiscopal court at Canterbury before receiving a bishopric himself, that of Chartres, late in his life.[83] He wrote his major work, *Policraticus*, in the 1150s while at Canterbury. The subtitle of the treatise is *On the Frivolities of*

---

82. Emil Friedberg, ed., *Corpus Iuris Canonici*, 2 vols. (1879–81; repr., Graz, 1955), 1:cols 1019–46. On Gratian and later legal traditions, see Patrick Hersperger, *Kirche, Magie, und "Aberglaube": Superstitio in der Kanonistik des 12. und 13. Jahrhunderts* (Cologne, 2010).

83. A good, brief introduction is Cary J. Nederman, *John of Salisbury* (Tempe, Ariz., 2005).

Courtiers (*De nugis curialium*), indicating John's satirical intent. He meant to ridicule the corrupt or simply nonsensical practices he had seen developing at various courts in his day, and among these were superstitious practices of courtiers and clerics. Astrology was beginning to assume a significant presence in the courts of John's time, and would grow only more prevalent in subsequent centuries. Like Isidore, John distinguished the licit science of the stars from the superstition of divinatory astrology, which "exceeds the bounds of sobriety." Such divination was illicit because its predictions extended far beyond anything immediately affected by natural astral forces and it claimed to provide a foreknowledge that only God truly possessed. In the realm of human action, on which horoscopes and other astrological prognostications typically focused, it trampled on the idea of free will.[84]

John also addressed various forms of magic, offering categories and definitions mainly from Isidore and the classical authorities on which Isidore himself had drawn.[85] He mentioned necromancy in particular, and provided a long discussion of its locus classicus in the Christian tradition: the biblical account of the Israelite king Saul turning to a female diviner, later designated the "witch" of Endor, who supposedly conjured the spirit of the dead prophet Samuel to predict the outcome of an impending battle with the Philistines (1 Samuel 28). Although the original text offers no indication that Samuel's shade was anything other than genuine, in keeping with what had become the standard interpretation by this time, John specified that it was actually a demon summoned by necromantic rites. In the very next chapter, he recounted his own experience as a young pupil with a necromantic rite, discussed above, and he condemned the art of scrying (conjuring images in a crystal, liquid, or any reflective surface) generally.[86] He also dismissed a plethora of omens, including observances of the behaviors of various birds and beasts. Most of these he drew from standard omen condemnations in earlier sources, but he also brought the practice up to his own day, noting in particular how many of his contemporaries considered encountering a toad a sign of good luck, although he found the sight of these little creatures repulsive.[87] More generally, he maintained that all supposed omens were meaningless and only the foolish put any faith in them, but he conceded (as would all later authors) that some future occurrences could be predicted by natural signs. Farmers and sailors, for example, knew

---

84. John of Salisbury, *Policraticus* 2.19, pp. 111–19, quote at 112.
85. Ibid., 1.11–12, pp. 57–61.
86. Ibid., 2.27–28, pp. 147–69.
87. Ibid., 1.13, pp. 61–70, toad at p. 66.

well how to judge coming weather from the behavior of certain birds, for birds were very sensitive to changing atmospheric conditions. Such entirely natural methods of prediction were not so much divination, however, as diagnosis, akin to the work of physicians.[88] This comparison of legitimate predictions based on reading astrological or other natural signs to medical diagnosis based on natural bodily symptoms extended back in Christian thought at least to the time of Augustine, and would continue into the late medieval period as well.[89]

John also discussed dreams as a potential source of divination at some length, and he acknowledged that this was a difficult subject, for portentous dreams might sometimes prove true, but they were often false and superstitious. The complexity stemmed from the fact that dreams could have several possible origins. They might arise from entirely natural causes, such as changes in bodily humors that could indicate some sickness or disease, or changes in the atmosphere that could be used to help predict the weather. They might also be instigated by angels in order to convey entirely wholesome revelations. They could also, of course, very easily be caused by demons.[90] Late medieval authors would struggle with these same complexities, and they would generally come to conclusions similar to John's that trying to discern portents in dreams should generally be avoided because the danger of unintended error or deliberate demonic deception was simply too great.[91]

The authors of the twelfth century offer a sense of both the innovations and continuities in scholastic thought on many forms of magic and divination that late medieval authorities would treat capaciously in their writings on superstition. In terms of direct influence on late medieval writers, however, they pale in comparison to the great figures of the thirteenth century. By the 1200s, scholastic systems of theology and Aristotelian natural philosophy were being perfected, and academics, above all at the great university in Paris, were thinking ever more precisely about how both natural forces and spiritual powers operated in the world. One of the most important such thinkers, perhaps the leading demonologist of the thirteenth century, and with Thomas Aquinas one of the two high medieval scholastics most cited

---

88. Ibid., 2.1–2, pp. 71–75.

89. Cf. Augustine, *De civitate dei* 10.32; anonymous, *De superstitionibus* (M), 55v; Nikolaus of Jauer, *De superstitionibus*, 50r.

90. John of Salisbury, *Policraticus* 2.14–17, pp. 93–106.

91. Anonymous, *De superstitionibus* (M), 65v–66v, 68r–68v; Carpenter, *Destructorium viciorum* 6.50; Denys the Carthusian, *Contra vitia superstitionum*, 615–17; Jakob of Paradise, *De potestate demonum*, 266v; Nikolaus of Jauer, *De superstitionibus*, 52r; Laurens Pignon, *Contra les devineurs*, 283–84; Johannes Schwarz, *De divinacionibus*, 318r; Ulrich of Pottenstein, *Dekalog-Auslegung*, 95–101.

by writers addressing superstition in the fourteenth and fifteenth centuries, was William of Auvergne.[92] Born around 1180, William was first a pupil and then a master in Paris, and finally bishop there from 1228 until his death in 1249. He clearly encountered magical texts as a student. Like John of Salisbury, he may even have been involved in superstitious rites in his youth, although the evidence for this is somewhat obscure.[93] Certainly in his later work he discussed practices similar to those John described of learned clerical magicians using children for demonic scrying in mirrors or liquids.[94]

In the first half of the thirteenth century, scholastics increasingly situated the apparent wonders thought possible through demonic and other forms of magical art within a framework of Aristotelian natural philosophy. More detailed consideration of potentially occult forces in nature (emanating from the stars or inherent in plants or minerals) led to the articulation of a separate category of "natural magic" (*magica naturalis*) operating without the taint of demonic involvement that Christian authorities had always associated with magical operations, and William may well have been the first scholar to use the term.[95] He introduced the notion of natural magic in his treatise *On Laws* (*De legibus*), where he seemed to emphasize the scope of natural occult forces, arguing that many people attributed entirely natural wonders far too readily to demonic activity, thereby exaggerating the degree of demonic influence in the world.[96] In his much longer *On the Universe* (*De universo*), however, after again discussing natural magic he stressed that most varieties of magical art were nevertheless indeed demonic, and that demons possessed tremendous knowledge of occult natural forces, such that they often employed natural magic themselves.[97]

Long sections of *On the Universe* deal with the nature of demonic existence and power.[98] William expounded on the capacities of the airy bodies that scholastic theologians argued demons assumed when seeking to interact with the physical world, and he analyzed at length how they could affect physical substances and cause movement ("locomotion") in material bodies.

92. On those aspects of William's life and career relevant here, see Thomas B. de Mayo, *The Demonology of William of Auvergne: By Fire and Sword* (Lewiston, N.Y., 2007); Lynn Thorndike, *A History of Magic and Experimental Science*, 8 vols. (New York, 1923–58), 2:338–71.

93. De Mayo, *Demonology*, 31.

94. William of Auvergne, *De universo* 2.3.18, in William, *Opera omnia* (Venice, 1591), 988–90.

95. Jean-Patrice Boudet, *Entre science et nigromance: Astrologie, divination et magie dans l'Occident médiéval (XIIe–XVe siècle)* (Paris, 2006), 128.

96. William, *De legibus* 24, in *Opera omnia*, 67.

97. William, *De universo* 2.3.22, pp. 998–1000.

98. Ibid., 2.2.33–34, pp. 825–27, 2.2.69–70, pp. 868–72, and all of 2.3.1–26, pp. 957–1012.

Among his most arresting illustrations of demonic action within the constraints of natural law was his explanation of how demonic incubi appeared to impregnate human women. In William's rigorous and logical system, demons and human beings could not naturally reproduce with one another because they were creatures of entirely different orders. Moreover, as immortal spiritual beings, demons had no need and hence no natural capacity for reproduction of any kind. Instead, they employed their ability to assume illusory forms, to transport matter, and to move at tremendous speed in order to mimic such ability. Thus they would first appear as succubi to men, seduce and have sex with them, collect the emitted semen, and then rush off to impregnate women with it.[99] Sex with demons was of course sinful, and any resulting offspring would be bastards, but at least this argument concluded that such children were still fully human and not unnatural, half-demonic monstrosities.

William also expounded on demonic knowledge, especially as it applied to divination, largely following the well-worn path established by Augustine.[100] He was critical of astrology. As someone who recognized and indeed had emphasized the existence of natural forces permeating the universe, he could hardly deny the long tradition in Christian thought asserting that careful study of the stars could be used to predict any events that astral energies directly caused or at least strongly influenced. He warned, however, that many aspects of astrology were false. Heavenly bodies had often been the focus of "superstitious" cults in antiquity, and still in his day some who studied the stars attributed to them properties and powers bordering on the "idolatrous"; such errors frequently originated with demons.[101] In brief, astrologers lapsed into superstition whenever they tried to extend their predictions beyond those areas that astral forces directly affected, mainly the weather and human health insofar as it was connected to the balance of the four bodily humors, believed to be subject to astral influences.[102]

In all of these areas—demonic power, astral forces, and other occult properties in nature—William provided a distillation of scholastic thought that

---

99. Ibid., 2.3.35, p. 1009. On the general emergence of incubi in scholastic thought, see Dyan Elliott, *The Bride of Christ Goes to Hell: Metaphor and Embodiment in the Lives of Pious Women, 200–1500* (Philadelphia, 2012), 236–43.

100. William, *De universo* 2.2.62, pp. 859–60.

101. William, *De legibus* 11, p. 43; *De universo* 1.1.46, pp. 626–28.

102. William, *De legibus* 25, pp. 77–78; *De universo* 2.2.76, pp. 876–77. Detailed discussion of William's positions especially on astral talismans is found in Nicolas Weill-Parot, *Les "images astrologiques" au Moyen Âge et à la Renaissance: Spéculations intellectuelles et pratiques magiques (XIIe–XVe siècle)* (Paris, 2002), 175–212.

became absolutely fundamental to many later medieval clerical writers addressing superstition. Despite his assertion of certain kinds of natural magic, his overriding emphasis was on the threat of demons and the danger that questionable rites might involve even inadvertent demonic invocation and worship. For this reason he often discussed as "idolatrous" practices that other authorities labeled as "superstitious." Of course idolatry, in the sense of a rite that in some way invoked or venerated demons either expressly or tacitly, was essentially a synonym for one of the principal definitions of superstition extending back to Saint Augustine. Nowhere was this clearer than in later writers' heavy reliance on William's ten general categories of idolatry in their works on superstition.[103] The Leipzig theologian Johannes of Wünschelburg, for one, drew extensively on William's categorizations of practice for his treatise *On Superstitions* (*De superstitionibus*), but no later authority drew more directly from William than the anonymous author of another fifteenth-century treatise *On Superstitions*, who structured the whole central section of his work around the question "whether idolatry is a form of superstition," and proved this point by systematically rehearsing and expanding William's ten categories.[104] Writing probably in the mid-fifteenth century, Denys the Carthusian almost certainly referred to one of these two treatises in his own *Against the Vices of Superstitions* (*Contra vitia superstitionum*), when he noted the valuable work of "a certain master in his treatise *On Superstitions*, which for the most part he drew from the book of the lord William of Paris *On Faith and Laws*."[105]

William's first category of idolatry consisted of rites performed explicitly through demonic agency. Then came other varieties, almost any of which might also involve demons in some more covert fashion. There were rites or observances directed to the stars, sun, or moon (the second category); practices entailing the four elements, such as those of hydromancers or pyromancers (the third); and, in what would have been blatant idolatry, the practice of crafting statues and worshipping them as "fabricated gods" (the fourth). People could employ images in other dubious ways, which many authorities readily interpreted as entailing demonic invocation or worship (the fifth category). Circles, triangles, or even pentagons often figured in the rites described in prohibited magical texts, such as those that magicians

---

103. Listed in William, *De legibus* 23, pp. 63–65, and explicated in *De legibus* 24–27, pp. 65–91.

104. Anonymous, *De superstitionibus* (M), 17r–51r.

105. Denys the Carthusian, *Contra vitia superstitionum*, 610: "Magister quidam in tractatu suo de superstitionibus, quem pro magna parte ex libro domini Guilielmi Parrhisiensis de fide et legibus collegit." He then drew on William himself (ibid., 610–13).

falsely attributed to Solomon.[106] Other errors involved the improper use of written characters or figures in magical rites (the sixth), or of spoken words or names (the seventh). William's eighth category entailed the observance of particular times, such as holding certain days to be inauspicious or unlucky while regarding other times as particularly favorable. The most famous such times were the so-called Egyptian Days, two or more days each month identified by long tradition as being ominous and unfavorable for most pursuits. Related to this, some people falsely ascribed ominous power or predictive force to "beginnings" of any sort (category nine): a mercantile or military venture might succeed or fail depending on the hour or day at which a ship set sail or a commander set forth, for example, while the weather at the outset of a new season could serve as a portent of future conditions. Some medieval people apparently believed that the weather on each of the twelve days before Christmas would predict conditions for each of the twelve months of the following year.[107] Still today one hears that if March comes in like a lion it will go out like a lamb. We tend not to think of this adage as entailing any kind of "divination," but some medieval authorities certainly would have.

William labeled his tenth and final category of idolatry that of "discovery" (*inventio*), by which he meant taking special account of various occurrences, items, or creatures that one simply came upon in the course of a day's activities and regarding them as omens. Spying certain animals, for instance, might foretell good or bad fortune. While some belief in the portentous power of black cats still exists in the modern West, medieval Europeans ascribed meaning to encounters with cats, hares, birds, and numerous other animals. For example, some regarded sparrows alighting on the roof of a house as a good omen for those within, while magpies were bad.[108] Others believed that crows on the roof of a house, an owl flying over it, or a rooster crowing before dawn were all negative signs.[109] Wolves, curiously enough, appear often to have foretold good fortune when encountered, while meeting a cleric on the road portended ill, although some people apparently distinguished between kinds of clergy, specifying that meeting a Cistercian monk was a bad sign, but meeting a Benedictine monk would bring good luck.[110] Sources also

106. On "magic circles," see Kieckhefer, *Magic in the Middle Ages*, 159–61; Richard Kieckhefer, *Forbidden Rites: A Necromancer's Manual of the Fifteenth Century* (University Park, Pa., 1998), 170–80.

107. Anonymous, *Dives and Pauper*, ed. Priscilla Heath Barnum, 3 vols., EETS 275, 280, 323 (London, 1976, 1980, 2004), 1:184.

108. Anonymous, *Évangiles* 2.7, p. 106.

109. Jean Gerson, *Contra superstitiosam dierum observantiam*, 118.

110. On wolves: Johannes Hartlieb, *Buch aller verbotenen Künste*, 80; Thomas Ebendorfer, *De decem praeceptis*, 9; Johannes of Wünschelburg, *De superstitionibus*, 238v; Ulrich of Pottenstein, *Dekalog-*

report superstitious beliefs concerning when and how often people sneezed, how they shook hands, whether their right or left ears itched, and omens of many other kinds. Then as now, finding a horseshoe meant good luck, and from William himself we learn that "many stupid people believe that it is better [luckier] to find a halfpenny (*obolus*) than a penny (*nummus*)."[111]

Among high medieval scholastics the only figure who equaled and indeed surpassed William of Auvergne in terms of direct influence on late medieval authors dealing with superstition was the bishop of Paris's slightly younger contemporary Thomas Aquinas.[112] As we have seen, along with Augustine he provided one of the two fundamental definitions of superstition used by late medieval clerical authorities, which he provided in his enormously influential *Summary of Theology* (*Summa theologiae*). He then posed the question whether divination was a kind of superstition. He first partitioned divinatory practices into three broad groups: necromantic rites (*quod pertinet ad nigromanticos*) that drew explicitly on demons; augury (*quod pertinet ad augures*), which involved the passive observation of signs or omens; and what could be called sorcery (*quod pertinet ad sortes*), which meant for him performing active rites, although not explicitly demonic ones, to divine the future, such as throwing dice or drawing straws. The casting of lots (*sortes,* whence the later medieval *sortilegium* or *sorceria,* and ultimately the English "sorcery") had a venerable history as a means for deciding a course of action when no rational grounds were available. Thomas noted that even Augustine had praised the use of lots to ascertain divine will in uncertain situations. Yet he stressed the possibility that such rites would inadvertently invoke demons, or that those malicious spirits would somehow involve themselves in the process, inevitably corrupting it. Hence he concluded that all forms of divination—by lots, by observing the stars, by augury or omens, or by interpreting dreams—were indeed superstitious. Likewise, he condemned the "magic art," healing spells or incantations, and medicinal amulets as forms of superstition, just as Augustine had. His reason, again, was that all these practices could involve demons, either patently or covertly.[113]

Auslegung, 108. On encountering clergy: Jakob of Paradise, *De potestate demonum,* 261r; Ulrich of Pottenstein, *Dekalog-Auslegung,* 108. Distinguishing Cistercians from Benedictines: anonymous, *Évangiles* 5.11, p. 164.

111. William of Auvergne, *De legibus* 27, p. 90.

112. Specifically on Thomas's thought on demonology, magic, or superstition, see Linsenmann, *Magie* (as above, n. 13). A useful summary is in Ostorero, *Diable au sabbat* (as above, n. 70), 223–33. For his thought on astral images and astral magic, see Weill-Parot, *Images astrologiques,* 223–59.

113. Aquinas, *Summa theologiae* 2.2.92.1, 2.2.95.2–8, 2.2.96.1–4, in *Summa theologiae: Latin Text and English Translation,* 60 vols. (New York, 1964–81).

Like William of Auvergne, Thomas Aquinas became a fundamental authority for later Christian writers on demonic power and especially how it interacted with the physical world and the laws of nature. At several points in his voluminous works, he addressed demons' essential nature as spiritual beings, how they could assume airy bodies and manifest in physical form, and how they could affect the physical world by causing motion in matter.[114] Importantly he stressed that, while demons possessed any number of amazing abilities, they could not do anything that lay entirely outside the order of nature. Their powers were preternatural, not supernatural, and while they could cause marvels (*mirabilia*) to astonish, delude, terrify, and tempt, they could not perform true miracles, which only God could accomplish.[115] As with William, Thomas's most memorable illustration of how demons operated within the bounds of natural law, frequently cited by later authors, was how they could seemingly generate human life by stealing semen from men as succubi and then impregnating women with it as incubi.[116]

Thomas also acknowledged the potency of occult but nevertheless fully natural forces, such as those of the stars. In terms of permissible natural predictions, he proceeded from the basic principle that "effects are known from their causes." That is, he continued to develop the position found already in William and in the work of other earlier authorities that observation of the stars could be used to predict anything that natural astral emanations directly caused or at least powerfully influenced, such as the weather. Such natural energies could also produce indirect signs of their coming effects. Birds again provided the principal example. They were sensitive to astral effects on the atmosphere, and so their behavior often also foreshadowed the changes in the weather in an entirely natural way.[117] Most occurrences in the natural world, however, were "accidents" that proceeded from the confluence of multiple causes, and for these the stars held no predictive power. Critically for the matter of astral divination of human actions, he offered extensive analysis of how astral forces could never directly affect the human mind or spirit. They could, however, make an "impression" on the gross matter of our bodies, and by causing desires or urges in this way they could "incline" certain people

---

114. On demonic bodies: Thomas Aquinas, *De malo* 16.1, in *The "De malo" of Thomas Aquinas*, ed. Brian Davies, trans. Richard Regan (Oxford, 2001); *Summa theologiae* 1.51. On interaction with matter and motion: Aquinas, *De malo* 16.10; *Summa theologiae* 1.110.3.

115. Aquinas, *Summa contra gentiles* 3.103, in Aquinas, *Opera omnia iussu Leonis XIII P.M. edita*, vols. 13–15 (Rome, 1918–30); *Summa theologiae* 1.110.4, 1.111.4.

116. Aquinas, *Summa theologiae* 1.51.3.

117. Ibid., 2.2.95.5 (stars), 2.2.95.7 (birds), 2.2.96.3 and 2.2.172.1 (natural signs generally).

toward certain behaviors. The mind could always overcome the influence of the body, however, so human will remained free and astrologers could never be certain of any predictions they might make about human behaviors or any events that stemmed from human action.[118] Thus he concluded that "if anyone tries to foretell contingent or chance events, or to know with certainty the future works of men, he proceeds from a false and empty supposition. . . . Hence this is superstitious and illicit divination."[119]

These points all needed to be argued at length because, while astrology had long been a debatable practice in the Christian tradition, "partly natural and partly superstitious," those debates were growing more intense amid the intellectual and scientific ferment of thirteenth-century western Europe. Astrological texts of ancient authority were now entering the West, along with learned Arabic writings based on that tradition. In Paris, the Englishman Roger Bacon championed astral science, and Aquinas's own teacher, Albertus Magnus, looked more tolerantly on many kinds of astrology than did his student, earning himself a reputation as a magician (*magus* rather than *magnus*) in the eyes of some later writers.[120] Albertus, Thomas, and Roger Bacon all agreed that there were superstitious forms of astrology. They even generally agreed on the basic criteria that might divide licit from illicit practice, certainly if a prediction seemed to negate human free will. They often clashed, however, on where exactly a particular practice would cross this nebulous boundary. As we will see repeatedly in later centuries as well, disagreements between authorities about the exact nature of superstition rarely focused on basic principles but instead on variable levels of skepticism and concern. While some authorities tended to promote practices unless they absolutely and evidently involved error, others tended to react against even a hint of potential error, fearing that the attendant dangers, above all of demonic involvement, were too great to allow.

Thomas clearly belonged to the second camp. He stressed that most forms of divination had absolutely no basis in correct understandings of natural causation and instead frequently involved demons.[121] He adhered closely to

---

118. Aquinas, *Summa contra gentiles* 3.84–87; *Summa theologiae* 1.115.4, 2.1.9.5, 2.2.95.5.

119. Aquinas, *Summa theologiae* 2.2.95.5.

120. Thorndike, *History of Magic*, 2:577–92, 659–77; Boudet, *Entre science et* nigromance, 214–39. On Bacon, see also Jeremiah Hackett, "Roger Bacon on Astronomy-Astrology: The Sources of the *Scientia Experimentalis*," in *Roger Bacon and the Sciences: Commemorative Essays*, ed. Jeremiah Hackett (Leiden, 1997), 174–98. On Albert's later reputation, see David J. Collins, "Albertus, Magnus or Magus? Magic, Natural Philosophy, and Religious Reform in the Late Middle Ages," *Renaissance Quarterly* 63 (2010): 1–44.

121. Aquinas, *Summa theologiae* 2.2.95.3.

Augustine when explaining how demons could sometimes accurately reveal secret information or predict the future through their long experience, their ability to move nearly instantly from place to place gathering information, and not least through their own thorough understanding of natural signs.[122] Such natural predictions would not have been corrupt per se, but obviously became so because of the involvement of these malevolent agents. Thomas extended this basic approach when considering forms of possibly natural magic. While William of Auvergne had, at one point, argued that many people attributed to demons wonders and marvels that were in fact entirely natural, Thomas more pessimistically warned that many rites and operations, even when seemingly natural, actually relied on demonic agency. He pointed to many rites of astral magic that, while supposedly operating by focusing and directing the power of the stars, actually aimed to achieve results that were entirely beyond the natural powers of astral bodies. He also pointed out that such rites frequently involved spoken invocations or employed written characters, and these, he maintained, could have no effect on natural astral emanations. They operated instead only as means of signification (*significationes*) directed toward some sentient intelligence, which, he went on to prove, had to be demonic.[123]

Since many learned, clerical necromancers readily admitted to summoning demons and exploiting their power but maintained that they commanded and controlled these wicked entities by means either natural or spiritual rather than supplicating and worshipping them, Thomas had to counter this assertion if he was to condemn such practices thoroughly. In terms of natural philosophy, he argued that, because natural forces such as those of the stars could influence a sentient will only by affecting the physical body to which it was attached, and because demons had no natural physical bodies, there was no possibility that the power of the stars or any other natural force that a necromancer might claim to wield could possibly control or coerce them.[124] In terms of spiritual compulsion, Thomas could hardly escape Christ's own statements in the Gospels that any Christian could exorcise demons in his name (Mark 3:15, Luke 9:1). Biblical texts presented exorcism exclusively in terms of commanding a demon to depart, but if the notion of command was expanded only a little, it could be regarded as conferring tremendous power indeed, for demons had prodigious abilities to move matter, create illusions,

122. Aquinas, *De malo* 16.7; *Summa contra gentiles* 3.154; *Summa theologiae* 1.57.3, 2.2.172.5.
123. Aquinas, *Summa contra gentiles* 3.104–6; *Summa theologiae* 2.2.96.2.
124. Aquinas, *Summa theologiae* 1.115.5.

inflict harm but also heal injuries, and impart secret knowledge. Thomas sought, therefore, to limit the range of possible command to the narrowest meaning of exorcism. Christians could expel demons, but they could not compel them into any kind of service. Seeking to do so meant abandoning forceful command and entering into "fellowship" (*societas*) with them. Drawing explicitly on the language with which Augustine had defined the essence of superstition, Aquinas would develop this notion of fellowship into the concept of a diabolical pact, entered into either explicitly or tacitly. Thus anyone engaging in a fairly wide gamut of practices could stand suspect of binding themselves to the terrible forces of hell.[125] Such reasoning would prove extremely important for many late medieval authorities striving to disentangle potentially licit rites and activities from baleful superstitions.

Late medieval writers were beholden to the early church fathers because they had created the Christian conception of superstition, altering Roman notions of excessive observances or secretive and vaguely subversive rites to fit the more dichotomous Christian universe split between God and the devil. In Augustine's classic and enduring formulation, the Christian church and all her members constituted the city of God. All that lay beyond the bounds of this city was pagan, demonic, and superstitious. The power of this conception held strong as Christianity came to dominate the ancient Mediterranean world and spread itself into the pagan wilds of northern Europe. Charting the process and the thoroughness of Christianization in the early medieval period is fraught with difficulty, but by around the turn of the first millennium at the latest, this dichotomous mentality no longer reflected the reality Christianity faced in most of the territories it encompassed. Certainly pagans still existed on the northern and eastern frontiers, Islam loomed to the south, and within Christian lands heretical groups of some sophistication were growing, or at least the church perceived them to be growing, in the eleventh, twelfth, and thirteenth centuries. Nevertheless, within the core area of Western Christendom during the high medieval period, no other remotely equivalent "city" threatened that of God. Without in any way diminishing their reliance on early Christian authorities, scholastic authors—particularly the great and culminating thirteenth-century figures of William of Auvergne and Thomas Aquinas—largely let go the old rhetoric of paganism. They restructured the simple dichotomy of Christianity versus pagan superstition into a more complicated divide with divine power and

---

125. Ibid., 2.2.90.2, 2.2.92.2.

fully natural operations on one hand (the two being made, in good scholastic fashion, to harmonize with one another) confronting bogus claims about nature and widespread demonic activity in the natural world on the other.

This was not a complete revolution, of course, for still the city of God (conceived to include his natural creation) stood opposed to demonic error. Yet neither was the shift an insignificant one, for by emphasizing natural operations and natural philosophy so much in their conceptions of superstition, these men introduced new dilemmas of definition and discernment. Like all scholastics, they sought to harmonize (Christian) faith with (Aristotelian) reason. That harmony was rarely easy to achieve or to maintain. Authorities in the fourteenth and fifteenth centuries worked within the intellectual framework developed in the twelfth and especially the thirteenth. They confronted new contexts as well as encountered what they perceived to be long-established errors, and they frequently struggled with the details of how to apply the clearly articulated theories they inherited to the often messy and vague world of actual practices. The problems they faced did not cause them to abandon their faith in earlier authorities, just as the scholastics had not abandoned the church fathers. Yet inevitably they moved European thought in all the important areas surrounding the issue of superstition in new directions, and they exposed certain cracks in the system that would only grow more pronounced in centuries to come.

Stretching across all these centuries is the entanglement of conceptions of superstition and concern over superstitious practices with the efforts of Christian authorities at pastoral ministration to their flocks. It is worth remembering that Thomas Aquinas's systematic scholastic parsing of all aspects of superstition, while hardly inspiring to the ear, was meant to instruct an order of preachers charged with promoting proper faith and devotion, and guiding the faithful away from any noxious practices that might be deemed superstitious. In the realms of both science (knowledge of natural operations and the effects they might produce) and religion (internal faith but also the external rites of devotion) the strict parameters of academic debate tended to increase concerns and reduce the possibilities of tolerable actions. While fear of the demonic was growing in some quarters, however, the trajectory of concern over superstition was never simply linear. For the next two centuries, while criticisms certainly grew more focused and intense, discussions of superstition always left room for natural operations, and even entirely natural errors, as opposed to the more threatening demonic kind. And always Christian authorities struggled with how to promote vibrant and intense devotions to their god while still shielding the uneducated laity, and the unwary clergy too, from dangerous superstition.

🪰 CHAPTER 2

Superstition in Court and Cloister

> If there is a sorcerer who attends at court, or magi-
> cian, or soothsayer, or augur, or one interpreting
> dreams by divinatory art . . . he shall be exposed to
> torments and tortured without regard for his rank.
> This law should be engraved in golden letters on the
> doors of princes, for they have no more dangerous
> plague in their retinue.
>
> —Jean Bodin, *On the Demon-Mania of Sorcerers*

Jean Bodin, the great sixteenth-century French
jurist and political philosopher, judged that sorcerers and diviners infested
courts like vermin, not only in his day but "from time immemorial"[1] Two
centuries earlier the canon lawyer Jacques Dueze, who reigned as Pope John
XXII from 1316 until 1334, would have agreed. The pontiff detested sorcerers, and he feared that his and other Christian courts were beset by them. He
instigated numerous investigations and trials, some targeting highly placed
clergy, and he ordered officials and inquisitors under his direction to do the
same. Generally counted among his proclamations condemning magical arts
is the important bull *Upon His Watchtower* (*Super illius specula*), which declared
that any Christian found guilty of demonic invocation was automatically
excommunicated.[2] He is emblematic, therefore, of the heightened concern
about one major category of superstition brewing within the courts of
some of the most powerful monarchs of the fourteenth century, namely the
"errors and abominations" of demonic sorcery.[3]

---

1. Jean Bodin, *De la démonomanie des sorciers* 4.5 (Paris, 1581), 200v.
2. Discussed at greater length later in this chapter.
3. John's phrasing in a letter to the archbishop of Narbonne and the inquisitors of Toulouse and
Carcassonne: *Quellen*, 6.

In tracing the long tradition of Christian thought about superstition from late antiquity through the thirteenth century, I focused on highly influential writers or broadly representative texts. I also concentrated more on their later influence or their general, representative aspects than on the particular contexts from which they emerged. In the fourteenth century, however, debate about superstition developed to a notable degree in some very specific settings. New and more sharply focused concerns radiated out from centers of both political power and advanced learning, and accusations of superstition now regularly implicated people of high social standing. This was largely due to the intellectual revival of the twelfth and thirteenth centuries, which had brought new occult learning into the Latin West and had reinvigorated many decidedly elite forms of magic and divination. Reaction against such practices, however, really crested in the fourteenth century. Educated clerics pursued spurious forms of astrology, and they endeavored to manipulate astral energies or, sometimes, to control what they perceived to be astral spirits. Some also sought to conjure demons through complex necromantic rites. They engaged in such practices both at the universities that trained them and at the courts of great princes, secular and ecclesiastic, where many of them found employment.

Stationed typically on the fringes of real political power, yet seeking influence and striving to curry favor, such men often drifted into a demimonde of sorcery and divination that existed at most courts.[4] This world could be quite dangerous, as indicated by a series of politically motivated sorcery trials that erupted in the fourteenth century, which both stemmed from and fed back into the increasingly fretful atmosphere evident at many courtly centers.[5] As discussed in the previous chapter, already in the mid-twelfth century John of Salisbury had criticized the "foolishness" of courtiers who engaged in sorcery or other superstitious practices. Such activities had in no way abated. Many feared that they were in fact escalating, and far from foolish trifles, they seemed now very threatening indeed.

In this chapter I will examine heightened debate about two broad categories of superstition that emerged from courts and university cloisters in the fourteenth century. The first category concerns what we might view as the mainly religious errors of demonic sorcery. The second involves certain

---

4. Edward Peters, *The Magician, the Witch, and the Law* (Philadelphia, 1978), 112–25.

5. Ibid., 120–25; Edward Peters, "The Medieval Church and State on Superstition, Magic and Witchcraft: From Augustine to the Sixteenth Century," in *Witchcraft and Magic in Europe: The Middle Ages*, ed. Bengt Ankarloo and Stuart Clark (Philadelphia, 2002), 173–245, at 218–22; William R. Jones, "Political Uses of Sorcery in Medieval Europe," *Historian* 34 (1972): 670–87.

seemingly more scientific errors associated with astrology. Such divisions are blurry at best when applied to the Middle Ages, since many authorities maintained that faulty and hence superstitious astrology could open the door to malevolent demonic influence, while rigorous scholastic understandings of demonic sorcery regularly situated demonic power within a physical world governed by Aristotelian natural philosophy. Nevertheless, I would argue that while the boundaries between these two kinds of superstition were fragile and permeable, they showed some signs of strengthening during the 1300s. Just as we have seen a category of natural magic develop in contrast to Christian authorities' more general assertion that magic always involved the invocation of demons, explicitly or tacitly, so I suggest that we can discern at least the outlines of a category of natural superstition contrasting with the enduring and in many ways intensifying demonic concerns also evident in this century.

Unlike with *magica naturalis*, no medieval writer ever coined the phrase "natural superstition," but some very important authorities who addressed astrology in the mid- to late fourteenth century chose quite clearly to downplay the threat of demons while still castigating various elements of the astral arts, especially those pertaining to prognostication, as superstitious purely because they were rooted in an incorrect understanding of natural philosophy. Although these men never succeeded in shifting the overall debate about superstition entirely to their terms, one could imagine that they might have, for they were situated at the very apex of intellectual and political power in this period. Certainly they demonstrate how false is the dichotomy that would define superstition in the Middle Ages always as a "perversion of religion" and would allow that only in the modern era did it become a "perversion of reason." They also exemplify the complexities and competing trajectories that characterize the developing debate over superstition in the late medieval period. While concern over the demonic grew notably in many corners, there were also powerful voices in which the tremor of such concerns cannot be heard very loudly at all.

We will begin tracing the paths of concern about various kinds of superstition that wind through the fourteenth century at the papal court under John XXII, located not in Rome but in Avignon (where the papacy resided after 1309), and we will also consider the work of some inquisitorial officials who operated under papal direction, although as we will see, their concerns were not always identical to those of the popes who commissioned them. Of particular interest here will be the Catalan inquisitor Nicolau Eymerich, connected to both papal Avignon and the Aragonese court in Barcelona, who wrote extensively about necromantic sorcery, as well as erroneous astrology and alchemy, and was furiously concerned with the threat of demons in all these areas. Then our focus will turn north to Paris, home of the greatest royal court as well as the greatest university in western Europe at this time. There, especially after midcentury, questions about the status of astrology as approved science or dangerous superstition attracted the attention of leading intellects, particularly the theologians Nicole Oresme and Heinrich of Langenstein. Both men produced rigorously academic treatments of these topics, addressed to their university peers, in which they engaged with significant questions of natural philosophy. Their concerns were not exclusively intellectual, however, but also moral and political, and they each wrote certain works for a decidedly more general courtly audience. Here they sought to instruct kings, princes, and other powerful lay figures about the harmful superstitions that clustered principally around astrological signs, omens, and divinatory practices. In both sets of writing they focused overwhelmingly on the erroneous understandings of natural philosophy and the physical world that underlay such practices and rendered them useless, rather than on the demonic menace that animated many of their contemporaries.

Papal Fears and Inquisitorial Reactions

The fourteenth century began with two famous trials, each featuring, to some degree, charges of demonic invocation and sorcery, and each setting the papacy against the French royal court. In 1303, at the behest of their king, Philip IV, French clergy leveled charges against Pope Boniface VIII of heresy and sodomy, of supposedly conjuring and consulting with a demon, and also of employing human diviners. In the late summer of that year, the royal councilor Guillaume of Nogaret led a force raised from among the pope's enemies in Italy to arrest the aged pontiff at his residence in Anagni, located in the foothills some twenty-five miles southeast of Rome. Soon freed by other local forces, Boniface never faced trial in Paris, but the French instigated posthumous proceedings against him in both Avignon and Rome a few years later, and accusations of sorcery, divination, necromantic conjuration, and demon worship again figured significantly in the charges brought against him.[6] In 1307, Philip IV also ordered the leadership of the powerful military order of Knights Templar to be arrested on charges including

---

6. See Agostino Paravicini Bagliani, *Boniface VIII: Un pape hérétique?* (Paris, 2003), 349–57. Documents in Jean Coste, ed., *Boniface VIII en procès: Articles d'accusation et depositions des témoins (1303–1311)* (Rome, 1995); see 895–908 for an evaluation of these charges.

heresy, sodomy, and some counts of sorcery and consultation with demons.[7] Both of these cases were clearly contrived by Philip and his officials to meet particular political objectives of the French Crown. Yet they were also grounded in real concerns. Dark suspicions had circulated about both Boniface and the Templars prior to these dramatic affairs, otherwise the charges against them could hardly have gained traction. The French court itself was awash in rumors of sorcery and diabolical plots at this time, and accusations similar to those brought against the pope and the Temple were also lodged against French courtiers and noblemen, notably Bishop Guichard of Troyes, an erstwhile confidant of Philip's queen who had fallen from favor. His case began in 1308 when a hermit from his diocese testified that he had seen the bishop performing sinister rites in the company of a known sorceress around the time when Queen Joan had suddenly died, and that Guichard was now plotting to poison other members of the royal family. The charges quickly swelled as court intrigue combined with authentic anxieties about supernatural attack: in addition to a sorceress the bishop had conspired with a learned necromancer of the Dominican order, he kept a demonic servant permanently bound in a glass bottle, and he himself had been fathered by an incubus.[8] Similarly (although rather less spectacularly) on the side of the papacy, as early as 1310 the theologian Augustine of Ancona, who had defended Boniface VIII against Philip's charges, addressed a treatise to his successor, Pope Clement V, warning him about the dangers of superstitious diviners at court.[9]

Concern about divination and sorcery blossomed in papal Avignon a few years later under John XXII. This stern and legalistically minded pontiff certainly would have recognized the usefulness of deploying charges of sorcery or other superstitious practices against political opponents, but he also appears to have been genuinely worried about demonic magic being practiced at his court and directed against his person.[10] Almost immediately on assum-

7. See Malcolm Barber, *The Trial of the Templars*, 2nd ed. (Cambridge, 2006).

8. Norman Cohn, *Europe's Inner Demons: The Demonization of Christians in Medieval Christendom*, 2nd ed. (Chicago, 2000), 123–30; Alain Provost, "On the Margins of the Templars' Trial: The Case of Bishop Guichard of Troyes," in *The Debate on the Trial of the Templars (1307–1314)*, ed. Jochen Burgtorf, Paul F. Crawford, and Helen J. Nicholson (Farnham, U.K., 2010), 117–27.

9. Julien Véronèse, "Contre la divination et la magie à la cour: Trois traités addressés à des grands aux XIVe et XVe siècles," *Micrologus: Natura, Scienze e Società Medievali—Nature, Sciences and Medieval Societies* 16 (2008): 405–31, at 408–10, 416–21.

10. Detailed accounts of John's actions are found in Anneliese Maier, "Eine Verfügung Johannes XXII. über die Züstandigkeit der Inquisition für Zaubereiprozesse," *Archivum Fratrum Praedicatorum* 22 (1952): 226–46; Alain Boureau, *Satan the Heretic: The Birth of Demonology in the Medieval West*, trans. Teresa Lavender Fagan (Chicago, 2006), 8–42.

ing the papal throne, he struck out against perceived enemies and sorcerous plots. In 1317, papal officials accused Hugues Géraud, bishop of Cahors, of trying to assassinate John by means of poison and through sorcery performed with wax images, the ashes of spiders and toads, and the gall of a pig. He was tried and burned at the stake. The next year, Robert Mauvoison, archbishop of Aix, was accused of engaging in improper astrological divination, as well as other forms of malfeasance in office. Tried by a papal commission, he was largely exonerated but still had to resign his episcopal see. Also in 1318, John appointed the bishop of Fréjus and two other commissioners to investigate a number of clerics in Avignon on suspicion of practicing "necromancy, geomancy, and other magical arts," of possessing magical texts, and of performing rites involving mirrors, images, and magic circles intended to summon demons. The pope was adamant that such "superstitious pestilence" be eliminated from his court.[11] The following year, at John's instigation, the Franciscan Bernard Délicieux was condemned to perpetual imprisonment, primarily for supporting the Spiritual Franciscan movement, which John detested, but also for supposedly possessing necromantic texts.[12] In 1320, a Milanese cleric claimed to have been approached by the Visconti rulers of that city to participate in a magical plot to kill the pope, and from 1320 to 1325, John had his agents level a whole series of charges against various of his enemies and opponents in the March of Ancona, a region of the papal states along the Adriatic Sea. While politics clearly factored into many of these charges and trials, in several cases compelling evidence exists that real magical plots were afoot. Medieval rulers often sought to employ sorcery against their rivals, and medieval clerics often possessed magical books and engaged in demonic rites. John's fears were not entirely groundless.[13]

Moreover, the pope did not level charges of sorcery just at his own enemies or within his own court, but also involved himself in cases originating elsewhere. In 1319, he ordered the bishop of Pamiers to pursue two clerics, "sons of Belial" in the pope's words, and a woman suspected of image magic, incantations, demonic conjurations, and "various other superstitious inventions." In June 1320 he had the seneschal of Carcassonne remit

---

11. *Quellen*, 2–4.

12. Alan Friedlander, ed., *Processus Bernardi Delitiosi: The Trial of Fr. Bernard Délicieux, 3 September–8 December 1319* (Philadelphia, 1996); see also Friedlander, *The Hammer of the Inquisitors: Brother Bernard Délicieux and the Struggle against the Inquisition in Fourteenth-Century France* (Leiden, 2000).

13. See Frans van Liere, "Witchcraft as Political Tool? John XXII, Hugues Géraud, and Matteo Visconti," *Medieval Perspectives* 16 (2001): 165–73; Rainer Decker, *Witchcraft and the Papacy: An Account Drawing from the Formerly Secret Records of the Roman Inquisition*, trans. H. C. Erik Midelfort (Charlottesville, Va., 2008), 23–31.

a priest charged with sorcery and his accomplices to Avignon for judgment. Only two months later he issued a more general order to the inquisitors in Carcassonne and Toulouse to proceed vigorously against all practitioners of demonic sorcery within their jurisdictions.[14] The inquisitor of Toulouse at this time was Bernard Gui, probably most famous now for his villainous appearance in Umberto Eco's novel *The Name of the Rose*, in which, among other fanatical pursuits, he sentences a young woman to the flames as a witch. In fact, while Gui addressed various forms of magic and other kinds of superstitious rites in his inquisitor's manual *The Practice of Inquisition* (*Practica inquisitionis*) and outlined how inquisitors should proceed against them, there is no record of his ever personally conducting a trial for sorcery. Other inquisitors in this region did conduct such trials, however, so John's mandate appears to have had an effect.[15] A few years later, in 1323, the pope acted again, appointing officials to try a certain Guillaume Robert, a monk in the monastery of Figeac who stood accused of necromancy, divination, and image magic. Three years after that, he appointed Cardinal Bertrand of Monfavès to proceed against a canon in Agen who possessed various forbidden books and supposedly conjured demons to cause thunderstorms and hail. Only a few months later he again appointed Bertrand, this time along with two other cardinals, to handle a case involving both clergy and laity in the diocese of Toulouse and Cahors who were supposedly conjuring demons and fashioning magical gems and images crafted out of lead.[16]

Carcassonne, Toulouse, Pamier, Figeac, and Agen all lie in the south of France. Clearly the anxiety over sorcerous and superstitious rites developing in Avignon spilled out most immediately to the surrounding regions (although Agen lies nearly two hundred miles west of the papal seat). Yet John could also turn his attention further afield, especially in response to concerns coming from another court. In 1331, he wrote to the bishop of Paris, commanding him to take action against a number of clergy whom the French king, Philip VI, believed were plotting to deploy harmful sorcery (*maleficium*) against him and his court.[17] One could even propose that the fears brewing in Avignon produced repercussions as far afield as distant Kilkenny, Ireland,

14. J.-M. Vidal, ed., *Bullaire de l'inquisition française au XIVe siècle et jusqu'à la fin du grand schisme* (Paris, 1913), 53, 60; *Quellen*, 4–5.

15. On Gui, see Michael D. Bailey, "From Sorcery to Witchcraft: Clerical Conceptions of Magic in the Later Middle Ages," *Speculum* 76 (2001): 960–90, at 967–71; on other inquisitorial activity, see Henry Charles Lea, *A History of the Inquisition of the Middle Ages*, 3 vols. (New York, 1888), 2:454.

16. Vidal, *Bullaire*, 87–88, 113–14, 118–19.

17. *Quellen*, 7–8.

where in 1324 the bishop of Ossory, Richard Ledrede, brought charges of demonic sorcery against Lady Alice Kyteler.[18] The Kyteler case is famous for its precociousness, and indeed its overall peculiarity. Trials for diabolical sorcery were exceedingly rare in medieval Ireland, which even during the height of Europe's early modern witch hunts produced a total of only four known criminal executions for witchcraft.[19] The character and intensity of the Kyteler inquest were completely unprecedented and have been attributed in large part to the individual zeal of Bishop Ledrede. An Irish Franciscan, he was educated by his order in France, where he spent time at the papal court in Avignon. Indeed he owed his appointment to the bishopric of Ossory to John XXII. Whether he directly imbibed any of the pope's concerns about demonically tinged superstition or not, he clearly brought new, "Continental" ideas about demonology and fears that demonic sorcery might flourish even in the upper echelons of courtly society when he returned to his island home.

At the papal court, John's intellectual engagement with issues of demonic sorcery and superstition went far deeper than responses to individual cases. Already in 1320, he had impaneled a committee of ten theologians and canon lawyers to consider the matter of demonic magic and issue a decision as to whether it was "merely" erroneous and sinful or whether it entailed manifest heresy.[20] This was not just a legal technicality that would allow papal inquisitors, designated to root out "heretical depravity," clear jurisdiction to pursue cases of sorcery and divination, as John would order the inquisitors of Toulouse and Carcassonne to do in that same year. It involved some serious reconceptualization of the basic issues such cases entailed. In theological terms, heresy was fundamentally a matter of belief, of the deliberate and pernicious rejection of church doctrine. Magical rites, however terrible their form or effect, were actions. Some church authorities, including canon lawyers and even early inquisitors, were already accustomed to addressing heresy mainly in terms of actions.[21] Yet to bring demonic magic incontrovertibly

---

18. The fullest study is Maeve B. Callan, "'No Such Art in This Land': Heresy and Witchcraft in Ireland, 1310–1360" (PhD diss., Northwestern University, 2002), 137–216. See also L. S. Davidson and J. O. Ward, eds. and trans., *The Sorcery Trial of Alice Kyteler: A Contemporary Account (1324) Together with Related Documents in English Translation, with Introduction and Notes* (Binghamton, N.Y., 1993).

19. Wolfgang Behringer, *Witches and Witch-Hunts: A Global History* (Cambridge, 2004), 150.

20. Boureau, *Satan the Heretic*, 14–15, 43–67. For another interpretation, see Isabel Iribarren, "From Black Magic to Heresy: A Doctrinal Leap in the Pontificate of John XXII," *Church History* 76 (2007): 32–60.

21. Richard Kieckhefer, "Witchcraft, Necromancy and Sorcery as Heresy," in *Chasse aux sorcières et démonologie: Entre discours et pratiques (XIVe–XVIIe siècles)*, ed. Martine Ostorero, Georg Modestin, and Kathrin Utz Tremp, ML 36 (Florence, 2010), 133–53, esp. 137–38.

under inquisitorial jurisdiction, members of the papal commission felt compelled to declare that certain actions automatically and inevitably entailed an
underlying heretical belief, regardless of whether the practitioner consciously
intended the error or was even aware of it. The explicit equation of demonic
sorcery with superstition in the Augustinian sense of an action opposing the
tenets of true Christian religion provided a major component of their argument, and apparently one of particular interest to John, since the manuscript
copy of their ruling contains a marginal annotation in the pope's own hand
at the point where the issue of superstition was first addressed.[22] This connection would also inform most future inquisitorial theory about magic, as
well as much learned discussion of superstition.

Since Augustine, Christian authorities had accepted the possibility of
magic involving a tacit pact with demons, unknown and unwished for but
sealed nonetheless by engagement in a superstitious rite. Until now, ignorance had largely shielded those who performed such rites at least from
charges of heresy. John's commission, however, signaled a major development
in the long debate over the consequential relationship between superstitious
action and erroneous belief. Ultimately, it ruled that the performance of
demonic magic was in and of itself a heresy. This decision probably helped
clear the way for one of the most important papal rulings on demonic sorcery, the decretal *Upon His Watchtower*, generally held to have been issued by
John in 1326.[23] The titular phrase, referring to standing on the watchtower
of the Lord, is likely a reference to Isaiah 21:8–9, in which a sentry positioned on a watchtower sees approaching horsemen who proclaim the fall
of Babylon and, crucially for this condemnation of demonic sorcery, the
destruction of her graven images. The bull then declared that any Christians
who "ally with death and make a pact with hell," who sacrifice to demons
and worship them, or craft images, rings, mirrors, or vials for use in magical
rites, were heretics under the law, and were automatically excommunicated
from the church. This decree would eventually become an important basis
for inquisitorial action against demonic sorcerers and later for witch trials,
although only after some significant delay.

While the long-term importance of *Upon His Watchtower* cannot be
doubted, its immediate impact appears to have been relatively muted. It addressed all Christians but not any specific audience of receptive officials, and
it curiously was not included in the *Extravagantes*, the canon law collection

---

22. Alain Boureau, *Le pape et les sorciers: Une consultation de Jean XXII sur la magie en 1320 (Manuscrit B.A.V. Borghese 348)* (Rome, 2004), 50.
23. *Quellen*, 5–6.

associated with John. If fact, it seems not to have received any exposure for fifty years, until the inquisitor Nicolau Eymerich made it a cornerstone of the condemnation of demonic magic in his highly influential *Directory of Inquisitors (Directorium inquisitorum)*, written in 1376. Some scholars therefore question the authenticity of its attribution to John.[24] Yet it clearly captured the basic tenor of the pope's attitude toward what he regarded as demonic superstition. Another of John's decretals titled *They Promise [Riches] Which They Do Not Produce (Spondent quas non exhibent)* is unquestionably genuine. Directed against perfidious alchemists, it appears in the *Extravagantes*, but nevertheless it too does not seem to have been very influential until much later in the century, when (again) Nicolau Eymerich presented it as the basis for his own condemnation of alchemy.[25]

As for the other great arena of potential elite superstition, astrology, although John certainly dealt with divination and cases of astral magic during his pontificate, he issued no general pronouncements about it.[26] This too is perhaps somewhat surprising, for astrology flourished at the courts of this era, although its real heyday began more toward midcentury, after John's reign had ended.[27] Rulers at most of the major courts across the Continent employed astrologers. In France, already in the 1350s the future king Charles V began to assemble an enormous library of astrological texts, and around 1371 he endowed a college of astrology and medicine at the University of Paris.[28] England lagged somewhat behind France (and Italy) in this trend, but even there, the presence of astrology at court and university grew steadily in

---

24. Most skeptical is Patrick Nold, "Thomas of Braunceston O.M./O.P.," in *Kirchenbild und Spiritualität: Dominikanische Beiträge zur Ekklesiologie und zum kirchlichen Leben in Mittelalter; Festschrift für Ulrich Horst O.P.*, ed. Thomas Prügl and Marianne Schlosser (Paderborn, 2007), 179–95, at 184–85; Boureau, *Satan the Heretic*, 12–14, is inclined to accept its attribution to John, as am I.

25. *Spondent* is found in Extrav. comm. 5.6.un; Emil Friedberg, ed., *Corpus Iuris Canonici*, 2 vols. (1879–81; repr., Graz, 1955), 2:cols. 1295–96. See Nold, "Thomas of Braunceston," 183–84. Eymerich's 1396 tract *Contra alchimistas* is discussed below.

26. Jean-Patrice Boudet, "La papauté d'Avignon et l'astrologie," in *Fin du monde et signes des temps: Visionnaires et prophètes en France méridionale (fin XIIIe–début XVe siècle)* (Toulouse, 1992), 257–93, esp. 262; Nicolas Weill-Parot, *Les "images astrologiques" au Moyen Âge et à la Renaissance: Spéculations intellectuelles et pratiques magiques (XIIe–XVe siècle)* (Paris, 2002), 380–85.

27. Lynn Thorndike, *A History of Magic and Experimental Science*, 8 vols. (New York, 1923–58), 3:585–90. Jean-Patrice Boudet, *Entre science et* nigromance: *Astrologie, divination et magie dans l'Occident médiéval (XIIe–XVe siècle)* (Paris, 2006), 283, notes a "golden age" for astrology beginning ca. 1350 and lasting into the early modern period.

28. Jean-Patrice Boudet, "A 'College of Astrology and Medicine'? Charles V, Gervais Chrétien, and the Scientific Manuscripts of Maître Gervais's College," *Studies in History and Philosophy of Biological and Biomedical Sciences* 41 (2010): 99–108. On Charles's library, see Boudet, *Entre science et nigromance*, 303–4.

the 1300s.[29] By the middle of the century, certain kinds of astrology even found success at the papal court, although Avignon was never among the great centers of astrological art.[30] Astrology also flourished in Iberia, in particular at the court of the count-kings of Aragon in Barcelona. Both Pere III (reigned 1336–87) and his son Joan I (1387–96) patronized astrology extensively, as well as alchemy and other forms of divination.[31]

As papal inquisitor-general for the Crown of Aragon, Nicolau Eymerich had affiliations with both the Avignon and Barcelona courts. He clearly admired John XXII for his stance against superstitious demonic magic, since he helped bring to prominence several of the pope's rulings, making John perhaps more influential in this area in the late fourteenth century than he was during his own lifetime. The Catalan inquisitor was himself an extremely influential figure who helped define concerns about sorcery and superstition (and about sorcery as superstition) both in his own day and for centuries thereafter. His writings on necromancy, astrology, and alchemy can, therefore, provide us with a sense of certain general trajectories of clerical authorities' thought about these matters over the latter half of the fourteenth century, before we turn our attention finally to the important developments taking place specifically at the court and university in Paris.

Nicolau Eymerich was born in the Catalonian city of Gerona around 1320. He entered the Dominican order in 1334, studied in Barcelona and then briefly in Paris around 1351, before returning to the Crown of Aragon, where he took up duties as an inquisitor by around 1357. Inquisitorial activity in Aragon was closely tied to royal power at this time, and the irascible Eymerich quickly came into conflict with the count-kings. He was removed from office briefly in 1358, although reinstated by 1359 at the latest. This was but the first of many such conflicts, and suspensions from office, throughout his career. The most significant of these were his two periods of major exile, spent mostly at the papal court at Avignon, from 1375 to 1386 and again from 1393 to 1397. Perhaps not coincidentally, all his major writings against magic and superstition are linked to these periods of professional and political turmoil in his life. He composed his earliest work on this subject, *Against Invokers of Demons* (*Contra demonum invocatores*), in 1359; he completed his great inquisitorial handbook, the *Directory of Inquisitors*, in Avignon in 1376;

---

29. Hilary Carey, *Courting Disaster: Astrology at the English Court and University in the Later Middle Ages* (London, 1992), 10.

30. Boudet, "La papauté d'Avignon et l'astrologie."

31. Michael A. Ryan, *A Kingdom of Stargazers: Astrology and Authority in the Late Medieval Crown of Aragon* (Ithaca, N.Y., 2011).

and he wrote two treatises about astrology and alchemy during his second exile, completing *Against Ignorant Astrologers* (*Contra astrologos imperitos*) in late 1395 or early 1396, and *Against Alchemists* (*Contra alchimistas*) in 1396.[32]

Undoubtedly Eymerich attained his greatest and most enduring influence through his monumental *Directory*, which circulated widely in manuscript copies and remained the leading inquisitorial manual well into the early modern period, going through nine printed editions in the sixteenth and early seventeenth centuries (the last in 1607).[33] He dealt with sorcery and superstition mainly in two "questions" in the second book of this long work, "On Sorcerers and Diviners" and "On Those Invoking Demons," and here he established the basic perspective, both legal and theological, from which subsequent inquisitorial courts would view the practice of demonic sorcery, as well as their own authority over it.[34] Somewhat remarkably, perhaps, this matter was still under debate in the later fourteenth century. As already noted, the jurisdiction of "inquisitors of heretical depravity" over cases of demonic magic was by no means clear-cut, and the history of its development is rather tangled. Almost a century and a half before Eymerich penned his *Directory*, in 1231, Pope Gregory IX had empowered special papally designated inquisitors to investigate heresy and other errors in the faith. Their purpose was to augment the efforts of local bishops, who were also obligated to inquire into such offenses. Inquisitorial investigations into heretical depravity appear almost immediately to have spilled over into areas of superstition and sorcery, such that in 1258 Pope Alexander IV had to instruct papal inquisitors that they should refrain from involving themselves in such matters unless the activity under investigation entailed "manifest" heresy.[35] Many scholars have questioned how limiting this prohibition proved to be in practice, since an inquisitorial manual from around 1270 or perhaps even earlier still contains a section offering guidance on how to handle cases of demonic invocation, idolatry, and augury.[36] In the early fourteenth century, as we have seen, John XXII took up the question, impaneling his special commission to consider the matter in 1320, and specifically ordering inquisitors in Toulouse and Carcassonne to pursue cases of sorcery and divination that same year.

---

32. Claudia Heimann, *Nicolaus Eymerich (vor 1320–1399)—praedicator veridicus, inquisitor intrepidus, doctor egregious: Leben und Werk eines Inquisitors* (Münster, 2001).

33. Thomas Kaeppeli, *Scriptores Ordinis Praedicatorum Medii Aevi*, 4 vols. (Rome, 1970–93), 3:158–59; Heimann, *Nicolaus Eymerich*, 175–82.

34. Eymerich, *Directorium* 2.42–43, pp. 335–48.

35. *Quellen*, 1.

36. Ibid., 42–44, which dates this *Summa de officio inquisitionis* to around 1270. Boudet, *Entre science et nigromance*, 557–58, suggests a date around 1260.

A decade later, in 1330, the pope temporarily withdrew that directive, although not, it would seem, because his basic concern had lessened. He noted that the "errors and abominations" he had outlined in his earlier order "still thrived," but he now wanted to review all cases personally before allowing them to proceed.[37] And of course the basic conclusion reached by his special commission in 1320 still held, namely that any rite thought to rely on demonic invocation was inherently heretical and so inarguably within the bounds of papal inquisitors' jurisdiction.

Decades later, Nicolau Eymerich's central concern remained precisely the same as John XXII's had been. He sought to prove the inherently superstitious and automatically heretical nature of any act of sorcery that involved the conjuration of demons, either expressly or tacitly.[38] Like the theologians who served on John's commission, he too drew on Augustine's fundamental definition from *On Christian Doctrine*, which stated that the essence of superstition entailed some fundamental opposition to Christian religion. Thus he was able, even more directly and concisely than they had done, to link superstitious magical rites to idolatrous demon worship and so to heresy. "Superstition," he wrote by way of swift conclusion, "is a vice opposed to the directive of Christian religion or worship; therefore in a Christian it is a heresy, and as a consequence those offering sacrifices to demons must be held to be heretics."[39] Shortly thereafter, he introduced John XXII's major decree condemning demonic sorcery, *Upon His Watchtower*, referring to it as a decree "against magicians and magical superstitions."[40]

Like John, Eymerich focused in his great inquisitorial manual almost entirely on elite necromantic practices of the sort common in at least the more shadowy corners of many courts and universities. He specifically mentioned a number of necromantic texts that he had seized from magicians whom he had prosecuted, noting that he had burned the books along with the men.[41] He also mentioned astrology and alchemy briefly, commenting at

---

37. *Quellen*, 6–7.

38. On Eymerich's efforts to conceptualize heresy, see Claudia Heimann, "*Quis proprie hereticus est?* Nicolaus Eymerichs Häresiebegriff und dessen Anwendung auf die Juden," in *Praedicatores Inquisitores I: The Dominicans and the Medieval Inquisition, Acts of the 1st International Seminar on the Dominicans and the Inquisition, 23–25 February 2002*, ed. Wolfram Hoyer (Rome, 2004), 595–624, esp. 599–605.

39. Eymerich, *Directorium* 2.43.5, p. 339: "Superstitio est etiam vitium oppositum de directo religionis Christianae seu latriae: ergo in Christiano haeresis in est, et per consequens daemonibus sacrificantes haeretici habendi sunt."

40. Ibid., 2.43.9, p. 341: "Extravagans Ioannis XXII contra magos magicasque superstitiones."

41. Ibid., 2.43.1, p. 338.

various points that so long as they remained free of any demonic taint they should not be judged heretical, even if they involved some other kind of error. Ultimately, however, he warned that these arts often relied on demons in essentially the same way as necromancy did.[42] In each of these areas the *Directory* contains the most influential expressions of his thought. His more focused treatises offer greater detail, however, and more insight into how he reasoned about these matters.

Eymerich had been concerned about demonic magic from very early in his inquisitorial career. Two decades before he composed his general handbook, and only a few years after completing his education, he wrote specifically *Against Invokers of Demons*. That treatise is a long and detailed work, and it would seem a fairly popular one, given its survival in a dozen known manuscript copies.[43] Indeed, after the *Directory of Inquisitors*, which would recapitulate many of its arguments in a more condensed and manageable form, this was the Catalan inquisitor's most widely distributed work. In the first three sections of this treatise, all of which are relatively short, Eymerich examined the basic nature of heresy. Here he noted that certain kinds of superstitious errors were not heretical, including some errors associated with astrology, but he also warned that many apparently astrological predictions actually involved consultations with demons.[44] The final two sections of the treatise are quite extensive, in contrast to the first three, and here Eymerich addressed the crux of his concern, demonstrating that any form of demonic invocation, whether overt or tacit, deliberate or accidental, indicated manifest heresy. While this emphasis on proving heresy was, of course, a reflection of his work as an inquisitor, it was also to some extent a particular articulation of a more general concern that Eymerich shared with the theologians and canonists on Pope John's commission nearly forty years earlier and with all subsequent theological and legal authorities writing against superstition in the decades to come; namely, to parse how superstitious actions related to or might be indicative of erroneous beliefs, and to determine whether and to what degree faulty understanding of some action might mitigate the error entailed in its performance, or magnify it.

Also akin to many later critics of superstition, Eymerich quickly turned in his treatise to a consideration of the scope and scale of demonic power. For the Catalan Dominican, well trained in Thomistic thought, demons were

---

42. Ibid., 2.42.2, p. 336.
43. Kaeppeli, *Scriptores*, 3:159–60; Heimann, *Nicolaus Eymerich*, 171–73.
44. Eymerich, *Contra demonum invocatores*, 102r–108v.

extremely powerful entities, but still their abilities were decidedly limited. Their power was not truly supernatural but only preternatural, capable of prodigious feats but nevertheless conforming to the prescripts of natural law. Grounding himself in Augustine's work on demonic abilities, he considered first to what extent demons might be capable of divination, and like the sainted bishop of Hippo he determined that while they could predict any number of occurrences thanks to their knowledge of natural signs and causation, they had no power to predict any action that depended on human will.[45] Another cornerstone of Eymerich's argumentation was that demons were entirely evil and inimical to human beings. Thus they would never respond to an invocation or obey a command unless a pact had been consecrated (again either overtly or tacitly, so human intention might make little difference) binding the "invoker" to the demons he summoned and involving some kind of worship or devotion being shown to them.[46] In fact, given that the malevolence of demons was an essential doctrine of the church, Eymerich could even argue that simply believing a demon would ever respond to a human invocation without some kind of supplication or offering being made was itself heretical.[47] For the Catalan inquisitor, however, the central error and indeed heresy of demonic invocation was that by such an act a Christian seemed to elevate a demon above God. This could occur either because the conjuring rite might contain some overt form of worship or devotion that should properly be directed only to God (the essential Thomistic definition of superstition), or simply because the act of invoking a demon itself seemed to proclaim that creature to be superior to the deity. When calling on a powerful entity for any purpose, Eymerich reasoned, one would naturally choose the most powerful entity possible, and the one most inclined to offer aid. To conceive of demons as either more powerful or more beneficent than God was clearly heretical.[48]

Ultimately, however, Eymerich had to confront the same issue that had faced Pope John and his commission: in theological terms, the essence of heresy was belief, not behavior. What if a Christian performed a demonic invocation, even one that included some explicit offering or honor shown to demons, but (a) did not truly believe that demons deserved such worship or devotion; (b) did not believe that they were in any way superior to God; (c) sought only to have them accomplish something that lay within their

45. Ibid., 110v–112r, 118v.
46. Ibid., 112v, 114r, 149r.
47. Ibid., 119v.
48. Ibid., 116v, 120r.

natural abilities; and (d) firmly believed that whatever they might accomplish would be possible only if God allowed it to occur? The thorough inquisitor would structure the entire fifth and final section of *Against Invokers of Demons* around this (for him) very thorny hypothetical question. At the heart of his reasoning was the unique nature of the reverence owed to God, so exalted that a Christian might fall into heresy simply by demonstrating it to any lesser creature, no matter how he or she might understand or intend that act. Heresy by action, even in the absence of any deliberately improper belief, thus became conceivable. Eymerich here was working out a complex relationship between internal belief and its external manifestations, one that other legal authorities sometimes had accepted in practice but that he now intended to explicate in full. Religious devotion, he would write, consisted of both internal and external elements, with external acts functioning as the visible demonstrations of internal beliefs, but also clearly connected to them in even more essential ways.[49]

Proceeding from this premise, Eymerich then cataloged various devotional acts and demonstrated how they corresponded to the ritual conjurations of necromancers. One could show devotion by praying to some entity or invoking its name in a prayer or blessing, by genuflecting or prostrating oneself before it, by observing vows such as keeping oneself chaste, by burning candles or incense in its honor, or in some cases by performing bloody animal sacrifices.[50] He capped this long discussion by noting how he had found all of these devotions and more laid out in various handbooks of ritual conjuration that he had seized.

> In the aforesaid books and in many others and through inquests [*inquisitionibus*] it appears indeed that invokers of demons manifestly exhibit the honor of worship to the demons they invoke, especially by sacrificing to them, adoring them, offering up execrable prayers, . . . by genuflecting, by prostrating themselves, by observing chastity out of reverence for the demon or by its instruction, by fasting or otherwise afflicting their flesh, . . . by lighting candles, by burning incense or spices or other aromatics, by sacrificing birds or other animals.[51]

Actual necromantic texts from the late medieval period confirm that magicians did indeed perform such rites, although in most cases they conceived

---

49. Ibid., 120r–122v, 154r.
50. Ibid., 124r–127v.
51. Ibid., 128v; the passage is repeated verbatim in Eymerich, *Directorium inquisitorum* 2.43.2, p. 338.

of them quite differently than did their inquisitorial opponents. Regarding the sacrifice of birds, for example, one text notes that hoopoes in particular were "possessed of great virtue for necromancers and invokers of demons."[52] What critics saw as superstitious forms of devotion, necessary to get a hostile demon to respond to a human invocation, might therefore be presented by practicing magicians quite explicitly as necessary and powerful elements of their ritual conjurations. Even when such rites appeared to be absent, however, Eymerich cautioned that they could merely be hidden—a trap laid by demons for an unsuspecting conjurer. Just like the pact it consecrated, a demonic invocation itself might be "tacit" rather than "express."[53] Thus some rite putatively drawing on astral energies but employing a crafted figure, especially if it contained any kind of inscribed symbols or writing, could in fact be a conjuration expressing reverence and devotion to a demon and thus thrusting any who performed it, whether they understood its true nature or not, into an alliance with the forces of hell. A simple spell that contained strange or unknown words or a curative rite that involved burning herbs could be seen in the same way.

In the final analysis, Eymerich would tolerate only one form of demonic conjuration, and this was when demons were piously commanded in the name of Christ rather than supplicated or propitiated. By this he meant the power of exorcism. In the Bible, Christ had clearly demonstrated command over demons, and he had with equal clarity conferred this power on his disciples and all faithful Christians. Moreover, many saints of the church had demonstrated their holiness in part through their power over demons. Neither Eymerich nor any other authority writing about the dangers of demonic superstition could deny that such rites, sanctioned by divine mandate and performed via divine power, were entirely legitimate. As we have seen, however, Thomas Aquinas had already provided the standard solution to this dilemma, and Eymerich faithfully repeated the position of his fellow Dominican, limiting legitimate exorcism strictly to the expulsion of demons, and forbidding efforts to compel them to perform any tasks, respond to any questions, or impart any kind of information.[54]

There was also a biblical precedent implying that certain natural items might exert power over demons and could legitimately be used to master them. The chief example came from the book of Tobit (Tobias), in which the

---

52. Richard Kieckhefer, *Forbidden Rites: A Necromancer's Manual of the Fifteenth Century* (University Park, Pa., 1998), 49.

53. Eymerich, *Contra demonum invocatores*, 114v.

54. Ibid., 156r–159v. On Aquinas, see chap. 1, n. 125.

angel Raphael instructed young Tobit to drive away demons by burning the heart and liver of a fish (Tobit 6:8, 6:19). Here Eymerich railed against the superstition inherent in believing that any natural items possessed the power to repel demonic spirits. In deference to biblical precedent, however, he conceded that including such items in rites of exorcism was not categorically impermissible, so long as people understood that the demons were actually expelled by divine power, not by virtue of any paraphernalia employed in the rite.[55] With this concession, he left open another dilemma that later authors would have to confront as they struggled to delineate clearly which practices they could confidently deem superstitious and which ones they must grit their teeth and tolerate, for discerning what people believed about how a rite operated was far more difficult than simply observing what items they employed when performing it.

If even explicitly demonic conjurations left some room for debate about the precise nature of their operations, and hence whether they might be legitimate or superstitious, the realm of astrology, grounded in natural philosophy and claiming to operate entirely by natural force, was fraught with contestation. As we have seen, proponents stressed astrology's scientific credentials, while admitting the potential for error or even deliberate malfeasance among less well-trained or morally upright practitioners. Critics, for their part, readily allowed the possibility of entirely licit astrology, stressing that they were, by definition, only concerned with its illicit, superstitious aspects. Debate then raged over where exactly those all-important boundary lines fell. Eymerich addressed astrology briefly in both *Against Invokers of Demons* and the *Directory of Inquisitors*, already warning of a possible link between astrological arts—both divination and astral magic—and the errors of necromancers. Only late in his life, however, did he examine this topic at length in his treatise *Against Ignorant Astrologers*, written toward the end of 1395, during his second period of exile from the Crown of Aragon. If *Against Invokers of Demons* and the *Directory of Inquisitors* each demonstrate a clear focus on the elite necromantic rites so feared in papal Avignon and other power centers of Europe, *Against Ignorant Astrologers* reveals an even more explicit courtly context. Eymerich addressed the treatise, examining a ubiquitous form of courtly magic, to the Franciscan friar Thomas Ulzine, the confessor to King Joan I of Aragon, who could be expected to bear considerable responsibility for controlling the king's well-known—and

---

55. Eymerich, *Contra demonum invocatores*, 157v, 159r.

in the eyes of his critics altogether excessive—fascination with astrological divination.[56]

In his opening letter to Ulzine, the exiled inquisitor touted legitimate astrology, readily admitting that one could, by studying the movement of heavenly bodies, make valid predictions regarding any terrestrial occurrence that proceeded naturally and necessarily from the effects of astral forces in the sublunar world. He warned, however, that many predictions supposedly derived from astrological science actually involved demons in some way. His central concern was to determine when astrologers crossed the line and became illicit diviners (whom he labeled here *mathematici*, adopting Augustine's and Isidore's term for those who pressed astrological prediction beyond its natural capacities) or even outright necromancers (*nigromantici*).[57] Yet first he felt the need to demonstrate that he himself understood the natural properties of the heavens, the science of their movements, and the force of their "influences" on the earth. Organizing the first part of his treatise into twelve articles, he spent fully ten of them (albeit each relatively short) discussing the substance and nature of the heavens, their form and movements, and the effects of their emanations on the terrestrial world.[58] At the beginning of each article, he carefully noted that his arguments drew on both "traditions of astrologers and of theologians," thereby stressing his own natural philosophical as well as doctrinal expertise, and demonstrating his support for legitimate astral science as much as his condemnation of improper superstition. Doctrine, however, always trumped philosophy, and in his eleventh article, Eymerich based himself "mainly" (*maxime*) in theology.[59] Here he addressed how astral forces might influence human beings and human "liberty." While the stars could affect the physical matter of human bodies, church doctrine clearly indicated that human will was free and inviolable. Thus if astrologers asserted any natural basis for predictions of human actions, they fell into serious error and their craft became superstitious.

---

56. On this work, see Julien Véronèse, "Le *Contra astrologos imperitos atque nigromanticos* (1395–96) de Nicolas Eymerich (O. P.): Contexte de rédaction, classification des arts magiques et divinatoires, édition critique partielle," in *Chasses aux sorcières et démonologie: Entre discours et pratiques (XIVe–XVIIe siècles)*, ed. Martine Ostorero, Georg Modestin, and Kathrin Utz Tremp, ML 36 (Florence, 2010), 271–329. While Véronèse dates King Joan's death to May 1395, many other scholars place his death in a hunting accident in May 1396, such that he was still alive when Eymerich completed *Contra astrologos*.

57. Eymerich, *Contra astrologos*, 75r–v.

58. Ibid., 75v–78v.

59. Ibid., 79r.

In his long twelfth article (itself almost as long as the first ten articles combined), Eymerich delved deeper into the errors of superstitious astrology.[60]
He again stressed that the stars could not control human will. So long as
astrologers limited themselves strictly (and appropriately) to observance of
heavenly bodies and calculation of their natural effects, they would never be
able to predict human actions with absolute certainty. Such prediction was
possible only regarding those events that arose "always and necessarily" from
heavenly motion. For example, astrologers could predict eclipses and other
heavenly phenomenon, but very few earthly ones. Eymerich did allow that
astrologers might predict some terrestrial events "not always, but often" (*non
semper sed sepe*), that is, not with complete certainty but with a fair degree
of accuracy.[61] For example, since the heavens exerted significant although
not absolute influence on earth's atmosphere, astrologers could often reliably forecast the weather. If they ever claimed absolute certainty in such
prognostications, however, they would again be guilty of error. They might
simply be lying about their abilities, or they might be engaging in forms of
divination beyond pure observation of heavenly bodies and calculation of
their natural effects. Ultimately, Eymerich echoed Isidore that astrology was
in part natural, good, and a "true science," but also in part "superstitious, evil,
and therefore illicit."[62] He even went so far as to rank legitimate astrology
among the seven liberal arts, a place usually held by its more clearly legitimate
cousin astronomy (although again it must be noted that medieval authorities
regularly interchanged these two seemingly distinct terms). In particular, the
inquisitor noted, physicians often needed to determine how astral influences
might affect illness or its treatment. When used by "magicians and *mathematici*," however, astrology became a "superstitious" and "divinatory" art.[63]

Having demonstrated astrology's limitations as a predictive science, Eymerich then hammered home the demonic danger inherent in superstitious astrological divination not through further direct arguments about astrological
practices per se, but instead by relying on the power of guilt by association.
In the second half of his treatise, he addressed twenty different forms of divination, beginning with necromancy and moving through other traditional
categories such as geomancy, aeromancy, pyromancy, and hydromancy, also

---

60. Ibid., 79v–81v.

61. Ibid., 81r.

62. Ibid., 81r: "Astrologia partim est naturalis et bona, qui vera sciencia et ideo licita, partim est
supersticiosa et mala et ideo illicita."

63. Ibid., 81v: "Hec etiam astrologia est supersticiosa in quantum magi et mathematici utuntur
ea ut arte divinatoria."

augury, divination by dreams, and the so-called notory art (*ars notoria*), which consisted of rites supposedly derived from Solomon and intended to bestow knowledge and wisdom by invoking angels or even the Holy Spirit itself, but which suspicious authorities believed actually invoked demons.[64] His treatment of necromancy provided the model for how he dealt with each of these practices in turn. First he defined the practice: in the case of necromancy, divination by means of a corpse or ghost. Then he demonstrated how the practice actually relied on demons. With necromancy, a conjured demon animated the corpse or assumed the form of a dead person's spirit. With phitomancy, an art deriving its name from the mythological python at Delphi, which had supposedly bestowed prophetic powers on the priestesses there, a demon inhabited the body of an animal to offer prognostications. With aeromancy, demons would control the movements of clouds or the force of the winds or whatever aspect of the elements was essential in the divination.[65] Then Eymerich argued—at length for necromancy and more briefly in each subsequent case, since the basic point was always the same—that demons hated human beings and would render such services only if human diviners offered them some form of sacrifice or worship. He also stressed that even when propitiated in these ways demons remained inherently deceptive creatures and the responses they offered could never be trusted.

Eymerich never, in fact, returned directly to astrology in this treatise, but his point was clear. When they extended their predictions into areas other than those directly affected by natural astral influences, astrologers became diviners, and almost all forms of divination involved at least a tacit alliance with demons. The inquisitor allowed only a handful of possible exceptions among the last few of his twenty categories.[66] Bearing a particular relation to astrology was his discussion of augury, or divination by observing the flight of birds. Following that strand of Christian thought that had long offered some justification for this practice, Eymerich proposed that augurs could make relatively reliable predictions of changes in weather or climate, because birds were naturally attuned to changes in the atmosphere that might herald such developments.[67] Similarly he noted that physicians might legitimately utilize *aruspiomancia*, meaning the observance of specific times, since natural factors and especially the strength of certain astral forces at particular times

---

64. Ibid., 81v–89v. The notory art will be discussed at greater length in the next chapter.
65. Ibid., 81v, 82v, 83r.
66. Véronèse, "Le *Contra astrologos*," 281, emphasizes this subtle shift.
67. Eymerich, *Contra astrologos*, 87v.

of the day or year could affect the human body in significant ways.[68] Beyond these and a few other exceptions, however, divination always involved some type of demonic invocation, in certain cases explicit but more often tacit and perhaps entirely unsuspected by the foolish practitioners of such arts. This was the message Eymerich assumedly expected Thomas Ulzine to pass along to an Aragonese king and court dangerously enraptured, so the inquisitor clearly felt, with superstitious astrology.

Not many months after completing *Against Ignorant Astrologers*, and still exiled in Avignon, Eymerich wrote a shorter, even more focused treatise, *Against Alchemists*. One might easily imagine these two works as companion pieces, since astrology and alchemy were two of the main branches of occult science at the courts of late medieval Europe. The courtly connection of this second treatise, however, is not as obvious as that of *Against Ignorant Astrologers*. For example, Eymerich dedicated it not to the king's confessor or any other court figure but instead to his friend and former companion Bernardo Estrucio, abbot of the Benedictine monastery of Rosis.[69] Moreover, while late medieval opponents of superstition often focused intently on astrology and debated its many forms and permutations at great length in numerous treatises, they appear generally to have been far less preoccupied with alchemy. Although they regularly included it in lists of damnable superstitions, they typically discussed it only briefly, if at all. Thus Eymerich's short treatise against alchemy (considerably shorter than what he wrote on astrology) was actually something of an anomaly in the corpus of late medieval writings about superstition.

Nevertheless, there are some basic similarities between the two treatises. As with astrology, when confronting alchemy Eymerich had to work his way through alchemists' claims that theirs was a legitimate form of knowledge (*scientia*) firmly grounded in natural philosophy, not any kind of erroneous superstition. He thus focused roughly the first third of his treatise on establishing his own credentials as an expert on the natural properties of gold, silver, and precious gems.[70] He then argued that, while natural substances could be purified and refined by human craft, they could not be created or fundamentally transformed by artificial means, as alchemists claimed to

---

68. Ibid., 88r.

69. Eymerich, however, also dedicated his 1395 treatise *Contra prefigentes certum terminum fini mundi* to Bernardo, which Michael Ryan has analyzed as a critique of courtly divinatory practices, so perhaps there is reason to think that Eymerich saw the abbot as a conduit to court. See Ryan, *Kingdom of Stargazers*, 133.

70. Eymerich, *Contra alchimistas*, 108–18.

accomplish in their furnaces.[71] He admitted that human art could alter the appearance of various substances, and he was quite ready to tolerate such artifice so long as it was put only to essentially inconsequential uses. Those not quite wealthy enough to afford the real thing, for example, could lay out a setting of alchemical "gold" or "silver" tableware, or adorn themselves with alchemical jewelry to impress anyone not clever enough to detect the fabrication. To try to use alchemical coins as true currency, on the other hand, was obviously to commit the crime of forgery. He also warned against using alchemically disguised materials in medicine, since their essential substance, and so their natural effects on the human body, would not match that of the true materials they mimicked.[72]

Only in his final chapter did Eymerich address the possible demonic component of alchemical practices. He noted that demons, bound by the strictures of natural law just as much as alchemists themselves were, could neither create precious materials nor transform nonprecious matter in any essential way. Yet demons knew where all the hidden treasures of the earth lay, and they could transport any amount of such material around the world in the blink of an eye. If, therefore, an alchemist were to draw any real gold from his furnace, the most likely explanation would be that he had contracted with a demon to bring it there, either deliberately or inadvertently through the various superstitious practices included in his efforts at transmutation.[73] Eymerich appears to have suspected more the former. Although he acknowledged that there were natural and permissible aspects to alchemical transformations, he concluded that, "just like astrologers," alchemists were "much disposed" to conjuring and consulting dangerous demonic spirits.[74]

While the circulation and influence of his later treatises against astrology and alchemy were probably not great, the concerns Eymerich expressed in them, as in his earlier work against demonic invocation and in his massively influential inquisitor's manual, are in many ways representative of general concerns growing among clerical elites in the fourteenth century, and persisting throughout the fifteenth century as well. Although some of his specific points of argument derived narrowly from his profession as an inquisitor, they nevertheless reveal a range of abiding issues that all Christian authorities would confront when seeking to link erroneous, superstitious rites to entanglements with demons. In particular Eymerich addressed

---

71. Ibid., 118–20, 124.
72. Ibid., 128.
73. Ibid., 128–32.
74. Ibid., 132.

the scope of demonic power within the natural world, the troublesome matter of how incorrect belief and improper action related to and potentially entailed one another, and the question whether and to what ends humans might ever master demons (or compel divine power, for that matter) through ritual acts or even by means of natural forces. In his writings against alchemy and astrology, he explored the potential power conferred by knowledge of natural forces and the capacity of humans to manipulate those forces, yet he mainly stressed the dangers of improper understanding or misguided action, especially that they might lead, even if unintentionally, to the unforgivable invocation of demonic spirits. By the time Eymerich penned *Against Ignorant Astrologers* in Avignon, in fact, these issues had already been addressed at some length by authorities connected to the greatest intellectual center and the most powerful royal court in western Europe. The debates that raged in Paris about the precarious position of astrology between admirable science and dangerous superstition, however, reveal a different kind of concern and different direction in which the debate about superstition could develop.

Astral Anxieties in Fourteenth-Century Paris

Uncertainty about astrology was, as we have seen, deeply embedded in Christian thought, grounded in the ambivalence of such early authorities as Augustine and Isidore of Seville. Debate only intensified in the twelfth and thirteenth centuries, as all aspects of astral science were reinvigorated in western Europe by the influx of ancient and Arab texts about the power of the stars and the spirits who might be thought to animate them. Major intellects such as Albertus Magnus and Roger Bacon looked favorably on many forms of astrology and emphasized its legitimate potential, while of course always noting the danger of illicit superstition. Others, including Albertus's own student Thomas Aquinas, were more suspicious, judging that the risks of this nebulous art often outweighed its beneficial uses. The very existence of such debate was troubling to many. In the late thirteenth century, first in 1270 and then much more fully in 1277, the bishop of Paris Etienne Tempier reacted against the new philosophy derived primarily from Aristotle and his Arab commentators, condemning a number of "manifest and execrable errors," including many dealing with astral science and astrological divination. In the introductory letter to the 1277 condemnation, he also inveighed against magical texts, including books of geomancy, necromancy, sorcery, demonic invocation, and "conjurations imperiling souls."[75] In 1290, the bishops of Paris and Sens jointly condemned a number of magical texts, including books of necromancy containing, in the view of later authorities, "horrible" and "detestable" demonic invocations.[76]

Fears also coursed through the French royal court, initially less about astral prediction than about possible sorcerous intrigues. When Philip IV's queen Joan of Navarre died suddenly in 1305, at the age of thirty-two, suspicions flourished, and in 1308 charges of poisoning and maleficent sorcery were brought against Bishop Guichard of Troyes.[77] Then, when Philip himself died in 1314, the royal chamberlain Enguerrand of Marigny faced charges of magically plotting against the royal family, as did Pierre of Latilly, bishop of Chalons. French kings underwent a period of particularly bad luck after Philip IV. His eldest son, Louis X, died in 1316 after only two years on the throne, and his younger son Philip V died in 1322. During his life, some believed Philip V had been ensorcelled by his mother-in-law, Mahaut of Artois, to revive his waning affections for her daughter Joan of Burgundy. Mahaut had also been accused of poisoning Louis X in 1316 in order to maneuver her son-in-law onto the throne in the first place. A third son of Philip IV, Charles IV, died in 1328. Then in 1331 the next king, Philip VI, complained to Pope John XXII about sorcerers plotting against him at his court, and the pope ordered the bishop of Paris to investigate.[78]

By the middle of the fourteenth century, the sorcerous fervor at the Parisian court had calmed somewhat, and with the Hundred Years War in full effect, French kings had other pressing matters to occupy their energies. Yet Paris remained a great center for intellectual debate about magic, divination, and especially astrology. Partly because of the vicissitudes of the war, in fact, astrologers became increasingly prevalent and popular at the royal court.[79] This, in turn, sparked warnings about astrological superstition from experts at the University of Paris, chief among them the theologians Nicole Oresme, writing mainly in the 1350s and 1360s, and Heinrich of Langenstein, writing in the late 1360s and early 1370s (see the timeline, Major Parisian Theologians, 1330–1430). Both valued legitimate astrological *scientia*, while at the

75. David Piché, ed. and trans., *La condamnation parisienne de 1277: Nouvelle édition du texte latin, traduction, introduction et commentaire* (Paris, 1999), quotes at 72 and 76.

76. On both sets of condemnations, see Boudet, *Entre science et* nigromance, 251–57.

77. See n. 8 above.

78. See n. 17 above; also Peters, *Magician*, 120–22; Jones, "Political Uses of Sorcery," 676–81.

79. Carey, *Courting Disaster*, 128.

same time recognizing the potential for astral prognostications to lead into error. Indeed, they probed the scientific foundations of the astral arts more fully than virtually any other contemporary authorities, and most earlier ones.[80] They wrote not only to clarify the true science of the stars to their academic colleagues, but also to warn princes and other powerful members of the Parisian court against the "superstitious curiosities" that they feared were all too common in their day.[81] Both, however, ultimately downplayed the threat of demons encroaching into the realm of even mangled or fallacious astrology. Unlike their contemporary Nicolau Eymerich, or indeed other important Parisian masters in years to come, they did not draw a straight line connecting superstition of every sort with diabolism and heresy, and even when they admitted the possibility of such a connection, they did not stress it in their writings. Superstition still needed to be identified, castigated, and corrected, in their view, but their understanding of superstition was more "scientific" than "religious." Together they illuminate another perspective on superstition in this period, one that might have become a dominant view, but did not. Of the two, Oresme was not only earlier but also more radical in his positions.

Born around 1320 in Normandy, Nicole Oresme came to Paris to study perhaps around 1340. He progressed through an arts degree and then moved on to the course in theology at the College of Navarre. By 1356 he had completed his theology degree and became master of the college. Also by this time he had formed a close relationship with the Dauphin, the future Charles V (crowned in 1364), that would continue until Charles's death in 1380. Thus, although after 1362 Oresme's residency in the French capital was often irregular and he held a number of other ecclesiastical posts, he always remained tied to Paris, both its university and its court, until he died (as bishop of Lisieux) in 1382.[82] One of the greatest intellectual figures of the fourteenth century, he is often regarded particularly by historians of science as an important precursor of modern scientific thought.[83] This evaluation is

---

80. Weill-Parot, *Images astrologiques* (as above, n. 26), 422.

81. Nicole Oresme, *Contra judiciarios astronomos*, 129.

82. For brief biographies, see J. Gautier-Dalché, "Oresme et son temps," in *Nicolas Oresme: Tradition et innovation chez un intellectuel du XIVe siècle*, ed. P. Souffrin and A. P. Segonds (Paris, 1988), 7–11; Dan Burton, *Nicole Oresme's* De visione stellarum *(On Seeing the Stars): A Critical Edition of Oresme's Treatise on Optics and Atmospheric Refraction, with an Introduction, Commentary, and English Translation* (Leiden, 2007), 5–17.

83. Marshall Clagett, *Nicole Oresme and the Medieval Geometry of Qualities and Motions: A Treatise on the Uniformity and Difformity of Intensities Known as* Tractatus de configurationibus qualitatum et motuum (Madison, 1968), 3; Joel Kaye, "Law, Magic, and Science: Constructing a Border between

Major Parisian Theologians, 1330–1430

Year	Monarch	Nicole Oresme	Heinrich of Langenstein	Pierre d'Ailly	Jean Gerson
1330	King Philip VI (1328–50)				
1340		**Nicole Oresme** studies in Paris (ca. 1340)			
1350	King John II (1350–64)				
1360	King Charles V (1364–80)	Appointed master of College of Navarre (1356) / Relinquishes post as master (1362)	**Heinrich of Langenstein** studies in Paris (ca. 1360)	**Pierre d'Ailly** studies in Paris (ca. 1364)	
1370		Becomes bishop of Lisieux (1377)	Receives theology degree (1373)		**Jean Gerson** studies in Paris (1377)
1380	King Charles VI (1380–1422)	(d. 1382)	Departs Paris (1382) / Settles in Vienna (1384)	Receives theology degree (1381)	
1390				Becomes chancellor of Paris (1389)	Receives theology degree (1392)
1400		Twenty-eight articles of sorcery condemned by Paris theological faculty (1398)	(d. 1397)	Becomes bishop of Cambrai (1397)	Becomes chancellor of Paris (1395)
1410				Becomes cardinal (1411)	
				Attends Council of Constance (1414–18)	Attends Council of Constance (1415–18) / Settles in Lyon (1419)
1420	King Charles VII (1422–61)			(d. 1420)	
					(d. 1429)
1430					

due at least in part to Oresme's criticisms of magic and superstition—one scholar goes so far as to say his efforts to "disenchant" his world.[84] In fact, while he never rejected the existence of demons or the theoretical possibility of their power (or that of divine miracle), he came to envision an extremely limited role for active spiritual forces in material creation, and this view informed some aspects of his critique of superstition. Other elements of his opposition to astrological divination, however, were much more practically grounded in a political as well as an intellectual context. Not surprisingly, his less extreme ideas were more immediately influential on subsequent authorities addressing superstitious practices.

Oresme wrote many works dealing with astrology, astral science, and the potential for error and superstition in the sidereal arts, as well as other forms of divination and natural wonders.[85] Unfortunately, the exact chronology of these works is uncertain. Many scholars date his *On Configurations of Qualities and Motions* (*De configurationibus qualitatum et motuum*) to the early 1350s, his vernacular *Book on Divinations* (*Livre de divinacions*) to the early 1360s, and the Latin treatise *Against Judicial Astrologers* (*Contra judiciarios astronomos*), seemingly closely related to the *Book*, just prior to that. They set his *Question against Astrological Diviners* (*Quaestio contra divinatores horoscopios*) and the more general *On the Causes of Wonders* (*De causis mirabilium*) around 1370. This sequence, however, is not without its problems or its challengers. In particular, some suggest that both the *Question against Astrological Diviners* and *On the Causes of Wonders* may be significantly earlier, in the 1350s, and the relationship between the *Book on Divinations* and *Against Judicial Astrologers* has been questioned.[86] Another important work on the mathematics of heavenly motion, *On the Commensurability or Incommensurability of Heavenly Motions* (*De commensurabilitate vel incommensurabilitate motuum celi*), which

---

Licit and Illicit Knowledge in the Writings of Nicole Oresme," in *Law and the Illicit in Medieval Europe*, ed. Ruth Mazo Karras, Joel Kaye, and E. Ann Matter (Philadelphia, 2008), 225–37, at 231; and to some extent also Lorraine Daston and Katharine Park, *Wonders and the Order of Nature, 1150–1750* (New York, 1998), 130–32.

84. Jeannine Quillet, "Enchantements et désenchantement de la nature selon Nicole Oresme," in *Mensch und Natur im Mittelalter*, ed. Albert Zimmermann and Andreas Speer (Berlin, 1991), 321–29.

85. Overviews in Thorndike, *History of Magic*, 3:398–471; Stefano Caroti, "La critica contro l'astrologia di Nicole Oresme e la sua influenza nel Medioevo e nel Rinascimento," *Atti della Accademia Nazionale dei Lincei: Memorie, Classe di Scienze morali, storiche e filologiche*, ser. 8, vol. 23 (1979): 545–685. See also Stefano Caroti, "Nicole Oresme's Polemic against Astrology in his 'Quodlibeta,'" in *Astrology, Science and Society: Historical Essays*, ed. Patrick Curry (Woodbridge, U.K., 1987), 75–93.

86. Max Lejbowicz, "Chronologie des écrits anti-astrologiques de Nicole Oresme: Étude sur un cas de scepticisme dans la deuxième moitié du XIVe siècle," in *Autour de Nicole Oresme: Actes du Colloque Oresme organisé à l'Université de Paris XII*, ed. Jeannine Quillet (Paris, 1990), 119–76.

undermined the possibility of precise astrological calculations, was probably written in the 1350s or very early 1360s, but the only fixed dates are that it was composed (conditionally) sometime after 1351 and certainly before 1377. To tease out developments in Oresme's thought over time, exact dating or at least sequencing of his work is essential, but here, to get a sense of the overall shape of his thought, we can simply move from his more focused anti-astrology treatises to his more general works on magic and "marvels" (*mirabilia*), regardless of precisely when he wrote them.

Among his works addressing astrological divination, Oresme wrote both *Against Judicial Astrologers* and its longer vernacular companion piece, the *Book on Divinations,* explicitly for a courtly audience, to warn princes and magnates about the dangers of probing into "occult matters" or predicting the future by means of astrology (or, as the *Book* added, by other forms of divination such as necromancy).[87] In addition to addressing these works to princes, he also included in each a lengthy recitation of historical rulers who had come to bad ends owing to their excessive infatuation with astrology.[88] He wisely steered clear of concluding these historical accounts with his own friend and patron Charles V, who was at this very time busy assembling one of the largest astrological libraries medieval Europe had ever seen. He did, however, include for castigation the (nearly) contemporary example of Jaume III of Majorca. Having lost his island kingdom to his mainland cousin the king of Aragon, Jaume consulted with astrologers on a propitious date to march forth and attempt to regain his crown, but his confidence in the power of astrological prognostication was misplaced and he died on the battlefield in 1349.[89]

Like all medieval Christian authorities, Oresme, drawing largely on Isidore of Seville's distinctions, accepted that astrology could be "beautiful and honest" and a "very noble and excellent science." Nevertheless, it often entailed elements that were "false and superstitious."[90] In his more voluminous *Book on Divinations,* he identified six elements of astrology. The first three were legitimate. They concerned observing and measuring the movements of heavenly bodies, studying the natural influences those bodies exerted on the earth, and making some general predictions based on effects that astral

87. Oresme, *Contra judiciarios astronomos,* 123; Oresme, *Livre,* 50. For a comparison of these two works, see esp. Caroti, "Critica contro l'astrologia di Nicole Oresme," 555–71.

88. Oresme, *Contra judiciarios astronomos,* 125–27; Oresme, *Livre,* 70–74.

89. Oresme, *Contra judiciarios astronomos,* 127; Oresme, *Livre,* 72. On Jaume, see Ryan, *Kingdom of Stargazers,* 77–78.

90. Oresme, *Contra judiciarios astronomos,* 132, 134; Oresme, *Livre,* 54.

energies might produce relatively directly, such as atmospheric changes and storms, famine or disease that might be caused by weather or climate, or illnesses arising from an imbalance of humors in the human body, which the stars could also affect. The final three elements, however, were highly suspect: nativities, interrogations, and elections. Nativities referred to drawing natal horoscopes meant to determine people's essential characteristics, supposedly imprinted on them by the force of the stars at the moment of their births, and then using that information in turn to make general predictions about the future course of their lives. Interrogations involved consulting the heavens in order to make specific predictions about some upcoming event or occurrence, such as the fate of a pending marriage or outcome of a looming battle. In the related practice of elections, one turned to the stars in order to choose a particular course of action or to select a propitious time for undertaking some action, as the ill-fated Jaume of Majorca had done.[91]

All these practices were fraught with error, with the latter two categories being particularly egregious. They constituted "judicial" astrology, that is, astrology used to render relatively narrow "judgments" in particular circumstances, as opposed to the more general information provided by a natal horoscope, which typically concerned a person's underlying character and capacities.[92] Since all authorities recognized that the stars exerted some general influences on the earth, and even on human beings, they almost always became more skeptical and suspicious as astrological prognostications became more precise. Opponents declared that judicial astrology had no basis in any proper understanding of natural philosophy, and Oresme condemned such practices polemically in *Against Judicial Astrologers* and the *Book on Divinations*, and more mathematically and "philosophically" in his *On Commensurability* and *Question against Astrological Diviners*.

In *On Commensurability*, Oresme noted what "arrogance" astrologers exhibited when they claimed to base their predictions on reliable knowledge of the heavens and careful calculation of their motion. Such absolutely precise calculations were impossible, in his view, and so was all knowledge supposedly based on them. Moreover, only some terrestrial events were subject to any astral influence at all.[93] Although he admitted that astrologers could le-

---

91. Oresme, *Livre*, 54–56.

92. For an overview, see Hilary M. Carey, "Judicial Astrology in Theory and Practice in Later Medieval Europe," *Studies in History and Philosophy of Biological and Biomedical Sciences* 41 (2010): 90–98.

93. Oresme, *De commensurabilitate*, 320.

gitimately predict the weather to a certain extent, since astral energies directly influenced atmospheric conditions, nevertheless in his *Book on Divinations* he wryly commented that most of the time they could not even get their weather forecasts right. How then could anyone trust them to make more complicated prognostications?[94] In the *Question against Astrological Diviners* he noted that when making any type of prediction, no two astrologers ever seemed to agree with one another, calling into serious question the scientific basis of their craft.[95] Regarding natal horoscopes, he offered the standard argument from Augustine regarding the different natures or fates of many twins, born under the same or at least similar astral influences: the biblical Jacob and Esau, for example, or the classical Romulus and Remus, who came to quite different ends. While he admitted that astral energies might "incline" human beings toward certain behaviors, owing to the physical effects they had on the human body, he denied that they could in any way control human action, as that would, of course, forfeit divinely ordained free will.[96]

Most basically, though, Oresme argued against using astrology to make any specific predictions because he regarded the natural effects of astral bodies on the earth to be general and universal, not localized in any way. This challenged the notion held dear by many astrologers, and certainly by astral magicians, that the effects of heavenly bodies were naturally concentrated, or could be artificially focused, at specific places or points in time.[97] Oresme reasoned, however, that variable effects and outcomes on earth were more likely caused by differing terrestrial conditions, not anything to do with the heavens themselves. For example, if two fields lay side by side, but crops flourished in one while withering in the other, this was probably due not to some beneficial astral force being focused on the first field and not the second, but to differences in the soil.[98] Arguing more generally, he asserted that a "remote cause" should not be considered an "efficient cause"; in other words, even when the stars did influence some terrestrial event, they usually did so only indirectly, which did not allow for reliable prediction. Too many other factors intervened. He went on to assert that no mysterious or occult powers inhered in any of the heavenly bodies; their natural properties consisted only of observable light and motion.[99]

---

94. Oresme, *Livre*, 90.
95. Oresme, *Quaestio*, 232.
96. Oresme, *Contra judiciarios astronomos*, 130–31; Oresme, *Quaestio*, 228, 234.
97. Oresme, *Quaestio*, 229–30, 241–42, 259–60.
98. Ibid., 242, 246.
99. Ibid., 270, 274.

Returning to practical implications, how should a prince respond to all of this? Since heavenly bodies did transmit certain natural energies (although never any secret or "occult" ones) toward the earth, and these in turn could produce some broad, generalized natural effects that might indirectly influence more specific matters of consequence to rulers, Oresme counseled the wise prince to be knowledgeable of general astrological principles and to support with all due honor the legitimate astrologers at his court. He should not, however, pay too much serious attention to them. He should also know enough to ignore and shun those "superstitious astrologers" who "abuse the [astral] sciences" through their ignorance or malice, for they were no better than practitioners of other fraudulent magical arts.[100] Some astrologers were simply mistaken about the natural limits of their craft, while others were deliberate frauds, either claiming to "predict" events that had already happened and about which they had secretly learned, or simply making such vague and garbled prognostications that they could, after almost any outcome transpired, claim to have foreseen it.[101] Many astrologers also deluded themselves, clinging to those few instances when, purely by chance, they made a correct prediction, and using that as evidence of their own power. Here Oresme drew a parallel between astrology and alchemy, noting that just one or two successful transmutations would draw alchemists fully into their false art no matter how many failures they suffered. Likewise he concluded that "just as alchemists are commonly deceived and wretched, so are those who put their trust in divinations."[102]

Linking astrology to other forms of "magical" fraud raised the possibility of demonic error infecting the astral arts, and Oresme in fact commented briefly that both astrologers and alchemists could be seduced by the temptations and machinations of the devil.[103] He proved remarkably restrained on this point, however, especially when compared to the vehemence of someone like Nicolau Eymerich. Of course Oresme acknowledged the existence and malevolence of the devil and his demonic minions. Particularly in the vernacular *Book on Divinations*, he occasionally lumped astrological divination together with the demonic art of necromancy (along with many other forms of divination, from augury to palm reading and the interpretation of dreams, it must be said).[104] But these were rhetorical conglomerations, simply lists of

---

100. Oresme, *Contra judiciarios astronomos*, 135–36; Oresme, *Livre*, 104–6.
101. Oresme, *Livre*, 94, 98.
102. Ibid., 98–100, quote at 100.
103. Ibid., 100.
104. Ibid., 51, 55.

the sort of divinatory practices one might expect to find in a princely court, not reasoned arguments equating different forms of practice. In fact, while Oresme occasionally noted that the devil might tempt or trick astrologers into superstitious error, such statements typically constitute only minor interjections into his arguments. For him, astrological superstition was more about scientific error than religious infraction. Indeed, while he admitted that some effects that astrologers attributed to the stars could in fact derive from demons, he warned against making that leap of judgment too readily. Most of the wonders and marvels that people fearfully ascribed to demons, he repeatedly maintained, were entirely natural occurrences.[105]

With this point, we move from Oresme's critiques of erroneous astrology to his more general position on magic, marvels, and wondrous spiritual powers operating in the world. While most critics regarded the greatest danger presented by superstitions to be the possibility that they somehow garbled devotion to God or invoked demons (explicitly or tacitly) in their operations, Oresme took the position—and here we can see why many now regard him as such a protomodern thinker—that superstitious people simply failed to understand the basic natural laws by which the universe operated, with neither demons, nor occult astral forces, nor the deity himself typically being involved. He began his treatise *On the Causes of Wonders*, in fact, with the challenging statement: "there is no need to turn immediately to the heavens, the last refuge of the pitiful, or to demons, or to glorious God, as if he would create these effects directly, more so than other effects whose [natural] causes we believe are well enough known to us."[106] Simply put, Oresme thought that most apparent marvels occurred naturally. If a magician acted at all in the process, it was typically only to deceive or mislead people from seeing the real causes of whatever occurrence he claimed to have produced by his rites.[107] Oresme did not deny the reality of demonic power, or the real possibility of miracles for that matter; he simply cautioned that people "should not believe too quickly" in such things. Natural causes were, for him, always more likely than demonic ones.[108]

Similarly, Oresme accepted the possibility of demonic conjuration and necromancy, but he contended that most often demonic magicians achieved

---

105. Oresme, *Quaestio*, 293, 295, 298.

106. Oresme, *De causis*, 136: "Nec propter hoc oportet ad celum tanquam ad ultimum et miserorum refugium currere, nec ad demones, nec ad Deum gloriosum quod scilicet illos effectus faciat immediate plus quam alios quorum causas credimus nobis satis notas."

107. Oresme, *De configurationibus*, 336.

108. Oresme, *De causis*, 138, 264, 360 (quote at 264); Oresme, *De configurationibus*, 372.

their supposed effects through deception and misdirection. Like alchemists and astrologers, sometimes necromancers deceived themselves with their own arts, but their results were unreal nonetheless.[109] Many "magical" effects, for example, arose from simple sensory misperception. Oresme criticized conjurers for operating typically at night or in dark, secluded spots that naturally produced fear and frenzied imaginings in anyone witnessing the rite (potentially including the conjurers themselves). He also noted that different dispositions could cause people to perceive the same event quite differently. A naturally fearful person seeing a cat enter a room, for example, would be convinced that it was a demon in disguise, while a fundamentally pious person might think it was an angel. Necromancers often had young boys gaze into mirrors or polished surfaces in divinatory rites precisely because their active imaginations caused them more readily to think that they saw apparitions in those surfaces. Magicians also frequently burned herbs or other plants in their rites, or concocted potions from them, which affected the senses, or they devised "mathematical" illusions, employing mirrors or other devices to alter perspective and perception.[110]

While in principle Oresme maintained space in his system for active and effective spiritual entities, in practice this space appears to have been small indeed. He made a point to criticize those people even more skeptical than he, who asserted that absolutely every occurrence must have a natural cause, such as followers of the Muslim astrologer al-Kindi, who attributed all events in nature to the influence of astral rays.[111] But even in such areas as spoken spells and incantations, let alone scientific astrology, he gravitated toward natural explanations to a tremendous degree. Most Christian authorities from Augustine to Aquinas had steadfastly maintained that words functioned only through "signification," that is, by conveying meaning to some receptive intelligence, which in the case of all superstitious rites they typically judged to be demonic. Words possessed no inherent power and certainly exerted no natural energies such as the stars did. In the thirteenth and fourteenth centuries, however, some intellectuals argued for more direct, physical ways in which words might produce effects. Oresme stood among them, suggesting that spoken words projected natural power through the sound waves of

109. Oresme, *De configurationibus*, 336–38.

110. Oresme, *De causis*, 154 and 160 (example of the cat); Oresme, *De configurationibus*, 336–38, 346–58.

111. Oresme, *De configurationibus*, 374. On al-Kindi, see Weill-Parot, *Images astrologiques* (as above, n. 26), 155–74.

which they were composed, their "formation and figuration," as he put it.[112] Again we can see Oresme's appeal to those who want to read modern or protomodern "skepticism" and "rationality" back into at least some figures in the Middle Ages. In fact, however, while he was fairly extreme in some of his positions, he was engaged in fully medieval debates.

While subsequent critics of superstition tended to draw on the less radical aspects of Oresme's thought, he nevertheless exerted a notable influence for the rest of the fourteenth century and into the fifteenth.[113] Pierre d'Ailly, undoubtedly the greatest authority on astrology in Paris in the early fifteenth century, studied at Oresme's College of Navarre when he first came to the university in the 1360s. Although the two men did not quite overlap as student and master at the same college (see timeline, p. 97), d'Ailly nevertheless later drew on Oresme in many of his own works.[114] D'Ailly's pupil Jean Gerson would also make significant, if not always sympathetic, use of Oresme in his condemnations of erroneous astrology, as we will see in the next chapter. Within the Parisian court, the vernacular writer Philippe of Mézières took most of the material on astrology and superstition in his allegorical *Dream of the Old Pilgrim* (*Songe du vieil pelerin*) of 1389 directly from Oresme's *Book on Divinations*.[115] Over a century later, the Italian humanist Pico della Mirandola drew on Oresme in his powerful and very influential condemnation of astrological divination *Disputations Opposing Divinatory Astrology* (*Disputationes adversus astrologiam divinatricem*).[116] More immediately, Oresme also influenced the other major figure associated with the critique of astrology in later fourteenth century Paris, the German theologian Heinrich of Langenstein.

Heinrich was Nicole Oresme's younger contemporary. His date of birth is uncertain, but was probably around 1325. He came to Paris from the Hessian town of Langenstein (he is also referred to as Heinrich of Hesse) to study probably in 1360 or 1361, completing his arts degree in 1363, so he overlapped with Oresme and must have known him either through the university or through the royal court. Completing his theology degree in 1373,

---

112. Oresme, *De configurationibus*, 368. On this important debate, see Béatrice Delaurenti, *La puissance des mots—"Virtus verborum": Débats doctrinaux sur le pouvoir des incantations au Moyen Âge* (Paris, 2007).

113. See Caroti, "Critica contro l'astrologia di Nicole Oresme," 613–76.

114. In addition to Caroti, see Laura Ackerman Smoller, *History, Prophecy, and the Stars: The Christian Astrology of Pierre d'Ailly, 1350–1420* (Princeton, N.J.: 1994), 36, 38–41.

115. Philippe Mézières, *Le songe du vieil pelerin*, ed. G. W. Coopland, 2 vols. (Cambridge, 1969), discussion of borrowing at 1:24; section on superstition at 1:590–619.

116. On Pico and astral magic, see Weill-Parot, *Images astrologiques*, 675–706; esp. 705–6 on connections to Oresme.

he quickly became a leading figure at the university. In 1378, he served as one of three delegates sent to Rome to express the opinion of the university on the papal schism that had just erupted. This split in the church would shape the rest of his life.[117] The French king supported the Avignon pope Clement VII, and soon pressured his university to back Clement as well. This put German scholars in Paris in a difficult position, potentially due to their own conscience, but also due to the fact that many territorial princes in the fragmented German Empire to whom they might owe allegiance adhered to Urban VI in Rome. For Langenstein, the situation quickly became untenable, and in 1382 he left Paris forever, settling two years later at the recently revived University of Vienna, where he would remain until his death in 1397. That institution had just received papal approval (from the Roman pope Urban VI) to develop a theological faculty, and Langenstein was one of the prize stars that Vienna captured from Paris at this time.[118]

Although Vienna was a major center for astronomy and astrology, both at its university and court, by the time Heinrich of Langenstein arrived in Austria, he had largely moved on to other intellectual interests.[119] He touched on astrology in one major work written during his Vienna years, his massive *Lectures on Genesis* (*Lecturae super Genesim*), composed likely between 1385 and 1392 or 1393. Here he addressed the influence of astral forces on the earth in his analysis of the fourth day of creation, when God had set the stars in the heavens.[120] We will concern ourselves, however, with his earlier, more focused work on astrology: his *Question on a Comet* (*Questio de cometa*), written in response to the appearance of a comet over Paris in 1368, and his treatise *Against Conjunctionist Astrologers* (*Contra astrologos coniunctionistas de eventibus futurorum*) from 1373.

The comet that blazed over Paris in 1368 ignited concern among many that it was a portent of terrible things to come. Thus it provided a perfect occasion for an academic author to wade into the realm of public opinion against astrological error and superstition. As a scholastic *questio*, *On a Comet* apparently arose from a disputation held at the university, and the treatise's

---

117. Basic biography in Nicholas H. Steneck, *Science and Creation in the Middle Ages: Henry of Langenstein (d. 1397) on Genesis* (Notre Dame, Ind., 1976), 9–14; more detail, especially on the schism, in Georg Kreuzer, *Heinrich von Langenstein: Studien zur Biographie und zu den Schismatraktaten unter besonderer Berücksichtigung der Epistola pacis und der Epistola concilii pacis* (Paderborn, 1987), 47–149.

118. Michael H. Shank, *"Unless You Believe, You Shall Not Understand": Logic, University, and Society in Late Medieval Vienna* (Princeton, N.J., 1988), x.

119. Ibid., ix–x; Michael H. Shank, "Academic Consulting in Fifteenth-Century Vienna: The Case of Astrology," in *Texts and Contexts in Ancient and Medieval Science: Studies on the Occasion of John E. Murdoch's Seventieth Birthday*, ed. Edith Sylla and Michael McVaugh (Leiden, 1997), 245–70.

120. Steneck, *Science and Creation*, 19, 100–104.

incipit indicates that it stemmed from a direct royal command. Why of all the scholars in Paris Heinrich of Langenstein should have been chosen to conduct such an important disputation is, however, less clear. At this time he was still a relatively young scholar, credentialed with an arts degree and well along but still not yet finished with his theological studies. He had already written a treatise on astral motion, *On the Rejection of Eccentrics and Epicycles* (*De reprobatione eccentricorum et epicyclorum*), in 1364, and evidence suggests he may have written another work even before that, but he was hardly a renowned astrological expert.[121] Perhaps hoping to make his reputation, he threw himself into his comet treatise with gusto, discrediting any grounds for reading occult meaning into its spectacular passage. Like other heavenly bodies, the comet would have affected the terrestrial world through natural forces that it emanated toward the earth, its "exhalations," as Heinrich described them. Yet these, he argued, were minimal. In fact, rather than the comet affecting the earth, it appeared that the earth's atmosphere exerted a major effect on the comet, shearing away its material and causing it to grow smaller.[122] He admitted that this shed matter might disturb the atmosphere, leading possibly to storms or even pestilence, which was considered to be very dependent on atmospheric conditions. Only twenty years earlier, in 1348, the Paris medical faculty had issued a report on the Black Death that linked its terrible advent to astral influences on the earth's atmosphere.[123] Heinrich avoided mention of the great plague, but argued that any atmospheric disturbances deriving from one comet would be slight. In the final analysis, the comet was an "inferior" astral event, far less potent in its natural effects than the "superior" stars.[124]

This conclusion brought Langenstein to a second major argument. Many astrologers promoted, and many people accepted, the notion that astral conjunctions were deeply significant because, as bodies moved into proximity with one another in the heavens, they augmented or altered each others' effects in various ways. Langenstein, however, argued tersely that a mere comet could not alter the natural influences of the superior stars to any degree as it shot across the sky.[125] In addition, he frequently noted in *On a Comet* the profound challenge of making precise observations of the comet or measurements of its movement in relation to that of other heavenly bodies, further

---

121. Ibid., 14–17.
122. Heinrich of Langenstein, *Questio*, 89–90.
123. Rosemary Horrox, ed. and trans., *The Black Death* (Manchester, 1994), 158–63.
124. Heinrich of Langenstein, *Questio*, 95–96.
125. Ibid., 99, 101.

undermining any claim that predictions could be based on calculations of the comet's natural effects, since knowledge of its true natural aspect was never more than an imperfect estimation.[126] At the very end of the work, he expanded this critique of prognosticating from the comet into a condemnation of all judicial astrology. The same problems—failure to properly understand the general nature of astral forces and how they did or did not affect each other or influence terrestrial conditions, as well as the basic impossibility of observing and calculating rapid and distant heavenly motion with any real precision—negated astrologers' claims to be able to make detailed predictions or answer specific questions based solely on a scientific study of the heavens. There was no more scientific basis to this (literally, "nothing related to philosophy") than there was in such magical arts as geomancy or necromancy, and the operations of this kind of astrology were clearly superstitious. He also alluded here to the dangers of astral magic, condemning texts that contained instructions for crafting inscribed images, which purported to attract and focus natural astral energies but actually functioned only thanks to the power of demons.[127]

Five years after debunking superstitions surrounding the comet of 1368, Heinrich addressed the topic of astrology more generally in *Against Conjunctionist Astrologers*. No single event seems to have precipitated its composition; instead it appears to respond to the general atmosphere in Paris and at the university at this time. He opened the treatise by declaring that "the University of Paris hates those who observe useless vanities," and he enjoined the faculty to be especially careful that no superstitious beliefs emanated from within learned circles. Instead, the university should always act as a careful "examiner of beliefs" and a "destroyer of superstitions" (*examinatrix opinionum, exstirpatrix superstitionum*). Yet in 1373 fantastical rumors and predictions of war and death, sterility, terrible storms, and other events abounded, apparently either originating within the university or at least finding no substantial opposition there.[128] He directed his treatise specifically against superstitious understandings of astral conjunctions, which he determined, as in his earlier *On a Comet*, had no bearing on natural astral forces or their effects on earth.[129] Since so much astrological divination claimed to be based

---

126. Ibid., 120–25, 133–34.
127. Ibid., 136: "Nichil igitur ad philosophiam de istorum huiusmodi auctoritate sicut nec de auctoritate auctorum geomancie, magice et nigromancie, etc. . . . Et cum isti scienciam de iudiciis astrorum in suis superstitionibus manifeste fateantur proficere et requiri et per eam operentur."
128. Heinrich of Langenstein, *Contra astrologos*, 139.
129. Ibid., 155, 159.

on the specific modulations of astral power these conjunctions supposedly produced, the work actually became a broad critique of all judicial astrology.

To summarize Langenstein's basic conclusions, he again admitted, as he had already acknowledged in his earlier work, that the stars radiated energies toward the earth, especially affecting the atmosphere, and possibly contributing to disease, although astral forces were never the "immediate" cause of great pestilence but only interacted with the air to create conditions that might be favorable to it.[130] Astral emanations also affected the behavior of animals attuned to such natural forces (the main focus here, as always, fell on birds and the possible natural, rational workings of augury), and they could "incline" any humans who submitted to their more bestial instincts to act in certain ways, because of their effects on the humors and other components of the human body to create physical urges. They could not, however, act directly on the mind or sway human free will.[131] Like Oresme, he advised princes to learn basic astrological principles, so that they would be aware of the general effects the stars might produce, but never to give any credence to the specific predictions of judicial astrologers.[132]

Against the claims of such astrologers regarding the scientific operation of their art, Langenstein marshaled three basic arguments. Drawing on Augustine, and seemingly (although not explicitly) on Oresme, he pointed out, as he had in the case of the 1368 comet, that even the best intentioned astrologers could not make absolutely precise observations of the distant and often obscure movements of the stars, so their calculations based on those observations would inevitably falter.[133] Also echoing Oresme, he maintained that heavenly bodies imparted their energies uniformly across the entire earth, so any local or individual variation in their force or effect, which would allow for specific and narrow predictions, was due entirely to terrestrial conditions, not the heavenly movement over which astrologers obsessed. He also stressed that a multitude of stellar forces always worked on the earth, and that it was impossible to accurately calculate all their interlocked and overlapping effects. He firmly insisted that nature itself never "lied," that is, it never presented false signs, but the signals it imparted were enormously complex and very easy to misinterpret.[134]

---

130. Ibid., 197–98.

131. Ibid., 170–71.

132. Ibid., 173.

133. Ibid., 140, 159. On Heinrich's debt to Oresme on the issue of incommensurability, see Edward Grant, *Nicole Oresme and the Kinematics of Circular Motion: Tractatus de commensurabilitate vel incommensurabilitate motuum celi* (Madison, Wis., 1971), 127.

134. Heinrich of Langenstein, *Contra astrologos*, 171, 175, 177, 179, 189.

This ready possibility of error led Langenstein to a final, dire objection to judicial astrology. Those who attempted to make precise predictions from the stars presented an inviting target to demons, and just like other kinds of diviners, astrologers laid themselves open to "demonic suggestion," whether they meant to or not.[135] This was why all the church fathers had censured astrological divination. Rather than citing any of those early fathers directly, however, Langenstein instead relied here on Nicole Oresme. This move is more than a little surprising. Langenstein's summation of the position of the fathers is true enough, and Oresme had also duly recapitulated it in his works. Nevertheless, as we have seen, the larger position he had actually advanced was to downplay the potential threat of demonic involvement in astrological errors, not to highlight it. Langenstein did not follow Oresme explicitly into the earlier master's more radical conclusions, so perhaps he meant to eschew them, as many subsequent authorities did. Or perhaps the citation itself was a telling indication of where he really stood on the spectrum of concern. By raising the possibility of demonic involvement in putatively natural divinatory practices at the end of his arguments against judicial astrology, he gave this concern more prominence, and potentially more credence, than Oresme had. Yet by invoking Oresme's authority, he would have somewhat undermined that credence for any reader who knew the subject well, at least raising certain doubts, albeit without directly advocating them himself. Certainly, aside from this admission of the possible threat of demonic involvement in divinatory practices, Langenstein, like Oresme, largely avoided any discussion of demons in his arguments against astral practices.

Langenstein would cite Oresme one more time before concluding *Against Conjunctionist Astrologers*, and not in a deeply serious vein. As a rhetorical aside, Oresme had sniped in his *Book on Divinations* that astrologers rarely even predicted the weather correctly although this was among the terrestrial conditions most directly affected by the stars, and so had warned princes that they should certainly scoff at any more complex prognostications astrologers might attempt.[136] To this, Langenstein added that great floods had struck both France and Germany in 1373, but no astrologer had managed to foresee them. Why then, he asked, should anyone fear the other dire predictions they were now spreading?[137] That parting shot probably conveys his true measure of the threat that erroneous astrology posed—not embroiled in diabolism but

135. Ibid., 192–93.
136. Oresme, *Livre*, 91.
137. Heinrich of Langenstein, *Contra astrologos*, 200–201.

simply incapable of comprehending the awesome and complex variability of the natural world.

Nicole Oresme and Heinrich of Langenstein possessed two of the keenest intellects of the fourteenth century. They helped move medieval natural philosophy in new directions, and it is not wrong to regard Oresme especially (and with proper qualifications) as something of a forerunner of modern scientific rationality. Yet their concern over astrology and astrological superstition stemmed not from any prescient, forward-looking quality in their thought, but rather from contemporary debates taking place at the University of Paris. They were also inspired to write by sorcerous intrigues and astrological infatuations at the French court. Similarly, earlier in the century John XXII had focused much of his attention on superstitious demonic sorcery that he thought threatened his court and his person, and Nicolau Eymerich, ultimately the most influential inquisitorial theorist of the medieval period, gave renewed voice to John's concerns and added his own, drawn in part from his experience at the courts of Avignon and Barcelona. Given the status of these men and the contexts in which they worked, we should not be surprised that they focused almost exclusively on elite forms of superstition: the conjurations of clerical necromancers and the divinations of court astrologers. Heinrich of Langenstein briefly mentioned certain uneducated "semi-astrologers" spreading wild and erroneous predictions among the populace, but that is virtually the only indication in all the tracts, treatises, and pronouncements cited here that these men were alert to superstitious practices at other social levels.[138] They were not ignorant of common superstitions, nor did they exempt them in any way from the condemnations they formulated. But superstitions of that sort—the simple charms, divinations, and observances of the average layperson—were nowhere near the forefront of their concern.

Being intellectuals, they used the issue of superstition to address some fundamental intellectual problems of their day. For John XXII and Nicolau Eymerich, as ecclesiastical authorities who saw themselves very much as guardians of the faith (standing on the watchtower of the Lord, after all), this involved constructing a virtually inevitable link between superstitious rites and demonic invocation and worship, and from this the connection between superstitious act and heretical belief. For Oresme and Langenstein, each a theologian but also, when addressing astrology, working as a natural

---

138. Ibid., 180.

philosopher, this meant carefully defining the extent of natural astral forces and their effects on the earth and its creatures, separating legitimate knowledge and prediction based on natural causation from superstitious divination, and considering the potential for spiritual (mainly demonic, but by extension also divine) involvement in the operations of the physical world. On this last point, Oresme pressed especially far toward a seemingly modern conception of a material universe from which spiritual action was largely excluded, allowing us to see the sometimes quite remarkable reach of medieval thinkers. Whether or not their particular conclusions carried the day, these men all helped sharpen the terms of debate about superstition. The issues they raised and tried so diligently to resolve, both in theology and natural philosophy, continued to pose problems for authorities addressing superstition into the next century.

Academic and courtly concern over sorcery, divination, and other forms of superstitious practice intensified further in Paris in the final decades of the 1300s and into the early 1400s as well, so the themes of this chapter carry over very directly into the next. Yet that period can also be seen as an important turning point in how Christian authorities addressed superstition, and what superstitions they chose to address. What I have here labeled the more "scientific" approach to superstition, focusing on erroneous understanding of the natural world and only rarely invoking the specter of demonic menace, continued to be evident in the work of some writers, but most (and certainly the most influential) now firmly emphasized the more traditional tendency to regard almost any superstitious error as indicating some kind of "fellowship" with demons. Also, while much concern remained focused on elite practices, highly placed authorities now regularly began to address common practices as well. The danger of demonic entanglement and increasing attention to common rites and observances would come to frame issues of superstition in the coming century and beyond. As always, however, the path forward was in no way direct or uncontested.

❦ CHAPTER 3

The Cardinal, the Confessor, and the Chancellor

> For I say that just as there are those superstitious
> astrologers who, against theological truth, excessively
> extol astrology beyond that of which it is capable,
> so too there are those superstitious theologians who,
> against philosophical reason, excessively disparage the
> potential of astrology, or exalt it absolutely.
>
> —Pierre d'Ailly, *Defensive Apology for Astrology*

Concerns over judicial astrology, astral magic, and other forms of divination and sorcery seem to have escalated dramatically in Paris in the final years of the fourteenth century, culminating in 1398 when the theological faculty of the university issued a broad condemnation of what it saw as "a filthy swill of error newly rising up from ancient hiding places." Before listing these errors in twenty-eight articles, the faculty noted in particular "the declaration of the most wise doctor Augustine concerning superstitious observances, that those who believe in such things . . . have sinned against the Christian faith and their baptism . . . and have incurred the wrath of God." Recognizing the contested nature of superstition, they declared that "it is not our intention in any way to disparage licit and true traditions, sciences, and arts." Nevertheless, the faculty members asserted, they would endeavor to "uproot entirely the mad and sacrilegious errors of the foolish and the deadly rites that harm, contaminate, and infect orthodox faith and Christian religion." Castigating magic arts, sorcery, and superstition in many forms, their articles of condemnation focused mainly on demonic invocation and sorcery, although they also touched on false astrology and astral magic.[1]

---

1. Heinrich Denifle, ed., *Chartularium Universitatis Parisiensis*, 4 vols. (1889–97; repr., Brussels, 1964), 4:32–36. Also appended to Jean Gerson, *De erroribus*, 86–90. See Jean-Patrice Boudet, "Les condemnations de la magie à Paris en 1398," *Revue Mabillon* 12 (2001): 121–57.

While anxiety about elite modes of superstitious sorcery and divination practiced in both court and university settings persisted into the 1400s, critical accounts also began more frequently to mention common superstitions such as simple healing rites and protective charms, and the unsophisticated laity, particularly women, who typically employed them, thereby inaugurating trends that would increasingly define the debate about superstition in the fifteenth century. In this chapter, Cardinal Pierre d'Ailly will represent continuities of concern, addressing learned astrology and the superstitious errors to which it could lead (although in fact he was mainly positive about astrology, emphasizing its legitimate aspects and useful potential). Another theologian, Laurens Pignon, educated in Paris and later the confessor to a future duke of Burgundy, will demonstrate broader concerns, as he stressed the links between judicial astrology and other forms of superstitious divination, varieties of elite magic, and also common sorcery. Finally, d'Ailly's greatest pupil, his successor as chancellor of the University of Paris, and one of the leading intellectual figures of the early fifteenth century, Jean Gerson, will exemplify both continuity and change. He continued the critique of erroneous astrology developed in the fourteenth century by Nicole Oresme, Heinrich of Langenstein, and others, although he advanced it in new directions and with a vehemence that at times alarmed his friend and teacher d'Ailly. He also brought this same vehemence to his condemnation of other forms of superstition, writing against magical and superstitious rites of various sorts that flourished, so he was convinced, at all levels of Christian society. Behind these practices, he saw the malevolent action of demons, hardly a new feature in Christian thought, but he declaimed against the demonic threat with particular force, setting a tone that would characterize much discourse about superstition in the new century, when ultimately, of course, common sorcery and superstitious rites would blur into the horrors of diabolical witchcraft.

Yet we must be careful in our judgment of Gerson on this and other points, for it is easy to miscast him in light of developments to come. The full-blown concept of diabolical, conspiratorial witchcraft lay still just over the horizon during his lifetime. Viewed from even a few decades later, his strong condemnations of demonic presence underlying almost all forms of superstition and his far from pervasive but nevertheless notable references to common magical practices and the superstitions of simple old women can appear prescient and indicative of a significant new course about to be taken in European history. If kindling was being laid, however, and perhaps even sparks were being struck, still the coming bonfires of the witch hunts were not yet fully ablaze in the early 1400s, and so, before we rush too deeply into fifteenth-century developments, we should return to the specific situation in Paris at the close of the fourteenth.

Fin de (Fourteenth) Siècle

As the fourteenth century neared its end, the Parisian court experienced a powerful swell of magical intrigue. The intermittent madness of King Charles VI, and the fierce, ultimately deadly political rivalry between the dukes of Burgundy and Orléans (the king's cousin and younger brother, respectively) to become the power behind the throne as the monarch faltered created fertile ground in which plots and suspicions would grow.[2] Charles VI assumed the crown in 1380, at the age of eleven. Just over a decade later, in 1392, the first of his fits of madness struck, as they would continue to do for the next thirty years until his death in 1422. Almost immediately, conjecture raced through the court that sorcery and a magical plot lay behind the king's insanity. Some courtiers and court observers dismissed such rumors as themselves superstitious, but others began to look seriously for a magical cure. In 1393, a sorcerer from Guienne named Arnaud Guillaume arrived at court. He appeared uneducated but carried with him a book of mainly astral magic. He proclaimed that he could cure the king with a single word, and his was only the first in a succession of such attempts.[3] In 1397, Louis of Sancerre, the marshal of France, brought to Paris two more Guienne magicians who claimed to be Augustinian friars. They assured the court, and particularly the duke of Orléans, that the royal madness did indeed arise from sorcery, and they eventually accused the king's barber and a housekeeper of having afflicted him. The housekeeper was in the service of Louis of Orléans, however, and when accusations eventually drifted toward Louis himself, he had the two friars executed. Only a year later, in 1398, the king's own physician, Jean of Bar, suspected by many of being a necromancer in the pay of the duke

---

2. Most of what follows draws on Jan R. Veenstra, *Magic and Divination at the Courts of Burgundy and France: Text and Context of Laurens Pignon's "Contra les devineurs" (1411)* (Leiden, 1998), 59–89. See also Edward Peters, "The Medieval Church and State on Superstition, Magic and Witchcraft: From Augustine to the Sixteenth Century," in *Witchcraft and Magic in Europe: The Middle Ages*, ed. Bengt Ankarloo and Stuart Clark (Philadelphia, 2002), 173–245, at 218–22.

3. On Arnaud, in addition to Veenstra, *Magic and Divination*, see also Jan R. Veenstra, "Cataloguing Superstition: A Paradigmatic Shift in the Art of Knowing the Future," in *Pre-Modern Encyclopaedic Texts: Proceedings of the Second COMERS Congress, Groningen, 1–4 July 1996*, ed. Peter Binkley (Leiden, 1997), 169–80.

of Burgundy, was executed after a lurid confession.[4] The twenty articles of sorcery to which he confessed are closely related to the twenty-eight articles of sorcery and superstition condemned that same year by the Paris theological faculty. Yet neither capital punishment nor university pronouncements could dissuade ambitious magicians from coming to Paris and throwing themselves into court intrigues. In 1403, two Burgundian sorcerers claimed to be able to cure the king. Sources describe them performing a fantastically elaborate rite that involved chaining twelve citizens of Dijon into a huge iron circle they had constructed in the woods outside that town, but this apparently produced no effect on the royal health. These men, too, were arrested and burned.

In 1407, the political struggle between Burgundy and Orléans climaxed when henchmen in the service of the Burgundian duke John II (John the Fearless) assassinated Louis of Orléans in a Paris street. John acknowledged ordering the murder but argued that Louis had been a tyrant attempting to lead the kingdom into ruin and so the killing was justified. As part of his defense, he had a theologian in his pay, Jean Petit, write a *Justification* of his action. In this work, Jean accused Louis of using sorcery to drive his older brother Charles VI insane and seeking to kill the king on several occasions by means of magic poisons. These allegations formed the very "backbone" of his defense of Duke John. He also asserted that Louis had hired sorcerers, including a knight and an apostate monk, to fashion magical items for him, such as a ring and a pouch containing some pulverized bone and pubic hair from a corpse. Louis supposedly carried these with him at all times. His contracted magicians also purportedly gave him a wand consecrated with the blood of a rooster that he could use to make women fall in love with him.[5]

Opponents at court also suspected Louis's wife, Valentina Visconti, of being a sorceress or at least a sponsor of sorcerers. In fact, these slanders long predated any suspicions directed against her husband, beginning soon after she married Louis in 1389. That King Charles's bouts of madness often calmed when Valentina was present fueled both the jealousy of the French queen Isabeau of Bavaria toward her sister-in-law and speculations about sorcery. Despite the king's obvious affection for his younger brother's wife, rumors abounded that she sought his death in order to advance her husband.

---

4. Edited and examined in Veenstra, *Magic and Divination*, 343–55; also in Jean-Patrice Boudet, *Entre science et* nigromance: *Astrologie, divination et magie dans l'Occident médiéval (XIIe–XVe siècle)* (Paris, 2006), 459–64.

5. Veenstra, *Magic and Divination*, 48–59.

According to Jean Froissart, the famous—and famously pro-Burgundian—chronicler of the Hundred Years War, she had once used a proverbial poisoned apple to try to kill the king and his progeny. In 1396, over a decade before her husband's murder, suspicions such as these, and the enmity of Queen Isabeau, had already driven her from Paris and she spent the rest of her life in exile from the royal court. Not that physical absence, or even death, slowed the Parisian rumor mill. In the second version of his *Justification*, written in 1408 just after the duchess had died, Jean Petit continued his character assassination against the house of Orléans by alleging that she had possessed a steel mirror in which she conjured divinatory images, and that she had in her pay in the French capital an Italian sorcerer whom she directed to perform various magical rites against the king.

This brief catalog of the plots and accusations rife in Paris at the turn of the century is worth recounting to establish the context in which the intellectual figures associated with the court and university in the early fifteenth century operated. Chief among them were Pierre d'Ailly and his star pupil, Jean Gerson. They were, in succession, chancellors of the great University of Paris. Each advised kings and negotiated with popes. D'Ailly rose to become a cardinal, while Gerson retained only his academic title until the end of his life, but the younger man unquestionably exerted more intellectual influence. They both opposed superstition, although they disagreed over where its exact boundaries lay, at least in the area of elite astrological practices. Between them, they illustrate many of the dilemmas and developments that characterized Parisian thought on these matters in the first decades of the fifteenth century.

The Cardinal

Pierre d'Ailly was a Parisian theologian, an eventual cardinal of the church (his elevation came in 1411), and at least in the later part of his life a serious student of astrology.[6] He was roughly one generation younger than Nicole Oresme and Heinrich of Langenstein, although he began his studies in Paris only a few years after Langenstein did. (The older German beat him to a theology degree by nearly a decade, however.) Born in 1350 or 1351 in

---

6. The definitive study is Laura Ackerman Smoller, *History, Prophecy, and the Stars: The Christian Astrology of Pierre d'Ailly, 1350–1420* (Princeton, N.J., 1994). For a general biography, see Bernard Guenée, *Between Church and State: The Lives of Four French Prelates in the Late Middle Ages*, trans. Arthur Goldhammer (Chicago, 1991), 102–258.

Compiègne, just north of Paris, he came to the capital in 1363 or 1364 and began to study at Oresme's alma mater, the College of Navarre. This was only a year or two after Oresme had stepped down as master. He received his arts degree in 1367 and his theology degree in 1381. Thereafter he rose through a number of important positions to become chancellor of the University of Paris in 1389. As head of the most prestigious academic institution in northern Europe, he became centrally embroiled in the disputes of the papal schism that had erupted roughly a decade before. Although early in the 1380s the French king had compelled the university to support the Avignon papacy, d'Ailly realized that backing either Avignon or Rome against the other would only prolong their split, and he came to promote quite strongly the idea of resolving the schism by means of an ecumenical council. Subsequently, he played a leading role at both the Council of Pisa (in 1409, long after he had passed the office of chancellor to his pupil Gerson) and the Council of Constance (1414–18), which finally elected a single pope recognized within the church and by virtually all the major powers in Europe.[7] Shortly after that success, he died in 1420.

D'Ailly produced all of his major works on astrology within a mere six years (1410–15), while enmeshed in the tumultuous final phase of schismatic politics, and these works all relate very much to those troubled times.[8] Unlike Oresme and Langenstein before him or Gerson after, he forcefully supported the astrological arts and championed some of their predictive possibilities, although technically this was a matter of differing emphasis, not outright disagreement, since all these men recognized both legitimate and superstitious aspects and applications of astrology. D'Ailly's first work, completed at the very end of 1410, was in fact titled *On Laws and Sects against Superstitious Astrologers* (*De legibus et sectis contra superstitiosos astronomos*). Then in quick succession, all in 1414, came his *Vigintiloquium on the Concordance of Astrological Truth with Theology* (*Vigintiloquium de concordantia astronomice veritatis cum theologia*), *Concordance of Astrology with Historical Narration* (*Concordantia astronomie cum hystorica narratione*), and the *Elucidation of Astrological Concord with Theological and Historical Truth* (*Elucidarium astronomice concordie cum theologica et historica veritate*), as well as two short defenses: *Apologetic Defense of Astrological Truth* (*Apologetica defensio astronomice veritatis*) and *Second Apologetic Defense of Astrological Truth* (*Alia secunda apologetica defensio eiusdem*). His final

---

7. On his political efforts, see Francis Oakley, *The Political Thought of Pierre d'Ailly: The Voluntarist Tradition* (New Haven, Conn., 1964).

8. Smoller, *History, Prophecy, and the Stars*, 4.

effort, completed early in 1415, was *On the Concord of Discordant Astrologers* (*De concordia discordantium astronomorum*).

A few years later, toward the end of 1419, d'Ailly composed a final, brief *Defensive Apology for Astrology* (*Apologia astrologie defensiva*), which he sent to Jean Gerson in response to his former student's newly published work attacking superstitious astrology, *Trilogium of Theological Astrology* (*Trilogium astrologiae theologizatae*). Here he indicated his agreement with Gerson on many points, but also his reservations about his colleague's tone. While superstitions within astrology should certainly be opposed, d'Ailly noted (in the passage that provides the epigraph for this chapter) how there were not only superstitious astrologers who pushed too far in their art, but also superstitious theologians who pressed too far in their condemnations.[9] He stressed that the early church fathers had opposed only astrological error, and that "true" astrology was in full accord with Christian theology, as he himself had argued in many works. Like Gerson, and like Oresme and Langenstein decades earlier, he worried about the dangers of superstitious astrology, especially the ways in which the illicit knowledge it promised might seduce powerful princes and magnates. Years before his exchange with his former pupil, d'Ailly had preached before the French king about separating true from false astral learning, and in a follow-up letter to Gerson after the *Defensive Apology*, he mentioned his intention to write soon to the Dauphin, the future Charles VII, specifically "so that he should beware of such superstitions" infecting astrological science.[10] Yet in general, d'Ailly's favored method of opposing superstition was not to attack what was wrong in astrology but to point out and praise what was legitimate and good.

The cardinal fully understood astrology's long and checkered intellectual history. He cited Heinrich of Langenstein, and ultimately Augustine, that the stars did not imprint particular characters on children at birth or consign them to certain fates, as astrologers who drew natal horoscopes claimed, and he repeated Nicole Oresme's warnings that princes and magnates should not pay undue attention to astrologers at their courts.[11] But he also noted that

---

9. D'Ailly, *Apologia astrologie defensiva*, 219: "Nam sicut illos dico superstitiosos astronomos qui contra theologicam veritatem astrologiam ultra id quod potest nimis extollunt, sic et illos superstitiosos theologos qui contra philosophicam rationem astronomiae potestatem nimis deprimunt vel penitus tollunt."

10. D'Ailly, *Apologetica defensio*, 138r; d'Ailly's letter is in *OC*, 2:222: "Intendo domino Regenti scribere ut caveat a talibus superstitiosis."

11. D'Ailly, *Apologetica defensio*, 138r–v (on Langenstein); *Alia secunda apologetica defensio*, 140v–141r (on Oresme).

Albertus Magnus had carefully distinguished true astrology from magic and superstitious divination, and that both Albertus and Thomas Aquinas had demonstrated how legitimate astrology, including some general predictions based on the natural influences of the stars, accorded with and complemented proper theology.[12] D'Ailly felt a pressing need to defend astrology's limited but useful predictive potential. By the second decade of the fifteenth century, over thirty years of papal schism had kindled widespread apocalyptic fears, and many worried that the seemingly intractable confusion in the church presaged the end of days. The cardinal wanted to marshal astrology to prove that the end of the Christian dispensation on earth still lay far in the future. This, he reasoned, would help motivate princes and prelates to work toward the resolution of the schism that he fervently sought, rather than waiting in resignation for the Last Judgment to settle matters.[13]

In several of his works, d'Ailly argued at length how astrology accorded with both Christian theology and the course of history. By divine plan major astrological events corresponded to great changes on earth, including shifts from one historical age to another, and in particular the beginnings (and endings) of major religions. Following Roger Bacon, who drew from the Arab astrologer Abū Ma'shar (Latinized as Albumasar), d'Ailly identified five great religious "sects" that had defined the course of human history: the Hebrews, Chaldeans, Egyptians, Saracens, and Christians. Each one's rise in the course of history and the period of its particular dominance corresponded to an astrological age. One more sect, that of Antichrist, had yet to appear. Thus calculating the future course of the heavens in search of an appropriately calamitous sign could help reveal when the final age of the world would begin.[14]

D'Ailly's particular eschatological use of astrology is not my principal concern here, but it provides the backdrop for his generally positive stance toward that art. Both when extolling the virtues of astrology and when occasionally opposing its superstitious elements, the cardinal rehearsed many of the basic arguments we have already encountered, although naturally with a different emphasis to suit his mainly pro-astrological purposes. While he

---

12. D'Ailly, *Vigintiloquium* 3 (on Albertus distinguishing astrology from magic); *De legibus et sectis*, 39r; *Apologetica defensio*, 138v; and *Apologia astrologie defensiva*, 221.

13. The relationship of schism to apocalypse, and d'Ailly's turn to astrology in response, is the main theme of Smoller, *History, Prophecy, and the Stars*. More broadly on the schism as a sign of the apocalypse, see Renate Blumenfeld-Kosinski, *Poets, Saints, and Visionaries of the Great Schism, 1378–1417* (University Park, Pa., 2006).

14. D'Ailly, *De legibus et sectis*, 39r. This theme is also central to *Vigintiloquium* 13–20; and throughout *Concordantia astronomie cum hystorica narratione* and *Elucidarium*.

admitted that astrology could become infected with superstition, at heart it was a legitimate *scientia* (which no critic would have denied).[15] The heavenly bodies radiated natural energies toward the earth, and inferior terrestrial material was affected by those superior emanations. On earth, celestial forces influenced some things quite directly (such as the atmosphere and weather), some things only indirectly, and some things not at all. Obviously, astrologers would make their most effective and least problematic predictions when they limited themselves to the first category of events.[16] Anyone seeking to employ the services of astrologers needed to be able to distinguish between proper and excessive aspects of the astral arts. At one point, d'Ailly even used different terminology, contrasting true "astronomy" to false "astrology," but in the fashion typical of most medieval writers on these topics he did not maintain such terminological distinctions with any consistency.[17] Conceptually, though, he was quite clear. Legitimate astrology studied the movements of the heavenly bodies and their direct natural effects on earth, and "great theologians" and other learned men regularly praised this art. "Nevertheless they have condemned judicial astrology to the utmost degree" because of its erroneous claims and the illicit predictions it sought to provide about things over which the stars exerted only indirect influence at best.[18]

Like Oresme and Langenstein, d'Ailly recognized that a basic problem with judicial astrology lay in the fearsome complexity of heavenly motion, which, following Oresme, he judged to be "incommensurable," that is, unable to be mathematically measured or calculated. Since human observers could never hope to perceive all astral movements, and since astrologers themselves maintained that even slight shifts in the positions of the stars altered the effect of their energies on the earth, drawing any kind of precise conclusions based on astral observations was simply impossible. Thus, while astrologers could make some valuable general predictions regarding very major conditions or events, they would founder when attempting any kind of narrow, specific prognostication.[19] Although he referred to the complexity of astral motion,

---

15. D'Ailly, *De legibus et sectis*, 45r.

16. Ibid., 44r; *Vigintiloquium* 3–4; *Alia secunda apologetica defensio*, 141v.

17. D'Ailly, *Vigintiloquium* 2. I have therefore generally translated both *astrologia* and *astronomia* as "astrology" unless the context clearly warrants contrasting those terms.

18. D'Ailly, *Alia secunda apologetica defensio*, 140v: "Astronomiam de iudiciis nihilominus extreme condemnauerunt."

19. D'Ailly, *De legibus et sectis*, 45v–49r, 51r; *Alia secunda apologetica defensio*, 141v, 142v; *De concordia discordantium astronomorum*, 152r. On d'Ailly's debt to Oresme, see Smoller, *History, Prophecy, and the Stars*, 39; and more fully Edward Grant, *Nicole Oresme and the Kinematics of Circular Motion: Tractatus de commensurabilitate vel incommensurabilitate motuum celi* (Madison, Wis., 1971), 130–32.

d'Ailly did not make a particular point of the multiplicity of stellar effects and their overlap on earth. Neither did he directly address Oresme's and Langenstein's argument that most earthly occurrences depended far more on terrestrial factors than on astral emanations, although he did mention in a few places that the stars produced varying general effects in different regions of the world because of how their energies refracted through different atmospheric conditions.[20] Of course he rejected the notion that the stars could be used to predict anything on which they exerted no natural influence, above all human action, for they could not impinge on free will (although, drawing the usual exception, he asserted that they could "incline" the weak-willed to certain actions through their physical effects on the human body).[21] As Christian authorities writing on astrology had done since Augustine, he dusted off the old chestnut about Jacob and Esau, the twins who could not have been more different, to demonstrate that the stars exerted no immutable control over human personality or behavior.[22]

One of d'Ailly's particular points of emphasis, in this regard, was that human beings should never use supposed astral influences to excuse wicked behavior. Doing so not only disparaged divinely ordained free will but also seemed to imply that at least some heavenly bodies exerted distinctly evil influences. Many people regarded Saturn, for example, as an especially wicked planet. Yet all the heavens were God's creation, d'Ailly asserted, and thus it was wrong, sinful, and blasphemous to regard any part of them as inherently evil.[23] In labeling the idea that certain stars or planets exerted an evil or inimical force a blasphemy, since it impugned the creator's ultimately benevolent design for the universe, the cardinal drew directly on the earlier Parisian master William of Auvergne. William had gone on to note that this false "idolatry" of the stars had originally been taught to humans by demons, but tellingly d'Ailly did not pick up on this latter point.[24] Like Nicole Oresme and Heinrich of Langenstein, he chose not to emphasize the darker possibilities that many medieval authorities imputed to astral error, but instead kept his focus more on the natural science of the heavens.

In this vein, d'Ailly paid considerable attention to the prospect that the stars exerted particularly strong natural influence over the impressionable bodies of children forming in the womb. Much of this theory appeared

20. D'Ailly, *Alia secunda apologetica defensio*, 142v; *De concordia discordantium astronomorum*, 151v.
21. D'Ailly, *De legibus et sectis*, 42v, 43v; *Vigintiloquium* 3.
22. D'Ailly, *Alia secunda apologetica defensio*, 141v.
23. D'Ailly, *De legibus et sectis*, 43r, 44v.
24. William of Auvergne, *De universo* 1.1.46, in William, *Opera omnia* (Venice, 1591), 618, 626–27.

eminently reasonable within the generally accepted parameters of medieval natural philosophy. Gestating fetuses were regarded as highly susceptible to all kinds of external influence. The matter became quite fraught for theologians, however, because of the problem presented by Christ. Could God himself, as incarnated in Mary's womb, be said to have been shaped partly by the stars? Many authorities recoiled. Yet d'Ailly accepted that, insofar as Christ partook fully of human flesh, he subjected himself to all natural influences that acted on that flesh.[25] This was, in fact, the central point of one of his short works, the *Apologetic Defense of Astrological Truth*, although in terms of predictive potential, he stressed that while the principle of astral forces exerting influence on fetuses was sound, determining their precise effects on any particular child—to say nothing of an infant who was so complicated in his basic constitution as the Christ child—was extremely problematic.[26]

Despite the manifold uncertainties of the sidereal arts, however, one danger d'Ailly never mentioned directly was that of demons involving themselves in astral divinations. As we have seen, he positively ducked the issue when drawing on William of Auvergne, and nowhere else did he address it directly. At most he may be seen as alluding to this threat when he discussed how the authors of erroneous astrological texts included in them "many execrable superstitions of magical art."[27] His fellow theologians and other church authorities would have known that both "superstition" and "magic" could be read to imply demons, but the cardinal, wanting to put the best face possible on astrology, simply did not delve into that side of this craft.

The Confessor

Much more vocal about the involvement of demons in astrology, and the connections between astrology and other magical and divinatory arts, was Laurens Pignon, a Dominican theologian (he too had studied in Paris) attached to the Burgundian court, where in 1412 he became confessor to the future duke Philip the Good, the son of the reigning duke, John the Fearless, the same who in 1407 had arranged the murder of his rival Louis of Orléans and then vilified him as a practitioner and patron of superstitious sorcery. In 1411, Pignon wrote a vernacular treatise *Against Diviners* (*Contre les devineurs*), which he dedicated to Duke John. Thus the courtly context

---

25. D'Ailly, *De legibus et sectis*, 43v; and the whole of *Apologetica defensio*.
26. D'Ailly, *Apologetica defensio*, 140v.
27. D'Ailly, *Vigintiloquium* 2.

of this work is clear. At the outset, Pignon noted that many nobles and notable men were drawn to illicit forms of divination, and he intended to counter this trend.[28] Jan Veenstra has studied this work thoroughly, editing the text, and setting it in its Burgundian (and Parisian) context. He calls it a "minor treatise on a major theme."[29] Clearly Pignon did not possess the same stature as Pierre d'Ailly or Jean Gerson. Nevertheless, we can usefully consider his treatise, briefly, as providing another perspective on discourse about superstition in the Francophone courtly world at the outset of the fifteenth century. In particular, while he too focused in large measure on issues of courtly astrology, he devoted much more space to other forms of superstitious divination than Oresme or Langenstein did, and certainly more than the proponent of astrology d'Ailly did. He drew fundamentally the same distinctions between superstition and *scientia* as did those more esteemed figures, and he posited the same basic connections between different varieties of superstition, but such allegations flowed more steadily from Pignon's pen. Like his fellow Dominican Nicolau Eymerich, he did not just accept the possibility of demonic involvement in divinatory rites but stressed this danger repeatedly.[30] He also looked beyond courtly circles and included some superstitions found among the common folk of Burgundy in his considerations. These are all tendencies that we will see in the writings of Jean Gerson as well, and then continuing in the world of the mainly German writers who predominately sustained the discourse of superstition into the mid-fifteenth century.

Regarding astrology, Pignon drew the usual distinction between legitimate and superstitious varieties. He recognized true *astronomie* (he also frequently jumbled his terminology) as a science that should never be considered a form of divination. The knowledge it provided was useful for predicting storms and other weather, and was valuable to physicians as they sought the causes of disease and planned their treatments. In fact, consulting the heavens was a useful way to gain knowledge of any occurrence that the stars directly affected through their natural emanations. There was, however, "another kind of astrology which is superstitious" (again Pignon used the term *astronomie*, but his meaning was clear). It entailed divination, made false claims

---

28. Pignon, *Contre les devineurs*, 223, 225.

29. Veenstra, *Magic and Divination*, 5. In addition to Veenstra, see Julien Véronèse, "Jean sans Peur et la 'foie secte' des devins: Enjeux et circonstances de la rédaction du traité *Contre les devineurs* (1411) de Laurent Pignon," *Médiévales* 40 (2001): 113–32.

30. Véronèse, "Jean sans Peur," 126–32, discusses Pignon's expanded concerns.

to knowledge, and promised to reveal secrets that could not be known by natural means. Hence it was always illicit.[31]

Pignon minced no words about the true nature of all kinds of "superstitious and divinatory art." They were devised by the devil and inevitably invoked and honored demons, even if only tacitly.[32] Like Eymerich, he saw demon worship—"idolatry"—underlying most forms of divination, and other kinds of magic as well. Some diviners crafted and consulted images, which they might claim to be imbued with astral energy or astral spirits, but which in fact could only be empowered by demons. Furthermore, any effort to gain knowledge or make predictions that was not based on natural signs or causes rebelled against divine order and invited demonic deception and temptation. Above all, Pignon condemned divination pertaining to human affairs as impinging on uniquely divine foreknowledge and violating God's promise of free will.[33] He accepted and reiterated the standard position that the stars exerted no control over human will, although of course with the usual qualification that they could influence base urges and carnal desires by their natural effects on the body. Similarly, while reading the flight of birds as signs of coming events was generally superstitious divination, observing avian behavior to predict the weather was not, since, as other authorities so often stressed, birds were naturally sensitive to weather conditions.[34]

When addressing divination by observing the flight of birds, Pignon avoided using the classical term "augury," but he did explicitly discuss other classic varieties of diviners, drawn mainly from Isidore of Seville's authoritative catalog of terms: necromancers, geomancers, hydromancers, and so on, as well as sorcerers, enchanters, and *maleficieurs*.[35] This last term was his rendering of Isidore's *malefici*, meaning practitioners of harmful magic, which would soon become a standard Latin term for those thought to engage in diabolical, conspiratorial witchcraft. The word certainly did not mean "witch" in that sense for Isidore and should almost certainly not be translated as such for Pignon. There is no indication that he thought of these *maleficieurs* as members of secret satanic cults. Neither is it clear that he meant the term necessarily to imply ordinary, uneducated laypeople practicing relatively simple sorcery, who would become the main focus of witchcraft accusations, as opposed to elite magicians performing more elaborate rites. We are certainly on the very

31. Pignon, *Contre les devineurs*, 231, 233 (quote), 269–70, 315.
32. Ibid., 231.
33. Ibid., 261–62, 289–90.
34. Ibid., 288–89 (augury), 305 and 310 (human behavior).
35. Ibid., 235.

cusp of such ideas in the early fifteenth century, as we will see just below, but we are not in that mental world just yet.

Like the earlier authorities we have surveyed up to this point, Pignon still clearly addressed much of his treatise to elite practices, among them the notory art (ars notoria), which he called the "art of Toledo," because that Spanish city was long rumored to harbor schools of learned but clearly wicked magical arts.[36] The "notory art" is itself the victim of some terminological mangling. As mentioned briefly in the previous chapter (because of its brief inclusion in the work of Nicolau Eymerich), it was a supposedly Solomonic form of ritual magic intended to impart knowledge and wisdom by invoking angelic spirits. Its name derived from the figures (notae) on which a practitioner was to concentrate while performing the invocations and awaiting enlightenment.[37] Thus some scholars prefer the designation ars notaria, or notarial art. Notoria literally means "well known" or "notorious," and certainly, given that authorities considered its angelic claims to mask demonic invocations, it was a "notorious art" indeed. Thomas Aquinas had condemned it at length.[38] Pignon followed him in this, as well as in his treatment of astral magic (unsurprisingly the Dominican confessor turned to the great scholastic master of his order throughout his treatise), agreeing with Thomas's conviction that most supposedly astral rites were in fact demonic necromancy.[39]

In addition to discussing sophisticated ritual practices largely confined to an educated clerical elite, however, Pignon also mentioned some specifically nonelite varieties of superstition. Of particular interest, in light of coming developments, is the fact that he noted how people known as "vaudois" were present in many parts of Burgundy. He described them as "old women who go with the good ones [les bonnes choses] at night," referring to beliefs in night-wandering spirits and supposed pagan deities whom church authorities had long recognized as demons in disguise. These elements of

---

36. Ibid., 294.

37. See Frank Klaassen, "English Manuscripts of Magic, 1300–1500: A Preliminary Survey," in Conjuring Spirits: Texts and Traditions of Ritual Magic, ed. Claire Fanger (University Park, Pa., 1998), 3–31, at 14–19; Michael Camille, "Visual Art in Two Manuscripts of the Ars Notoria," in Fanger, Conjuring Spirits, 110–39 (esp. on the notae per se); Claire Fanger, "Plundering the Egyptian Treasure: John the Monk's Book of Visions and Its Relation to the Ars Notoria of Solomon," in Fanger, Conjuring Spirits, 216–49; Julien Véronèse, L'Ars notoria au Moyen Âge: Introduction et édition critique, ML 21 (Florence, 2007); Véronèse, "Magic, Theurgy, and Spirituality in the Medieval Ritual of the Ars notoria," in Invoking Angels: Theurgic Ideas and Practices, Thirteenth to Sixteenth Centuries, ed. Claire Fanger (University Park, Pa., 2012), 37–78.

38. Aquinas, Summa theologiae 2.2.96.1, in Summa theologiae: Latin Text and English Translation, 60 vols. (New York, 1964–81).

39. Pignon, Contre les devineurs, 300.

popular folklore were clearly related to the superstition of certain women who believed that they traveled at night in the train of the goddess Diana, which had been decried by the canon *Episcopi* nearly five hundred years before.[40] Soon, the ideas in *Episcopi* would become an important component in the emerging notion of witches' night-flight to diabolical sabbaths, and *vaudois* would become a standard term for a witch in Francophone lands.[41] A major witch hunt directed against *vauderie* would in fact take place in the Burgundian-controlled city of Arras and its environs in 1459 and 1460.[42] As with *maleficieurs*, there is no indication in Pignon's account that *vaudois* meant "witch" in the coming sense, but it clearly denoted a form of superstition believed to be particularly common among old women. He also discussed the widespread practice of wearing protective magical amulets, common among all levels of medieval society. Again drawing on Aquinas, he remarked that such devices might be legitimate, but only so long as they did not contain any overtly demonic names, or any unfamiliar words, symbols, or characters that could secretly refer to demons.[43]

While Pignon does not yet appear fearful of witches haunting the Burgundian night, he clearly was more attuned to common superstitions than were such leading intellects as Oresme, Langenstein, or d'Ailly. His treatise indicates how for many authorities concerns over superstitions thought to exist at different levels of society intermingled. It also begins to show how a discourse about superstition developed at courts and universities and focused mainly on elite forms of practice could spill over to affect how authorities perceived common beliefs and practices as well. Jean Gerson shared this trait with Pignon, and unlike the good confessor, the great chancellor of the University of Paris was very much a leading intellectual figure and trendsetter of his day.

The Chancellor

Jean Gerson is unquestionably the most famous intellectual figure associated with the late medieval history of superstition. Indeed, he is considered

---

40. Ibid., 235, 248 (quote at 235).

41. On shifting meanings of the term *vaudois*, see Wolfgang Behringer, "How Waldensians Became Witches: Heretics and Their Journey to the Other World," in *Communicating with the Spirits*, ed. Gábor Klaniczay and Éva Pócs, in collaboration with Eszter Csonka-Takács (Budapest, 2005), 155–92; Kathrin Utz Tremp, *Von der Häresie zur Hexerei: "Wirkliche" und imaginäre Sekten im Spätmittelalter* (Hannover, 2008), 441–47.

42. See Franck Mercier, *La Vauderie d'Arras: Une chasse aux sorcières à l'Automne du Moyen Âge* (Rennes, 2006).

43. Pignon, *Contre les devineurs*, 303–4.

by many experts to have been the most influential theologian and academic writer working north of the Alps in the early fifteenth century.[44] Born in 1363, he was fourteen when he began his studies in Paris in 1377, where, like his mentor Pierre d'Ailly, he attended the College of Navarre. Receiving his arts degree in 1381 and his theology degree in 1392, he succeeded d'Ailly as chancellor of the University of Paris in 1395 and retained this title for the rest of his life.[45] He resided mainly in Paris for the next two decades, and in 1402 he wrote the first in a series of works condemning magical and superstitious practices, On Errors concerning the Magic Art (De erroribus circa artem magicam). Here he criticized the medical faculty of his own university for employing and thus sanctioning many erroneous and superstitious healing practices—amulets, inscribed figures, spells that included strange or foreign-sounding words—and he went on to lambast the magical arts more generally. He warned physicians first to "heal themselves," not to include anything "impious or superstitious or against divine laws" in their remedies, and then not to tolerate such practices when they learned of them being performed by others.[46]

Gerson's basic concern with superstition preceded his tract on the medical and magical arts by at least a decade, however. He first mentioned "sorcery, superstition, and foolish belief" in a sermon delivered likely in 1391.[47] He did so again several times in 1396 and 1397.[48] Then probably in early 1402, perhaps just days before completing On Errors concerning the Magic Art, he preached to a Parisian audience about how the devil strove to sow discord and division within Christian society. To illustrate his point, he focused mainly on demonic possession and exorcism, but he also reminded his audience of certain sorcerers executed in 1398.[49] That, of course, was the fateful

44. Daniel Hobbins, Authorship and Publicity before Print: Jean Gerson and the Transformation of Late Medieval Learning (Philadelphia, 2009), 5–6; Yelena Mazour-Matusevich, "Gerson's Legacy," in A Companion to Jean Gerson, ed. Brian Patrick McGuire (Leiden, 2006), 357–99, at 357.

45. For basic biography, see Brian Patrick McGuire, "In Search of Jean Gerson: Chronology of His Life and Works," in McGuire, Companion to Jean Gerson, 1–39; and McGuire, Jean Gerson and the Last Medieval Reformation (University Park, Pa., 2005).

46. Gerson, De erroribus, 77.

47. Sermon Regnum celorum in OC, 7.2:992–1005, quote at 1001; identified as his first known mention of superstition by Louis Mourin, Jean Gerson: Prédicateur français (Bruges, 1952), 111–13.

48. Sermons In nomine patris (OC, 7.2:671–79), Suscepimus Deus misericordiam tuam (OC, 7.2:1049–57), and Ave Maria (OC, 7.2:538–49). Gerson also mentions "supersticion, c'est a dire fole ou dampnable assercion commes des sorciers" and "supersticion fole et sorcerie contraire a Dieu et a nostre foy" in the sermon Gloria in altissimis deo (OC, 7.2:639–50, at 647 and 649), dated in OC to December 25, 1402, but by Mourin, Jean Gerson, 113, to 1397.

49. Sermon Omne regnum (OC, 7.2:753–62, at 759); see also Mourin, Jean Gerson, 133. The sermon is dated to February 26, likely 1402, and the tract to most likely March 8.

year when King Charles VI's physician Jean of Bar was burned along with his books of magic, and when the Paris theological faculty issued its proclamation condemning twenty-eight articles of superstition, with which Gerson had been intimately involved.[50] He certainly had the events of 1398 on his mind in 1402, for he appended the full text of the theological faculty's condemnation at the end of *On Errors concerning the Magic Art.*

The remainder of Gerson's works on various aspects of superstition date to some two decades after this first flurry of activity and were written while he was far from the university that had been his home for so long. He spent several periods away from Paris during the course of his life, but the longest, which would last until his death in 1429, began in 1415. Early in that year, Gerson departed Paris for the southern German city of Constance, where the great church council that would eventually end the papal schism was convening. He remained there until 1418, when the council concluded, but he found that he could not return to Paris, for in May of that year, just as Gerson was preparing to depart from Constance, the French capital had fallen to Burgundian forces, who were then allied with the English in the Hundred Years War. The chancellor was a royalist, not in the Burgundian camp, and so Paris suddenly became hostile territory to him. Moving from Constance briefly to the monastery of Melk in Austria, and then even more briefly through Vienna, he returned to France in 1419, settling in Lyon, where he would live out the remaining ten years of his life in a kind of exile.

In his final decade, Gerson would write half a dozen more works against various kinds of superstitious practices. Perhaps just on the verge of his arrival in Lyon, he completed his major critique of the astrological arts, *Trilogium of Theological Astrology.* Whereas his former mentor d'Ailly had generally emphasized the positive potential of astral science, Gerson took a sterner view. Granting, of course, that proper astrology was a worthy science, he went on to warn that some practitioners had defiled it with many "vain observances, impious errors, and superstitious sacrilege."[51] Despite their differing stances, Gerson nevertheless cited d'Ailly in this tract and sent him a copy for comment when he had completed it, prompting the cardinal to write his *Defensive Apology for Astrology* in reply. Noting their shared principles but different perspectives, the cardinal warned his erstwhile student in strong language that he might be among those whom d'Ailly regarded as "superstitious theologians" if he unfairly and excessively disparaged the

---

50. McGuire, *Jean Gerson*, 91, declares the language of the articles to be "pure Gerson."
51. Gerson, *Trilogium*, 90.

astral arts.[52] But Gerson was not deterred. Confident in his own view, he would write two more brief works critical of astrology and astral magic: *Regarding the Heavenly Stars* (*De respectu coelestium siderum*) in 1419, and *Against the Superstition of a Lion Sculpture* (*Contra superstitionem sculpturae leonis*) in 1428. In this latter tract, too, he positioned himself against some potentially formidable authorities who were more favorable to various astral arts. The superstitious image in question was an amulet shaped like a lion and crafted "under a certain constellation" (one would assume Leo) to cure kidney stones. It was made by a university physician, Nicolas Colne (Nikolaus Kolne), a native of Berlin who was at this time dean of the prestigious medical faculty at the University of Montpellier.[53] As we have already seen from his *On Errors concerning the Magic Art*, however, Gerson had no hesitation about criticizing trained physicians for employing what he regarded as superstitious practices. He also wrote two tracts on superstitions pertaining to certain days and times: *Against the Superstitious Observance of Days* (*Contra superstitiosam dierum observantiam*) in 1421, and the very brief *On the Observance of Days with Respect to Works* (*De observatione dierum quantum ad opera*) in 1425. Finally, just before he died in 1429 he wrote *Opposing Superstition in Hearing Mass* (*Adversus superstitionem in audiendo missam*) challenging various practical protections and benefits (beyond the good to one's soul) that many people believed derived from attending a Mass.

Whether in Paris or Lyon, Gerson always focused a good deal of his concern on superstitious errors in elite practices, which he feared educated schoolmen like himself and powerful nobles at court were increasingly willing to accept and tolerate. Under his direction the Parisian theological faculty as a whole had declared that the practices it condemned in 1398 represented a "filthy swill of error newly rising up from ancient hiding places," and likewise Gerson himself exclaimed dramatically in his 1402 tract *Against Errors concerning the Magic Art* about "superstitious errors growing beyond all measure in, oh the horror!, our own times."[54] A decade earlier, in his first known sermon on the subject, he was already warning that superstition appeared to be flourishing "among many great lords and nobles," and in a long

---

52. See n. 9 above; Gerson had mentioned d'Ailly in *Trilogium*, 92.

53. Gerson, *Contra superstitionem sculpturae leonis*, 131. See E. Vansteenberghe, "Le traité contre Nicolas Colne," *Revue des sciences religieuses* 15 (1935): 532–39; Nicolas Weill-Parot, *Les "images astrologiques" au Moyen Âge et à la Renaissance: Spéculations intellectuelles et pratiques magiques (XIIe–XVe siècle)* (Paris, 2002), 595–602. The case is discussed further below.

54. Gerson, *De erroribus*, 77: "Superstitiosas observationes nostra, pro nefas, tempestate nimis et nimis invalescentes."

sermon from 1405 he noted that "sorcerers, charmers, and magicians" accepted at court, or at least not strongly repudiated, were among the greatest
threats to the spiritual health of the kingdom.[55] In fact, he delivered most of
his sermons criticizing sorcery and superstition to noble audiences, and he
exhorted his listeners to reject these errors themselves and to exert leadership
to help combat them in society.[56]

These concerns, evident from the beginning of his career, did not dimin-
ish with time or distance. Two decades after orchestrating the Paris faculty
condemnations of 1398 and then criticizing the Paris medical faculty in
his *On Errors concerning the Magic Art*, Gerson sent a copy of his *Trilogium
of Theological Astrology* not only to his former master d'Ailly but also to his
prince, the Dauphin Charles (to whom, as mentioned above, d'Ailly also
promised to write), to warn him against the many errors infecting legitimate
astrology and to instruct him, as Oresme and Langenstein had instructed
his grandfather, about how to distinguish "admirable science" from "vain
observations, impious errors, and superstitious sacrilege."[57] At the conclusion
of the *Trilogium*, Gerson echoed those earlier critics of courtly astrology by
warning that princes should be very careful about how much attention they
paid to astrologers. He added that they should also protect their people by
issuing frequent declarations about astrology, both in writing and through
public proclamations. While texts containing legitimate astrological learning
should of course be preserved (Gerson gave as an example the works of the
great classical astronomer Ptolemy), a prince should consign any texts found
to contain astral superstitions to the flames, as had been done in 1398 with
the books (as well as the person) of Jean of Bar.[58]

In his critique of astrology, Gerson echoed many positions that we have
already encountered, although sometimes with harsher tone or sharper intent. Legitimate astrology was a "noble and admirable science," but all too
often it became riddled with errors and superstition.[59] Purely in terms of
empirical data, one could never observe all astral movement in perfect detail, nor could one ever make absolutely precise calculations based on all the
complex motions of the heavens without any error (the issue of incommensurability).[60] Thus completely accurate predictions even of the stars' natural

---

55. Sermons *Regnum celorum* of 1391 (*OC*, 7.2:1001), and *Vivat rex* of 1405 (*OC*, 7.2:1183).
56. Mourin, *Jean Gerson*, 274.
57. Gerson repeated this phrase from the *Trilogium* (see n. 51 above) in his letter to the Dauphin
(*OC*, 2:223).
58. Gerson, *Trilogium*, 105–8.
59. Ibid., 90.
60. Ibid., 95–96.

effects were impossible. He also noted the overlapping and often contrary effects of celestial emanations as they bombarded the earth, and, like Oresme in particular, he stressed how terrestrial conditions themselves frequently altered the influence exerted by the stars.[61] Seemingly drawing on Oresme, but to different effect (and notably not citing him directly), Gerson derided those, like the followers of great Arab authority al-Kindi, who attributed all earthy events solely to the influence of astral forces. Oresme had also voiced this critique of al-Kindi at the end of his *On Configurations of Qualities and Motions* in order to leave some possibility for divine action in the world, but ultimately he felt that truly miraculous acts by the deity were very rare and he sought to emphasize the natural but terrestrial causation of most occurrences on earth. Gerson made the same reference in the midst of a section of the *Trilogium* arguing for divine action in the world, and clearly the chancellor regarded the likelihood of such action to be much greater.[62] As we will see, Gerson was generally much more concerned with the potential operations of spiritual powers, sometimes divine but mostly demonic, than the great fourteenth-century Parisian authorities on astrology and possible astrological superstitions had been.

Of course Gerson did not deny the natural effects of astral forces. They acted on the air, affecting the weather, and they could influence the flight of birds (so often held to carry divinatory import) by causing subtle changes in the atmosphere. Their energies permeated the earth, and even the human body, affecting the balance of the four bodily humors, contributing to health or sickness, and potentially even becoming the font of dreams (again, often thought to impart divinatory messages). Such natural operations allowed certain general predictions to be made, but did not justify augury or other divinatory "traditions" as practiced by "magicians." Indeed, while these traditions might have impressive intellectual pedigrees stretching back to the Arabs, Romans, or even ancient Indian civilizations, they were nonetheless erroneous and superstitious.[63] Neither could one use the stars to determine particular times that would be favorable for specific activities, nor to divine the outcome of any particular endeavor based on their position when it was undertaken. Finally, while medieval authorities were typically more comfortable attributing general natural effects to the stars rather than specific ones, Gerson cautioned that the stars could no more render particular days or other

---

61. Ibid., 84, 96.
62. Ibid., 93–94.
63. Ibid., 97.

periods of time generally propitious or entirely ill-fated than they could make a specific time favorable for a specific activity.[64]

Regarding natal horoscopes, while he accepted that the stars exerted significant influence on the highly impressionable bodies of infants at birth and in the womb, he rejected the claim that such influence allowed for reliable prognostication about a person's future actions or character. In the course of this discussion, Gerson fervently rejected his teacher d'Ailly's position that even Christ had been subject to natural stellar influence, arguing instead that the savior had enjoyed an entirely miraculous and supernatural gestation.[65] He politely refrained from referencing his friend's contrary position directly here, but he did cite d'Ailly, along with Oresme, regarding one important conclusion on which they all agreed, namely, that of stellar incommensurability. Given all the complexities involved in observing the stars and all the uncertainties in deducing their effects, any specific, detailed prediction an astrologer claimed to make was almost certainly grounded in some error. Yet few astrologers limited themselves to the sort of broad speculations about general conditions now and in the future that their art actually allowed. Here again, although Gerson began by citing d'Ailly as an authority on this position, he ultimately parted ways from his mentor, arguing strongly that when astrologers' overweening ambition to make precise predictions led them out of the realm of licit science and into that of illicit divination, it also led them directly into the waiting snares of demons.[66]

While Oresme minimized active demonic power, and d'Ailly was essentially silent about demonic fraud infecting astrology, such issues were central for Gerson. For a large portion of the *Trilogium*, he focused not on the stars per se, but on angels and demons. Some astrologers—more properly astral magicians—posited that spirits inhabited the celestial spheres, guiding their motions and directing their energies. Such magicians claimed to be able to control these beings and thus harness the power of the heavens through their rites. Gerson eviscerated this position, deriding the astrologers' claims to controlling power, although not the real presence and potency of demons in these arts. Angels and demons did not animate the stars, he asserted. Heavenly motion had been established by divine mandate, and whatever forces the stars radiated toward the earth was natural and constant. Nevertheless, spiritual beings could, through their powers of motion, exert some influence over astral energies. Thus he opened the door to demonic operations possibly lying

---

64. Gerson, *Contra superstitiosam dierum observantiam*, 109–17.
65. Gerson, *De respectu coelestium siderum*, 110–12.
66. Gerson, *Trilogium*, 95–97.

at the heart of any apparently astral rites. As for the contention of some astral conjurers that they employed celestial forces to bind and control demons, Gerson scoffed. Natural astral energies had no effect on spiritual beings, and so, like so many other church authorities since the time of Augustine, he grimly asserted that whenever an inherently hostile and inimical demon appeared to serve a human conjurer, it did so only because a pact, express or tacit, had been consecrated between it and its human foil.[67]

Astral images were a source of especially grave debate. As we have seen, no less an authority than Thomas Aquinas had declared that these objects operated only by means of "signification" to demons, that is, communication and implied supplication, particularly when symbols or characters were engraved on them.[68] Yet such talismans were widely employed and widely lauded, especially for their healing potency, by authorities across Europe and even to the very pinnacle of the ecclesiastical hierarchy. A powerful intellectual tradition defending their use and arguing that their power could be entirely natural and fully in accord with the principles of natural philosophy extended back to the thirteenth-century *Mirror of Astronomy* (*Speculum astronomie*), regularly attributed in the later Middle Ages to the great Dominican theologian, and Thomas Aquinas's own teacher, Albertus Magnus.[69] Of course, as in all matters pertaining to astrology and the power of the stars, the potential for superstitious error existed. While the author of the *Mirror* maintained that properly crafted and appropriately deployed images would draw only on natural astral energies, he recognized that they could also be used in an "abominable way" explicitly to summon demons. He further admitted a dangerous ambiguity; namely, that images engraved with certain unknown words or characters, or employed in conjunction with certain rites, might also draw on demonic power.[70] Again we find that the real difference between medieval authorities approving or opposing astrological practices lay not in absolute arguments pro or con, but in whether they chose to emphasize legitimate potentialities or corruptive dangers.

---

67. Ibid., 97–100.

68. Aquinas, *Summa contra gentiles* 3.105–6, in Aquinas, *Opera omnia iussu Leonis XIII P.M. edita*, vols. 13–15 (Rome, 1918–30); *Summa theologiae* 2.2.96.2; cited in Gerson, *Contra superstitionem sculpturae leonis*, 132.

69. While scholars now debate Albertus's genuine authorship of the *Speculum*, all late medieval writers identified the work with him. See Weill-Parot, *Images astrologiques*, 27–90, on the *Speculum*, and ibid., 223–302, contrasting Albert to Thomas in regard to astral images. On later reception of the *Speculum*, see Scott E. Hendrix, *How Albert the Great's* Speculum Astronomiae *Was Interpreted and Used by Four Centuries of Readers: A Study in Late Medieval Medicine, Astronomy, and Astrology* (Lewiston, N.Y., 2010).

70. Weill-Parot, *Images astrologiques*, 34–37.

This divide was as evident in the early fifteenth century as in the mid-thirteenth. In his *Against the Superstition of a Lion Sculpture*, written in 1428, Gerson criticized physicians in Montpellier for using an astral talisman fashioned in the form of a lion to relieve kidney stones. At virtually the same time, however, the English Dominican Alexander Carpenter, in a treatise otherwise dedicated to stamping out superstition, boldly praised a London physician who employed an astral lion-image crafted out of gold to cure fevers. For Carpenter, the cure was "entirely natural," and so there were no grounds for condemnation.[71] While he did not elaborate on the point, he most likely meant to imply that the image derived its power not from its particular form or the methods used in its crafting but from its basic substance. Gold was widely regarded as being naturally attuned to the beneficial energies of the sun, capable of attracting and focusing them to effect or augment medical remedies. Undoubtedly the most famous medieval case of such a talismanic cure had occurred a century earlier, when the Catalan physician Arnau of Vilanova had used a golden image crafted in the shape of a lion to channel astral energies and cure Pope Boniface VIII's kidney stones, apparently successfully and without any official sanction, although reportedly to the shock of some of the cardinals.[72] Arnau chose not to mention this treatment in his medical treatise on kidney stones, written about the same time as he performed this cure, but a treatise *On Seals* (*De sigillis*) attributed to him did circulate, which provided directions concerning how to craft such an image, which could then be used against stones, fevers, and other maladies.[73] There is also evidence that aspects of such thought, at least to the extent of connecting the power of the sun to the affliction of gallstones, circulated in the realm of folk wisdom as well. The mid-fifteenth-century Franco-Flemish *Distaff Gospels* (*Évangiles des quenouilles*) offered no cure, either amuletic or otherwise, but warned that anyone who urinated while facing the

---

71. Carpenter, *Destructorium viciorum* 6.52: "Item quondam londiniis quidam dicebatur curare a quartana per ymaginem leonis auream secundum certas constellationes factam, sed hec non fiebant nisi per naturam, igitur vti huismodi ymaginibus ad curam hominum spectantibus est naturale, et per consequens non rationabiliter prohibitum."

72. See inter alia Agostino Paravicini Bagliani, *Boniface VIII: Un pape hérétique?* (Paris, 2003), 287–89; Robert E. Lerner, "The Pope and the Doctor," *Yale Review* 78, no. 1 (1988/89): 62–79, at 70–71; documents in Heinrich Finke, *Aus den Tagen Bonifaz VIII: Funde und Forschungen* (Münster, 1902), 200–209.

73. Nicolas Weill-Parot, "Astrologie, médecine et art talismanique à Montpellier: Les sceaux astrologiques pseudo-Arnaldiens," in *L'Université de Médecine de Montpellier et son rayonnement (XIIIe–XVe siècles)*, ed. Daniel Le Blévec (Turnhout, 2004), 157–74. Most fully on Arnau and astral images, see Weill-Parot, *Images astrologiques*, 456–500.

sun would suffer from stones later in life.[74] One can only assume that the sun was imagined not to tolerate such disrespect and to strike out against those who would be so impertinent toward it, or perhaps like yellow gold so too a stream of urine exposed directly to sunlight was thought to attract and focus its power, only here to inimical effect.

We have no way of knowing whether Gerson, a native of northern France, knew about the taboo against urinating toward the sun, but he certainly knew the history of leonine astral figures. The talisman he criticized in *Against the Superstition of a Lion Sculpture* had been crafted by none other than the dean of the Montpellier medical faculty. Thus he could hardly avoid considering the astral-medicinal efforts of that school's famous alumnus, Arnau of Vilanova. Nor did he need to, because although Arnau had used an astral talisman when treating Boniface VIII, the Catalan physician regularly condemned what he regarded as magical or superstitious elements in such cures.[75] Gerson therefore invoked Arnau at the very start of his treatise, referring to him as a "most Christian doctor." The chancellor fully acknowledged the possibility that such images as Arnau had employed to heal the pope might indeed have a legitimate place in medical practice, drawing only on natural forces to effect a cure. He further acknowledged that Nicolas Colne, the Montpellier dean, was an "exceptional physician," and that the charges of superstition leveled against him, which had come to Gerson's attention and motivated him to write, stemmed explicitly from the "jealousy" of a colleague who had been unsuccessful in effecting his own cures for kidney stones. Nevertheless, in his overall evaluation of the case, Gerson remained deeply concerned, cautioning that astral images, however useful they might prove, were "very much suspect of superstition, idolatry, and magical observance." Agreeing with Aquinas, he noted that they frequently signified pacts with demons, either "express or hidden," and that they generally achieved their results by means of demonic operations.[76] Again we see the chancellor stressing the darkest possibilities of debatable practices. Where others emphasized the benefits of legitimate medical science, he worried that the risks of superstitious error were too great to allow.

---

74. Anonymous, *Évangiles* 3.21, p. 136. Doing so could also lead to eye infections: ibid., 3.1, p. 122.

75. Jospeh Ziegler, *Medicine and Religion c. 1300: The Case of Arnau de Vilanova* (Oxford, 1998), 246–47.

76. All quotes at Gerson, *Contra superstitionem sculpturae leonis*, 131; then discussion of demonic operations throughout the rest of that tract.

For Gerson, the slightest possibility of demonic involvement in astral rites was fatal. Even though a practice might be "healthy and holy" in ten, or twenty, or a hundred ways, if even a single element was tinged with idolatry, heresy, or apostasy, or was even suspected of being tainted in such a terrible way, then the entire practice should be declared "suspect and infected."[77] As a theological position, this was unassailable. As a prescription for action against rites or observances that were almost always muddled or uncertain in some way, it seems to exude an air of rigid intolerance. Scholars have noted that, in fact, Gerson could be fairly accommodating of confused and thus potentially superstitious behaviors especially among the common laity if these were grounded in basically pious intent.[78] Certainly, we should not read too much into a single clearly rhetorical statement that he penned against a case of patently elite, learned practice. Yet overall, the marked emphasis he placed on demonic infection of astral as well as other superstitious rites sets him in stark contrast to other leading intellects like Oresme, who downplayed demonic power altogether, or even Langenstein, who discussed the danger but did not dwell on it at length. Certainly it sets him apart from his astrophile teacher d'Ailly, who recognized the potential for superstition but chose to stress instead positive and valuable aspects of legitimate astrology. Unlike these great Parisian thinkers, and more in tune with the thought of John XXII and Nicolau Eymerich, Gerson saw a world under assault by demonic forces, and he sought to motivate all Christians—great princes and university elites, certainly, but also ordinary lay men and women—to resist this threat by guiding them to stronger faith and away from superstitious practice.

This heightened, or at least more extensively expressed, anxiety about demons pervaded most of Gerson's writing against superstition. Much of *On Errors concerning the Magic Art* dealt not with the magical arts per se but with the range and scope of demonic power that undergirded them. A decade before this, Gerson had made clear in his first sermon on the topic that all superstition stemmed from the devil, and that superstitious people in fact "worship the devil and make sacrifice to him" through their erroneous rites.[79] In a sermon of 1397, he declared that those who practiced

---

77. Ibid., 132: "Omnis observatione quantumcumque sancta et salubris videatur in decem aut viginti aut centum particulis, si habeat unicam particulam de idolatria vel haeresis vel de apostasia suspectam aut infectam, debet tota suspecta et infecta reputari."

78. Daniel B. Hobbins, "Gerson on Lay Devotion," in McGuire, *Companion to Jean Gerson* (as above, n. 44), 41–78, at 44.

79. Sermon *Regnum* (*OC*, 7.2:1001); also sermon *Factum est prelium magnum* of 1393 (*OC*, 7.2:628).

"superstition, sorcery, and magic . . . deny their baptism and the Christian faith, worship the devil, and make sacrifices to him."[80] Again in *On Errors concerning the Magic Art* he stated that demonic activity must be suspected to lie behind any occurrence that did not stem from clear and direct natural causes, that demons acted on human behalf only when some kind of pact had been formed between them, and that, as Augustine had declared long ago, any kind of fellowship with demons entailed superstition and idolatry.[81]

This frequent linkage of superstition with sorcery and magic (that is, of the term *superstitio* with the terms *magia* or *sortilegia*), repeated in various forms in several of the chancellor's works, may itself indicate an important point that Gerson was trying to make. Consider the fact that Nicolau Eymerich and the theologians directed by John XXII had worked very deliberately to connect demonic magic to superstition because *superstitio*, in the Augustinian sense, implied a clear violation of Christian faith. Thus the connection they drew helped bolster their argument that any act of demonic invocation was inherently heretical. Gerson may now have sought to achieve a similar kind of conceptual transference, but in the opposite direction. That is, he wanted to conflate the broad category of superstition with the (somewhat) more precise categories of magic or sorcery because these latter terms now carried a clearer implication of demonic entanglement to many intellectual authorities, and he sought to expand that threat of demonic menace to superstitions of any kind. He certainly did not hesitate, when the opportunity presented, to argue explicitly that the taint of demonic evil extended beyond rites of active conjuration and into the realm of entirely passive superstitious observances as well. In *Against the Superstitious Observance of Days*, for example, he declared that the long-standing common practice of regarding certain days as especially propitious or unlucky stemmed from the devil, and that demons perpetuated such beliefs among the unwary through their deceptive actions.[82] Here too, where more complacent authorities might be inclined to see, at worst, harmless foolishness, he stressed the potential for dire, diabolical threat.

Gerson would also brook no arguments that might mitigate the profound evil of involvement with demonic forces. As he denied astral magicians' claims to be masters of demons, rather than supplicants and devotees, so he dismissed the potential of magical rites generally to control or compel demons in any way.[83] Of course, like all Christian authorities, he was forced to

---

80. *OC*, 7.2:1055.
81. Gerson, *De erroribus*, 79.
82. Gerson, *Contra superstitiosam dierum observantiam*, 119.
83. Gerson, *De erroribus*, 84–85.

recognize the valid power of exorcism, and in fact he strongly approved of a number of churchly rites and consecrated items that pious Christians could employ against the threat posed by hostile demonic spirits. Certain processions, holy water, or even icons and images all offered a means of defense, provided the faithful properly understood that no special power lay in these actions or items themselves, but rather came from God or his saints or angels responding to the devotion focused on an image or enacted through a rite.[84] The allowance for appropriate use of church ceremonies, sacramental items, and devotional objects, while essential, was not without problem for the chancellor, nor for other opponents of superstition. Such practices all carried the risk that people might misuse or simply misunderstand them, and so render them superstitious. Gerson took pastoral obligations very seriously, and he wanted to encourage the laity in any devotional practices, even unofficial ones so long as they were grounded in real faith.[85] Yet, like Nicolau Eymerich writing decades earlier against the pretended pieties of necromancers, he vigorously argued that "sanctity" did not inhere automatically in prayer or apparently devotional acts like fasting, observing chastity or other forms of purification, or even receiving the sacrament of the Eucharist. Rather, even the "best and most holy things" could be abused, and such abuse should never be tolerated.[86]

Another contention Gerson sought to counter was that Christians might legitimately employ demonic rites to undo other devilish magic used against them. "Is it not licit to drive out vanities with vanities just as to knock out one nail with another?" Most decidedly not, he retorted, primarily because demons always sought to harm humanity, even when appearing to do good. If they effected a cure or alleviated some suffering, they did so only to corrupt and deceive both those performing the cure and those receiving it.[87] As he noted in a sermon, the faithful must cultivate the wisdom to avoid recourse to sorcery even in great tribulation or need.[88] The only proper response to suffering lay in the legitimate medical arts, and in increased devotion to God: "not in superstitious observances but in pious supplications, not in demonic invocations but in the emendation of life."[89] The injunction

---

84. Ibid., 83; on appropriate devotion to images, see also Gerson, *Le miroire de l'ame* (*OC*, 7.1:196).
85. See Hobbins, "Gerson on Lay Devotion"; more broadly D. Catherine Brown, *Pastor and Laity in the Theology of Jean Gerson* (Cambridge, 1987).
86. Gerson, *De erroribus*, 82–83.
87. Ibid., 84–85. The image of the nail goes back at least to Aristotle, *Politics* 5.11.
88. Sermon *Dedit illis scientiam sanctorum* of January 1403 (*OC*, 7.2:596).
89. Gerson, *De erroribus*, 85.

to "amend one's life" was common among religious reformers in the late medieval period, and, among many other hats that he wore, Gerson was a major proponent of reform, not only within the institutions of the church, damaged and degraded by the convulsions of the schism, but also within Christian society as a whole.[90]

Like his desire for reform, Gerson's concern over superstition, while rooted in his own experiences at court and university, extended to all levels of society, and he explicitly addressed the inclination of common people toward superstition, as well as discussing elite practices. This broadening of concern was one of Gerson's most important contributions to the debate about superstition, for it would set patterns that endured for the rest of the fifteenth century. He was, of course, not entirely innovative in this maneuver. Such connections were clearly in the air around the year 1400. As we have already seen, Laurens Pignon shared this trait, but it need hardly be said that the Burgundian confessor's voice carried much less force than the Parisian chancellor's. Certainly, no earlier figure nearly as influential as Gerson ever addressed superstitions among the common laity to the extent that he did. That said, Gerson himself never wrote exclusively about common superstitions. What we typically find in his works are brief but telling indications of a broader perspective. In his first known condemnation of superstition in a sermon likely of 1391, for example, he stated directly that erroneous beliefs and practices flourished among common people as well as the courtly classes.[91] In fact, the sermon gives the distinct impression that superstitions were to be expected among the lower orders, while it conveys a certain shock and indignation that they have now filtered up through society to infect those who should know better.

Gerson expressed this idea of upward social contagion more concretely a decade later in *On Errors concerning the Magic Art*. There he rebuked the learned Parisian medical faculty for employing superstitious practices just like those found in common magical healing rites: ligatures, amulets, and strange words or characters. Educated members of the medical profession, he charged, complained bitterly about the "pernicious and foolish superstitions of magicians and old sorceresses who through their cursed rites promised to heal patients," but they were often just as guilty of superstition themselves.[92]

---

90. On Gerson as an institutional reformer, and particularly on church reform culminating in "personal reform," see Louis B. Pascoe, *Jean Gerson: Principles of Church Reform* (Leiden, 1973), esp. 175–206.

91. Sermon *Regnum* (*OC*, 7.2:1000, 1001).

92. Gerson, *De erroribus*, 77.

Again at the very end of his life, in *Opposing Superstition in Hearing Mass*, Gerson criticized preachers who, instead of instructing the laity in proper faith, perpetuated through their sermons many common superstitious beliefs concerning the ceremony of the Mass, such as that one could not go blind, go hungry, or die on a day when one attended a Mass.[93] The promise of such protection obviously appealed to many average Christians, and the thought of filling their churches no doubt appealed to many preachers.

In two successive tracts, Gerson addressed a very widespread category of superstition, namely the "observance of days"; that is, the belief that certain days and times were either particularly auspicious or inauspicious. Such observances permeated elite classes as well and could be grounded in learned astrology, but clearly they also had enormous popular appeal. As if to emphasize that popular aspect of this superstition, Gerson included in one of these two tracts a catalog of distinctly "vulgar" beliefs regarding portents and omens. For example, encountering a cat or rabbit when leaving one's house in the morning was a sign of impending misfortune. So was striking one's foot when stepping out the door, or putting one's shirt on backward or one's shoes on the wrong feet when dressing. If an owl hooted or a crow croaked while flying over a house, or if a rooster crowed before dawn, people took it as a portent of doom. All these beliefs were foolish and stupid, he maintained, as was the equally ridiculous superstition of attributing misfortune to certain supposedly unlucky days.[94]

There was, of course, a long tradition in the medieval West (as indeed in antiquity) of elite authorities deriding the foolish superstitions of the common masses. Among the beliefs Gerson listed we will recognize some basic varieties that had been the target of clerical scorn since the time of Augustine. Here we again encounter a basic uncertainty regarding to what degree any authority's catalog of such superstitions might accurately reflect real beliefs or practices among contemporary laypeople. Yet the chancellor surely knew something about the world beyond university walls and the halls of courtly power, and there is at least some resonance between his list and apparently widely held beliefs in the early fifteenth century known from other sources. His assertion that people generally believed that encountering a hare was a bad portent would seem to be confirmed by the "wisdom of women" collected in the *Distaff Gospels*, for example, which made the same point.[95]

---

93. Gerson, *Adversus superstitionem in audiendo missam*, 141.
94. Gerson, *Contra superstitiosam dierum observantiam*, 117–18.
95. Anonymous, *Évangiles* 2.3, p. 102.

In other cases, however, the resonance is indirect or even inverted. While Gerson derided people who maintained that accidentally putting a shirt on backward when dressing in the morning was a sign of coming misfortune, the *Gospels* recommended that a man deliberately wear his shirt reversed, or inside out, if he wanted to ensure himself of success in either war or business.[96] As for the divinatory power of barnyard fowl, while Gerson decried the notion that a rooster crowing before dawn should be regarded with foreboding, the *Gospels* advised in a more homey manner that hens gathering in the shelter of a henhouse might be taken as a sign of coming rain.[97] This seems a relatively straightforward and commonsense sort of prediction, and had he addressed it, Gerson might well have concluded that it was entirely legitimate. Animals did, after all, have a heightened but entirely natural sensitivity to changes in the weather, as Christian authorities diligently maintained throughout the Middle Ages. One wonders, then, what the chancellor would have made of one of the *Gospels'* most colorful descriptions of animal prognostication: "when you see a cat sitting in a window in the sun, lifting its leg to its ear and licking its own behind, it is certain that it will rain that very day."[98]

Of course, texts like the *Distaff Gospels* are also not direct accounts of common beliefs. As a piece of courtly literature, and one that framed itself very much in terms of the derision of common foolishness, the *Gospels* might no more accurately reflect the everyday "reality" of early fifteenth-century superstition than did Gerson's critique. At the very least, however, these accounts let us know the sort of superstitions in which two writers presenting somewhat different perspectives both thought ordinary people engaged. They also tell us what sort of people those men believed were most likely to be superstitious, and here we find another resonance. Like the anonymous author of the *Distaff Gospels*, Jean Gerson clearly thought that among ordinary laypeople—the *stulti* and *vulgari* (implying mainly a lack of Latin education and literacy)—women were particularly prone to superstitious belief and practice. In this, he drew on a tradition long embedded in Christian thought, but also one that was becoming increasingly evident in both the theological and medical literature of the late medieval period.[99] He mentioned women in his very first sermon on superstition to the French

---

96. Ibid., 4.17, p. 148.
97. Ibid., 4.12, p. 146.
98. Ibid., 2.22, p. 118.
99. Jole Agrimi and Chiara Crisciani, "Savoir médical et anthropologie religieuse: Les représentations et les fonctions de la vetula (XIIIe–XVe siècle)," *Annales ESC* 48.5 (1993): 1281–1308.

court, noting with "abomination" that foolish beliefs held sway not merely among "old women sorcerers" (*vielles sorcières*), but now also among great lords of the court.[100] At the very outset of *On Errors concerning the Magic Art*, he located the roots of the "pernicious and foolish superstitions" that he believed were infecting the healing arts as lying among (male) magicians but also "old women sorcerers" (*vetulae sortilegae*). Later in this work he warned his readers not to put faith in the rites of "mere uneducated women" (*indoctae mulierculae*).[101] And in another tract, he yet again decried the superstitions of "old women sorcerers," this time in two languages as "vetulae sortilegae, gallice vieilles sorcières."[102]

As much as such references attract our sharp attention because of what we know them to foreshadow, however, we must also be careful not to overstate their implications. Gerson never expounded at length on why women were particularly implicated in sorcery and superstition, as some later witchcraft theorists such as Johannes Nider or the infamous Heinrich Kramer were to do.[103] Indeed, he explicitly referenced the superstitions of women only occasionally and quite briefly. He was far from oblivious to gendered components of spirituality, as witnessed by his often (although again never entirely) strident condemnation of female mystics and visionaries.[104] Regarding superstition, however, the far greater part his language, and seemingly of his thought, was gender neutral. Nevertheless, he was clearly a signal figure in terms of the increasingly intense linkage that late medieval intellectual authorities would come to draw between women and various kinds of superstitious error and magical transgression. Compared to the notable silence regarding women that we have encountered in so many other systematic treatments of superstition up to this point, Gerson's sporadic but very direct pronouncements reverberate loudly indeed.

We should also be cautious here because Gerson can be, and has been, too easily cast as an opponent of all women and all forms of female spirituality.[105] A few statements about "old women sorcerers" should not serve to reinforce

---

100. Sermon *Regnum* (*OC*, 7.2:1001).

101. Gerson, *De erroribus*, 77, 83.

102. Gerson, *Contra superstitiosam dierum observantiam*, 120.

103. Both will be discussed in following chapters.

104. Nancy Caciola, *Discerning Spirits: Divine and Demonic Possession in the Middle Ages* (Ithaca, N.Y., 2003), 289–91, 302–8; Dyan Elliott, *Proving Woman: Female Spirituality and Inquisitional Culture in the Later Middle Ages* (Princeton, N.J., 2004), 264–96; also Elliott, *The Bride of Christ Goes to Hell: Metaphor and Embodiment in the Lives of Pious Women, 200–1500* (Philadelphia, 2012), 245–56.

105. For nuanced views, see Hobbins, "Gerson on Lay Devotion," 62–67; Wendy Love Anderson, "Gerson's Stance on Women," in McGuire, *Companion to Jean Gerson*, 293–315.

any sweeping conclusions. Against them might be set the fact that Gerson was strongly supportive of the most famous "superstitious woman" of the early fifteenth century, Joan of Arc. The political reality surrounding Joan's case cannot be ignored. Gerson, a staunch French royalist, wrote a tract defending the veracity of her visions and her mission just days after the Maid's remarkable victory over the English at Orléans in May 1429. He was thus defending the evident savior of France against the charges already beginning to circulate that her "voices" were demonic and she was in league with the devil. Still, as the most thorough study of this text concludes, he defended Joan "fully and without hesitation."[106]

We would do well to recall that, from a modern perspective, some basic misogyny was a constant element in the thinking of almost all medieval intellectuals, a "ground base" that rumbles through an endless variety of texts.[107] Given the absolutely pervasive medieval conviction in the mental and spiritual inferiority of women, rooted in both classical philosophy and Christian theology, that a medieval intellectual should have considered women more vulnerable than men to the errors of superstition is only to be expected. No doubt such ideas prevailed also among the laity, including among women themselves. Still, knowing that major witch hunts predominantly targeting women lay in Europe's immediate future, we cannot ignore that at the outset of the fifteenth century a figure as influential as Gerson both linked superstition resolutely to demonic evil and pointed specifically toward women as a particular source of superstitious error.

Jean Gerson was perhaps the most important intellectual figure of his day, and his stature, at least north of the Alps, only grew for the remainder of the fifteenth century. His influence lay particularly heavily on German lands, even though he himself spent only the briefest of periods traveling through them.[108] His works announce (although of course they neither uniquely embodied nor single-handedly created) several trends that will be apparent in the intense discourse about superstition that emerged in the fifteenth century primarily among German theologians. Perhaps most fundamentally we have seen in Gerson's work a tremendous concern with demonic presence and

---

106. Daniel Hobbins, "Jean Gerson's Authentic Tract on Joan of Arc: *Super facto puellae et credulitate sibi praestanda* (14 May 1429)," *Mediaeval Studies* 67 (2005): 99–155, quote at 102.

107. Barbara Newman, *From Virile Woman to WomanChrist: Studies in Medieval Religion and Literature* (Philadelphia, 1995), 2.

108. Mazour-Matusevich, "Gerson's Legacy," 359–71; Hobbins, *Authorship and Publicity before Print*, 193–205.

power, not just as the real force underlying most superstitious operations, but more broadly threatening to disrupt and disorder all Christian society. Opposition to demonic superstition became therefore not just an intellectual exercise to correct error, but a pastoral call to arms, to "amend life" and amend the world by promoting proper devotion in both thought and action. Here concern over superstition coincided with desires for reform that, while prevalent to some degree across all of Europe in this period, would also become especially pronounced in German lands. Insofar as opposition to superstition was linked to positive reformist agendas of any sort (and of course, it need not be), a problem emerged: How might authorities stringently repress dangerous errors without also stifling, in an atmosphere of unmitigated fear, numerous expressions of genuine if perhaps somewhat confused or disordered piety on the part of the common laity? Gerson struggled with this dilemma, as would other writers after him.[109]

At root here lay the problem of discernment. Any devotion directed toward God was appropriate so long as it remained free of corruption. Yet such corruption need not be intentional. People could inadvertently summon demons or succumb to their temptations, and a tacit pact with such a fiend was as terrible as an express and deliberate one. Similarly, authorities were prepared to deem legitimate any operation that worked through some natural force or power, be it terrestrial or emanating from the heavens. Yet even educated elites often held erroneous ideas about how such forces operated and what they might accomplish. Moreover, many feared that demons perpetually sought to involve themselves in otherwise natural operations. Authorities struggled to find firm grounds on which they could assign often muddled practices to one or another of their theoretically distinct categories, and they debated the proper level of suspicion one needed to maintain. In this regard, Gerson appears to have set a bad example with his statement that a practice must be deemed corrupt if it was suspect in even one one-hundredth of its parts.[110] Yet he penned that statement as part of a short tract focused on a single, very specific issue: an educated physician's use of astral image magic to cure kidney stones. It was not part of a carefully considered program for the "discernment of superstition." Gerson offered no such program.

For all his brilliance, the chancellor of Paris was no systematizer. He worked in a new métier, an "applied moral theology" that concentrated on addressing specific, practical, and often pastoral problems.[111] Issues of superstition

---

109. On Gerson, see Hobbins, "Gerson on Lay Devotion," 44.
110. See n. 77 above.
111. See Hobbins, *Authorship and Publicity before Print*, 51–71 (term at 71).

fit this category nicely. By the early fifteenth century, all the great categorical statements had been pronounced time and again, whether on the demonic nature of virtually all magic or the erroneous potential in so much astrology. The mainly German writers who carried debate about superstition forward into the fifteenth century continued to expound on such matters, advancing, for the most part, the same theoretical positions based on the same authorities we have already encountered. They become most interesting when they enter the messy world of common practices, which they struggled to categorize by rigid scholastic logic. This is the most significant of the subsequent trends that Gerson marked. While Nicolau Eymerich railed against the demonic heresy inherent in all sorcery, and while he composed a handbook for inquisitors, he dealt always with elite forms of necromancy. A magistrate who had read his Eymerich but found himself confronted with a common healing charm or some peasant muttering a protective spell over his cow would hardly know how to proceed. Heinrich of Langenstein and Pierre d'Ailly both addressed the nebulous world of interaction with spirits in treatises on discernment, but such questions appear to have exerted relatively little influence on their writings on superstitious astrology, which remained for the most part strictly focused on the "scientific," natural philosophical aspects and errors of that craft, not spiritual ones.[112]

The story revealed in these past two chapters is not quite the standard narrative of steadily growing concern over the magical and the demonic in late medieval Europe, particularly among religious and intellectual elites. That trajectory is certainly evident, but by expanding our focus to the broader category of superstition, we have discovered some interesting connections and intriguing byways. The encompassing category of superstition, with its broad meaning and yet also specific definition going back to Augustine, helped authorities first label elite necromancy a heresy, and then extend the demonic menace implied by that kind of magic to all sorts of other spells, charms, rites, and observances. Yet the term *superstitio* also served in this period to establish boundaries between proper and improper understandings of natural science, particularly in relation to astrology, and the possibility existed for these debates about superstition to proceed almost entirely shorn of any

---

112. For Langenstein and d'Ailly on discernment of spirits, see Caciola, *Discerning Spirits*, 284–89, 298–302; Elliott, *Proving Woman*, 259–62, 266–67. D'Ailly treated discernment and astrology jointly in his relatively early (1380s) treatise *De falsis prophetis II* (commonly so labeled, although likely written before another treatise *De falsis prophetis I*). Notably, *De falsis prophetis II* is relatively hostile to astrology, in contrast to the cardinal's later approach. See Smoller, *History, Prophecy, and the Stars*, on this work.

demonic overtones. It was ultimately from this intellectual tradition of the Parisian masters Orseme, Langenstein, and d'Ailly that Jean Gerson arose, and yet he effected another crucial change. Seeking to apply moral theology more practically, he addressed superstition of every kind, from astrological error to elite necromancy to the common spells and simple divinatory observances of ordinary lay men and women. This was the broad territory whose often confusing contours and indistinct edges would challenge late medieval authorities addressing superstition for much of the fifteenth century.

❧ CHAPTER 4

Dilemmas of Discernment

> However much the aforesaid blessings and adjura-
> tions may not be superstitious or illicit in themselves,
> if they should be performed as has been set forth they
> must nevertheless be shunned and forbidden due to
> attendant dangers, because often some superstitions get
> mingled into them.
>
> —Denys the Carthusian, *Against the Vices of
> Superstitions*

In the introduction of this book, I mentioned a
case of alleged superstition in the German Rhineland at the very beginning
of the fifteenth century. A woman wanted to use a questionable blessing to
help her son, who had injured his finger. She sought, and ultimately found,
a clergyman who told her that such healing rites were perfectly permissible.
The woman lived in the town of Neustadt, just west of the episcopal city
of Speyer. Despite her obvious concern for her boy, she had initially held
back from using what healing rites she knew because the local clergy, and
in particular a certain "Lord Nikolaus," opposed them. The woman found
occasion, however, to travel to Landau, about ten miles south of Neustadt,
where she consulted another clergyman, an Augustinian friar, probably in the
course of confession. This man, Werner of Friedberg, told her that she could
help her son with a clear conscience. He did not consider such rites "false" or
illegitimate in any way. After all, he would later note with some apparent indignation, if all blessings were false, why would the church officially sanction
the blessing of ashes, palm fronds, eggs, and meat at Easter? He also admitted
that he personally knew a curative incantation in the German vernacular that
he had used on himself, had found to be effective, and had even taught to a
novice of his order. For all this, along with several other questionable positions that he held, in January and February of 1405 he found himself hauled

in for interrogation first by an official of the bishop of Speyer and then by theologians at the nearby University of Heidelberg.[1]

This woman's question to Werner and his response illustrate the multilayered concerns and uncertainties that surrounded common superstitions, or more accurately the dilemmas faced by anyone endeavoring to determine whether particular practices were or were not superstitious. Not just clergy struggled to discern legitimate blessings from illegitimate spells. A concerned mother apparently refrained from aiding her son, worried by frequent clerical condemnations of potentially superstitious healing rites. She also seems to have known, however, that not all the clergy spoke with one voice on such matters. No record remains of how she came upon Werner of Friedberg. Did she just happen to be in Landau, perhaps for a market, a religious festival, or even making a local pilgrimage on behalf of her boy? Had she been cornering clergymen wherever she could find them, posing her question and hoping for a positive response? Did she know of Werner specifically and perhaps deliberately set out to meet him? During his inquest, he admitted that he had preached openly about the value of blessings, and that he had advised many people about such healing rites in the course of hearing confessions. In all cases he was fairly tolerant and encouraged people to use what rites they knew, as long as these did not blatantly seem directed toward demonic forces.[2] Perhaps he had acquired a reputation for leniency in such matters, one that spread up the road to Neustadt. "Forget what Lord Nikolaus says about the danger of superstition," I imagine some friend or relative telling our concerned mother. "There's a friar in Landau who will tell you to go ahead and help your boy."

Such speculations aside, Werner's case clearly illustrates ongoing debates among clerical authorities in German-speaking central Europe regarding potentially superstitious practices among both the common laity and educated clergy in the fifteenth century. Particularly at the many universities now scattered across the politically fragmented German Empire (the oldest of them, including Heidelberg, were only a few years or at most a few decades old when the new century dawned) a group of writers produced a string of works about superstition that spanned the first half of the 1400s. In many ways, these men were similar to the authorities we have already examined. They were almost

---

1. Werner, *Revocatio*, 198r; Werner, *Responsiones*, 280. On Werner's trial, see Robert E. Lerner, "Werner di Friedberg intrappolato dalla legge," in *La parola all'accusato*, ed. Jean-Claude Maire Vigueur and Agostino Paravicini Bagliani (Palermo, 1991), 268–81; also briefly treated in Euan Cameron, *Enchanted Europe: Superstition, Reason, and Religion, 1250–1750* (Oxford, 2010), 51–52.

2. Werner, *Revocatio*, 198r; Werner, *Responsiones*, 280.

all schoolmen, mainly theologians. They continued to address and denounce elite superstitions: erroneous astrology, astral magic, necromancy, and the like. They tended to view all superstition through a framework provided by those elite practices, and yet, following the path largely blazed by Jean Gerson, they also tended to work mainly in the mode of an applied, practical, and pastoral theology. Thus, like the Parisian chancellor, their focus increasingly fell on common superstitions as well.[3]

The more these men tried to apply their scholastic distinctions to common practices, however, the more disquieting confusion they encountered. Despite the magnitude of their concerns, a few demonstrated considerable leniency, like Werner of Friedberg banning only those rites that appeared overtly demonic. In this they perhaps sought to follow Gerson's imperative of promoting lay devotion as much as possible, some pressing their tolerance further than his would ever extend. The chancellor's own guidelines for distinguishing licit from illicit devotional practices appear, in the words of one expert, "like lines drawn in blowing sand," so we should hardly be surprised to find that other authorities were equally flummoxed about where to establish these all-important boundaries.[4] Many, as we will see, determined that the wisest course was to err on the side of caution. Again in what could be seen as adherence to an example set by Gerson, they decided to draw a line excluding all practices that seemed in any way suspect, even if the risk lay in only one part out of one hundred. This is not to say that these authors constantly cited Gerson or sprinkled his dictums throughout their works. Their stated sources of authority were, in fact, very much what his had been: the early church fathers and the great systematizers of scholastic thought in the thirteenth century, above all Thomas Aquinas and William of Auvergne. But they focused on basically the same issues as Gerson, and they faced the same dilemmas.

In this chapter I introduce a core group of German writers addressing superstition in the fifteenth century and explore the particular contexts in which they wrote. I will only briefly recount the commonalities they shared with earlier authorities and how they perpetuated many well-established critiques, for we have already seen these points made time and time again. Instead,

---

3. On these men as a group, see Lynn Thorndike, *A History of Magic and Experimental Science*, 8 vols. (New York, 1923–58), 4:274–307; Françoise Bonney, "Autour de Jean Gerson: Opinions de théologiens sur les superstitions et la sorcellerie au début du XVe siècle," *Moyen Âge* 77 (1971): 85–98; Jan R. Veenstra, *Magic and Divination at the Courts of Burgundy and France: Text and Context of Laurens Pignon's "Contre les devineurs" (1411)* (Leiden, 1998), 137–53.

4. Daniel B. Hobbins, "Gerson on Lay Devotion," in *A Companion to Jean Gerson*, ed. Brian Patrick McGuire (Leiden, 2006), 41–78, at 60.

I want mainly to examine new points of emphasis found in their works. These men were not deliberate innovators, and we should not be surprised to find that virtually nothing in their basic argumentation was original in an absolute sense. Yet their increased engagement, at a practical level, with common superstitions required them to focus to a considerable degree on elements of lay religiosity and the murky, troublesome "twilight zone" in which the practical use of prayers, blessings, and appropriated sacramental items might signal either admirable faith or damnable superstition.[5]

Such considerations led them to write at length on the nature and extent of demonic power, for like Gerson they tended to emphasize the threat of demons behind most forms of common superstition. Inevitably, however, they also had to consider what limits pertained to human invocations of divine power, and how God responded to such pleas. The underlying question here was whether particular rites might automatically invoke a divine response. Church doctrine established that sacraments were always valid, regardless of the personal qualities of the priests who performed them, for God had promised that his grace would always flow through the sacramental act itself. Would an item blessed by a priest then also carry inherent power in all contexts? Would a prayer, properly said, always exert some force? Such questions bore to the heart of late medieval religion, and to some extent of all religion: What is the correct relationship between internal faith and the external enactments of that faith? The authorities who wrote about superstition in the fifteenth century did not necessarily want to sail into such deep waters, but ironically the more practical and focused their concerns became, the further they found themselves blown into them. Ahead lay the storm clouds of the Reformation, when theologians and ministers both Protestant and Catholic would address these issues much more directly and deliberately, although often enough still through the framework of superstition.[6]

Of course, no one in the early fifteenth century imagined the tumults of the sixteenth, and Reformation-era religiosity will not be our focus here. Neither, at least in this chapter, will be the other great, and more immediate, shadow looming over the history of superstition in the 1400s. As the century progressed, authorities' vilest conceptions of common superstition came to

---

5. On this "twilight zone," see R. W. Scribner, "Ritual and Popular Religion in Catholic Germany at the Time of the Reformation," *Journal of Ecclesiastical History* 35 (1984): 47–77 (term introduced at 71). On the relation of common "magic" to official church practices, see also Eamon Duffy, *The Stripping of the Altars: Traditional Religion in England, 1400–1580* (New Haven, Conn., 1992), 266–87.

6. See Cameron, *Enchanted Europe*, 156–239.

entail not basically pious laity mangling certain rites but wicked malefactors deliberately swearing service to Satan: witches, now frequently believed to operate as members of conspiratorial diabolical cults. As early as the 1430s, some writers were describing gatherings of witches at horrific sabbaths, and within decades stereotypes of witchcraft were circulating in many regions of western Europe and witch hunts were becoming increasingly common. Witchcraft always entailed superstition. The demonologists who wrote about witchcraft all addressed other superstitions to some extent, and writers dealing with superstition in general increasingly addressed witchcraft as the century wore on. There are reasons, however, for keeping the two topics apart, both practical, since so much has already been written about witchcraft, and conceptual, since by no means did all forms of superstition entail witchcraft.[7] Here, in order to consider superstition more broadly in its own right, I will simply bracket off the matter of witches, leaving it until the next chapter.

Like witchcraft would eventually become, superstition in the fifteenth century was an issue and a concern that was both universal across Western Christendom and particularly pronounced in the central European lands of the German Empire. I focus here almost entirely on German authors because they produced by far the largest cluster of treatises specifically addressing this topic in this period, forming a body of evidence both coherent in itself and representative of wider concerns.[8] Also, insofar as concern about superstition bled into and promoted later fears of witchcraft, it clearly bore its most bitter and consequential fruit in German soil. At the end of the chapter I will suggest some reasons why superstition should have been addressed so frequently and to such effect in German lands. But first we need to introduce these authors, many of whom will not be especially well known even to experts in this period.

The Authors and Their Audience

In this chapter, we are no longer dealing with a fairly linear succession of highly placed authorities but rather a cluster of writers. In just over six decades, more than a dozen men across the German Empire penned a score of works dealing in significant ways with the issue of superstition. Many of these were substantial

---

7. Notably Cameron, *Enchanted Europe*, does not discuss witchcraft at all.

8. On other regions, see Marina Montesano, *"Supra acqua et supra ad vento": "Superstizioni,"* maleficia e incantamenta nei predicatori francescani osservanti (Italia, sec. XV) (Rome, 1999); Fabián Alejandro Campagne, *Homo Catholicus, Homo Superstitiosus: El discurso antisupersticioso en la España de los siglos XV a XVIII* (Madrid, 2002); Kathleen Kamerick, "Shaping Superstition in Late Medieval England," *MRW* 3 (2008): 29–53.

Fifteenth-Century Central European Works on Superstition

Date	Author	Title	Location
ca. 1400	Ulrich of Pottenstein	Explanation of the Decalogue	Vienna
1405	Johannes of Frankfurt	Question: Whether the Power to Control Demons . . .	Heidelberg
1405	Nikolaus of Jauer	On Superstitions	Heidelberg
ca. 1415	Anonymous	On Divinations	Cologne
1423	Nikolaus of Dinkelsbühl	On the Commandments of the Decalogue	Vienna
ca. 1425	Heinrich of Gorkum	On Certain Superstitious Occurrences	Cologne
1436–38	Johannes Nider	Anthill	Vienna
1438	Johannes Nider	Preceptor of Divine Law	Vienna
1438/39	Thomas Ebendorfer	On the Ten Commandments	Vienna
ca. 1440	Johannes of Wünschelburg	On Superstitions	Leipzig
before ca. 1445	Anonymous	On Superstitions	Erlangen?
1451/52	Felix Hemmerli	Treatise of Exorcisms and Adjurations	Zurich
ca. 1451/52	Felix Hemmerli	On Blessings of the Air with the Sacrament	Zurich
1452	Jakob of Paradise	On the Power of Demons	Erfurt
1450s?	Denys the Carthusian	Against the Vices of Superstitions	Roermond
1455 or after	Felix Hemmerli	On Showing Credulity to Demons	Zurich
1456 or after	Johannes Hartlieb	Book of All Forbidden Arts	Munich
1456/57	Felix Hemmerli	On Exorcisms	Zurich
before 1459	Anonymous	On Superstitions	Bavaria?
1466	Johannes Schwarz	On Divinations	Eichstätt?

treatises composed specifically "on superstitions" (*de superstitionibus*). Some were shorter, more focused tracts, in the style of Gerson.[9] One was a traditional scholastic *quaestio* (literally a "question") designating a point for academic debate. Some writers approached superstition by addressing the nature and extent of demonic power. Others came to this topic when they wrote commentaries on the Ten Commandments, in which they treated superstition under the rubric of the first commandment, as a form of idolatry. They form a diverse array, but they also share a number of common traits and connections.

One of the most important German authorities to address superstition, clearly very influential in his own time yet subsequently soon forgotten, was

---

9. On Gerson's approach to writing, see Daniel Hobbins, "The Schoolman as Public Intellectual: Jean Gerson and the Late Medieval Tract," *AHR* 108 (2003): 1308–37; Hobbins, *Authorship*

the Heidelberg theologian Nikolaus Magni of Jauer (Jawor, in modern Polish Silesia).[10] Born around 1355, he studied briefly at the University of Vienna, but was educated mainly at the University of Prague, obtaining his theology degree in 1395. He then taught at Prague for a few years before moving in 1402 to Heidelberg, where he died in 1435. In 1405 he wrote the first major treatise *On Superstitions* (*De superstitionibus*) of the fifteenth century. The immediate context was Werner of Friedberg's interrogation by members of the Heidelberg theological faculty earlier that year. Nikolaus played a leading role in that process, authoring the official "refutation" of Werner's positions.[11] That document was itself a substantial comment on superstition in general, but Nikolaus then wrote the far larger *On Superstitions*, a long and mostly theoretical treatise that aimed to provide a systematic statement on all aspects of superstitious beliefs and practices. The work was extremely influential, or at least extremely widely distributed, as it still survives in well over one hundred known manuscript copies produced during the remainder of the century.[12] It then appears to have been just as suddenly forgotten, for as the printing revolution swept over Europe, *On Superstitions* never found its way to press. Perhaps by the end of the 1400s, when printing began to take hold, intellectual authorities interested in such things had become sufficiently focused on witchcraft that Nikolaus's sprawling treatise on superstition in general provided little immediately useful information.[13] Earlier in the century, though, this work was clearly of great interest to a widespread readership.

Nikolaus of Jauer's biographer Adolph Franz noted that the Heidelberg theologian's treatise tapped into concerns at many German universities.[14] He missed one significant connection at Heidelberg itself, however, owing to his misdating of another important work on superstition, the Heidelberg theologian Johannes of Frankfurt's formal academic "question" *Whether the Power to Control Demons Can Be Achieved through Inscriptions, Figures, and the Utterance of Words* (*Quaestio utrum potestas cohercendi demones fieri possit per caracteres,*

---

and Publicity before Print: Jean Gerson and the Transformation of Late Medieval Learning (Philadelphia, 2009), 128–51.

10. Adolph Franz, *Der Magister Nikolaus Magni de Jawor: Ein Beitrag zur Literatur- und Gelehrtengeschichte des 14. und 15. Jahrhunderts* (Freiburg im/Br., 1898); Krzysztof Bracha, *Teolog, diabeł i zabobony: Świadectwo traktatu Mikołaja Magni z Jawora 'De superstitionibus' (1405 r.)* (Warsaw, 1999).

11. Franz, *Magister Nikolaus Magni*, 154; Lerner, "Werner di Friedberg," 269.

12. Franz, *Magister Nikolaus Magni*, 255–64, lists 58 manuscripts, which Bracha, *Teolog*, 216–21, more than doubles to 119. In a personal communication of February 26, 2012, Dr. Bracha indicated to me that he has now extended his list to 141 manuscripts.

13. Franz, *Magister Nikolaus Magni*, 191–92.

14. Ibid., 154–55, 160.

figuras atque verborum prolationes). Franz (and many scholars following him) dated this scholastic disputation on the power of demons and the capacity for human magicians to control them through various ritual means to 1412, whereas it appears to have occurred in early January 1405, just as Werner's case was beginning to unfold.[15] Perhaps the two events were directly connected, although there is no clear indication of this in any source. Theologians in Heidelberg could easily have been focusing on issues of demonic sorcery and superstition even before the bishop of Speyer's court laid a specific case at their feet. Johannes of Frankfurt was certainly an important figure at the university. Educated in Paris, he came to Heidelberg in 1401. Over the course of his life he served as a professor of theology, rector, and then vice-chancellor of the university. He also operated as an inquisitor against heresy in the upper Rhineland before dying in 1440.[16]

While Johannes's 1405 *Question* dealt with one important element of debate regarding superstition, namely the potential for humans to control demons via certain rites, about a decade later and somewhat further down the Rhine valley in Cologne, another treatise appeared dealing with another major aspect of this broad topic, the anonymous *On Divinations* (*De divinacionibus*), dating to around 1415. Almost certainly written by a theologian, the treatise may have been the work of the Cologne professor Dietrich of Münster.[17] Meanwhile, in the eastern part of the empire, the Austrian curate Ulrich of Pottenstein had already by this time discussed superstition in a vernacular exegesis of the Ten Commandments.[18] Others would follow in this vein. In 1423, the prominent Viennese theologian Nikolaus of Dinkelsbühl made it a focus of his treatise *On the Commandments of the Decalogue* (*De preceptis decalogi*), originally presented as a series of sermons.[19] Nikolaus had come to Vienna in 1385 to study under Heinrich of Langenstein, himself newly arrived from Paris. He would eventually become one of Langenstein's most important pupils and a

---

15. Among those following the earlier dating is, regrettably, Michael D. Bailey, *Magic and Superstition in Europe: A Concise History from Antiquity to the Present* (Lanham, Md., 2007), 127. On issues of textual dating, see appendix.

16. For basic biography, see Dorothea Walz et al., eds., *Zwölf Werke des Heidelberger Theologen und Inquisitors* (Heidelberg, 2000), ix–xxii.

17. *Quellen*, 82.

18. On Ulrich, see Gabriele Baptist-Hlawatsch, *Das katechetische Werk Ulrichs von Pottenstein: Sprachliche und rezeptionsgeschichtliche Untersuchungen* (Tübingen, 1980); Emilie Lasson, *Superstitions médiévales: Une analyse d'après l'exégèse du premier commandement d'Ulrich de Pottenstein* (Paris, 2010).

19. On Nikolaus, see Alois Madre, *Nikolaus von Dinkelsbühl Leben und Schriften: Ein Beitrag zur theologischen Literaturgeschichte* (Münster, 1965); Karin Baumann, *Aberglaube für Laien: Zur Programmatik und Überlieferung spätmittelalterlicher Superstitionenkritik*, 2 vols. (Würzburg, 1989), esp. 1:199–207.

key member of the so-called Vienna school of theologians and other clergy, for whom opposition to superstition was a matter of major importance.[20]

Another key member of the Vienna school was the Dominican Johannes Nider. Having studied at Cologne and then, in the mid-1420s, at Vienna, he served as prior of the Dominican convents in Nuremberg and then Basel before returning to Vienna as a professor of theology in 1434, where he remained until his death four years later. Best known as one of the major early theorists of witchcraft in the 1430s, Nider also dealt with superstition more generally, particularly in his Decalogue commentary, *Preceptor of Divine Law* (*Preceptorium divine legis*), written at the very end of his life in 1438.[21] Although heavily tinged with concern about witchcraft, this work can still reasonably be considered more a superstition treatise than a witchcraft one (although admittedly drawing distinctions of this kind is a bit silly, and would probably have befuddled Nider or any other writer of this period). A popular work in a popular genre, the *Preceptor* survives in over sixty known manuscript copies and went through five early printed editions.[22] At virtually the same time, in 1438 and 1439, another Vienna theologian, Thomas Ebendorfer, delivered a series of sermons that became yet another treatise *On the Ten Commandments* (*De decem preceptis*), as always addressing superstition as a violation of the first commandment's proclamation against idolatry.[23]

To return from Vienna to the Rhineland, and to turn back the clock slightly, around 1425 the Cologne theologian Heinrich of Gorkum wrote *On Certain Superstitious Occurrences* (*De superstitiosis quibusdam casibus*). A Dutchman (Hendrik van Gorinchem) born around 1378, Heinrich was educated in Paris. In 1419, however, he moved to Cologne, where he taught for the rest of his life, and, like Johannes of Frankfurt in Heidelberg, he served as rector and then vice-chancellor of his university.[24] Moving again to the east, in Leipzig we find the theologian Johannes of Wünschelburg (now Radków, Poland) writing a treatise again simply titled *On Superstitions* (*De superstitionibus*) at roughly the same time Johannes Nider and Thomas Ebendorfer were composing their

20. Baumann, *Aberglaube für Laien*, 1:201, 203. More fully on the Vienna school, see Lasson, *Superstitions médiévales*, 23–40.

21. On Nider, see Michael D. Bailey, *Battling Demons: Witchcraft, Heresy, and Reform in the Late Middle Ages* (University Park, Pa., 2003); Werner Tschacher, *Der Formicarius des Johannes Nider von 1437/38: Studien zu den Anfängen der europäischen Hexenverfolgungen im Spätmittelalter* (Aachen, 2000).

22. Thomas Kaeppeli, *Scriptores Ordinis Praedicatorum Medii Aevi,* 4 vols. (Rome, 1970–93), 2:507–8; Bailey, *Battling Demons*, 155.

23. See Alphons Lhotsky, *Thomas Ebendorfer: Ein österreichischer Geschichtschreiber, Theologe und Diplomat des 15. Jahrhunderts* (Stuttgart, 1957).

24. See A. G. Weiler, *Heinrich von Gorkum († 1431): Seine Stellung in der Philosophie und der Theologie des Spätmittelalters* (Hilversum, Neth., 1962).

treatises on the Ten Commandments in Vienna. Johannes of Wünschelburg was among the founding generation of the University of Leipzig, present there since at least 1409.[25] He probably wrote his superstition treatise in the later 1430s or in the 1440s. Also by the mid-1440s at the latest, another anonymous work *On Superstitions* had been composed, this time a short tract that survives in a single manuscript copy in Erlangen.[26]

Moving into the 1450s, the Zurich canon Felix Hemmerli wrote a series of short tracts over the space of several years dealing with common blessings and spells, exorcism, and the power of demons. A lawyer rather than a theologian, he had studied both at Erfurt in Germany and at the ancient legal center of Bologna in Italy.[27] Unlike so many of his theological colleagues, he exhibited a notably tolerant attitude toward common rites and practices. His position was basically, if the anachronism may be forgiven, innocent until proven guilty; that is, authorities should regard common practices as legitimate unless they exhibited clear evidence of diabolical involvement or other illicit components. Also at this time, in 1452, the Erfurt Carthusian Jakob of Paradise wrote a treatise *On the Power of Demons* (*De potestate demonum*) in which he addressed the various abilities that demons possessed and their role as the fundamental actors in most superstitious practices. Born near the town of Jüterbog, south of Berlin, Jakob was a Cistercian monk for several decades at the monastery of Paradise (hence his name) in Meseritz (Polish: Międzyrzecz), in the diocese of Posen. He studied and then taught theology at the University of Krakow in the 1430s and into the 1440s, until 1442 when he became a Carthusian in Erfurt. Like many members of that bookish order, he continued to write essentially academic works even after his withdrawal from university life.[28]

Another famous Carthusian, Denys of Rijkel, commonly known simply as Denys the Carthusian, wrote his treatise *Against the Vices of Superstitions* (*Contra vitia superstitionum*) also most likely around the midpoint of the fifteenth century. Early lists of his works compiled in the fifteenth and sixteenth centuries

25. The fullest biography is in *Die deutsche Literatur des Mittelalters: Verfasserlexikon*, 2nd ed., ed. Kurt Ruh, 14 vols. (Berlin, 1978–2008), 4:818–22.

26. My thanks to Jonathan Green, who told me of this work at an Alexander von Humboldt Foundation conference for fellows in Berlin in June 2007, and who subsequently provided images of the manuscript and a transcription.

27. For biography, see Catherine Chène, *Juger les vers: Exorcismes et procès d'animaux dans le diocese de Lausanne (XVe–XVIe s.)*, CLHM 14 (Lausanne, 1995), 23–30; Frank Fürbeth, *Heilquellen in der deutschen Wissensliteratur des Spätmittelalters: Zur Genese und Funktion eines Paradigmas der Wissensvermittlung am Beispiel des "Tractatus de balneis naturalibus" von Felix Hemmerli und seiner Rezeption, mit einer Edition des Textes und seiner frühneuhochdeutschen Übersetzung* (Wiesbaden, 2004), 109–24.

28. On Jakob, see Ludger Meier, *Die Werke des Erfurter Kartäusers Jakob von Jüterbog in ihrer handschriftlichen Überlieferung* (Münster, 1955); Dieter Mertens, *Iacobus Carthusiensis: Untersuchungen*

also show a treatise *Against Magic Arts and Errors of Waldensians* (*Contra artes magicas et errores waldensium*), but no copies are known to have survived.[29] Born in the Limburg region of what is now Belgium, he studied at Cologne in the early 1420s. While Denys was pursuing his arts degree, Heinrich of Gorkum, just then about to write his own treatise on superstition, was teaching theology at Cologne and it seems likely that their paths would have crossed.[30] Departing Cologne, he entered the Carthusian monastery at Roermond (in that part of his native Limburg now in the modern Netherlands) in 1424 or 1425, where he remained until his death in 1471. Denys became one of the most prolific writers of the late medieval period, advancing new ideas and transmitting the ideas of others. In *Against the Vices of Superstitions*, he drew explicitly and extensively on the work of William of Auvergne. He also cited "a certain master" who had likewise relied heavily on William.[31] This may well be a reference to Heinrich of Gorkum, although Heinrich was certainly not the only other fifteenth-century author dealing with superstition who cribbed from the great thirteenth-century Parisian master. An extensive anonymous treatise *On Superstitions*, composed no later than the 1450s and to all appearances of central European provenance, also structures a major portion of its commentary around William's ten categories of superstitious "idolatry."[32]

To this substantial list of theological and legal tracts and treatises we might also add the work of Johannes Hartlieb, court physician to the dukes of Bavaria in Munich in the mid-fifteenth century. Although a medical doctor, he was familiar with contemporary theological writings on superstition, and he was especially influenced by Thomas Aquinas. His work also manifested a pastoral bent, as he originally studied at Vienna before taking his medical degree at Padua in 1439, and he was clearly familiar with the Vienna school of practical, pastoral theology.[33] Beginning in 1456 he wrote, in the vernacular, his *Book of All Forbidden Arts* (*Buch aller verbotenen Künste*) as a warning to princes about the dangers of superstition. Working in a well-established genre, he held many

---

zur Rezeption der Werke des Kartäusers Jakob von Paradies (1381–1465) (Göttingen, 1976). Specifically regarding superstition, see Krzysztof Bracha, "Die Kritik des Aberglaubens, der Irrtümer und Mißbräuche im Kult bei Jacobus Cartusiensis," in *Bücher, Bibliotheken und Schriftkultur der Kartäuser: Festgabe zum 65. Geburtstag von Edward Potkowski*, ed. Sönke Lorenz (Stuttgart, 2002), 151–63.

29. Kent Emery, ed., *Dionysii Cartusiensis Opera Selecta*, CCCM 121–121a (Turnhout, 1991), 129.

30. Ibid., 16. On Denys's life, see ibid., 15–38; Dirk Wasserman, *Dionysius der Kartäuser: Einführung in Werk und Gedankenwelt* (Salzburg, 1996), 7–12.

31. Denys the Carthusian, *Contra vitia superstitionum*, 610.

32. Anonymous, *De superstitionibus* (M), 17r–51r.

33. Frank Fürbeth, *Johannes Hartlieb: Untersuchung zu Leben und Werk* (Tübingen, 1992), esp. 88–132.

elite, courtly magical practices up for censure, but addressed a number of common practices as well, including some discussion of witches and witchcraft.[34] Also among the outliers of this group we can include the Dominican Johannes Schwarz (also known by the Latinate version of his name, Johannes Nigri). Born in the Bohemian town of Kaaden, he entered the Dominican order in Nuremberg in 1452, studied briefly in Bologna, and served in the priories at Nuremberg and then Eichstätt before transferring to Regensberg in 1475. He obtained his degree in theology from the University of Ingolstadt (later to become the University of Munich) only in 1476, but already a decade earlier, in 1466, he had written a treatise *On Divinations* (*De divinacionibus*). Although slightly late for my purposes, since my focus here really falls on the first half of the fifteenth century, his work deserves attention not only in its own right but because of the degree to which Schwarz appears indebted to writers from earlier in the century. He began his treatise by quoting Nikolaus of Jauer's *On Superstitions*, and he also cited extensively from his fellow Dominican Johannes Nider.[35]

Another curious and more distant outlier who nevertheless can be appended at least tangentially to our group of "German" writers is the Pamplona archdeacon Martin of Arles. He wrote a treatise again simply titled *On Superstitions* likely at the very outset of the sixteenth century. Efforts to date this work are mostly speculative, with the only certain date being that provided by the first printed edition in Lyon in 1510. Much of the confusion has been due to this work's curiously Germanic content, despite its clearly northern-Iberian provenance. Martin began the treatise by explaining that his impetus for writing came from a colleague's question about the legitimacy of a popular rite performed near Pamplona, in which local clergy and villagers consecrated a statue of Saint Peter and carried it in a procession in order to implore God, through his saint, to send them rain.[36] He also indicated his Iberian context quite directly when, at one point, he stated that superstition was so prevalent in his day mainly because of the many "new Christians," that is, converted Jews and Muslims in the Iberian kingdoms.[37] Yet for all this, he also drew heavily on northern European superstition critiques, citing Jean Gerson and in particular Johannes Nider with great frequency. The fact that he drew so extensively from Nider, who wrote in the 1430s, but failed even to mention the infamous *Hammer of Witches* (*Malleus maleficarum*) of 1486 has led several

---

34. Several other works on divination, magic, or superstition are often attributed to Hartlieb, but Fürbeth, ibid., 49–75 and 130–32, questions his authorship of any of them.

35. Johannes Schwarz, *De divinacionibus*, 297v, 312r–v.

36. Martin of Arles, *De superstitionibus*, 1r–2r.

37. Ibid., 33r.

scholars to reason that he must have written sometime before that latter work appeared.[38] Such speculation is not terribly reliable for the purposes of dating a work, and the most reasonable supposition now appears to be that Martin wrote within a few years of 1500. Nevertheless, conceptually he can justifiably be linked to earlier northern critiques, and especially to the German context of the early fifteenth century.

These men produced a diverse array of works for a variety of audiences. While some helpfully announced exactly when, why, and for whom they wrote, often such basic facts remain obscure. Some obviously addressed a courtly audience, as had so many writers in fourteenth- and early fifteenth-century France. The clearest example of this in the German context is Johannes Hartlieb, who dedicated his *Book of All Forbidden Arts* to Johannes II, known as Johannes the Alchemist, margrave of Brandenburg-Kulmbach, a territory centered around the northern Bavarian city of Bayreuth.[39] Martin of Arles also, although he wrote directly at the request of a fellow clergyman, included in his treatise several warnings to princes to guard against superstitious error and to set a clear example for their subjects by punishing any superstition discovered in their territories.[40] The majority of these men wrote at universities and therefore, to varying degrees, for university audiences. Most obvious of this group would be Johannes of Frankfurt, working at Heidelberg, whose tract on demonic power and the possibility of controlling demons through various rites took the form of a traditional academic *quaestio*. Also at Heidelberg, Nikolaus of Jauer wrote the official *Refutation* of the errors of Werner of Friedberg, after the theological faculty had questioned the suspect friar and found his positions deserving of condemnation. He went on to compose his own treatise *On Superstitions*, and such a long and systematic work would seem primarily intended for other schoolmen, although its impressive circulation points to a broad and diverse readership.

Those who addressed superstition via sermons or commentaries on the Ten Commandments (or sermons that became Decalogue commentaries) worked in a thriving fifteenth-century genre.[41] They wrote immediately for their fellow clergymen but ultimately for the instruction of the laity, who could be expected to receive the lessons contained in these treatises through popular

---

38. See appendix.

39. Hartlieb, *Buch*, 16.

40. Martin of Arles, *De superstitionibus*, 59r, 60r.

41. Lasson, *Superstitions médiévales*, 56–62; Dieter Harmening, "Spätmittelalterliche Aberglaubenskritik in Dekalog- und Beichtliteratur," in *Volksreligion im hohen und späten Mittelalter*, ed. Peter Dinzelbacher and Dieter R. Bauer (Paderborn, 1990), 243–51. Baumann, *Aberglaube für Laien*, examines this genre most fully.

preaching, the mechanisms of confession, or other means of moral instruction. Such basic catechetical efforts, in which critiques of superstition played a clear role, formed a fundamental part of the "applied moral theology" pioneered by Gerson and championed by the influential Vienna school, of which our Decalogue authors Nikolaus of Dinkelsbühl, Johannes Nider, and Thomas Ebendorfer were all members.[42] Efforts to instruct the laity about superstition extended beyond commentaries on the first commandment, of course. Denys the Carthusian explicitly addressed his *Against the Vices of Superstitions* to parish clergy, whose task was then to "reprove, correct, and inform" the laity.[43] Johannes of Wünschelburg, in his *On Superstitions*, reprimanded "useless pastors" who failed to correct superstitious practices among their flocks. He also captured the underlying pastoral sentiment here rather more poetically in the very opening of this treatise, where he quoted the Song of Songs that "the time of pruning has come."[44] The image was ultimately a hopeful one: spring had come, and with it new flowers in the land, but first the dead matter of superstitious error needed to be cut away to allow for proper growth.

These men all firmly agreed that superstition should be cut off and uprooted. Yet amid the exuberant growth of late medieval piety and lay devotion, one could not always or easily tell the flowers from the weeds.[45] Thus arose Gerson's deep concern over how to promote vibrant lay devotion yet still guard against errors. Notable in the writings of this group of German authors is how often they focused on specific cases, yet again following a format set by Gerson. Even expansive treatises often stemmed from a particular case or question. Heinrich of Gorkum stated explicitly that he wrote his aptly titled *On Certain Superstitious Occurrences* to respond to specific examples of superstitious practice that had been brought to his attention.[46] Martin of Arles addressed a colleague's concern about the legitimacy of a local rainmaking rite. Even Nikolaus of Jauer wrote his exhaustive, mostly theoretical treatise *On Superstitions* in connection with the specific case of Werner of Friedberg. As much as these men worked to clarify these "occurrences" to their fellow theologians, parish clergy, and finally a broad audience of the laity, they also struggled to clarify for themselves exactly where and what boundaries needed

---

42. Baumann, *Aberglaube für Laien*, 1:14 and 1:32.

43. Denys the Carthusian, *Contra vitia superstitionum*, 599: "Pertinetque ad pastores ut illos [laicos] corripiant, corrigant et informant."

44. Johannes of Wünschelburg, *De superstitionibus*, 228r–v.

45. On the vibrancy of late medieval lay religiosity, see Duffy, *Stripping of the Altars*; the seminal study for German lands is Bernd Moeller, "Frömmigkeit in Deutschland um 1500," *Archiv für Reformationsgeschichte* 56 (1965): 3–31.

46. Heinrich of Gorkum, *De superstitiosis quibusdam casibus*, 1r.

to be drawn in the myriad rites and practices they saw all around them. They conformed to the parameters established by earlier authorities as much as they could, and stood on reasonably solid ground as they rehearsed yet again the standard positions on astrology, necromancy, and the like. Ultimately, however, the common spells, blessings, prayers, and charms of the laity they sought to instruct would leave them somewhat confounded.

Continuing Concerns

The tracts and treatises on superstition written in central Europe in the first half of the fifteenth century continued to discuss elite practices of astrology, astral magic, and demonic invocation in considerable detail. Indeed these remain the primary focus of many of these works. In the fourteenth century, though, authorities had often deployed the concept of superstition in the course of innovative arguments affecting broader understandings of religion or science, while most fifteenth-century writers were content to repeat pat and comfortable condemnations. Only rarely did they need to cite their immediate precursors, generally relying instead on the more deeply rooted authority of the church fathers or the great thirteenth-century scholastic systematizers. Since they mainly reiterated positions that we have already encountered, I want to survey their treatment of elite practices as expeditiously as possible while still giving a sense of what was, after all, a significant component of almost all of their writings.

Astrology remained an enormous area of concern for central European authorities, and they covered—often at great length—all the standard positions that we have seen explicated (and more aggressively debated) by earlier writers. They all acknowledged that astrology was at root a perfectly legitimate science, valuable for making some general predictions based on knowledge of natural causation and the calculation of astral influences. This was not so much divination as diagnosis, and, drawing on a comparison that appears to have originated with William of Auvergne, both Denys the Carthusian and Nikolaus of Jauer described legitimate astrologers as being like physicians who could predict the course of an illness by observing its symptoms in the human body.[47] Nikolaus, however, also compared medical doctors to demons, noting that just as physicians could read the course of a disease through a patient's symptoms, demons could often read sinful desires or other secrets of the human soul in telltale bodily signs or behaviors.[48]

---

47. Denys the Carthusian, *Contra vitia superstitionum*, 601; Nikolaus of Jauer, *De superstitionibus*, 50r. See also anonymous, *De superstitionibus* (M), 51v, 55v.
48. Nikolaus of Jauer, *De superstitionibus*, 37r.

Back in the realm of heavenly cause and effect, the basic adage for all these writers remained that astrologers might permissibly make general predictions about anything caused fairly directly by astral emanations. The favored example was always the weather. Since the force of the stars was believed to operate very directly on the atmosphere, astrologers could legitimately offer meteorological forecasts. Likewise the flight of birds or the behavior of any animals naturally attuned to atmospheric changes could be used to similar effect. The Carthusian Jakob of Paradise wrote explicitly that when astrologers predicted the weather, they were acting exactly like physicians diagnosing a disease.[49] Such predictions could never be completely certain, because countless other factors impinged on any specific event, but so long as astrologers acknowledged their limitations, they could avoid the taint of superstition. Absolutely illicit and unforgivable was any attempt to foresee specific human actions or to predict any events that depended on human volition, since this seemed to trample on the notion of free will. Here authorities frequently targeted those astrologers specialized in drawing natal horoscopes, although the critics of such practices themselves generally admitted that the physical bodies of newborn babes were particularly impressionable, and moreover that the stars continually acted on human bodies throughout life, creating physical urges and inclination that could sway the weak-minded and the carnal.[50]

Ignoring the more skeptical or scientifically minded critiques of astrology from the fourteenth century, most authorities now warned stridently about the threat of demons entering into erroneous astrological practices, corrupting them even more terribly, and leading astray both those who offered and those who accepted any kind of astrological divination. Wondering how astrologers so often made correct predictions in areas that completely exceeded the natural capacities of their craft, for example, Denys the Carthusian warned that they could do so only "because, so it is said, demons often meddle in the more excessive, prying inquiries of astrologers."[51] Nikolaus of Jauer noted that although many kinds of astrological rites did not appear to invoke or rely on

---

49. Jakob of Paradise, *De potestate demonum*, 263r.

50. Anonymous, *De divinacionibus* 168r–v; anonymous, *De superstitionibus* (M), 55v, 63v–64v, 68v–69v; Denys the Carthusian, *Contra vitia superstitionum*, 614, 618–19; Heinrich of Gorkum, *De superstitiosis quibusdam casibus*, 1r; Jakob of Paradise, *De potestate demonum*, 264v–265v; Johannes of Wünschelburg, *De superstitionibus*, 237r; Schwarz, *De divinacionibus*, 305r; Nider, *Preceptorium* 1.11.36(rr), 1.11.38(tt), 1.11.40(xx); Nikolaus of Jauer, *De superstitionibus*, 40r, 53r–v, 61r; Ulrich of Pottenstein, *Dekalog-Auslegung*, 85–86.

51. Denys the Carthusian, *Contra vitia superstitionum*, 615: "Quia (vt dictum est) curiosis inquisitionibus astrologorum immiscent frequenter se daemones." See also anonymous, *De superstitionibus* (M), 65r; Jakob of Paradise, *De potestate demonum*, 264v; Nider, *Preceptorium* 1.11.39(vv).

demons explicitly, nevertheless they did so tacitly, "on account of which the demons secretly obtrude themselves" into these practices.[52] They might impart preternaturally obtained information to querying astrologers, or they might themselves simply cause the events that astrologers believed that they had foreseen in the heavens. In fact, as Nikolaus went on to observe, given the limited range of purely natural astral influences on the earth and the great difficulties inherent in accurately calculating astral movements or the effects of astral energies, the stars actually held very little predictive power on their own.[53]

As with astrological prognostication, so astral magic enjoyed some limited possibilities for legitimate use, but the concern that astral rites might mask demonic invocations overshadowed all of these. Authorities typically maintained that certain substances had natural affinities with, and could therefore attract or focus, particular celestial emanations.[54] Thus various amulets, rings, stones, or gems might exhibit certain wondrous but still entirely natural properties. Any implication that human actions could augment the natural capacities of basic substances, however, entailed superstition, and authorities were therefore leery of items shaped into any kind of symbolic form, or fashioned at particular times or under specific astral signs.[55] Relying mainly on arguments derived from Thomas Aquinas and William of Auvergne, fifteenth-century writers maintained that such ritually crafted items served primarily as a means of concourse with demons. Sometimes deceitful spirits inhabited rings or mirrors, or spoke from statues or images.[56] This was hardly a new allegation. At the beginning of the fourteenth century, enemies of Pope Boniface VIII had declared that the pontiff had bound a demon into a ring that he always wore, and the basic Christian notion of demons inhabiting statues extended fully back to the fifth century, when Augustine had contended that malign spirits often resided in pagan idols, animating them and causing them to speak and prophesy.[57] More often the communication went in the other direction, however, and authorities were convinced that any kind of writing or symbols inscribed on astral images must secretly invoke

---

52. Nikolaus of Jauer, *De superstitionibus*, 50v: "Et habet sub se multas species in quibus licet non fiet expresse demonum vocacio sit tamen tacita, propter quam demones ingerant se occulte." See also ibid., 40v, 53v, 54v.

53. Ibid., 52v.

54. Heinrich of Gorkum, *De superstitiosis quibusdam casibus*, 3v; Martin of Arles, *De superstitionibus*, 15v–16r.

55. Anonymous, *De divinacionibus*, 170v–171r.

56. Anonymous, *De superstitionibus* (M), 30r.

57. Jean Coste, ed., *Boniface VIII en procès: Articles d'accusation et depositions des témoins (1303–1311)* (Rome, 1995), 281–84; Augustine, *De civitate dei* 8:23, ed. Bernard Dombart and Alphonse Kalb, CCSL 47–48 (Turnhout, 1955).

and supplicate demonic spirits.[58] While some magicians claimed to command demons by virtue of arcane figures and formulas, authorities responded that mere characters and signs possessed no power of that sort.[59] An even more basic argument was that the stars exerted no natural influence over spiritual beings, and so images supposedly deriving their power from the stars could not compel demons in any way.[60]

The possibility previously evident at least among certain intellectual authorities that discussion of astrological superstitions might focus on natural errors rather than demonic menace had faded with Gerson, and it is entirely absent from the works of these central European writers. Instead, following the more traditional course of Christian authorities since the time of the fathers, they concerned themselves, when addressing superstition, very directly with issues of demonic presence and power. Applying a description of Leviathan from the book of Job to Satan and his minions, several of them declared that "there is no power on earth that can be compared to him."[61] They relished describing the might of demons, although in cataloging demonic powers, they again relied on long-standing tradition. From Augustine they drew the notion that, while demons could not know the future per se, they could often correctly deduce future events due to their extensive knowledge and experience.[62] Demons also understood and could employ all the forces in nature, both patent and occult. Most basic was their capacity, although spirits themselves, to cause movement in matter. They could stir storms, bring disease, or agitate and unbalance the humors of the human body.[63] Like the stars in the heavens, demons could not overcome human free will, but by affecting the body they could "incline" weak-willed people to certain actions.[64]

Such recitations of demonic power helped buttress the conclusion that mere humans could never control the might of demons or harness it for legitimate

---

58. Anonymous, *De divinacionibus*, 174r; anonymous, *De superstitionibus* (M), 31v–32r; Jakob of Paradise, *De potestate demonum*, 259v; Nikolaus of Jauer, *De superstitionibus*, 48v; Nider, *Preceptorium* 1.11.23(dd); Martin of Arles, *De superstitionibus*, 16v.

59. Johannes of Frankfurt, *Quaestio*, 73, 78; Jakob of Paradise, *De potestate demonum*, 251r.

60. Anonymous, *De divinacionibus*, 181r; anonymous, *De superstitionibus* (M), 39r–v; Nikolaus of Jauer, *De superstitionibus*, 43r.

61. Johannes of Frankfurt, *Quaestio*, 72; Schwarz, *De divinacionibus*, 307r; Nider, *Preceptorium* 1.11.28(ii); Nikolaus of Jauer, *De superstitionibus*, 42r.

62. Anonymous, *De superstitionibus* (M), 56v–57r; Felix Hemmerli, *De credulitate*, 112v; Jakob of Paradise, *De potestate demonum*, 247r–v; Schwarz, *De divinacionibus*, 299r; Nikolaus of Jauer, *De superstitionibus*, 39r–v; Nider, *Preceptorium* 1.9(g); Ulrich of Pottenstein, *Dekalog-Auslegung*, 93–95.

63. Denys the Carthusian, *Contra vitia superstitionum*, 608; Jakob of Paradise, *De potestate demonum*, 246r–v, 251v; Johannes of Frankfurt, *Quaestio*, 72; Nikolaus of Jauer, *De superstitionibus*, 44r.

64. Hartlieb, *Buch*, 20; Jakob of Paradise, *De potestate demonum*, 257r–v; Nikolaus of Jauer, *De superstitionibus*, 35r–36r, 38r–v; Schwarz, *De divinacionibus*, 300r.

ends. As noted above, authorities insisted that the energies of the stars could not affect or sway demons. Neither could herbs, gems, or any natural substances control them, nor could spoken words, written characters, or ritual actions compel them in any way, although they might feign submission in order to fool unwary humans and lure them into superstitious actions.[65] In making these contentions, our central European writers were particularly concerned to explain away the account in the book of Tobit in which the angel Raphael taught Tobit's son, also called Tobit, to drive away demons by burning the heart or liver of a fish (Tobit 6). This seemed to imply that some natural substances did indeed exert power over demons, and worse still, to late medieval writers it smacked of the sort of ritual immolation and suffumigation that necromancers frequently performed. Nicolau Eymerich had addressed the issue briefly in his treatise *Against Invokers of Demons*, but in the fifteenth century a number of our central European writers sought to explain this account.[66] The explanation, of course, was always that, despite all appearances in the story, the ritual burning and certainly the physical substance of the fish were powerless over demons, and instead young Tobit was protected by divine grace. Only Jakob of Paradise offered an interesting addendum. Building on the story of Tobit, he discussed various materials—mainly herbs, but also stones, and even human urine used in some magical ceremonies—that supposedly compelled demons. None possessed such power, he asserted, but demons did have cause to despise any herbs that were naturally healthful or beneficial to humans. One could not use these herbs to exert real command over them, but demons might nonetheless be repelled simply because of how much they "hated" these plants.[67]

Quirky natural antipathies aside, the only reason demons ever cooperated with or appeared to obey human conjurers, our fifteenth-century writers echoed centuries of church tradition in asserting, was because of pacts made between them. Such pacts could of course be tacit as well as express, conse-

---

65. Anonymous, *De superstitionibus* (M), 39v, 43v; Hartlieb, *Buch*, 36; Johannes of Frankfurt, *Quaestio*, 78–79; Jakob of Paradise, *De potestate demonum*, 251r, 259v, 270v; Nikolaus of Jauer, *De superstitionibus*, 42v.

66. Eymerich, *Contra demonum invocatores*, 158v. Then in the fifteenth century: anonymous, *De divinacionibus*, 177r; anonymous, *De superstitionibus* (M), 34v, 44v; Jakob of Paradise, *De potestate demonum*, 270r; Johannes of Frankfurt, *Quaestio*, 72, 81; Nikolaus of Jauer, *De superstitionibus*, 42v; Schwarz, *De divinacionibus*, 307r.

67. Jakob of Paradise, *De potestate demonum*, 270v: "Et quidam dictum esse de herbis et aliis que fugant demones, racio est quia odiunt omnia que sciunt esse hominibus salubria. Ideo creditur fugere a bethonica quia habet magnas virtutes hominibus utiles. Licet nec hec herba nec alia cogat demones recedere, tamen demones per se fugiunt ex odio istarum herbarum."

crated by even seemingly innocuous rites.[68] The one exception to this dire conviction lay in all Christians' capacity to exorcise demons in Christ's name, so long as they sought only to expel malevolent spirits, never to compel them into any kind of service.[69] Above all, the faithful must avoid any "fellowship" (*societas*) with demons, which was, of course, Augustine's ancient stricture. Nor did these writers admit any possibility of spiritual magic that was not essentially demonic. The notory art, for example, held by its practitioners to be angelic or theurgic, they uniformly condemned as demonic and superstitious.[70] Given the wiles of demons and their capacity to act covertly, few practices indeed must have seemed entirely secure to the most suspicious authorities. If even educated men could succumb to error and superstition in elite arts, the common laity were surely even more vulnerable.

New Concerns, New Complexities

That (mostly) clerical authors would condemn superstitious practices as demonic is hardly shocking. Neither is the fact that significant confusion prevailed over the exact boundaries between demonic superstitions and legitimate devotions. Fifteenth-century writers probably felt some affinity with Augustine and his struggles against deeply rooted pagan practices as they endeavored to convince people—princes, clergy, the general laity—of the range and scope of demonic power, and to warn them that seemingly beneficial rites might be riddled with dangerous error. As beholden to the past as they were, however, these men also recognized their distance from it. Nikolaus of Jauer, for instance, noted how rites that were perfectly permissible among ancient pagans, because of their ignorance of proper religion, were now proscribed for Christians.[71] The author of an anonymous central European treatise *On Superstitions* carried this thinking a step further, stating that even some forms of Christian prayer or exorcism that had been effective and legitimate in

---

68. Anonymous, *De superstitionibus* (M), 4r, 32v; Denys the Carthusian, *Contra vitia superstitionum*, 613–14; Johannes of Frankfurt, *Quaestio*, 80; Johannes of Wünschelburg, *De superstitionibus*, 231r; Nikolaus of Dinkelsbühl, *De preceptis decalogi*, 27v; Schwarz, *De divinacionibus*, 317r.

69. Anonymous, *De superstitionibus* (M), 60r; Jakob of Paradise, *De potestate demonum*, 259v–260r; Johannes of Frankfurt, *Quaestio*, 71–72; Nider, *Preceptorium* 1.11.29(kk); Nikolaus of Jauer, *De superstitionibus*, 48r–v.

70. Anonymous, *De superstitionibus* (M), 33r–34r; Denys the Carthusian, *Contra vitia superstitionum*, 600, 622; Jakob of Paradise, *De potestate demonum*, 262r–v; Johannes of Frankfurt, *Quaestio*, 80–81; Johannes of Wünschelburg, *De superstitionibus*, 231r; Nider, *Preceptorium* 1.11.43(zz); Nikolaus of Jauer, *De superstitionibus*, 56r.

71. Nikolaus of Jauer, *De superstitionibus*, 55v.

the age of the primitive church could no longer be condoned.[72] Underlying such arguments was a basic position widely held by medieval churchmen that flamboyant expulsions of demons, astonishing healings, and the whole panoply of wondrous acts regularly performed by early Christian saints had been appropriate in that heroic age, as the church struggled to establish itself and the truth of its message in a thoroughly pagan world, but had become unnecessary in the more humdrum present.[73] God no longer sanctioned them, and so if they still appeared to occur one must suspect demonic rather than divine power at work.

In no sense were late medieval writers attempting to craft a truly historicized analysis of superstition. Instead, by recognizing some degree of change over time, they sought to construct a bulwark against arguments defending and indeed valorizing what they regarded as dangerously superstitious practices by pointing to seemingly similar effects achieved by early Christian holy men. Jakob of Paradise wrote specifically of the practice of exorcism (problematic, as we have repeatedly seen, precisely because of its indisputable biblical foundation) that exorcisms in the time of Christ and the apostles were quite different from contemporary ones, or at least existed in a very different context, "because this time is no longer a time of performing miracles."[74]

Leaving aside the great divide separating the primitive from the late medieval church, we can recognize a much more recent shift in debate about wondrous acts and powerful rites. While in the fifteenth century writers continued to deploy many of the basic arguments and principles regarding superstition evident already in the fourteenth century (and earlier), the scope of their concern had become more comprehensive. Either at particular points or pervasively in their works, they now all regularly addressed common practices, most often those used to heal illness or injury. Nikolaus of Jauer and Johannes of Wünschelburg both mentioned common rites to reduce fevers, for example, and Johannes indicated a particular remedy by which people invoked Christ's wounds. Other writers mentioned rites against toothache, which sometimes involved elements of prayer or gargling with holy water. Still others mentioned

---

72. Anonymous, *De superstitionibus* (M), 39r: "Licet verba oratoria uel exorcisatoria recta intencione dicta frequenter consecuta fuit effectus corporales in primitiua ecclesia, non tamen oportet regulariter sic fieri tempore pro presenti."

73. Johannes of Wünschelburg, *De superstitionibus*, 252v; echoed in the English work *Dives and Pauper*, ed. Priscilla Heath Barnum, 3 vols., EETS 275, 280, 323 (London, 1976, 1980, 2004), 1:209–10.

74. Jakob of Paradise, *De potestate demonum*, 270r: "Quia hoc tempus non esse tempus miraculorum faciendorum."

remedies for sore eyes or backaches.[75] In Zurich, the lawyer Felix Hemmerli dedicated an entire tract to defending a vernacular incantation meant to heal cows suffering some kind of throat ailment, and he also approved of common charms to relieve animals of worms.[76] Writing in an opposite bent, Johannes of Wünschelburg criticized the notion of curing horses of worms by muttering in their ears or by hanging charms around their necks.[77] Protective rites often focused on warding off dangerous animals such as wolves and serpents, but also caterpillars, insects, and mice, which might harm crops or food stores.[78] Heinrich of Gorkum described an elaborate protective rite in which a pig's shoulder blade was placed on an altar and the four Gospels were read over it, thereby supposedly charging it with broad power to shield people "from perils at sea and from bodily harm, from robbers and from all misfortunes."[79] He also mentioned superstitious rites intended to spark passionate love between two people, although without going into any interesting detail, and Nikolaus of Jauer discussed rites meant to arouse either love or discord between spouses.[80]

Practices such as these were in most ways worlds apart from those of court astrologers or astral magicians who walked the fine line between natural science and superstitious error, or of clerical necromancers who deliberately incorporated elements of prayer, liturgy, or even official exorcism into elaborate demonic invocations. The writers who addressed superstition in the early fifteenth century, however, could not openly confront the expanded horizons of their concern. For them superstition was, and had to be, basically perennial, founded as it was on the unwavering hostility and deceitfulness of the church's eternal demonic foes. Thus they moved unhesitatingly from elite to common practices, recognizing no real distinctions, and applying the same basic strictures and frames of analysis to both.

---

75. Anonymous, *De superstitionibus* (E), 176r (eyes); Denys the Carthusian, *Contra vitia superstitionum*, 612 (toothache); Thomas Ebendorfer, *De decem praeceptis*, 7 (toothache); Johannes of Wünschelburg, *De superstitionibus*, 232v–233r (fever, toothache, backache); Nikolaus of Jauer, *De superstitionibus*, 56v (fever and toothache).

76. Hemmerli, *De exorcismis*, spell at 103v: "Ob das sy das Maria magt oder iungfrow eyn kindt Jesum gebar, so kumme disem thier das blatt ab, in namen des vatters, etc." Against worms: Hemmerli, *Tractatus exorcismorum*, 110r.

77. Johannes of Wünschelburg, *De superstitionibus*, 233v.

78. Anonymous, *De superstitionibus* (E), 176r; Hartlieb, *Buch*, 76; Hemmerli, *Tractatus exorcismorum*, 109v–110r; Johannes of Wünschelburg, *De superstitionibus*, 232v, 233r, 235v.

79. Heinrich of Gorkum, *De superstitiosis quibusdam casibus*, 3r–v: ". . . virtutem preseruandi homines a periculis maris et ab inimicis corporalibus scilicet raptoribus et ab omnibus infortuniis."

80. Ibid., 1v; Nikolaus of Jauer, *De superstitionibus*, 45v.

To evoke the important shift occurring underneath all the traditional critiques of superstition in these texts, let me relate two stories of demonic treachery. In his 1405 *Question* concerning whether demons could be controlled or manipulated by certain rites, Johannes of Frankfurt related an exemplary tale redolent of the world of elite, courtly necromancy. A certain bishop had taken up the magic arts for the material "honors" they could confer. Having thus gained wealth and power, however, he also acquired many enemies, who eventually besieged his castle. He summoned his attendant demon and asked whether he should flee the coming assault. The demon responded, so the bishop thought, "No, stand fast, your enemies will come meekly and will be subject to you." His foes successfully stormed the castle, however, captured the bishop, and ultimately burned him at the stake. Before his execution, he again conjured his demonic servant and demanded to know how its prediction had been so terribly wrong. The creature explained that the bishop simply had not understood properly, for it had actually said, "Don't stand fast, your enemies will come thrice in strength and will set a fire beneath you." The alternate meaning emerged from several twists in the Latin so abstruse that their finer points had to be explained in the text itself.[81] Possibly this intricate play on Latin grammar and vocabulary had them rolling in the ecclesiastical aisles of a university town like Heidelberg, but the story's impact would have been quite literally lost in translation if any parish clergyman sought to use it as a sobering tale to warn his parishioners away from magical entanglements with demons.

Half a century later, the Zurich canon Felix Hemmerli told a tale of demonic deception in a rather different vein in his tract *On Showing Credulity to Demons* (*De credulitate demonibus adhibenda*). A certain parish priest enjoyed fornicating quite "ardently" with the wives of his parishioners, until finally the cuckolded husbands drove him from their village. While wandering terrified in some nearby woods, he encountered a "wise monk" who was, of course, the devil in disguise. Inquiring into his problems, the monk noted that if only the priest no longer possessed his "wicked member," he could safely return home. At the monk's instruction, the priest lifted his clothes, the monk touched his penis, and immediately it disappeared. The priest then returned to his village where, eager to proclaim his newfound irreproachability, he rang the church

---

81. Johannes of Frankfurt, *Quaestio*, 79; discussed in Richard Kieckhefer, *Magic in the Middle Ages* (Cambridge, 1989), 174. Instead of "Non, sta secure, venient inimici tui suaviter et subdentur tibi," the demon claimed to have said "Non sta secure, venient inimici tui sua vi ter et subdent ur tibi." The text clarifies that *sua vi ter* meant *trina vice sua fortitudine* (literally: thrice in their strength); that the obscure *subdent* (from *subdere*, literally meaning "to submit oneself," and therefore figuratively "to place under") meant the more common *subponent* (to place beneath); and that *ur*, an invented noun derived from the verb *urere* (to burn), meant *ignem* (fire).

bell to gather a crowd. Standing before his parishioners at the communion rail, he again raised his vestments, and, of course, there was his penis, completely visible and "in even greater fullness than before."[82] Hemmerli's account ends at this point. One assumes that the men of the priest's village were not amused, but most people who heard the tale probably were, as well as being memorably instructed in the dangers of demonic deceit and the lack of lasting benefit to be gained from dabbling in any kind of superstitious sorcery. The story also obviously foreshadowed Heinrich Kramer's more famous accounts three decades later in the *Hammer of Witches* of witches stealing penises, sometimes keeping as many as twenty or thirty of them in a chest or hiding them in birds' nests. Invariably the larger ones always belonged to parish clergymen.[83]

These accounts by Johannes of Frankfurt and Felix Hemmerli are at one level identical: both highlight the inherent deceitfulness of demons and the inevitably bad end met by anyone who traffics with them. Obviously, however, at another level the stories could not be more different, and they aimed at quite different audiences, as indicated by the main character in each. While both victims of demonic deception were clergymen, the bishop was clearly of high status and presumably well educated. He succumbed to his demon's ruse not because of bad Latin on his part, but because of the creature's own ornate linguistic chicanery. The randy priest of Hemmerli's account, on the other hand, was a bumbling fool, no wiser to the devil's frauds than the laity he was supposed to instruct. Yet at a theoretical level, his guilt was the same as the necromancer bishop's, thanks to the notion of tacit pacts and of potential tacit invocations of demons. And if the devil could ensnare corrupt clergy, he could also certainly capture laypeople through corrupted uses of church rites.

Writers addressing superstition in fifteenth-century central Europe were particularly troubled by the potential misuse of prayer or its incorporation into superstitious acts. Not that this was a new concern. Johannes of Frankfurt clearly echoed Nicolau Eymerich, for example, when he condemned learned necromancers for using elements of prayer in their rituals and invocations and then claiming that this proved their actions were pious. In fact demons reveled in the degradation of legitimate prayer.[84] At a more quotidian level, Denys the Carthusian worried about the widespread practice of uttering prayers while

---

82. Hemmerli, *De credulitate*, 112r: "Stans in cancellis et confidenter eleuatis vestimentis, mox membrum suum abundantius quam prius apparuit."

83. Kramer, *Malleus* 2.1.7, pp. 428–34. The connection to Hemmerli's story is noted in Hans Peter Broedel, *The Malleus Maleficarum and the Construction of Witchcraft: Theology and Popular Belief* (Manchester, 2003), 45. On the humor here, see introduction, n. 6.

84. Johannes of Frankfurt, *Quaestio*, 76–77.

gathering medicinal herbs. He noted that prayer in this context had nothing to do with properly honoring God. Nevertheless, he agreed with numerous other authorities that people might permissibly say the Lord's Prayer or Apostles' Creed, and those two prayers alone, while collecting herbs.[85] The reason for this uniform exception was that canon law had explicitly sanctioned this use of these prayers for nearly a millennium.[86] Yet fifteenth-century authors dwelled on the use and misuse of prayer at greater length and in more varied contexts than had earlier been the case, and they struggled to define the exact parameters of permissible uses.

Thomas Ebendorfer noted that the Lord's Prayer and Apostles' Creed could drive away demons, and so presumably could relieve any illness or suffering that demons had caused, but he lamented that people often combined legitimate prayer with many "vain and stupid observances" in their efforts to cure common fevers, headaches, toothaches, or other ailments. Those saying a prayer might enfold their thumb in their hand, or otherwise conceal their fingers in a ritual gesture, or pray while walking backward around a church. Such extraneous elements had no bearing on "divine reverence" and so, drawing on the authority of the same decree in canon law that validated the proper use of these prayers when picking medicinal herbs, Ebendorfer asserted that any such addition "ought to be judged superstitious."[87] There can be little doubt that many people in the early fifteenth century sought to augment the effectiveness of official prayers in many ways, as they had no doubt done throughout Christian history. The English poem *Dives and Pauper* (Rich Man and Poor Man) condemned just as did church officials and theologians any rite or formula used to heal "but it be Pater noster, Ave, or þe crede or holy wordis of þe gospel" alone.[88] The French vernacular *Distaff Gospels* noted that people could treat fevers by writing the first three words of the Lord's Prayer on sage leaves and eating these on three consecutive mornings.[89]

---

85. Denys the Carthusian, *Contra vitia superstitionum*, 603. Also Johannes of Wünschelburg, *De superstitionibus*, 235r; Nikolaus of Jauer, *De superstitionibus*, 59v; Ulrich of Pottenstein, *Dekalog-Auslegung*, 105.

86. We have encountered this sanction in Burchard of Worm's eleventh-century *Decretum* (see chap. 1, n. 63), but such decrees are traceable as early as the sixth-century Second Council of Braga. See José Vives, ed., in collaboration with Tomás Marín Martínez and Gonzalo Martínez Díez, *Concilios Visigóticos e Hispano-Romanos* (Barcelona, 1963), 27. The standard canon law citation became C. 26, q. 5, c. 3; see Emil Friedberg, ed., *Corpus Iuris Canonici*, 2 vols. (1879–81; repr., Graz, 1955), 1:1028.

87. Ebendorfer, *De decem praeceptis*, 7: "Hoc tamen debet judicari superstitiosum, sicut 26 q. 5 Non liceat."

88. Anonymous, *Dives and Pauper*, 1:158.

89. Anonymous, *Évangiles* 6.7, p. 178.

In addition to canonical prayers included in suspicious rites, special prayers intended to heal particular ailments also proliferated in the late medieval period, which would have disquieted concerned authorities. A Latin book of hours produced for English merchants in Bruges, for example, contained a formula that could have been judged superstitious on several counts. Its heading reads: "A good prayer for fevers through the thousand names of the Lord." Then follows a string of nonsense words, "Theobald quith et quth Kanai," which authorities would have feared concealed a demonic invocation. Ostensibly the prayer was directed against wicked demons. Its actual opening read: "Through the truth of our Lord Jesus Christ, may all malignant spirits flee from me. In the name of my Lord Jesus Christ sign me + with this sign + AΩ." But its complex and ritualized formula (it continues for several more paragraphs) would have raised yet more concern. It was followed in the manuscript by a prayer to Mary for general benefaction, but before the Latin text itself, a rubric in English instructed people to say the prayer while holding "certain alms" in their hands.[90]

For all their suspicious elements, however, we should note that the prayers above were included in a pious devotional handbook, not a condemned necromantic text. Far from being consigned to the flames along with its owners, this book, which contained a number of other such "quasi-magical material," passed from the markets of Bruges to a respectable gentry family in Middlesex.[91] Despite fretting over the potential for superstition, many theologians and other clerical authorities chose to emphasize the positive value of proper prayer, both in terms of the devotion it encouraged and for more immediately salubrious effects as well. Certainly this was true of our central European writers. The author of an anonymous treatise *On Superstitions* held that "it is licit to say the holy words" of the Lord's Prayer, Apostles' Creed, and Ave Maria, because they could drive away demons and so might help cure any number of injuries and afflictions.[92] Johannes Nider felt that writing the Creed or Lord's Prayer on a slip of paper and laying this on a sick person was perfectly legitimate, as did Ulrich of Pottenstein. Ulrich also suggested that people could wear similar charms around their necks, so long as they did so in reverence of God, and did not believe that fashioning the amulets into any particular shape, for example folding them into triangles as was apparently sometimes done, would contribute to their effectiveness.[93] Although authori-

---

90. Eamon Duffy, *Marking the Hours: English People and Their Prayers 1240–1570* (New Haven, Conn., 2004), 91–92.

91. Ibid., 83–93.

92. Anonymous, *De superstitionibus* (M), 34v: "Aliqua sacra verba licitum est dicere que eciam efficacia sunt ad effectus corporales ut ad sanandum infirmos expellendos demones."

93. Nider, *Preceptorium* 1.9(e); Ulrich of Pottenstein, *Dekalog-Auslegung*, 105, 107.

ties had condemned such ligatures, especially those worn around the neck, as superstitious since the time of Augustine, a venerable Christian tradition of approved and powerful textual amulets also existed. No less a figure than the sainted Francis of Assisi had written protective prayers on a parchment that he then gave to his close companion Brother Leo, advising him to keep the amulet on his person for the rest of his life. Even after Leo's death in 1271, the so-called *chartula* retained its power. The great Franciscan theologian Bonaventure (who himself died in 1274) reported that it continued to perform healings, ultimately taking on the aura of a holy relic.[94]

If even the proclamation of Saint Augustine did not suffice for unproblematic condemnation, however, neither did the precedent of Saint Francis allow for complete confidence in any particular practice's legitimacy. Johannes of Wünschelburg was among the more suspicious authorities when he wondered whether it was ever licit for anyone "to carry such written words about one's person, or even to say the Our Father or Hail Mary over the sick."[95] Yet even he allowed that there was typically some possibility of legitimate use. Frustratingly for the historian struggling to understand where and how he drew his boundaries, he ultimately settled on a simple tautology. Drawing on William of Auvergne, he acknowledged that prayer or indeed any kind of spoken healing rite (*carminare* was his term, here meaning "to recite an incantation") might be used licitly "if nothing superstitious is said or done."[96] He then doubled back to suspicion, however, warning that such practices often provided an "occasion for scandal and abuse among simple people," and so, again, they should be forbidden. Whatever their disagreements over specific practices or their vacillating points of emphasis, fifteenth-century writers did agree on one fundamental principle. People must never believe that prayers themselves produced any automatic effects simply through the ritual act of their recitation. Rather, one needed to have faith in God, show this faith through prayer, and then wait for divine power to act in response.[97] This was solid theology, but offered little practical pastoral guidance in terms of actually judging specific cases.

A whole gamut of religious rites raised similar problems for anxious authorities. Like prayer, another protection from demonic assault was exorcism.

94. Don C. Skemer, *Binding Words: Textual Amulets in the Middle Ages* (University Park, Pa., 2006), 172–77.

95. Johannes of Wünschelburg, *De superstitionibus*, 235r: "Sed dubitatur . . . an liceat aliqua verba scripta circa se portare vel eciam super infirmos dicere pater noster vel ave maria."

96. Ibid.: ". . . quod liceat super pueros aut super infirmos carminare si nichil supersticiosum dicatur vel fiat."

97. Nikolaus of Dinkelsbühl, *Der Herrengebetskommentar des Nikolaus von Dinkelsbühl: Deutsche Übersetzung nach der textkritischen lateinischen Ausgabe*, trans. Rudolf Damerau (Giessen, 1972), 3–6.

Legitimized by Christ's own promise to the faithful, authorities could hardly deny its effect or condemn its practice. We have seen how concerned many became to hem in the permissible applications of exorcism, limited solely to the expulsion of demons without the potential for any kind of broader command. Now authorities also worried about proper understanding of the power behind exorcism. They would have meant, here, not just an official ecclesiastical ceremony but any effort to drive away demons in Christ's name. As with prayer, no automatic force clung to the specific words or rites that might be used. When exorcism worked, it did so because divine power had chosen to respond to a pious supplication.[98] Some authorities also began to stress reasons why exorcisms could fail. Johannes Nider maintained that either the exorcist himself could lack sufficient faith, or those presenting the possessed person for exorcism and witnessing the rite could lack faith, or the demoniac could be especially sinful (and so deserving of demonic affliction). Further, a rite might fail if other "appropriate remedies" such as prayer or fasting had not already been tried, or, finally, if hope for a cure had already been placed "in the powers of another." This implied that the possessed had been brought to some kind of healer or sorcerer (or sorcerer-healer) who would have used superstitious rites to attempt a cure.[99]

The cross and the sign of the cross were ubiquitous symbols of Christ and his church. Most directly, they symbolized his triumph over death and over hell's grip on humanity. Like prayer, they often served as a means for expressing and channeling his power against the dark threat of demons. Yet the cross was even more fraught with potential for superstition than were prayer or the rites of exorcism, for the cross as an object might slip from being a focal point for proper piety to become a false idol, worshipped in its own right.[100] While this danger had always existed in Christianity, Caroline Bynum has noted how the conflation between image and what it represented "radically intensifies" in the later medieval period, which would in turn have intensified such concerns.[101] As for practical uses of the cross to heal and protect, which were widely touted and certainly widely employed, again authorities worried that the laity would not grasp the necessary distinction: while divine power might operate

---

98. Anonymous, *De superstitionibus* (M), 42r; Denys the Carthusian, *Contra vitia superstitionum*, 602; Jakob of Paradise, *De potestate demonum*, 259v; Johannes of Frankfurt, *Quaestio*, 81; Johannes of Wünschelburg, *De superstitionibus*, 234v; Nider, *Preceptorium* 1.11.32(nn); Nikolaus of Jauer, *De superstitionibus*, 58v; Nikolaus of Jauer, *Refutatio*, 201v.

99. Nider, *Formicarius* 5.2, pp. 343–44.

100. Nikolaus of Dinkelsbühl, *De preceptis decalogi*, 28r; Ebendorfer, *De decem praeceptis*, 5.

101. Caroline Walker Bynum, *Christian Materiality: An Essay on Religion in Late Medieval Europe* (New York, 2011), 120.

through a cross or in response to devotion shown to it, no power inhered in the object itself. Heinrich of Gorkum scoffed at the notion that simply shaping some material into a cross-like form imbued it with any power. Yet all across medieval Europe peasants raised crude crosses in fields to protect crops from storms and other threats, and most authorities, including Heinrich himself, were loathe to condemn this widespread form of both practical defense and popular devotion.[102] Another problem lay in people believing that particular crosses were somehow more sacred or powerful than others. Authorities in Heidelberg suspected Werner of Friedberg of this superstition, and he had to recant his alleged belief that a cross in the possession of the Augustinian community in Landau possessed any special virtues, while Johannes of Wünschelburg castigated the citizenry of Bamberg for similarly asserting that a particularly ancient cross in their city was worthy of special reverence.[103]

The sign of the cross was no less problematic, and its myriad uses no less confusing. Again the essential dilemma was that, while divine power might often operate through or in response to the sign of the cross, people needed to understand that the gesture itself held no inherent power. On particular points, however, various authors staked out different positions. While Johannes of Frankfurt declared that using the sign of the cross to protect crops smacked of superstition, his Heidelberg colleague Nikolaus of Jauer affirmed that it could be employed to drive away demons, and demons could certainly afflict crops in the fields. In Vienna, Johannes Nider had no problem advising parents to protect their children from demonic assault by crossing them, and in Leipzig Johannes of Wünschelburg approvingly related one of those problematic tales of the wonder-working saints of old, recounting how Saint Benedict had avoided being poisoned by making the sign of the cross over his food and drink. Similarly Felix Hemmerli recalled that Saint Jerome had healed a lion's paw by making the sign of the cross over it, and he also noted how Gregory the Great and many other early Christian authorities advocated using the sign of the cross to protect crops from storms.[104] Given how easy it is to cross oneself, many pious or even not so pious people surely did so at the slightest provocation. The *Distaff Gospels* asserted that if people made the sign of the cross upon

---

102. Heinrich of Gorkum, *De superstitiosis quibusdam casibus*, 3v, 4v; Johannes of Wünschelburg, *De superstitionibus*, 232v; Nikolaus of Jauer, *De superstitionibus*, 57r.

103. Werner of Friedberg, *Revocatio*, 198r; Johannes of Wünschelburg, *De superstitionibus*, 245r.

104. Johannes of Frankfurt, *Quaestio*, 77; Nikolaus of Jauer, *De superstitionibus*, 42r; Nider, *Preceptorium* 1.11.12(q); Johannes of Wünschelburg, *De superstitionibus*, 236v; Hemmerli, *De exorcismis*, 103v (on lions); Hemmerli, *De benedictionibus*, 101v (on crops).

waking (as well as washing their hands before leaving the house), they would be protected from Satan's power all day. One might think that theologians would have been skittish about such a sweeping claim, but Johannes Nider related a story about a magistrate of the city of Bern who once failed to make the sign of the cross when rising and subsequently fell down a flight of stairs (having been pushed by demons, of course, to whom he had made himself vulnerable by forgetting this simple rite).[105]

Similar reasoning, concern, and at times apparent confusion as applied to the cross also pertained to other blessed or consecrated items, such as holy water. While stressing that even officially blessed water possessed no inherent virtue but only acted as a conduit for divine grace, some authorities still recommended it as a reliable and seemingly automatic defense against demons.[106] Certainly belief in its general protective qualities was widespread. If the sign of the cross made once in the morning would protect one from the devil for an entire day, the *Distaff Gospels* reported about holy water that receiving it at Mass would keep the devil at bay for an entire week. Indeed, the tempter would not be able to approach nearer than seven feet to a person so shielded.[107] Again, it was the seemingly automatic and inherent nature of the water's power in these practices that made theologians and other authorities nervous. Johannes Hartlieb, for example, castigated the false belief (*ungelaub*) of women who sprinkled garden plants with holy water to protect them from caterpillars, and Johannes of Wünschelburg condemned people who placed seeds in holy water before sowing, believing this would safeguard the resulting crops against insects. The physician Hartlieb also chided chivalric courtiers who dipped their spurs in holy water so the flanks of their horses would not swell when pricked, and he disparaged the notion that holy water had any special power to prevent wounds from becoming infected. Not just the laity, however, engaged in such superstitions. Both Johannes of Wünschelburg and Nikolaus of Jauer criticized parish clergy who administered holy water to animals to protect them against wolves.[108]

Such practices were superstitious because they constituted "irreverent" uses of specially consecrated items, but the line that separated irreverent from appropriate use was often blurry. Nikolaus of Jauer sternly maintained that no one should employ any sacramental item outside of the official, ecclesiastical

105. Anonymous, *Évangiles* 3.15, p. 132; Nider, *Formicarius* 5.7, pp. 380–81.
106. Anonymous, *De superstitionibus* (M), 42r; Jakob of Paradise, *De potestate demonum*, 260r.
107. Anonymous, *Évangiles*, 3.13, p. 130.
108. Hartlieb, *Buch*, 76–80; Johannes of Wünschelburg, *De superstitionibus*, 232v–233r; Nikolaus of Jauer, *De superstitionibus*, 57r.

context for which it had been consecrated, because the risk of superstition was too great.[109] Denys the Carthusian also typically railed against any lay appropriations of sacramental items. He made an exception, however, for holy water taken from a church and used to protect crops against storms. Some tempests, he reasoned, were raised by demons, and since holy water was officially consecrated to drive away demons during baptisms, so it might also be used to keep them from afflicting a farmer's fields. Yet he still considered using holy water to defend against wolves or to relieve toothaches to be patently superstitious.[110] Of course, demons would surely have been capable of engineering those afflictions as well, but Denys simply ignored that possibility here.

Beyond sacramental items stood the sacraments, and the greatest among them, the Eucharist, seemed to many a patent demonstration of the automatic efficacy of ritual action and the inherent power of consecrated matter. Throughout Christendom, priests spoke formulaic words and bits of bread transformed into God. These innumerable physical manifestations of divinity then provided a staggering potential for abuse, and the fear of Host desecration by Jews, heretics, magicians, and witches flourished in the fifteenth century.[111] Of course, the clergy also feared that ordinary laypeople might desecrate the Eucharist by employing it in unofficial ways, a concern only stoked by the profusion of popular devotions and miracle cults that sprang up around consecrated wafers in the late medieval period.[112] No clerical authority ever questioned that the Host really became God in the course of the sacramental ritual, for that itself would have been the gravest of heresies, but even here writers discussing superstition stressed that the rite per se possessed no inherent power. It functioned reliably, indeed immutably, only because God had contracted with his church always to perform a miracle whenever a duly consecrated priest performed a Mass. In fact, just as clerical authorities regularly described many superstitious rites as functioning only through pacts with demons, so quite literally the sacrament of the Eucharist, indeed all sacraments, functioned only because of a "pact" (*pactum*, also translatable as "covenant") with

---

109. Nikolaus of Jauer, *De superstitionibus*, 55v, 57r.

110. Denys the Carthusian, *Contra vitia superstitionum*, 611–12.

111. Among our authors, see Hartlieb, *Buch*, 104; Heinrich of Gorkum, *De superstitiosis quibusdam casibus*, 5v; Johannes of Wünschelburg, *De superstitionibus*, 234v; Martin of Arles, *De superstitionibus*, 48r–v. Seminal analysis in Peter Browe, "Die Eucharistie als Zaubermittel im Mittelalter," *Archiv für Kulturgeschichte* 20 (1930): 134–54. On Host desecrations by witches, see Walter Stephens, *Demon Lovers: Witchcraft, Sex, and the Crisis of Belief* (Chicago, 2002), 207–40.

112. A detailed study is Caroline Walker Bynum, *Wonderful Blood: Theology and Practice in Northern Germany and Beyond* (Philadelphia, 2007).

God.[113] If the laity did not understand this distinction, they fell into superstition. Yet so long as they did understand properly and treated the sacramental wafer with appropriate reverence, many authorities allowed and even encouraged devout laypeople to employ the sacred Host in unofficial contexts. Johannes Nider, for example, advocated the Eucharist (along with the ringing of church bells and prayer) as a valid means of protecting crops from storms raised by demons. The particularly permissive Felix Hemmerli wrote an entire tract arguing for the legitimate use of the consecrated wafer to "bless the air" and quell storms.[114]

The Eucharist highlights the convoluted issue of "inherent power" that underlay much debate about superstition, certainly those forms of superstition that related to religious rites.[115] From prayers to sacramental items to the sacraments themselves, Christian authorities seemed to imbue certain words, formulas, objects, and rites with special efficacy. This was the "magic of the medieval church," which Keith Thomas evocatively described in his magisterial study *Religion and the Decline of Magic*.[116] In fact, as we have seen, writers addressing superstition argued that no inherent power resided in any rite or sacral item, even the greatest. Rather these operated only as conduits for divine power. Yet neither were such forms entirely empty or meaningless. Again we return to an essential tension in debates about superstition: the relationship between internal belief (or intellectual understanding) and external act. Both components factored into our writers' condemnation, indeed their very definition, of superstitious practices. Yet the imperatives to regulate both belief and behavior were not always readily compatible.

Discerning Superstition in Common Practices

Like Christian authorities since the time of the church fathers, the cluster of writers in central Europe who focused on superstition in the first half of the fifteenth century regularly condemned both erroneous thought and illicit

---

113. Anonymous, *De superstitionibus* (M), 32v, 41v; Denys the Carthusian, *Contra vitia superstitionum*, 613; Johannes of Wünschelburg, *De superstitionibus*, 234r; Nikolaus of Jauer, *De superstitionibus*, 58r; also Nikolaus of Jauer, *Refutatio*, 201r. Fifteenth-century authors drew here on William of Auvergne, *De legibus* 27 (in William, *Opera omnia* [Venice, 1591], 87; on whom see Irène Rosier-Catach, "Signes sacramentels et signes magiques: Guillaume d'Auvergne et la théorie du pacte," in *Autour de Guillaume d'Auvergne († 1249)*, ed. Franco Morenzoni and Jean-Yves Tilliette (Turnhout, 2005), 93–116.

114. Nider, *Preceptorium* 1.11.34(pp); Hemmerli, *De benedictionibus*.

115. See Cameron, *Enchanted Europe*, 123–26.

116. Keith Thomas, *Religion and the Decline of Magic: Studies in Popular Beliefs in Sixteenth and Seventeenth Century England* (1971; repr., New York, 1997), 25–50.

practices. They clearly regarded the joint disciplining of faith and its enacted forms as necessary and complementary. Yet to an extent their efforts worked at cross-purposes. If, according to proper belief, no real power inhered even in officially consecrated items or sanctified rites, why should it matter if people used them in improper contexts or performed them in incorrect ways? And yet it did. In all their debate, none of our writers was ever so radical as to suggest stripping any official rite, prayer, blessing, or consecration of its special significance. Commenting on uses of the Lord's Prayer, for example, Nikolaus of Dinkelsbühl stated clearly that God did not heed the specific words recited but rather attended to the "heart" of the one praying. Likewise, Christians should not be "imprisoned" by particular verbal formulas when seeking to address God. He went on to argue at length, however, that official prayers like the Our Father, with their established and set formulas (that could, worrisomely, become corrupted by bungled utterance), were especially beneficial. After all, Christ himself had provided the words of the Lord's Prayer (Matthew 6:9–13 and Luke 11:2–4) and enjoined his disciples to use them above all others.[117] In a somewhat similar vein, Johannes Nider specified two forms of exorcism: the basic act of expelling a demon in Christ's name possible for all the faithful, and the official ecclesiastical ceremony performed by a cleric. In essence, the two forms of practice were identical. Neither possessed any inherent power; both succeeded only if divine power chose to respond, and needless to say the omnipotent divinity could never be compelled by mere human words or rites. Yet Nider also differentiated between the two methods, setting the official rite above the common practice and forbidding the laity to employ any element of the ecclesiastical ceremony, as it was above their station.[118]

One obvious clerical concern in all this had to do not with different modes of ritual efficacy, but simply with levels of education. While the laity might memorize a few proper Latin prayers, such as the Apostles' Creed, the Our Father, and perhaps the Hail Mary, they could not possibly make their way without error through an elaborate rite in a language they did not know. But this again raises the question, if rites themselves were essentially devoid of power and God attended only to pious intent, what would it matter if one garbled a rite from start to finish? Yet clearly for fifteenth-century authorities it did. Johannes Nider discussed how certain superstitious spells and blessings that many people now performed over the sick contained elements of healing practices that saints had performed in antiquity. They were laudable in

---

117. Nikolaus of Dinkelsbühl, *Herrengebetskommentar*, 21, 26–30, 137–38.
118. Nider, *Preceptorium* 1.9(d).

their essence, and educated men, including theologians like himself, could still use them quite legitimately. Yet the ordinary laymen and especially the "old women" who now typically employed them had, in his view, corrupted them beyond measure through the introduction of superstitious elements.[119] Similarly, Johannes of Wünschelburg advised that the laity avoid any prayers that had not been sanctioned "by divine decree or by statute or decree of the church," because improvised or misspoken language might lapse into superstition.[120]

Protestant reformers would later allege that debates of this sort confused essential distinctions between "religion" and "magic." In fact, however, these early fifteenth-century writers wanted to reinforce that very distinction by delineating the boundaries of superstition as clearly as they could, while still allowing as much space as safely possible for pious devotional practices. In doing so, they confronted the perennially complex interplay between intangible belief and its external enactment. That difficult and uncertain relationship had troubled Christian thinkers since the earliest days of the church. In various ways, the issue became exceptionally fraught in the late medieval period.[121] And in the sixteenth century, still bound to debate about superstition, it drove Protestant reformers' rejection of many medieval church rites and popular devotions. Yet even the Reformation would not resolve the issue. While Protestant leaders shifted certain boundaries and altered some points of emphasis, they did not "disenchant" their world or their faith. Stripped of many sacraments and sacramentals, of the intercession of the saints and the virtues of their relics, Protestants turned ever more fervently to the power of the Word given through scripture and sermon, and they were not above fetishizing items associated with great reforming leaders as ersatz relics.[122] The leaders of the Catholic Counter-Reformation also had to address the significance and special status of rites and rituals, and they came to their own conclusions, in large measure reaffirming and further elaborating the distinctions that late medieval authorities had drawn.[123]

---

119. Ibid., 1.11.27(hh): "Unde ortum habeant benedictiones et carminationes quas uetule hodie super infirmos et uiri quidam faciunt."

120. Johannes of Wünschelburg, *De superstitionibus*, 236r: "Non sunt ex dei ordinacione nec ex statuto uel ordinacione ecclesie."

121. A central theme of Bynum, *Christian Materiality*.

122. See R. W. Scribner, "'Incombustible Luther': The Image of the Reformer in Early Modern Germany," *Past and Present* 110 (1986): 38–68; Scribner, "The Reformation, Popular Magic, and the 'Disenchantment of the World,'" *Journal of Interdisciplinary History* 23 (1992–93): 475–94; reprinted in Scribner, *Religion and Culture in Germany (1400–1800)*, ed. Lyndal Roper (Leiden, 2001), 346–65; Scribner, "Magic and the Formation of Protestant Popular Culture in Germany," in *Religion and Culture in Germany*, 323–45.

123. On Catholic as well as Protestant thought, see Cameron, *Enchanted Europe*, 156–239.

In terms of the practical work they endeavored to accomplish, our fifteenth-century writers might well have found their going easier if they had, as
their later critics charged, emphasized only the seemingly inherent "magical"
power of word and rite. Discerning superstition, at least, would have been a
simpler task. Certain rites, performed precisely, would always produce specific
ascribed effects. If garbled in any way or employed for other purposes, they
would become superstitious. But this would have unacceptably restricted God's
freedom to aid the faithful, or withhold that aid as his will might mandate.
And at the level of human institutions, it could have restricted the church's
freedom to deploy its rites in various extramural ways. Across Europe, priests
processed consecrated Hosts around fields on Rogation Days to confer generalized blessing and protection. Bishops would sometimes "exorcise" fields
infested by worms and insects.[124] Our most permissive author, Felix Hemmerli, seized upon such officially performed mutations of church rites that he
knew from the diocese of Chur, Constance, and Lausanne to justify a whole
range of common blessings and charms that appropriated elements of sanctioned prayers or the liturgy to heal, protect, or otherwise benefit people, crops,
and cattle.[125] To him, God cared more about good intention than the correct
formulation of some consecration or official exorcism. He confidently used
this principle even to oppose the more restrictive decisions of other authorities, asserting, for example, that the Heidelberg theological faculty had erred
nearly fifty years earlier when it had condemned Werner of Friedberg for his
approval and use of well-intentioned but decidedly unofficial healing rites.[126]

Ultimately, while all fifteenth-century authorities asserted the importance
of good and pious intent, whether in devotional, curative, or protective rites,
none did this so absolutely as the lawyer Hemmerli, nor did any devalue the
need for correct formulaic action so completely. On a purely practical level,
of course, authorities could perceive and judge actions far more easily than
intentions. In his *Summary of Theology* (*Summa theologiae*) Thomas Aquinas
had given five conditions for discerning superstition, none of which bore
on the intent of the practitioner. First, there should be no overt demonic
invocation, nor, second, any strange or unknown words or names that might
indicate covert invocation. His third and fourth conditions were that the act
should contain nothing false (contrary to Christian faith) or vain (meaningless
or empty). Finally, no one should behave as if an act's power or efficacy derived

---

124. See Chène, *Juger les vers* (as n. 27 above).
125. Hemmerli, *De exorcismis* and *Tractatus exorcismorum*; also his *De benedictionibus*.
126. Hemmerli, *Tractatus exorcismorum*, 106v, 110v.

from the specific manner in which it was performed.[127] Fifteenth-century authors clung to these strictures. Denys the Carthusian, Jakob of Paradise, Johannes Schwarz, Nikolaus of Dinkelsbühl, and Nikolaus of Jauer all repeated them more or less exactly.[128] Johannes Nider added two more conditions, also derived from Thomas and really just elaborating on his final point. When people used holy words, he warned, they should regard them only as signs of reverence to God and a means of supplicating divine aid, not as possessing power in themselves; likewise people should entrust whatever outcome they hoped to achieve to the will of God rather than placing faith directly in words or rites.[129] A major anonymous treatise *On Superstitions* gave all but the last of Thomas's conditions, and then added four additional strictures against "testing" God, such as by imploring divine aid when more mundane remedies were available (for example, when sick, one should turn to a physician before demanding a miracle from the Almighty), or employing holy words with the intent of obtaining some effect that would be offensive to God (cursing a good person, for example, or seeking to gain unnecessary wealth for oneself).[130]

These conditions were straightforward enough in theory, but in practice they often required authorities to probe proper belief, understanding, and intent rather than just observe clearly discernible actions. And even in terms of overt practices, what precisely constituted a damning "falsehood" or "vanity"? Authorities could never entirely agree. Take the case of inscribed amulets, the very practice for which Aquinas had laid out his conditions for separating legitimate from superstitious behavior. Among the most prevalent amulets in the late medieval period were those bearing the names of the three biblical magi, widely held to ward off epilepsy.[131] In 1405, Nikolaus of Jauer and other Heidelberg theologians had included belief in the legitimacy of this practice

---

127. Aquinas, *Summa theologiae* 2.2.96.4, in *Summa theologiae: Latin Text and English Translation*, 60 vols. (New York, 1964–81). Here the conditions pertain specifically to fashioning protective amulets. I have paraphrased them in slightly generalized form, as they were understood and used by later writers.

128. Denys the Carthusian, *Contra vitia superstitionum*, 602–3; Nikolaus of Dinkelsbühl, *De preceptis decalogi*, 30v; Nikolaus of Jauer, *De superstitionibus*, 59r; Schwarz, *De divinacionibus*, 322v. Also Jakob of Paradise, *De potestate demonum*, in Munich, BSB, Clm 9105, fols. 167r–211r, at 190v–191r. They are not found in the copy of *De potestate demonum* I normally cite (in Clm 18378), where they would appear at 261r. Clm 18378 is considerably earlier than Clm 9105 (1470 as opposed to 1514). Nevertheless, after comparison with other copies in Augsburg and Berlin (see appendix), I am convinced the material was somehow omitted from Clm 18378 rather than added to the later Clm 9105, although a systematic manuscript study would be needed to prove this absolutely.

129. Nider, *Preceptorium* 1.11.26(gg).

130. Anonymous, *De superstitionibus* (M), 37r–38r. Thomas had discussed "tentatio Dei" immediately after superstition in *Summa theologiae* 2.2.97.1–4, but these specific points are not from him.

131. Skemer, *Binding Words*, 64–65.

among the charges of superstition they leveled against Werner of Friedberg. Twenty years later in Cologne, however, Heinrich of Gorkum explicitly supported the practice, so long, he stressed, as people properly understood that the operative power keeping the disease at bay came from God and not directly from some trinket they happened to wear around their necks.[132] Like Jean Gerson and Pierre d'Ailly debating astrology, these men did not disagree on the basic principles that divided permissible from superstitious action, but they could differ considerably in their application of those principles, a difference often only detectable in their tone and general manner of presentation. Heinrich of Gorkum seems to have been more willing to focus on the positive value of legitimate charms; Nikolaus of Jauer and his Heidelberg colleagues were more worried about the dangers of possible superstition.[133]

Similar uncertainties pervaded our writers' treatment of healing spells or blessings, and of written charms inscribed with holy words or Bible verses and then laid on the sick.[134] It can be unsettling to read again and again (and I often wonder how distressing it may have been for these men to write) some variation of the all-encompassing tautology that such-and-such practice might be perfectly licit "so long as nothing superstitious is mingled in," referring back to generic categories that, as we have just seen, were inevitably vague and required interpretation when applied to specific cases. If a prayer explicitly called on Satan or a rite violently desecrated the cross or Eucharist, that was clear enough. But how to tell when someone was "placing faith" in a ritual action rather than divine power, or how much someone "respected" the words of a prayer? Denys the Carthusian offered the most direct way out of this dilemma of discernment: simple reliance on the magisterial authority of the church. Discussing healing rites, he noted that many common practices were fundamentally licit and people could use them with a clear conscience—unless the church prohibited them. He further explained that the church might justifiably ban any practices, even ones that entailed no intrinsic superstition, simply because of the risk that "some superstitions" might

---

132. Werner of Friedberg, *Revocatio*, 198r; Werner of Friedberg, *Responsiones*, 280; Heinrich of Gorkum, *De superstitiosis quibusdam casibus*, 4r.

133. Nikolaus of Jauer, *De superstitionibus*, 59r, is generally negative about all protective amulets.

134. Denys the Carthusian, *Contra vitia superstitionum*, 602; Heinrich of Gorkum, *De superstitiosis quibusdam casibus*, 4v; Jakob of Paradise, *De potestate demonum*, 261r; Johannes of Wünschelburg, *De superstitionibus*, 235r; Nikolaus of Dinkelsbühl, *De preceptis decalogi*, 28v; Nider, *Preceptorium* 1.9(e); Ebendorfer, *De decem praeceptis*, 10.

"get mingled into them."[135] Here lay certainty: what the church proscribed became illicit, whether inherently so or not. Denys expressed this idea in its clearest, most distilled form, but he was hardly alone in proclaiming the basic concept. Johannes of Wünschelburg also discussed the inherently legitimate nature of many common healing practices, but he too noted that they could be condemned merely for presenting a potential "occasion for scandal and abuse among simple people."[136] And as we have seen already, Johannes Nider described healing rites that were licit when performed by educated clergy but that had been corrupted, or ran the risk of corruption, when used by "superstitious people," especially old women.[137]

Given the uncertainties inherent in determining whether specific practices were superstitious or not, authorities turned perhaps inevitably to judging the quality of the people performing them.[138] While our cluster of writers clearly thought that even well-educated clergymen could succumb to superstition, they also scattered references to "simple folk," and above all to simple women, throughout their works. As was the case with Gerson, the condemnation of women as especially susceptible to superstition never constituted a major component of analysis for most of the authorities considered in this chapter, but many referenced the idea, even if only by casual, passing mention.[139] They considered women naturally weaker than men in both body and mind, and thus more subject to demonic tricks and temptations that would draw them into superstition. In the concise formulation of Heinrich Kramer, who went on to expound against women at great length, the feminine sex was in all ways, including etymologically, "lesser in faith" (fe-minus).[140]

Kramer dealt not with superstition generally but with witchcraft, so I will discuss him mainly in the next chapter. Among the writers holding our atten-

---

135. Denys the Carthusian, *Contra vitia superstitionum*, 607: "Iam dictum est, quod quamuis benedictiones et adiurationes praefatae in seipsis non sint superstitiosae neque illicitae, si fiant sicut praehabitum est, nihilominus sunt vitandae ac prohibendae propter annexa pericula, quia in eis frequenter aliqua superstitiosa miscentur."

136. Johannes of Wünschelburg, *De superstitionibus*, 235r: "occasionem scandali simplicibus et abusus."

137. Nider, *Preceptorium* 1.11.27(hh) (as n. 119 above).

138. Similarly regarding discernment of spirits, see Nancy Caciola, *Discerning Spirits: Divine and Demonic Possession in the Middle Ages* (Ithaca, N.Y., 2003), 312–13; Dyan Elliott, *Proving Woman: Female Spirituality and Inquisitional Culture in the Later Middle Ages* (Princeton, N.J., 2004), 266–70.

139. Anonymous, *De divinacionibus*, 177v–178r; Hartlieb, *Buch*, 46; Jakob of Paradise, *De potestate demonum*, 245r and 263v; Johannes of Frankfurt, *Quaestio*, 76; Johannes of Wünschelburg, *De superstitionibus*, 232r; Nikolaus of Dinkelsbühl, *De preceptis decalogi*, 28v.

140. Kramer, *Malleus* 1.6, p. 286. The formulation was not original to Kramer but comes from the fifteenth-century Dominican reformer and bishop Antoninus of Florence.

tion here, Johannes Nider, later to become an important source for Heinrich Kramer, discussed the proclivity of women for superstition in general (as well as witchcraft specifically) at greatest length.[141] He offered three reasons for their susceptibility. Demons sought them out because of their weak faith. Physically, their bodies were more impressionable and susceptible to demonic influence than those of men. And finally, because women loved to gossip, whenever one woman found herself drawn into superstition, she quickly spread her error to others.[142] Elsewhere he discussed women's special vulnerability to visions and delusions, and he noted that one reason so many superstitions clustered around childbirth was that delivering and recovering mothers were secluded for so long in the company of other women, where they did little but pass superstitious notions back and forth among themselves.[143] Given the extreme risks that childbirth presented to both mother and baby in this era, a more charitable interpretation might be that women would consider almost any rite that promised some protection for them or their newborns at a moment of terrible vulnerability. Nider's fellow Viennese theologian Thomas Ebendorfer briefly noted how many mothers resorted to superstitious practices, not just during childbirth but at any time, to heal sick children. He expressed no compassion for them, however, nor any hint of sympathy for their maternal concerns, issuing instead only a warning about the danger they represented.[144]

Of course, one must wonder how well these clergymen really knew the practices of women. The *Distaff Gospels*, for example, mention many beliefs related to pregnancy but relatively few associated specifically with the period of birth or subsequent lying-in. One was that a newborn child should be given a cooked apple before being suckled to ensure that it would grow to be a courteous adult, or touched with the umbilical cord to ensure not only long life but "sweet breath" and "gracious speech." Another was that, to protect a boy against a bad death or to ensure that a girl grew into an honorable woman, newborns should be placed immediately on their father's or mother's chests, respectively. Mothers were also not to hold infants with their left arms anytime before baptism, lest the child grow to be left-handed.[145] None of these stric-

141. Nider, *Preceptorium* 1.11.21(bb). Also Nider, *Formicarius* 5.8, pp. 385–90. On Nider's gendered concerns, see Bailey, *Battling Demons* (as n. 21 above), 48–52, 110–11; also Dyan Elliott, *The Bride of Christ Goes to Hell: Metaphor and Embodiment in the Lives of Pious Women, 200–1500* (Philadelphia, 2012), 256–63.

142. Nider, *Preceptorium* 1.10(a).

143. Ibid., 1.11.25(ff).

144. Ebendorfer, *De decem praeceptis*, 11.

145. Anonymous, *Évangiles* 1.13, p. 90; 5.17, p. 168; 4.15, p. 148.

tures appear especially malevolent, but as we have seen, suspicious authorities could see danger in even the most seemingly benign practices. Nider does not mention midwives, only mothers in childbirth, but it is worth noting that at least in the towns of southern Germany, midwives were closely regulated by civic authorities at this time, and no ordinances pertaining to them mention or condemn superstitious practices, although such condemnations do appear elsewhere in Europe.[146] Nider spent years in Basel and Nuremberg, so presumably he was familiar with the southern German context. Whether he knew of these urban officials' lack of concern in this area or what he might have thought of it had he known is, however, a matter of complete speculation.

A clear vein of hostility and contempt for what they regarded as the particular weakness of women wove its way through the writings of clerical critics of superstition, but they were hardly alone in perceiving women in this way. Common opinion, too, held women to be generally more superstitious than men, and more easily ensnared by demons. Records of sorcery and witchcraft trials from this period reveal more women than men being accused, typically by their own neighbors. Moreover, women appear to have been tried in larger numbers in regions where local courts held jurisdiction, rather than church inquisitions, and where ideas of witchcraft grew more directly from local culture.[147] Johannes Nider may well have addressed the particular susceptibility of women to superstition and witchcraft at length in part because he and other clerical authorities were genuinely surprised by the numbers of women now being accused of such things.[148] Similarly, one study of the *Hammer of Witches* has stressed how Heinrich Kramer asserted "experience itself" as the best evidence that women were more prone to witchcraft than men and has argued that, far from driving the gendering of witchcraft, theologians and demonologists were themselves driven to this notion by the "reality" they encountered in contemporary trials.[149]

We would be foolish to downplay completely the importance of repeated references to "simple old women" drawn into superstition that we find in Gerson at the beginning of the fifteenth century and continuing through the central European writers examined here, especially since some of these writers themselves regarded their association of women with superstition and witch-

---

146. Merry E. Wiesner, *Working Women in Renaissance Germany* (New Brunswick, N.J., 1986), 64.

147. Kathrin Utz Tremp, *Von der Häresie zur Hexerei: "Wirkliche" und imaginäre Sekten im Spätmittelalter* (Hannover, 2008), 528–29.

148. Michael D. Bailey, "The Feminization of Magic and the Emerging Idea of the Female Witch in the Late Middle Ages," *Essays in Medieval Studies* 19 (2002): 120–34.

149. Broedel, *Malleus Maleficarum*, 167–70.

craft as significant and startling enough to require special comment. I have argued that as these men began to deal more with common superstitions than had previous authorities, and as they attempted to provide guidance to parish clergy and the laity as to what practices were and were not superstitious, they found no certain purchase in this slippery terrain. Among the strategies they fell back on was to evaluate the practitioner as much as the practice, warning about the dangers of inherently legitimate rites corrupted by the errors of simple, uneducated men and especially women. Yet they also lived in a world that already commonly associated superstition and simple sorcery more with women than with men. Their contribution to the gendering of superstition and subsequently of witchcraft makes up only one part of a large and complicated story.

Schools, Sermons, and Reforming Impulses

Many of the new concerns demonstrated by central European theologians and other authorities writing about superstition, not least their increasingly evident concern with women, have pointed toward witchcraft. I have focused on these men, rather than casting my net across all of western Europe in the early fifteenth century, in part because the history of late medieval superstition inevitably blends into the history of witchcraft, and the German Empire would soon become the proverbial heartland of early modern witch-hunting. Before turning to witchcraft in the next chapter, therefore, I want to suggest some reasons why concern about superstition, certainly evident across Western Christendom at this time, generated such a strong response specifically in German lands.

We might begin, simply enough, with Jean Gerson. He was the most widely read and respected critic of superstition at the outset of the fifteenth century, and, as noted at the end of the previous chapter, his influence was especially pervasive in the German Empire. He brought together two currents that largely characterized authoritative writing about superstition for the remainder of the century. First, he continued the critique of elite superstitions related to courtly astrology and clerical necromancy that had developed in the fourteenth century while placing strong emphasis on diabolical menace infecting almost all superstitious practices. Second, he extended the focus of his concern to include common practices as well, because of the essentially pastoral impulse that motivated his new applied moral theology.

Gerson's more practical, pastoral focus clearly appealed to theologians and other academics at the numerous relatively young universities in central Europe. The first university established in this region was that of Prague, founded in 1347 by papal decree and affirmed in 1348 by royal privilege. Krakow followed in 1364, and Vienna in 1365. Then came Heidelberg in 1386, Cologne in 1388, Erfurt in 1392, and Leipzig in 1409. The men who filled the faculties of these new institutions were eager to take up what they saw as the new and pressing concerns of their age. They were also ready to address specific and practical problems, in the manner advocated by Gerson. While Prague and Vienna certainly aimed to rival Paris (Krakow had faltered somewhat after its mid-fourteenth-century foundation but revived at the beginning of the fifteenth century), all these schools tended to be more "local" in their horizons than the ancient and self-consciously international center of learning by the Seine.[150] Typically founded by territorial princes, they provided regional repositories of practical expertise, as well as adding intellectual luster to a ruler's domain. A prince might turn to his local university faculty for guidance or consultation on almost any matter.[151] Theological faculties were often called on to help promote better pastoral care and general piety, and superstition became an obvious issue for them to address. Similar conditions existed at universities elsewhere in Europe, but they were clearly ripe in those in German lands. Perhaps the matter of superstition simply fit characteristically "German" intellectual interests at this time, which focused largely on spiritual and religious matters.[152] Whatever the cause, the stark fact is that some form of comment on superstition emerged from almost every central European university that existed in the early fifteenth century.

Werner of Friedberg's questioning before a commission of Heidelberg theologians, with which this chapter began, demonstrates how a particular university's faculty might come to address superstition. Werner had theological training himself. The positions he took were hardly matters of simple or foolish error, and he could defend his views fairly effectively.[153] The episcopal official who presided over the initial inquest against him could not see his way clearly through the issues involved, yet he needed a resolution, for if Werner was guilty of error, he was also leading others astray. Fortunately, the bishop's court could now refer the case to the nearby university at Heidelberg, which may already have been debating questions of superstition (if Johannes of Frankfurt's *Quaestio* correctly dates from early January 1405), and where

150. A. B. Cobban, *The Medieval Universities: Their Development and Organization* (London, 1975), 118–19; Jacques Verger, *Les universités au Moyen Âge* (Paris, 1973), 140–43.

151. See Michael H. Shank, "Academic Consulting in Fifteenth-Century Vienna: The Case of Astrology," in *Texts and Contexts in Ancient and Medieval Science: Studies on the Occasion of John E. Murdoch's Seventieth Birthday*, ed. Edith Sylla and Michael McVaugh (Leiden, 1997), 245–70.

152. Hobbins, *Authorship and Publicity before Print* (as n. 9 above), 215–16.

153. See Lerner, "Werner di Friedberg."

this case then sparked an abiding interest in the topic. The theological faculty issued an official refutation of Werner's positions, likely penned by Nikolaus of Jauer, who followed it with his influential treatise *On Superstitions*.

In focusing on a court case like Werner's inquest, and indeed in focusing on theological treatises and other didactic literature that confronted the issue of superstition in a (relatively) systematic way, we risk losing sight of the principle mechanism by which largely "academic" considerations of superstition entered the world of pastoral care and reached the masses, namely though sermons. Debate about superstition and condemnation of perceived superstitious activities had been intertwined with pastoral activity and preaching since the early days of the church. Many of Augustine's foundational pronouncements on the nature of superstition came in catechetical works, after all, and Caesarius of Arles addressed superstitious practices in the course of his sermons. Similarly the penitential literature of the early Middle Ages that often included "lists of superstitions" was basically pastoral in nature. Just as the basic theology and natural science that underlay late medieval debates about superstition was more immediately rooted in twelfth- and thirteenth-century scholastic developments, however, so the pastoral trends in the late medieval period stemmed in large measure from a more recent source, namely a series of pastoral programs initiated at the Fourth Lateran Council in 1215.[154] In chapter 1, I touched on the post-Lateran inquisitor but also preacher Stephen of Bourbon and his actions against what he regarded as a patently superstitious cult dedicated to a greyhound in the mid-thirteenth century. Preachers in the fourteenth and especially the fifteenth century continued to address issues of superstition in increasingly pronounced ways.[155]

My main excuse for sidelining the prodigious sermon literature of the late medieval period in this book is precisely that it is so vast. I have, of course, presented some examples of preaching material among the figures on whom I have focused. Aside from his various tracts on the subject, Jean Gerson also addressed superstition in a number of his sermons, and some of the treatises

---

154. Jean-Claude Schmitt, "Les 'superstitions,'" in *Histoire de la France religieuse*, vol. 1, *Des dieux de la Gaule à la papauté d'Avignon*, ed. Jacques Le Goff (Paris, 1988), 417–551, at 497–533; and esp. Krzysztof Bracha, "Der Einfluß der neuen Frömmigkeit auf die spätmittelalterliche Kritik am Aberglauben im Reformschrifttum Mitteleuropas," in *Die "Neue Frömmigkeit" in Europa im Spätmittelalter*, ed. Marek Derwich and Martial Staub (Göttingen, 2004), 225–48.

155. See Montesano, *Supra acqua et supra ad vento* (as n. 8 above); Krzysztof Bracha, "Magie und Aberglaubenskritik in der Predigten des Spätmittelalters in Polen," in *Religion und Magie in Ostmitteleuropa: Spielräume theologischer Normierungsprozesse in Spätmittelalter und Früher Neuzeit*, ed. Thomas Wünsch (Berlin, 2006), 197–215; Fabrizio Conti, "Preachers and Confessors against 'Superstitions': Bernardino Busti and Sermon 16 of His *Rosarium Sermonum*," *MRW* 6 (2011): 62–91.

composed by central European writers, especially those on the Decalogue, either began as sermons or were intended mainly as a resource for preachers. Sermons on superstition appeared across Europe. Probably the most famous fifteenth-century figure, in this regard, was Italian: the fiery Franciscan preacher Bernardino of Siena, who from the 1420s until his death in 1444 scourged the populaces of cities across Italy for their toleration of sorcery, superstition, and witchcraft.[156] The Spanish Dominican Vincent Ferrer (d. 1419) had preached on similar themes in Dauphiné and elsewhere in the western Alps just prior to this.[157] North of the Alps Johann Geiler of Kaysersberg (d. 1510) delivered a major series of sermons on sorcery and superstition in Strassburg in 1509, which were then published posthumously as *The Ants (Die Emeis)* in 1516/17. Although active into the early sixteenth century, Geiler was indebted to the early fifteenth-century Dominican preacher Johannes Nider and his great collection the *Anthill.*[158]

The sermons of this period reflect many of the same trends evident in tracts and treatises. Preachers might discuss elite practices, especially astrology, but they dealt mainly with common rites—indeed, much more so than in treatises, where writers often felt the need to reiterate the full tradition of intellectual debate on superstition. Sermons frequently focused on the powerful threat represented by demons, and many preachers chose to address the superstitious errors of women particularly, although they often recounted the special virtues of faithful and pious women as well.[159] Appealing directly to the masses, preachers often brought into stark relief the tension between the need to condemn perceived superstitious activities and the desire to promote a vibrant popular piety focused on prayer, the liturgy, and sacramental objects.[160] What some authorities regarded as dangerous error others supported as laudable devotion, either out of genuine conviction of because of personal interest. Even as Bernardino of Siena decried sorcery and witchcraft in rousing

---

156. See Franco Mormando, *The Preacher's Demons: Bernardino of Siena and the Social Underworld of Early Renaissance Italy* (Chicago, 1999).

157. Pierrette Paravy, *De la chrétienté romaine à la Réforme en Dauphiné: Évêques, fidèles et déviants (vers 1340–vers 1530),* 2 vols. (Rome, 1993), 2:904; Kathrin Utz Tremp, "Predigt und Inquisition: Der Kampf gegen die Häresie in der Stadt Freiburg (erste Hälfte des 15. Jahrhunderts)," in *Mirificus Praedicator: À l'occasion du sixième centenaire du passage de Saint Vincent Ferrier en pays romand,* ed. Paul-Bernard Hodel and Franco Morenzoni (Rome, 2006), 205–32.

158. Rita Voltmer, *Wie der Wächter auf dem Turm: Ein Prediger und seine Stadt: Johannes Geiler von Kaysersberg (1445–1510) und Straßburg* (Trier, 2005).

159. In addition to sources above, see Larissa Taylor, *Soldiers of Christ: Preaching in Late Medieval and Reformation France* (New York, 1992), 138–40, 171–74.

160. E.g., Krzysztof Bracha, "Between Learned and Popular Culture: The Example of Preaching in Poland during the Late Middle Ages: *Sermones dominicales et festivales* from the Collection Ascribed to Piotr of Miłosław," *Quaestiones Medii Aevi Novae* 8 (2003): 105–31.

sermons in the 1420s, for example, he was summoned to Rome to stand trial for heresy because of his strong promotion of the novel cult of the Holy Name of Jesus. Faith in the holy name, he had preached, would keep one safe from demons, thieves, plague, shipwreck, poison, and harm in battle.[161] Although he was ultimately acquitted, suspicion clung to him for years. Church authorities also often looked askance at enormously popular cults centered on Christ's blood that sprang up in the late Middle Ages, such as that of Wilsnack in northern Germany. This "blood piety" had vigorous defenders, however, certainly among local clergy who benefited from the flow of pilgrims, but among others as well.[162]

One factor underlying much of this activity and concern was the powerful effort to reform the church and Christian society in general in the late medieval period. While cynical motivations could always arise, and while the policing of popular beliefs and practices was of course an exercise in power, we must also give credence to the real drive among clerical leaders to heal the church and promote healthy religiosity, especially in the late days of the terrible papal schism that rent Western Christendom from 1378 until 1417, and then in the decades after its resolution. This impulse for reform extended across Europe, but it attained a particular intensity in central European lands.[163] One reason for this may have been the convocation of two great reforming councils at Constance (1414–18) and Basel (1431–49). Yet these were in fact major international assemblies, not particularly "German" in their composition. In terms of the special resonance that reforming impulses achieved in German lands, an important part of the answer may again be the new universities of this region. Years before the councils convened, calls for reform were already emerging from the universities at Prague and Vienna, and reformist thought spread from these schools to others in central Europe as they were founded.[164]

---

161. Mormando, *Preacher's Demons*, 88–89, 103–5.

162. Bynum, *Wonderful Blood*, esp. 25–81.

163. No single overview of all varieties of late medieval reform exists. See Kaspar Elm, ed., *Reformbemühungen und Observanzbestrebungen im spätmittelalterlichen Ordenswesen* (Berlin, 1989); Ivan Hlaváček and Alexander Patschovsky, eds., *Reform von Kirche und Reich zur Zeit der Konzilien von Konstanz (1414–1418) und Basel (1431–1449)* (Constance, 1996). An important contribution in English will be James Mixson and Bert Roest, eds., *A Companion to Observant Reform in the Later Middle Ages and Beyond* (Leiden, forthcoming).

164. Baumann, *Aberglaube für Laien*, 1:199–202; Bracha, "Einfluß," 227–29; Krzysztof Bracha, "Kritik an den Glaubens- und Verhaltensformen und an der Aberglaubenspraxis im kirchlichen reformatorischen Schrifttum des Spätmittelalters," in *Christianity in East Central Europe: Late Middle Ages*, ed. Paweł Kras and Wojciech Polak (Lublin, 1999), 271–82, at 271–72, 275–77, 280–81; František Šmahel, "Stärker als der Glaube: Magie, Aberglaube und Zauber in der Epoche des Hussitismus," *Bohemia: Zeitschrift für Geschichte und Kultur des böhmischen Länder/A Journal of History and Civilization in East Central Europe* 32 (1991): 316–37, at 333–34.

A number of the authorities who addressed the issue of superstition in the late fourteenth and early fifteenth centuries also engaged in varieties of reform: Heinrich of Langenstein, Pierre d'Ailly, Jean Gerson, Nikolaus of Jauer, Johannes of Frankfurt, Nikolaus of Dinkelsbühl, Johannes Nider, Thomas Ebendorfer, Felix Hemmerli, Jakob of Paradise, and Denys the Carthusian all had reformist credentials.[165] Their tracts and treatises on superstition did not deal with institutional ecclesiastical reform in any direct sense, but they certainly all aimed at correcting religious errors, restoring correct belief and practice among both clergy and the laity, and improving the overall moral and spiritual condition of Christendom. Of course, one did not need to be a reformer in any larger sense to write about superstition. But superstition was an important reform issue, especially as developed and deployed in fifteenth century central Europe. It would remain so throughout the sixteenth century as well.[166]

As Jean Gerson recognized, if one sought both to correct errors and to promote as much vibrant legitimate spirituality as possible, one had to wade into the complicated world of common superstitions. Particularly during the first half of the fifteenth century in central Europe, theologians and other intellectual authorities took his ideas to heart. More than ever, superstition became an important "boundary issue" against which to define certain key elements of belief and devotional practice in an age increasingly marked by a disturbing (to some) multiplicity of religious options.[167] The main dilemma authorities encountered was that clear boundaries were so difficult to perceive in the murky realm of common practices. Grappling with superstition at this level really meant confronting one of the most intractable conundrums of structured religion, namely the interplay of belief and practice, of personal faith and prescribed ritual. When they failed to cut clear paths through that tangled thicket, these men turned back to what they knew: respect for the authority of the church and an abiding suspicion of the uneducated laity and especially women.

In the course of the fifteenth century, indeed in some of the writings we have considered already, issues of superstition fed into witchcraft. Harmful

---

165. For more detail, see Michael D. Bailey, "Reformers on Sorcery and Superstition," forthcoming in Mixson and Roest, *A Companion to Observant Reform*; also Bailey, *Battling Demons*, esp. 75–117.

166. Stuart Clark, *Thinking with Demons: The Idea of Witchcraft in Early Modern Europe* (Oxford, 1997), 472–88; Cameron, *Enchanted Europe*, 156–239.

167. On "boundary issues," see John Van Engen, "The Future of Medieval Church History," *Church History* 71 (2002): 492–522, at 521; on "multiplicity," see Van Engen, "Multiple Options: The World of the Fifteenth-Century Church," *Church History* 77 (2008): 257–84.

demonic sorcery (*maleficium*) was by definition superstitious, and the drive to eradicate the *malefici* or more often female *maleficae* who supposedly practiced it was in a sense a natural outcome of intensifying concerns about common superstitions and the increasingly conspicuous demonic focus of those concerns. Yet stereotypes of fully diabolical, conspiratorial witchcraft that took shape in the mid- to late 1400s were decidedly darker than any earlier conceptions of superstition. They asserted not just that uneducated people might slip unknowingly into error, or even that educated elite magicians could be overwhelmed by natural or spiritual forces that they mistakenly thought they could master, but rather that monstrously derelict Christians deliberately forsook their faith, submitted to demons, and became members of a satanic cult that engaged in some of the most abominable acts imaginable. Against this terrible threat, good Christians had their faith, the rites of their church, and also an array of blessings, charms, protective amulets, and healing herbs that could themselves lead to suspicion of superstition. To a perhaps surprising degree, clerical authorities condoned and sometimes quite positively recommended these practices as legitimate defenses against witchcraft. After all, if nothing superstitious became "mingled in," these could be perfectly pious acts. Thus debate about superstition wended its way into tracts and treatises about witchcraft, too, as authorities continued to seek the precise balance that would allow them to promote even unofficial forms of piety, yet avoid condoning any error.

✒ CHAPTER 5

Witchcraft and Its Discontents

> Moreover, witchcraft differs from all other harmful
> and mysterious arts in this point, that of all superstition
> it is essentially the vilest, the most evil and the worst.
>
> —Montague Summers translation of the *Hammer
> of Witches*

The history of witchcraft in Europe is well-covered terrain. Since the later nineteenth century, scholars have mapped it from multiple perspectives and via diverse methodologies.[1] Most have drawn on the records of witch trials, using these particularly since the 1970s to explore not just the legal but also the social and cultural history of Europe. Others have focused on the writings of learned demonologists. While the great majority of studies have dealt with witch-hunting and witchcraft theory in the sixteenth and seventeenth centuries, when concern over this imagined crime peaked in western Europe, developments in the medieval period have also been well surveyed.[2] The fifteenth century, in particular, was the cradle of many later concerns. Here one finds the earliest true witch hunts in the sense of a series of related prosecutions (or waves of persecution, if you will) conducted by authorities committed to weeding out what they increasingly regarded as a pervasive menace, as opposed

---

1. Jonathan Barry and Owen Davies, eds., *Witchcraft Historiography* (Basingstoke, U.K., 2007).

2. The fundamental studies remain Jeffrey Burton Russell, *Witchcraft in the Middle Ages* (Ithaca, N.Y., 1972); Norman Cohn, *Europe's Inner Demons: The Demonization of Christians in Medieval Christendom*, 2nd ed. (Chicago, 2000 [1st ed., 1975]); Richard Kieckhefer, *European Witch Trials: Their Foundations in Popular and Learned Culture, 1300–1500* (Berkeley, 1976); Edward Peters, *The Magician, the Witch, and the Law* (Philadelphia, 1978).

to the more individual, isolated sorcery trials of earlier periods.[3] One also finds demonological literature in this period beginning to describe diabolical, conspiratorial sects of witches gathering at sabbaths (more typically referred to as synagogues in early sources), worshipping demons, and explicitly surrendering both their bodies and their souls to Satan, in whose service they then sought to afflict the church, undermine the true faith, and corrupt all of Christian society. The first such texts appeared in the 1430s, and many of these ideas reached an initial culmination (although profound developments were, of course, still to come) half a century later with the publication of the *Hammer of Witches* (*Malleus maleficarum*) in 1486.[4]

In this chapter I will not attempt a comprehensive survey of the emerging idea of witchcraft in the mid- to late fifteenth century, or even an examination of all aspects of superstition in the demonological literature of that era. For clerical writers, witchcraft was inherently superstitious, indeed it was the worst of superstitions, and a full treatment of this issue would inevitably require expanding our focus to encompass the totality of their work. Instead, I intend here to follow an important thread of discourse about superstition that I, not they, will isolate from the rest of witchcraft theory: their discussions of restorative rites and protective practices employed against maleficent witchcraft. Such rites could easily become superstitious, and authorities condemned them when they did. Yet they also allowed a perhaps surprising amount of space for faithful Christians to defend themselves against bewitchment, not just by official prayer and sacrament, although of course those came highly recommended, but by unofficial charms and rituals as well. In this sense, the same issues surrounded debate about superstition in witchcraft treatises as in the texts examined in the previous chapter. Authorities sought to control error while still encouraging as many potentially beneficial or even pious practices among the laity as possible. In this effort, they again confronted the frustrating dilemma of how to discern dangerous superstitious practices reliably from those that were salutary, laudable, or at the very least tolerable.

---

3. Much work has focused on lands around the western Alps, where the earliest trials clustered, and has been usefully summarized in Kathrin Utz Tremp, "Witches' Brooms and Magic Ointments: Twenty Years of Witchcraft Research at the University of Lausanne (1989–2009)," *MRW* 5 (2010): 173–87.

4. On early texts, see *L'imaginaire du sabbat: Edition critique des texts les plus anciens (1430 c.–1440 c.)*, ed. Martine Ostorero, Agostino Paravicini Bagliani, and Kathrin Utz Tremp, with Catherine Chène, CLHM 26 (Lausanne, 1999). On the *Malleus*, see below.

Demonologists and Their Practical Concerns

At the center of this chapter stand three prominent demonologists who together form a thread leading through the fifteenth century. All three were members of the Dominican order, all were trained as theologians, and two of the three were practicing inquisitors who personally tried witches. The first, and also the only one to lack that direct connection to witch-hunting, was Johannes Nider, whom we have already met as the author of an important commentary on the Ten Commandments. He is, however, better known to history as the author of a sprawling didactic treatise that took as its central metaphor for moral order the well-structured life of the industrious ant, and so which he titled the *Anthill* (*Formicarius*). The fifth book of this treatise in particular dealt with "Witches and Their Deceptions" (*De maleficis et eorum deceptionibus*), and among the cluster of early sources addressing witchcraft written in the 1430s, it was by far the most extensive. Born in the Swabian town of Isny, probably in the early 1380s, Nider entered the Dominican order at Colmar, in what is now French Alsace, in 1402. He studied at Cologne and then Vienna, where he taught briefly after obtaining his degree in theology in 1425. From 1427 to 1429, he served as prior of the Dominican convent in Nuremberg, and from 1429 until 1434 he was prior of the Dominicans in Basel, where he was also an important member of the great church council that convened there in 1431. Although he actually wrote the *Anthill* in Vienna, where he was again a professor from 1434 until his death in 1438, he clearly conceived of the work in Basel, and a number of his accounts of witchcraft come from what is now western Switzerland, particularly the region of the Bernese Oberland.[5] This work was tremendously influential and of enduring importance, surviving in at least twenty-six manuscripts and going through seven printed editions as late as 1692. A French translation was also published in Brussels in 1656. In addition, the fifth book of the *Anthill* was printed separately in certain editions of the *Hammer of Witches*, for which it served as a major source of information and ideas.[6]

The next figure is the French inquisitor Nicolas Jacquier. Born probably in Dijon around 1400, he was a generation younger than Nider but most likely met the senior Dominican when he attended the Council of Basel

---

5. Werner Tschacher, *Der Formicarius des Johannes Nider von 1437/38: Studien zu den Anfängen der europäischen Hexenverfolgungen im Spätmittelalter* (Aachen, 2000); Michael D. Bailey, *Battling Demons: Witchcraft, Heresy, and Reform in the Late Middle Ages* (University Park, Pa., 2003), esp. 91–138. Catherine Chène provides introduction and commentary in *Imaginaire du sabbat*, 101–20, 201–65.

6. Tschacher, *Der Formicarius*, 83–125.

in the early 1430s. He began his inquisitorial activities in the 1450s, first in the area around Lyon and then mainly in the Burgundian Low Countries. There he was based primarily in Lille, the site of one of the premier reformed Dominican priories in northern Europe and a major political and economic center of the Burgundian realm. A brief period in the late 1460s found him in central Europe, operating against heretical Hussites in Bohemia, but he soon returned to the Low Countries, dying in Ghent in 1472.[7] During his early years as an inquisitor, he wrote two treatises dealing with witchcraft: *On the Trampling of Demons* (*De calcatione daemonum*) in 1457, followed quickly by his major work, the *Scourge of Heretic Bewitchers* (*Flagellum haereticorum fascinariorum*) in 1458. Surviving in only nine known manuscript copies, and printed only once in 1581, Jacquier's *Scourge* was not so widely influential as Nider's *Anthill*, or certainly as the later *Hammer of Witches*.[8] Nevertheless, it was arguably the most important account of witchcraft written between those two treatises, and will serve here to cover the midcentury period.

Certainly other major demonological works appeared at this time. For example, the Dominican inquisitor Jean Vinet wrote a treatise *Against Invokers of Demons* (*Contra daemonum invocatores*) most likely in the early 1450s. Like Jacquier, he made important arguments for the reality, as opposed to the purely illusory nature, of witches' sabbaths. Educated in Paris and subsequently an inquisitor there and then in the southern French city of Carcassonne, however, he was at a greater remove from the mainly Germanic tradition I have focused on here. The same is true of Pierre Mamoris, a professor of theology at Poitiers, who wrote a *Scourge of Witches* (*Flagellum maleficorum*) between 1460 and 1462.[9] Jean (or Johann) Tinctor was born in Tournai, in the southern Low Countries, and served as a canon there at the end of his life. In between, he studied and taught for several decades at the University of Cologne, matriculating in 1423 and remaining on the faculty through the late 1450s. In Tournai around 1460 he wrote a treatise *Against the Sect of the Vaudois* (*Contra sectam Vaudensium*), drawing on the witch trials that had been conducted at nearby Arras beginning in 1459, and a French version of this work soon began to circulate as well.[10] Other figures could be

---

7. Martine Ostorero, *Le diable au sabbat: Littérature démonologique et sorcellerie (1440–1460)*, ML 38 (Florence, 2011), 117–48.

8. Ibid., 129–30, redates *De calcatione* from the traditional 1452 to 1457; ibid., 153–54, brings the list of known manuscripts of *Flagellum* to nine.

9. On both men, see ibid.

10. Brief excerpts in *Quellen*, 183–88. A full edition is available as Jean Tinctor, *Invectives contre la secte de vauderie*, ed. Émile Van Balberghe and Frédéric Duval (Tournai, 1999); Jan Veenstra is preparing a Latin edition (noted in Ostorero, *Diable au sabbat*, 13). On Tinctor, see Émile Van Balberghe

named from around Europe. Geography certainly played a role in shaping conceptions of witchcraft at this time, with particular aspects of the cumulative stereotype emerging from specific regions and diffusing at different rates into the general (educated) imagination.[11] Jacquier, however, will stand in (imperfectly) for them all.

Toward the end of the century, we encounter a truly towering figure, although also a deeply controversial one: Heinrich Kramer (Institoris). He completed his *Hammer of Witches* in 1486 and its subsequent influence is undeniable.[12] Over the next two hundred years it was printed in almost thirty separate editions. And yet it never became an absolutely definitive or universally accepted guide on witches and how to eradicate them. Its depiction of witchcraft was in fact as idiosyncratic as was Kramer himself. For such a well-known work, much about the *Hammer of Witches* remains uncertain or debated, including its authorship. Traditionally it has been attributed to both Kramer and his fellow Dominican Jakob Sprenger. Significant evidence, however, points to Kramer as the primary author. There is much in the *Hammer of Witches* that reflects his individual experience as a witch-hunter and his particular obsessions. Arguments then arise over the degree of Sprenger's participation. Some contend that he made at least modest contributions to the content of the treatise, others that he supplied virtually nothing but his name (he was more highly placed in the Dominican order and more respected as a theologian than Kramer). Still others assert that Kramer essentially stole his good name, presumably for the respectability it would confer, and that Sprenger either had no knowledge of the *Hammer of Witches* or that

and Jean-François Gilmont, "Les théologiens et la 'vauderie' au XVe siècle: À propos des oeuvres de Jean Tinctor à la bibliothèque de l'abbaye de Parc," in *Miscellanea codicologica F. Masai dicata*, ed. Pierre Cockshaw, Monique-Cécile Garand, and Pierre Jodogne (Ghent, 1979), 393–411. On the trials of 1459–60, see Franck Mercier, *La vauderie d'Arras: Une chasse aux sorcières à l'Automne du Moyen Âge* (Rennes, 2006).

11. Richard Kieckhefer, "Mythologies of Witchcraft in the Fifteenth Century," *MRW* 1 (2006): 79–108. Ostorero, *Diable au sabbat*, details nuanced differences between her three authors: Vinet, Jacquier, and Mamoris.

12. Aside from Hans Peter Broedel, *The Malleus Maleficarum and the Construction of Witchcraft: Theology and Popular Belief* (Manchester, 2003), much basic scholarship on Kramer and the *Malleus* has appeared in introductions to various editions and translations. See esp. André Schnyder, *Malleus Maleficarum von Heinrich Institoris (alias Kramer) unter Mithilfe Jakob Sprengers aufgrund der dämonologischen Tradition zusammengestellt: Kommentar zur Wiedergabe des Erstdrucks von 1487 (Hain 9238)* (Göppingen, 1993); Wolfgang Behringer and Günter Jerouschek, "'Das unheilvollste Buch der Weltliteratur'? Zur Entstehung- und Wirkungsgeschichte des Malleus Maleficarum und zu den Anfängen der Hexenverfolgung," in *Der Hexenhammer*, ed. and trans. Behringer, Jerouschek, and Werner Tschacher (Munich, 2000), 9–98; Christopher S. Mackay, "General Introduction," in *Malleus Maleficarum*, ed. and trans. Mackay, 2 vols. (Cambridge, 2006), 1:1–171.

he actually disapproved of it and of Kramer.[13] Hans Peter Broedel usefully cuts through much contention when he concludes, "Because the *Malleus* throughout reflects Institoris' [Kramer's] known preoccupations, it is likely that beyond lending the work the prestige of his name, Sprenger's contribution was probably minimal."[14] I agree, and I am content to refer to Kramer alone when discussing the author of the *Hammer of Witches*.

In his own day, as still in modern scholarship, Kramer was a polarizing figure. Born around 1430 in the German-Alsatian town of Schlettstadt (Sélestat, in what is now French Alsace), he joined the Dominican order there probably when he was around fifteen. By 1474, he had obtained a degree in theology, and in that year he began his career as an inquisitor. By the 1480s he was hunting witches. In the *Hammer of Witches* and other works he offered various accounts of his own exploits, all surely exaggerated. The first trials he conducted that can be confirmed by other records occurred in the Swabian town of Ravensburg in 1484. Here Kramer encountered significant resistance from local authorities, so much so that he petitioned Pope Innocent VIII for support and in December of that year obtained the famous "witch bull" *Desiring with Supreme Ardor* (*Summis desiderantes affectibus*), addressed to him and his senior colleague Jakob Sprenger, who was at this time also a papally appointed inquisitor, although he was much less active in that role than was Kramer. The bull proclaimed the danger that witches represented, clarified papal inquisitors' jurisdiction over them, and demanded that other officials, both ecclesiastical and secular, provide all due assistance in eradicating this menace. The bull had no connection to the later *Hammer of Witches*, but Kramer made sure it was included in the first printing (as it would be in most subsequent editions as well), thereby giving the work the luster of apparent papal approbation.

Kramer did not return to Ravensburg after obtaining Innocent's bull. Rather, he went to the Austrian Tyrol, where he conducted his next major witch hunt in 1485 at Innsbruck.[15] Arriving with all possible support, Kramer again quickly stirred up strong resistance from local officials. He clearly

---

13. Arguing that Sprenger had no input and even opposed Kramer is Peter Segl, "Heinrich Institoris: Persönlichkeit und literarisches Werk," in *Der Hexenhammer: Entstehung und Umfeld des Malleus maleficarum von 1487*, ed. Peter Segl (Cologne, 1988), 103–26; the position is strongly supported by Behringer and Jerouschek, "Das unheilvollste Buch," 31–37. Allowing Sprenger a greater role are Schnyder, *Malleus Maleficarum . . . Kommentar*, 419–25; and Mackay, "General Introduction," 103–21.

14. Broedel, *Malleus Maleficarum*, 18–19.

15. Richard Kieckhefer, "Magic at Innsbruck: The Case of 1485 Reexamined," in *Religion und Magie in Ostmitteleuropa: Spielräume theologischer Normierungsprozesse in Spätmittelalter und Früher Neuzeit*, ed. Thomas Wünsch (Berlin, 2006), 11–29.

possessed a confrontational personality, and even those who shared his concern about witches could find his methods extreme. By the end of the abortive hunt, the bishop of Brixen, Georg Golser, in whose diocese Innsbruck lay, declared that he thought Kramer to be senile and ordered him to leave the region in early 1486. Kramer retired to Cologne. Here he poured his energy into his magnum opus, the *Hammer of Witches*. Working quickly, he completed the long treatise that very year. No doubt resentful and suspicious of opposition after his failure in two major hunts, Kramer buttressed his text not only with Innocent VIII's papal bull, but also with an official declaration of approbation from the theological faculty at Cologne. Debates similar to those concerning the authorship of the *Hammer of Witches* rage around the authenticity of this document as well. Certainly Kramer obtained it in haste and probably by a somewhat irregular procedure. It actually represents two different documents merged into one, and it is not clear that all the signatories had read all or even any of the work in question. In short, the *Hammer of Witches* was far from a "standard" or especially authoritative witchcraft treatise in its origin, whatever its later influence would be. After its completion, Kramer's peripatetic life led him from the Rhineland to Augsburg, Regensburg, Salzburg, Venice, and briefly Rome, before finally taking him to Bohemia in 1500. Here he labored against the heretical Hussites until the end of his life, dying in Olomouc, a hundred miles east of Prague, in 1505.

The most well-known portions of the *Hammer of Witches* today are its long and often vitriolic attacks on women. More than any other demonologist, indeed far more than most, Kramer made the particular susceptibility of women to superstition, the deceptions of demons, and ultimately the sordid allures of witchcraft a centerpiece of his analysis.[16] Yet he was not an absolute misogynist. Like Johannes Nider, whose basic arguments about female weaknesses and proclivity for witchcraft he appropriated and greatly expanded, he could be strongly supportive of some female mystics and visionaries.[17]

---

16. See Broedel, *Malleus Maleficarum*, 167–84; also the provocative reading in Walter Stephens, *Demon Lovers: Witchcraft, Sex, and the Crisis of Belief* (Chicago, 2002), 32–57.

17. For contextualization of Kramer's broader gendered concerns, see Tamar Herzig, "Witches, Saints, and Heretics: Heinrich Kramer's Ties with Italian Women Mystics," *MRW* 1 (2006): 24–55; Herzig, "Flies, Heretics, and the Gendering of Witchcraft," *MRW* 5 (2010): 51–80. On connections between Nider and the *Malleus*, see Catherine Chène and Martine Ostorero, "Démonologie et misogynie: L'émergence d'un discours spécifique sur la femme dans l'élaboration doctrinale du sabbat au XVe siècle," in *Les femmes dans la société européenne / Die Frauen in der europäischen Gesellschaft: 8e Congrès des Historiennes suisses / 8. Schweizerische Historikerinnentagung*, ed. Anne-Lisa Head-König and Liliane Mottu-Weber (Geneva, 2000), 171–96.

He therefore provides a useful lesson that even in often formulaic demonological literature, and even in the thought of the purportedly most
focused—some would say monomaniacal—thinker, we can find unexpected
nuances.

Even more than Nider's *Anthill* or Jacquier's *Scourge*, the *Hammer of Witches*
will lie at the heart of my argument in this chapter. This is not because
Kramer's *Hammer* was somehow more representative of fifteenth-century
witchcraft theory than those other works. No one demonological treatise
ever defined the genre completely. While they all shared a common basis in
certain generally accepted scholastic doctrines, each followed its own approach and presented its own interpretation, with the *Hammer of Witches*
being as singular as any, and in many ways harsher than most. It will receive
so much of my attention here precisely because it was more severe, and
certainly more extensive, in its condemnations of witchcraft than any other
fifteenth-century source. It therefore provides more extensive discussion of
the potentially superstitious protective practices that interest me. An extreme
text in many ways, the *Hammer of Witches* could also be quite extreme in its
tolerance of such practices, although that is a judgment that requires a good
deal of nuancing.

The underlying question I want to broach in this chapter is this: For all of
their clearly stated concerns about the dangers of possible superstition, how
severely would the men whose thought we have been exploring actually have
reacted to the multitude of simple spells, charms, rites, and conjurations that
pervaded the world around them? This is a question that cannot be answered
definitively, as surprisingly little record of direct responses to specific cases
of perceived superstition survive. Werner of Friedberg, for example, was
hauled into court and interrogated about a number of erroneous beliefs and
practices. We know that he was forced to recant all the positions of which
he stood accused, but we do not know what further punishment or penance,
if any, he was required to undergo. The fate of the woman whose healing
blessing Werner had sanctioned, and who presumably returned to Neustadt,
used it on her son, and then probably taught it to her neighbors in the way
that many authorities were convinced loose-tongued women would, is lost
entirely to history. Even the effect of the case on the university community
in Heidelberg is uncertain. Among the theologians there, Nikolaus of Jauer
obviously continued to focus on superstition. As a remarkable surviving
manuscript reveals, however, at least one student at the university readily collected and recorded healing rites and other potentially superstitious practices
similar to some of Werner of Friedberg's only a few decades later, when

most of the men who sat in judgment over Werner were still active on the faculty.[18]

While witch trials cut a broad swath through the historiography of late medieval and early modern Europe, scholars have generally paid much less attention to the array of professional or semiprofessional healers and cunning-folk who actually constituted the vast majority of the "magic-users" of this era, to say nothing of the countless ordinary people who turned to spells and charms sporadically in times of need.[19] Theoretical literature is a poor substitute for complaints, accusations, and trials when attempting to track "real" levels of concern and perception of a supposed threat. These texts need not, and perhaps cannot, be read as referring to any kind of reality beyond their own intellectualized anxieties. Of course, the same could be said to some degree of trial records as well.[20] Moreover, surviving medieval trial records are extremely spotty, and a substantial number would need to be surveyed to yield anything other than impressionistic results. Instead, I will here tease what impressions I can from the theoretical literature.

Demonic Power and Defenses against Witchcraft

Like many other opponents of superstition, witchcraft theorists stressed the reality and imminent threat of demonic power. Their frequent and urgent injunctions are sometimes presented as clear evidence of widespread and growing fear of the devil in this period, but they can equally give the impression that no one else in late medieval society recognized the power of demons or gave much credence to the dire menace they represented.[21] Certainly there appears to have been at least some resistance to the notion that

---

18. Elizabeth I. Wade, "Magic and Superstition in a Fifteenth-Century Student Notebook," *Fifteenth-Century Studies* 28 (2003): 224–41; see also Elizabeth I. Wade-Sirabian, "Fifteenth-Century Medicine and Magic at the University of Heidelberg," *Fifteenth-Century Studies* 32 (2007): 191–208.

19. After the seminal work of Keith Thomas, *Religion and the Decline of Magic: Studies in Popular Beliefs in Sixteenth and Seventeenth Century England* (1971; repr., New York, 1997); see now Owen Davies, *Cunning-Folk: Popular Magic in English History* (London, 2003); Jonathan Roper, ed., *Charms and Charming in Europe* (Basingstoke, U.K., 2004). For Italy, David Gentilcore, *From Bishop to Witch: The System of the Sacred in Early Modern Terra d'Otranto* (Manchester, 1992), attempts to survey the entire spectrum of magical activity.

20. In lieu of an enormous body of postmodern theory, responses to it, and applications to the field of witchcraft, I will point here only to one recent, vigorous, and informative exchange: the special forum section "Contending Realities: Reactions to Edward Bever, *The Realities of Witchcraft and Popular Magic in Early Modern Europe: Culture, Cognition, and Everyday Life*," in *MRW* 5 (2010): 81–121.

21. Michael D. Bailey, "Concern over Superstition in Late Medieval Europe," in *The Religion of Fools? Superstition Past and Present*, ed. S. A. Smith and Alan Knight (Oxford, 2008), 115–33, at 126–27.

so terrible a danger would be embodied in the poor, illiterate old women who typically stood accused of witchcraft. The *Hammer of Witches* began by proposing the scholastic question "whether to assert that witches exist is such an orthodox position that stubbornly to defend its opposite is altogether heretical?"[22] The disbelief Kramer meant to challenge here was not in the reality of harmful sorcery (*maleficium*) per se, but that the *malefici* who performed it did so as sworn agents of the devil, as he would illustrate in the rest of his treatise. The context in which he wrote, in the immediate wake of two successive failed witch-hunting campaigns, is certainly also instructive. He felt a profound need to convince other ecclesiastical and secular authorities that the measures he had pursued against witches, which they clearly found excessive, were necessary in light of the magnitude of the danger.

Kramer was not alone in his basic concern on this point. Nicolas Jacquier also began his *Scourge of Heretic Bewitchers* by stressing that demons, and through them witches, were not an ephemeral threat, and that they could and did work real harm against faithful Christians.[23] In addition, Johannes Nider, although he did not foreground the material at the very outset of his work, joined Jacquier and Kramer in explaining at some length exactly how demons, and through them witches, could harm human beings, such as by causing illness, afflicting farm animals, and conjuring storms and hail to destroy crops.[24] He even presented several stories illustrating exactly how witches might perform such harmful magic. When a witch wanted to rouse a storm, for example, all she need do was stir a pail of water with the end of a broom. Nider assured his readers that this simple act had no efficacy in and of itself, but instead served as a signal given to a waiting demon with whom the witch had formed a preexisting pact. Kramer made a passing reference to this account in the *Hammer of Witches*, after he had already presented a more vulgar version: if a witch lacked water or pail, she might simply urinate in a ditch, then stir her own urine with her finger. Her attendant demon would understand the signal just as well, and would hasten to rouse a storm at her command.[25] Nider also related a more elaborate, and more overtly necromantic, form of weather magic. A male witch captured by a secular judge supposedly confessed that when he wished to conjure thunderstorms and

---

22. Kramer, *Malleus* 1.1, p. 217.

23. Jacquier, *Flagellum*, preface (unpaged).

24. Nider, *Formicarius* 5.3, pp. 348–49; also Nider, *Preceptorium* 1.11.15(t); Jacquier, *Flagellum* 12, pp. 85–90; 17, p. 119; Kramer, *Malleus* 2.1.11, pp. 455–58; 2.1.15, pp. 477–82.

25. Nider, *Preceptorium* 1.11.16(v); Kramer, *Malleus* 2.1.3, p. 409 (urine); 2.1.11, p. 458 (water in a pail).

hail, he would take a black fowl to a crossroads. There he would invoke the "prince of all demons," imploring him to dispatch a lesser demon to carry out the witch's desire. When that demon arrived, he would throw the fowl into the air as an offering to it, and it would then raise a storm to lay waste whatever fields or crops the witch indicated.[26]

One reason people may have questioned the real harmful power of demons, and so of witches, was that the church itself had long stressed how demons operated mainly by means of trickery and illusion rather than by physical action (although they were capable of both). Jacquier raised this issue with particular directness, noting that some people took the church's message on this point far too narrowly and concluded that demons could do nothing except tempt and deceive.[27] Perhaps the most canonical source for the idea of illusory demonic operations, and a deeply problematic one for fifteenth-century witchcraft theorists, was the late ninth- or early tenth-century canon *Episcopi*. Long since enshrined in canon law, this document stressed that women who believed that they traveled at night in the company of the goddess Diana had been "seduced by the illusions and phantasms of demons," and their experience had no physical reality.[28] To believe otherwise was superstitious, yet such beliefs persisted nonetheless.[29] In the fifteenth century, the notion of witches flying at night to demonic sabbaths gathered strength, although by no means was flight a necessary element of all descriptions of sabbaths in this period. Neither did authors need to deny *Episcopi* to accept an elaborate conception of the sabbath; the whole gathering could remain an illusion. Yet increasingly many authors stressed the reality of these fantastic and horrific assemblies, as a way to reinforce the terrible and degraded nature of witchcraft, and in order to reinforce the physical reality of demonic power and menace.[30]

Nicolas Jacquier was among the first demonologists to argue explicitly for the "difference between the sect and heresy of present-day witches and

26. Nider, *Formicarius* 5.4, p. 358.

27. Jacquier, *Flagellum* 1 and 4, pp. 2 and 26.

28. *Quellen*, 38.

29. Addressed, either with or without reference to *Episcopi*, in anonymous, *De divinacionibus*, 176v, 179r; anonymous, *De superstitionibus* (M), 296v–297r; Nicolau Eymerich, *Contra demonum invocatores*, 143v; Eymerich, *Directorium inquisitorum* 2.43, pp. 340–41; Hartlieb, *Buch*, 44; Johannes of Frankfurt, *Quaestio*, 76, 80; Nikolaus of Jauer, *De superstitionibus*, 43v; Pignon, *Contre les devineurs*, 235; Ulrich of Pottenstein, *Dekalog-Auslegung*, 81–82.

30. Werner Tschacher, "Der Flug durch die Luft zwischen Illusionstheorie und Realitätsbeweis: Studien zum sog. Kanon Episcopi und zum Hexenflug," *Zeitschrift der Savigny-Stiftung für Rechtsgeschichte* 116, Kan. Abt. 85 (1999): 225–76; Stephens, *Demon Lovers*, 125–44; Ostorero, *Diable au sabbat*, 574–617.

the deception of the women about whom the canon *Episcopi* speaks."[31] The ancient canon had not described witches gathering at a sabbath. The supposed nocturnal journeys with which it dealt (it never even specified flight, although this came to be assumed) were of an entirely different sort, consisting of women traveling through the night but toward no specified destination, with a demon who masqueraded as a pagan goddess. The canon remained authoritative, but the fact that demons acted only through the power of illusion in the particular case that it described, Jacquier argued, in no way precluded their ability to transport people physically in other circumstances. Thus the canon provided no basis to deny the material reality of witches' night-flight or of their unholy sabbaths. Like many other authorities, however, Jacquier also argued that even if the events of a sabbath were entirely illusory and witches participated in them only in spirit rather than in the flesh, that was still no reason to assert that these gatherings did not constitute "real" experiences and very real evil. In support of this point, he offered several examples of saints and biblical prophets transported spiritually by angels, which were, of course, the same order of being as demons and possessed the same abilities. These people, for example Ezekiel or Saint Paul, had certain experiences and revelations only in the spirit, but these were real and meaningful nonetheless. The same logic applied to the confessed experiences of witches.[32]

Writing twenty years earlier, Johannes Nider had not raised any explicit arguments either for or against the applicability of the canon *Episcopi* to cases of witchcraft. When he described gatherings of witches, they were entirely material, but also quite local and completely terrestrial affairs. No flight, real or illusory, was involved.[33] At one point, however, he strongly echoed the canon's position on illusory demonic flight. One of his own teachers, he claimed, had told him about a contemporary encounter between a Dominican friar and a woman who believed that she flew at night in the train of the goddess Diana. The skeptical friar asked if he could observe her as she did so, and she consented. Seating herself in a large bowl balanced on a bench, she lathered herself with an unguent, muttered a spell, and fell

---

31. "De differentia inter sectam et haeresim fascinariorum modernorum et illusionem mulierum de quibus loquitur c. Episcopi"; the title of Jacquier, *Flagellum* 7, pp. 36–51. For analysis, in addition to Ostorero, *Diable au sabbat*, see Matthew Champion, "Crushing the Canon: Nicolas Jacquier's Response to the Canon *Episcopi* in the *Flagellum haereticorum fascinariorum*," *MRW* 6 (2011): 183–211.

32. Jacquier, *Flagellum* 9, pp. 65–67.

33. Nider, *Formicarius* 5.3, pp. 350–52.

into a trance. Immediately she began to dream that she was in the company of the goddess. Rocking back and forth, she caused the bowl in which she had precariously perched herself to topple to the ground, but physically she traveled no further than that. Although a demon had clearly ensnared this woman, Nider did not call her a witch, and he did not place this account in book 5 of his *Anthill*, on witchcraft, but rather in book 2, on "revelations."[34] In the fifth book, he mentioned two witches who believed that they could fly with the aid of demons, although in this case the flight was not to a sabbath, and he also related a story about a knight who encountered a spectral troop while riding late one night near the Rhine. Mounting a horse they offered him, he flew with them to Jerusalem and back in the course of the night.[35] Nider would discuss such "armies of the night" more generally in his *Preceptor of Divine Law* (*Preceptorium divine legis*), and there too he would state unequivocally that demons could transport people physically through the air, although he hedged that many such experiences were only illusions.[36] Thus he validated the authority of *Episcopi* while still keeping open the possibility of "real" flight to a sabbath.

Heinrich Kramer, for his part, at the beginning of the *Hammer of Witches* explicitly differentiated the superstition of the women described in the canon *Episcopi* from that of contemporary witches. While he grouped the former, because of their visions, with other "pythonesses," he categorized the latter simply as witches (*malefici*)—a distinction unto themselves.[37] In terms of potential flight or "bodily transportation" worked by demons, he recognized that *Episcopi* might appear to present a problem, but like Nider he asserted that demons clearly possessed the necessary power to carry human bodies through the air, and he recounted several examples of captured witches who proclaimed that they had been transported in a fully waking and material state. Thus, agreeing with Jacquier, he concluded that while demons often worked through illusion as the canon *Episcopi* described, no one should assert on that basis that they could not also carry witches in the flesh to very real, substantial gatherings. In fact, he offered the testimony of a witch captured

---

34. Ibid., 2.4, pp. 123–24; also Nider, *Preceptorium* 1.10(a). On this aspect of the *Formicarius* see Gábor Klaniczay, "The Process of Trance: Heavenly and Diabolic Apparitions in Johannes Nider's *Formicarius*," in *Procession, Performance, Liturgy, and Ritual: Essays in Honor of Bryan R. Gillingham*, ed. Nancy Van Deusen (Ottawa, 2007), 203–58.

35. Nider, *Formicarius* 5.4, p. 354 (on the two witches); 5.1, pp. 337–38 (on the spectral army).

36. Nider, *Preceptorium* 1.11.5(i), 1.11.13(r).

37. Kramer, *Malleus* 1.1, p. 223: "Et species sub qua huiusmodi mulieres continentur vocatur species phitonum, in quibus demon vel loquitur vel mira operator, et est sepius prima in ordine, species autem sub qua malefici continentur vocatur species maleficorum."

in Breisach who reported that she often traveled in both states. If she did not want to attend a sabbath physically, but still wanted to keep in touch with her "associates" and know what had transpired, she would lie on her left side and a gray vapor would emerge from her mouth. In this way she would travel to the sabbath and participate in spirit.[38]

Asserting the physical reality of sabbaths and night-flight, at least as potentialities if not necessities, indirectly buttressed the reality of all other forms of demonic power to affect and afflict humanity in material ways. As Satan had once brought down terrible suffering on Job (the favorite biblical example of demonic power to harm), so now witches could assail their neighbors through the power they wielded by proxy. In the divine plan, the purpose of all these afflictions was the same: to test and temper the faithful. All clerical authorities agreed that demons, however great their power, could do nothing without God's tacit permission. Since their purpose was to test one's faith, the best defense most authorities could think to recommend against assault by witches was to maintain strong faith at all times. According to Johannes Nider, a demon itself had confirmed this. A witch captured by a secular magistrate had supposedly confessed that on one occasion he had been entirely unable to harm one of his neighbors. Annoyed at this, the witch summoned his demon and demanded to know why it was not fulfilling his commands. The creature responded that it could not directly harm anyone who had strong faith and who regularly used the sign of the cross as a defense.[39]

As this example illustrates, Nider also strongly recommended external actions to augment and exemplify internal integrity of faith. Specifically to ward off demons, the faithful could sprinkle their houses each Sunday with holy water. Every morning they should consume some consecrated salt. They should also frequently reinforce such defenses by making the sign of the cross, and they should not hesitate to call on the benevolent protection of guardian angels against the maleficent assaults of demons.[40] Separately, he enumerated five similar means of defense against witches (who of course operated solely by means of demonic power). First and foremost, maintain strong faith. Then faithfully employ the sign of the cross and official prayers sanctioned by the church. Attend Mass and other ecclesiastical ceremonies regularly. Then he included a point of public order: adhere carefully to "public justice" and secular law. Finally, ruminate as often as possible on the

---

38. Ibid., 2.1.3, pp. 403–11, witch of Breisach at p. 410.
39. Nider, *Formicarius* 5.4, p. 356.
40. Ibid., 5.2, p. 340.

passion of Christ.[41] None of these methods guaranteed complete protection. God had, after all, allowed Satan to plague even so righteous a man as Job. If, despite all one's best efforts, one nevertheless succumbed to some malevolent spell, Nider later outlined five remedies for bewitchment. One could undertake a pilgrimage to a saint's shrine. One could redouble one's use of the sign of the cross or legitimate prayers. Confession of sins could also serve to break the power of a bewitchment, presumably because those sins had rendered one vulnerable to witchcraft in the first place. People could employ "licit exorcism." Or they might seek to uncover a cursed item that, although functioning only as a signal to demons, was nevertheless somehow essential to the operation of a harmful spell and "cautiously" remove and destroy it.[42]

While this last remedy may seem, to modern sensibilities, to be of a rather different order from pious pilgrimage, prayer, confession, or even exorcism, Nider had no doubt of its efficacy. He related an account of a witch who had afflicted an entire household with infertility by placing a lizard under the threshold stone of the house. For years, the woman living there could not bring a child to term, nor could the few cattle that the couple possessed produce any calves. When the witch was eventually arrested and confessed to all this, authorities looked for the lizard but could not find it. Assuming that it had crumbled into dust in the course of years, they dug up and dispersed all the soil beneath the threshold, and soon both the woman and her livestock became fertile again.[43] Similarly Heinrich Kramer noted that when he was conducting his witch hunt in Innsbruck, a woman had recounted to him how she had been bewitched years earlier. Afflicted with tremendous pain throughout her body, she could find no relief until after four days the husband of the lady she served pointed out to her a bundle of white cloth that had been placed above the door of a local inn. Inside this package, she found white kernels of grain that resembled the pustules that had formed on her body, as well as seeds and plants and the bones of serpents and other animals. Burning all of this, she immediately recovered her health.[44] To return to Nider, when listing five remedies (seemingly the "magic number" in which groups of such cures always came) for people tormented sexually by an incubus or succubus, in addition to prayer, the sign of the cross, exorcism, and confession, he also noted that simply changing one's location

---

41. Ibid., 5.4, p. 356.
42. Ibid., 5.6, p. 370; also *Preceptorium* 1.11.17(x).
43. Nider, *Formicarius* 5.3, p. 350.
44. Kramer, *Malleus* 2.1.12, pp. 461–62.

might suffice. Here he related an account from the thirteenth-century Cistercian abbot Caesarius of Heisterbach's *Dialogue on Miracles* (*Dialogus miraculorum*) about the daughter of a certain priest who had freed herself from her incubus by crossing to the other side of the Rhine. Unfortunately the demon then turned on her father, who had remained behind, and tormented him so severely that he died within three days.[45] Still, the basic mechanism of moving across a river had worked. The one solution never permitted to those suffering under some bewitchment was to turn to further witchcraft for relief. Although witches could certainly cure as well as cause harm, Nider repeatedly asserted that Christians should suffer any malady or affliction, even to the point of death, rather than seek such aid as witches might promise.[46]

Nicolas Jacquier also sternly warned about the power of demons, and therefore of witches. Since they wielded forces greater than any in the world, no mere human art could counter their attacks.[47] Out of compassion for human frailty, however, God had provided faithful Christians with a number of means for protection. Not surprisingly, that number was five. In Jacquier's counting, these were prayer (especially the Lord's Prayer), the sign of the cross, holy water, pilgrimage or attendance at Mass, and the ministry of guardian angels.[48] Heinrich Kramer provided by far the most extensive account of remedies for witchcraft, dedicating the entire second "question" of the second part of the *Hammer of Witches* to this issue. While he offered more detail and colorfully illustrative stories, however, he did not vary in his substance from the recommendations of earlier authorities. In fact, in his assorted lists of remedies, he largely parroted Johannes Nider. He asserted strongly, and very notably at the start of this "question," that in addition to those who protected themselves by means of church sacramentals (holy water, blessed salt, candles, and so forth) and those who enjoyed the special protection of benevolent angels, any magistrate or legal authority would also be protected against witchcraft by virtue of his office, through which he maintained essential public order.[49] Nider had made this point fifty years before, citing the experience of a secular judge, Peter of Bern, who had provided him with much firsthand information about witches.[50] Kramer also

---

45. Nider, *Formicarius* 5.5, pp. 404–5.
46. Ibid., 5.3, pp. 352–51 (sic, misnumbered pagination); also 5.6, p. 371; likewise Nider, *Preceptorium* 1.11.17(x) and 1.11.33(oo).
47. Jacquier, *Flagellum* 10, p. 74.
48. Ibid., 14, pp. 96–108.
49. Kramer, *Malleus* 2.1, p. 378.
50. Nider, *Formicarius* 5.4, pp. 357–58.

repeated Nider's five remedies for people beset by incubi or succubi, his five general remedies for those afflicted by any sort of witchcraft (pilgrimage, confession, the sign of cross and prayer, exorcism, and the cautious removal of bewitched items—although Kramer listed them specifically as cures for those whom witches had rendered impotent or infertile), and his five general defenses against witches and demons (strong faith, the sign of cross and prayer, attendance at Mass and other church rites, observance of public justice, and meditation on Christ's passion).[51]

Not shockingly these men, all clerics and trained theologians, argued that against the very real harmful power of diabolical witchcraft good Christians should adhere ever more closely to the church, receiving its sacraments, imploring its saints, reciting its prayers, and shielding themselves by means of its sacramental items. The intensity and directness with which they did so could vary. While both Nider and Jacquier had recommended regular attendance at Mass as an effective means of protection from demonic assault, for example, Kramer added an illustrative story that drove the point home. Three men were walking down a road. Suddenly, two were blasted by bolts of lightning. The third heard a voice coming out of thin air saying, "Let's strike that one too," but another voice responded, "We cannot, because today the word was made flesh." The third man then understood that he was protected from these demons because he had attended Mass that day and had heard the opening of the Gospel of John leading up to the phrase "and the word was made flesh."[52] This example, clearly meant to reach the laity through sermons or other media, represents scare tactics at their most basic.

Beyond urging or frightening laypeople back into careful observance of church rite and ritual, however, several of the defenses and remedies that Nider, Jacquier, and Kramer recommended had a certain practicality to them as well. While one can easily imagine the theological justification for the automatic protection magistrates supposedly enjoyed by virtue of their office when proceeding against witches—that earthly justice was part of the divine order and so God sanctioned and supported its conduct—still Nider's account makes quite clear that without the promise of such protection the secular magistrate Peter of Bern would have had a very difficult time

---

51. Kramer, *Malleus* 2.2.1, p. 506; 2.2.2, p. 514; 2.2.7, pp. 550–51. Only in the first case, concerning incubi and succubi, did Kramer explicitly cite Nider as his source.

52. Ibid., 2.1, p. 382: "Sed et illi tres socij per viam ambulantes, duo eorum ictu fulminis percussi fuerant et tercius territus cum voces in aere clamantes audisset, 'Percutiamus et illam,' altera vox cum respondisset, 'Non possumus, quia hodie verbum caro factum est,' audiuit. Intellexerat quod ea de causa quia missam audierat et in fine misse euangelius Johannis 'In principio erat verbum et' etc. audisset, ideo preseruatus fuisset."

finding subordinates to help him conduct witch trials.[53] The discovery and removal of bewitched items carried no morally edifying or devotional quality. Moreover, by these demonologists' own theories, such items had no power in themselves and served only as a sign to demons, such that their removal and destruction should have carried no necessary beneficial consequence (unless one assumes that demons were perpetually forgetting whom witches had directed them to assail and needed these little markers to remind them of their targets). Presumably, however, the idea of witchcraft being performed through cursed items was deeply engrained in common culture, and stories of successful un-witchings by the discovery and destruction of such items must have abounded, so much so that authorities simply accommodated them within their schemes of possible protections and cures. They often extended this same accommodating tendency to any number of common protective charms or curative rites as well.

Legitimate Spells and Tolerable Superstitions

Beyond the realm of clearly approved ecclesiastical defenses against witchcraft, such as attending Mass, reciting the Lord's Prayer, or petitioning a saint or guardian angel for aid, lay an expansive world of common spells and charms, healing rites, and protective conjurations. Any theorist discussing witchcraft at any length had to address these potentially protective measures, and Heinrich Kramer in particular often expounded on them at considerable length. As a scholastic theologian, he shared the same basic premises regarding the boundaries separating legitimate rites and rituals from dangerous superstitions as did most of the other intellectual authorities whose thought we have explored. Certainly he sought to perform the same essential task as they did, namely to discern superstition reliably amid a great mass of legitimate, commendable, or at least tolerable common practices. Through the sheer volume of richly detailed examples he presented, most drawn supposedly from his own experiences and explicitly intended to instruct other witch-hunters, we can see a fifteenth-century mind working through this problem of discernment. True, Kramer's was but one mind, and one voice, opposing superstition and condemning witchcraft in this period, and we cannot take him as directly representative of any other late medieval theorist's, theologian's, inquisitor's, or magistrate's particular concerns. By all accounts, both those of his contemporaries and of later scholars, he was among the most

---

53. Nider, *Formicarius* 5.4, p. 358.

zealous, perhaps fanatical, witch-hunters of his day. Yet despite or possibly because of the intensity of his opposition to witchcraft, he carefully carved out a space for tolerable practices that bordered on the superstitious. He can, therefore, give us at least a sense of the modulations of concern operating in this period, and he can certainly provide insight into the intellectual work authorities had to perform as they tried to demarcate clear boundaries in this often uncertain terrain.

Perhaps the most basic practical boundary on which Kramer, like earlier authorities, insisted was that no one should resort to any kind of further witchcraft to remedy a bewitchment. Better to die than sink into such sin.[54] But how could one tell when a rite that yielded a positive effect was actually malevolent witchcraft? To have already identified the person who performed the rite as a witch provided an easy way out of this dilemma of discernment. No matter how benign a known witch's actions might seem or what beneficial ends they might appear to achieve, authorities could confidently declare that they were superstitious, demonic, and condemnable simply because of her inherent character as a disciple of Satan. Indeed, the *Hammer of Witches* proclaimed quite clearly that any cure performed by a known witch was illicit "as much on account of the one performing it as on account of the remedy itself."[55] That a witch contained within her very person at least some of the evil that rendered her actions illicit, as opposed to that evil inhering in the actions themselves, is apparent in Kramer's subsequent distinction. To effect a cure by means of "illicit and witch-like rites" but not through the person of a witch (*non quidem per maleficum sed per maleficiales ritus et illicitos*—Kramer does not clarify, but we must assume magical rites performed via demonic agency but not by a person who also participated in sabbaths or engaged in any other of the attendant horrors of the developing witch stereotype) was still superstitious and condemnable, but not quite to the same degree as witchcraft performed by a witch herself.[56]

Embedded in this discussion is one of the most convoluted sets of distinctions contained in the *Hammer of Witches*. Although Kramer ultimately labeled even the "witch-like rites" described above as basically illicit, albeit not as illicit as they might be if performed by a witch, he also declared that within that former category some rites had to be judged "vain and illicit" while others could in some sense be "vain [but] not illicit."[57] The clarification

54. Kramer, *Malleus* 2.2, p. 496.
55. Ibid., 2.2, p. 496: ". . . tam ex parte auctoris quam et ipsius remedii."
56. Ibid., 2.2, pp. 495–96.
57. Ibid., 2.2, p. 496: ". . . vel per illicitos et vanos ritus insimul vel per vanos et non illicitos."

(such as it is) of this tricky point comes in a further tripartite division that he subsequently developed. Once again, a bewitchment might be relieved by recourse to some witch who would perform further witchcraft (*per malefi-cum alium et per maleficia alia*). Alternately, a "respectable person" could effect a remedy, but in a "superstitious" way that merely transferred the injury or affliction to another person. Finally, the bewitchment might be undone completely (not merely transferred) in some manner that involved either the express or tacit invocation of demons but that did not rise to quite the same level of evil as witchcraft per se, that is, demonic magic practiced by a witch. Kramer proclaimed that he and all other theologians regarded each of these methods to be entirely illicit. Nevertheless, he conceded that "according to the canonists"—that is, the canon lawyers of the church—the second and third methods could sometimes be licit or at least "not vain," and "they can be tolerated when previously attempted church remedies . . . have not been effective."[58] Thus Kramer offered some sanction, although not his own, for certain explicitly superstitious and even demonic practices used to combat witchcraft. Much further in the *Hammer of Witches* he again invoked legal principles rather than theological ones (although here he noted that "certain theologians" actually agreed with their lawyer colleagues) to argue that, while explicit demonic invocation must always be condemned, rites that entailed only tacit invocations were "vain rather than illicit," and therefore should be tolerated by both secular and clerical authorities, including inquisitors like himself.[59] Kramer frequently and fully condemned numerous particular practices described in the *Hammer of Witches* that he evidently construed as involving only tacit invocations, however, so how he actually intended his own painstaking distinctions to be deployed remains a bit befuddling.

Demonologists were surely not alone in the fifteenth century in their confusion over the boundaries between legitimate or at least tolerable remedies for bewitchment and condemned superstitions or even witchcraft itself. Johannes Nider related a story about such ambiguities featuring two

---

58. Ibid.: "Vnde summarie dicere possumus quod per tria et tribus modis remedium redditur illicitum: quando videlicet tollitur per maleficum alium et per maleficia alia, videlicet virtute demonis alicuius; secundo quando non per maleficum sed honestam personam tollitur, sic tamen quod super-stitiosis remedijs maleficium quod vni persone aufertur alteri infertur, et hoc iterum illicitum; tertio, quando aufertur sine eo quod alteri infertur, vtitur tamen demonum inuocatione expressa vel tacita, tunc iterum illicitum. Et secundo hos modos dicitur a theologis quod potius mors sit preeligenda quam in talia consentire. Alijs vero duobus modis vltimis tollere maleficium potest esse vel licitum vel non vanum secundum canonistas, et quod tollerari possunt vbi remedia ecclesie prius attemptata, vt sunt exorcismi ecclesie, suffragia sanctorum implorata ac vera penitentia, nihil effecissent."

59. Ibid., 3.34, p. 702.

laypeople that supposedly played out in the diocese of Constance. In an area reported to be rife with witches, a man had suffered an injury to his foot and suspected witchcraft to be the cause. He tried many cures, but none brought any relief. Finally his friend, a pious old woman named Earnestine (*Seriosa*), visited him, and he begged her to bless his foot. She silently said the Lord's Prayer and the Apostles' Creed, made the sign of the cross, and immediately healed him. When he, mistaking her actions, asked her what "spells" (*carmina*) she had used, she angrily berated him for his weak faith and warned that he imperiled his soul every time he turned to such "spells and prohibited remedies."[60] Kramer repeated this account in the *Hammer of Witches*, and he felt compelled to add some commentary. Lest Earnestine's warning to her friend be taken too broadly, he explained that she had not intended to condemn all "blessings and incantations or even conjurations," but only illicit ones.[61] The dilemma of discernment illustrated by the story remained, however. One could be a direct witness to a rite, indeed be the object of its performance, and still be completely befuddled about what had transpired—legitimate blessing or illicit spell—as well as being uncertain about how such distinctions were to be drawn.

Like the man in the story, an inquisitor or secular magistrate could always ask a cunning-woman or healer what spells she had used and how they operated. Unfortunately, practitioners of rites that might be deemed superstitious had a habit of prevaricating when confronted by authorities. In a long story also recounting the cure of an injured foot, Kramer indicated what sort of details a careful inquisitor should notice to deduce the true character of a questionable rite.[62] A merchant from the city of Speyer, in the Rhineland, was traveling through the neighboring region of Swabia and stayed for some time with a local lord. He was walking one day with two other members of the lord's household when they saw a woman approaching. His companions warned him that she was a notorious witch and urged him to protect himself with the sign of the cross, as they both immediately did. The merchant scoffed at their trepidation, however, and refused to do so. No sooner had the woman passed by than he felt a crippling pain in his left foot. The two other men had to carry him back to the castle, where he lay suffering for three days. Finally his host sent for a peasant sorcerer and healer, a cunning-man, who knew how to counteract witchcraft. The merchant protested that he would not consent to be cured by any superstitious

---

60. Nider, *Formicarius* 5.4, p. 357.
61. Kramer, *Malleus* 2.2.6, p. 530.
62. Ibid., 2.2, pp. 500–501.

means, but the healer swore that he would apply only licit remedies. First, he needed to determine whether the injury was indeed the result of a bewitchment. He poured melted lead into water and observed the images that the cooling metal formed, concluding from these that the merchant had indeed been assaulted through witchcraft. This procedure drew entirely on natural forces, he explained to his troubled patient. Lead had an inherent affinity with the planet Saturn, and, because of the energies that Saturn radiated, when it was liquefied and poured into water in the vicinity of any witchcraft, it responded in certain clearly discernible ways. Having isolated the cause of the injury, the cunning-man turned next to his cure, which he was now confident he could perform. Asking the merchant how many days had passed since his encounter with the witch, he explained that the remedy would also require that long to operate. So for the next three days the peasant returned regularly to the castle, handling the merchant's foot and muttering words over it. On the third day, the cure took effect and the merchant could walk again.

Kramer then parsed this procedure. He praised the cunning-man's assertion that he would use only legitimate, nonsuperstitious methods to relieve the bewitchment, but clearly he did not trust it. He also praised the healer's contention that he had relied entirely on natural means to diagnose the existence of witchcraft. If these claims were true, the inquisitor observed, then the man was "irreproachable," indeed he should be "commended." Yet suspicions loomed. The actual forces that had caused the lead images to form in the water and especially the means by which the cunning-man had then carried out his cure remained in doubt (*sub dubio reliquitur*). Kramer was troubled by the fact that the man, once he had identified witchcraft as the cause of the injury, was absolutely certain that he could effect a cure, for this implied that he had access to the very same diabolical powers that had crippled the merchant. He noted that since the remedy involved only spoken words, and not the application of any material to the stricken foot, it could not be construed as drawing on any natural powers or curative properties. Above all, he homed in on the fact that the cunning-man had claimed that he needed to perform his rite over a specific number of days determined by the amount of time since the injury. Again this indicated a fearful equation between the healer's power and that of the witch herself. Kramer stated that he was fairly certain that the cunning-man was not actually a witch, yet still he had found more than enough grounds to suspect that the peasant had entered into at least a tacit pact with demonic forces through which he worked his cure. He recommended that the man be condemned.

Kramer went into similar detail about protective rites to ward off hailstorms caused by witches. Protecting crops or other property from storms was, understandably, a major concern for medieval peasants, and numerous rites and practices appear to have been common. Farmers raised crosses in their fields, or sought to have them blessed with the power of the Eucharist, or rang church bells at any sign of inclement weather so that the sound of the bells might divert the coming storm.[63] They apparently also gathered special herbs in midsummer on Saint John's Day and burned them in their fields, invoked Christ against coming storms, or hurled certain kinds of stones into the air to quell tempests.[64] The vernacular *Distaff Gospels* included a fairly elaborate rite to protect crops from storms that one of its female characters claimed she had learned in Savoy, a region that many church authorities strongly associated with witchcraft in this period. One should take four sticks of oak, fashion them into a cross, light them on fire, set them into the face of the wind, and make the sign of the cross. The coming storm would then alter its direction.[65] Authorities typically looked askance at such rites, although as we have seen their clear devotional elements (crosses, the sign of the cross, or prayers to Christ) induced some authorities to regard them as legitimate under certain conditions and within certain limitations. In his *Anthill*, for example, Johannes Nider mentioned with approval a rite designed to thwart hailstorms conjured by witches, revealed by a captured witch himself. Having confessed to raising hailstorms by demonic means, this man then explained that people could transform his destructive tempests into gentle rain by reciting a simple charm: "I adjure you, hail and winds, by the three holy nails of Christ, which pierced the hands and feet of Christ, and by the four evangelists, saints Matthew, Mark, Luke, and John, that you come down dissolved into water." Kramer repeated the example in the *Hammer of Witches*, with a similar sense of approbation.[66] In the absence of any detailed explication, one would assume that both Dominicans approved invoking divine power for protection, but that they would have rejected as superstitious any implication that the particular formula used, or any ritualized actions that might have accompanied it, bore any relevance to its efficacy. But perhaps this was not entirely so.

---

63. Heinrich of Gorkum, *De superstitiosis quibusdam casibus*, 4v; Johannes of Wünschelburg, *De superstitionibus*, 232v; Nikolaus of Jauer, *De superstitionibus*, 57r; Nider, *Preceptorium* 1.11.34(pp); Kramer, *Malleus* 2.2.7, p. 551.

64. Martin of Arles, *De superstitionibus*, 7v, 29v, and 61v respectively.

65. Anonymous, *Évangiles* 3.7, p. 126.

66. Nider, *Formicarius* 5.4, p. 358: "Adiuro vos grandines et ventos per tres Christi diuinos clauos qui Christi manus et pedes perforarunt, et per quator euangelistas sanctos Matthaeum, Marcum, Lucam, et Ioannem, vt in aqua resoluti descendatis"; Kramer, *Malleus* 2.2.7, p. 550.

Immediately before reiterating Nider's countercharm in the *Hammer of Witches*, Kramer had presented another much more complex rite that could also serve to defend against hailstorms raised by witchcraft. First, people should set up a cross in their fields. They must then kindle a fire into which they would cast hailstones while invoking the holy Trinity. Next they should repeat the Lord's Prayer two or three times, along with the Hail Mary, and recite the opening passage of the Gospel of John, "In the beginning was the word," while making the sign of the cross in all the cardinal directions. Finally they should proclaim "the word was made flesh" and "may this storm be put to flight by the words of this Gospel" three times each. Kramer declared such "experiments" (*experimenta*—a word also commonly applied to the elaborate rituals of elite necromancers[67]) to be "very true" and in no way suspicious (*hec verissima experimenta nec suspecta iudicantur*). He noted that simply throwing hailstones into a fire without invoking God would have been a superstitious act, and he explained that the rite could also be performed without casting any hailstones whatsoever. But he did not, as we might expect, altogether disparage the inclusion of such material components in this rite, nor did he regard them as a mysterious vanity that might signal a tacit demonic invocation. Rather than a corruption, he proclaimed the ritualized casting of hail into fire to be a perfectly legitimate act symbolizing the practitioner's desire to destroy the works of the devil.[68] Needless to say, not all authorities would have come to the same conclusion. In fact, Kramer himself can be seen coming to a somewhat different conclusion in his explication of another rite.

Witches, it would seem, often used their maleficent power to curse butter churns so that they would never produce butter no matter how long one might toil over them. Kramer reported that when women suspected that their churns has been bewitched and thought they knew who the responsible witch was, they would endeavor to obtain some pats of butter from her and would throw these into their churns while invoking the holy Trinity, thereby removing the bewitchment. This, Kramer declared, was rank superstition, the use of "vanity to crush vanities," but only because of the perceived need to obtain the witch's own butter to undo the spell. Rather than making some argument about how, by this act, women might symbolize their devout intention to churn all the works of witchcraft into oblivion, he argued instead

---

67. See Richard Kieckhefer, *Forbidden Rites: A Necromancer's Manual of the Fifteenth Century* (University Park, Pa., 1998), 23.

68. Kramer, *Malleus* 2.2.7, p. 550.

that they would be much better off using some of their own butter as a material component in the counterrite. Even that, however, would not be "commended." Instead, women should dispense with such vanities altogether and sprinkle their churns with holy water or blessed salt while invoking the Trinity.[69] One wonders whether the real reason for the differing levels of suspicion evident in these two cases was simply that the unwitching of butter churns was an expressly female practice, while presumably it was men who lit fires in the fields and ritually cast hailstones into them.

While a strongly gendered reading is never unwarranted with Kramer, he could also create some interesting space for superstitious but still tolerable acts, even when specifically performed by women. Among the various counterrites he discussed in the *Hammer of Witches*, Kramer presented several as typically being within the purview of women. One actually involved a method for striking back at a witch through the devil's own power. When village women suspected that a witch was preventing their cows from giving milk, they would hang a pitcher of milk over a fire, recite "certain superstitious words," and smash the pitcher with a stick. The witch, wherever she was, would feel as if she were being struck directly by this blow. This, Kramer explained, was because "the devil transfers all the blows to the back of the witch." Thus the rite operated quite explicitly through diabolical agency. Yet still he listed this practice as an at least marginally tolerable response to bewitchment, because, despite clear demonic involvement (clear to Kramer, that is), he declared that he saw no indication of a demonic pact, either explicit or implicit. Instead, his notion seems to have been that since the devil hated all humans, including his own servants, he was only too happy to see them suffer. Also, by bestowing efficacy on an at best borderline practice, he could also seduce some otherwise faithful women into more serious errors.[70]

Another questionable but ultimately permissible rite was intended to identify who had bewitched a cow. When a beast was so afflicted, Kramer asserted, women would sometimes place a man's breeches or other "foul thing" (*immundum*) on the animal and strike it, possibly even invoking the name of the devil as they did so. The beast would then charge to the house of the person who had bewitched it and ram its head repeatedly into her door. Again, the agent that directed the cow here was explicitly the devil. Thus Kramer saw much to be leery of in this practice. It was in no way "meritorious," and he entreated the women who employed it to give it up, do penance, and turn

---

69. Ibid., 2.2.7, p. 549.
70. The practice is described twice: Ibid., 2.2, pp. 494–95; 2.2, pp. 501–2.

to official remedies for witchcraft prescribed by the church. Nevertheless, at least in a strictly legalistic sense, the practice was to be tolerated.[71]

Kramer struck an even more suspicious but still grudgingly tolerant note regarding a custom that he associated with the women of Swabia. Before sunrise on the first day of May, women here would collect willow branches and weave them into wreaths that they would then hang over their barn doors, confident that this would protect the cows within from witchcraft for an entire year. We have seen, of course, how many authorities considered the gathering of herbs or other plants at specific times to be superstitious, and similar practices were common in many regions of Europe. The *Distaff Gospels*, for example, described women collecting herbs before dawn on Saint John's Day (Midsummer's Eve), which they would either rub in their milk pails or hang above their barn doors to ensure that their cows gave copious amounts of milk.[72] Kramer noted caustically that those who felt one could "crush vanities with vanities" might well approve of such rites. He stated that he wanted to proceed here "without offense" to anyone, so he did not argue against the legitimacy of this practice directly, but simply noted that women would be far better advised to collect whatever plants they wanted, while saying the Lord's Prayer or the Apostles' Creed, but without paying any special attention to the date or the time of day. If they then wanted to hang these over their barn doors while "in good faith entrusting the effect of protection to divine will," they need not be censured.[73]

One could multiply such examples, but in the end they would not reveal any completely coherent system for discerning superstitious responses to witchcraft from legitimate ones, or for distinguishing merely tolerable rites from commendable ones. And even if they did, such a system would pertain only to Kramer himself and could not be applied without careful study and modification to any other writers addressing these topics. Ultimately what the *Hammer of Witches* best reveals, because it was the most extensive demonological source written in the fifteenth century and because it was both a theoretical exploration of witchcraft and a practical guide to witch-hunting, is a fact that I suspect all intellectual authorities at this time must have known: despite their scholastic pursuit of clear categories and distinctions, practical discernment and appropriate response to superstition had to be worked out on a case-by-case basis. Kramer, for one, was completely confident that this

---

71. Ibid., 2.2, p. 502.
72. Anonymous, *Évangiles* 5.6, p. 162.
73. Kramer, *Malleus*, 2.2.7, pp. 547–48.

could be done, but the task required "diligent inquiry" by authorities in each situation.[74]

In one last effort at systematic guidance, toward the end of the *Hammer of Witches* he suggested four telltale signs of superstition that a judge should look for in any curative or protective rite employed against witchcraft. If cunning-folk accompanied their cures with some form of divination, for example pronouncing on their own where, when, or by whom the injured person had been afflicted instead of asking for this information, such knowledge could come only from a demon. If they could cure certain instances of magical harm but not other similar cases, this might indicate that they depended on the fickle assistance of demons rather than their own medicinal skills. If they introduced certain conditions under which they would or would not be able to effect a cure, this indicated superstition. For example, when a "respectable person" in the city of Speyer suffered a gash in her leg supposedly due to witchcraft, the cunning-woman who was summoned claimed that she would be able to heal the wound only if she found no scales or hair in it. Last, if they cured by means of "superstitious ceremonies," such as insisting on performing their rites at a particular time of day, Kramer recommended that they be held suspect.[75] He readily admitted that many other considerations could and should be added to these, however, and in the end he fell back on the most easily discernible point: the character of the person performing such rites. Judges should view with greater suspicion any rite practiced by people of bad repute, particularly when those people happened to be female. Although Kramer refrained from any final recitation of the shortcomings of women and their susceptibility to witchcraft and superstition here, he specifically used only the female forms of the terms he employed in a final, telling passage. Here he urged greater suspicion in cases involving *women* of bad repute, *women* who had committed adultery, and the children (literally, the "successors") of any *women* who had themselves been judged to be witches.[76]

Debates about superstition fed into and were perpetuated by debates about witchcraft. Again we have seen issues of discernment lying at the heart of

---

74. Ibid., 3.34, p. 703.
75. Ibid., 3.34, pp. 703–4.
76. Ibid., 3.34, p. 704: "Possunt et addi quamplures alie considerationes circa talium personarum conditiones, quia vt plurimum retroactis temporibus male et reprehensibilis vite fuerunt, diffamate seu adultere aut maleficarum superstites."

discussions of superstition, evident particularly in the sometimes tortuous considerations of which remedies for and defenses against witchcraft authorities should recommend, which ones they might at least tolerate, and which ones they had to condemn and strive to extirpate. Of all the antiwitch literature from the fifteenth century, the expansive *Hammer of Witches* shows this debate in fullest light. Kramer did not provide any kind of final summation of all thought on this subject, and we should not automatically extend his particular resolutions to other demonologists. Yet we need not do so in order to conclude that his laborious parsing of specific cases indicates his awareness of the uncertainties that confronted any authority dealing with potentially superstitious healing rites or protective charms.

Because authorities ultimately had to make most of the meaningful determinations about such cases—whether they lapsed into superstition, and if so to what degree; and whether they might still be tolerated in the face of the more terrible threat of full-blown witchcraft—on a very individual and situational basis, we cannot know how deeply and in what directions their concerns actually ran, in practice, without studying a broad sampling of accusations and their outcomes. What I have tried to suggest by pursuing the issue of superstition into the emerging witchcraft literature of the fifteenth century is that the issue of witchcraft and the developing image of the diabolical witch, while incorporating and in some cases greatly expanding many elements of earlier (and ongoing) concern, did not resolve or suppress any of the really fundamental debates about superstition. If anything, debate expanded, and while certain concerns became exacerbated, some intriguing new space also opened for a modulated toleration.

Most basically, I have argued that if even so dedicated and driven a witch-hunter as Heinrich Kramer, whom many contemporaries regarded as unacceptably ferocious in his pursuits, still carefully considered relatively fine points of various practices (as well as certain blunt points, such as whether the practitioner was male or female) and tried to allow as much opportunity for permissible but unofficial responses to witchcraft as possible, then we cannot conclude anything so simple about concern over superstition as that it grew steadily worse throughout the fifteenth century. Its relationship to emerging notions of witchcraft, and its history in general, is more complicated and nuanced than that straightforward judgment would allow.

CHAPTER 6

Toward Disenchantment?

> The fate of our times is characterized by rationaliza-
> tion and intellectualization and, above all, by the
> "disenchantment of the world."
>
> —Max Weber, "Science as a Vocation"

Concern about supposedly superstitious prac-
tices persisted long after the fifteenth century, figuring prominently in major
debates associated with the Reformation in the sixteenth century, the Scientific Revolution in the seventeenth, and the Enlightenment in the eighteenth.
In none of these periods did the history of superstition ever proceed along an
entirely straightforward trajectory. Oscillations continued, along with some
surprising connections and curious byways. Ultimately, superstition came
to be deeply implicated in one of the most important but also disputed
trajectories in all of history, namely Europe's progression from a supposedly
distinct medieval era to a discernibly modern one, and in the nineteenth
and twentieth centuries discourse about superstition helped shape the highly
charged theoretical category of modernity itself.[1] A rejection of "mysterious
incalculable forces" in the universe and of "magical means . . . to master or
implore the spirits" in favor of the cold calculations of scientific rationality
was a central feature of the German sociologist Max Weber's conception of
a disenchanted world in the early 1900s. So was an identification of much

---

1. Euan Cameron, *Enchanted Europe: Superstition, Reason, and Religion 1250–1750* (Oxford,
2010), 10.

religious ritual as "magical" and "superstitious."[2] In the years since Weber introduced the notion, disenchantment has been rigorously contested and critiqued, but has nevertheless established itself as a central pillar of Western modernity.

How then to end a history of "late medieval" superstition? One could, of course, simply stop, comfortable with the traditional periodization that a distinct historical epoch was nearing its end around the year 1500. Scholars focusing on the fourteenth and fifteenth centuries often confront the broad characterization of their chosen period, when it is set in the overall course of European history, as one of decrepitude and decline awaiting the sudden rejuvenation of nascent early modernity. As usual, the classic account of Johan Huizinga provides some of the most evocative expressions along these lines. Here he is writing of witchcraft:

> So towards the end of the Middle Ages this dark system of delusion and cruelty grew slowly to completion. All the deficiencies of medieval thinking and its inherent tendencies to gross error had contributed to its building. The fifteenth century transmitted it to the coming age like a horrible disease, which for a long time neither classical culture nor Protestant reformation nor the Catholic revival were able or even willing to cure.[3]

Yet specialized scholarship has long dispensed with such notions of autumnal "lateness."[4] In fact, many experts have noted that articulations of an inherently sick and waning late medieval period such as Huizinga's that appeared during the late nineteenth and early twentieth centuries had at least as much to do with the fin-de-siècle atmosphere of those times as with fourteenth- and fifteenth-century realities.[5]

---

2. Weber, "Science as a Vocation," in *From Max Weber: Essays in Sociology*, ed. and trans. H. H. Gerth and C. Wright Mills (New York, 1946), 129–56, at 139, 155; Weber, *The Protestant Ethic and the Spirit of Capitalism*, trans. Talcott Parsons (New York, 1958), 61.

3. Here from the older translation (really an English adaptation under Huizinga's direction) *The Waning of the Middle Ages: A Study of the Forms of Life, Thought, and Art in France and the Netherlands in the Dawn of the Renaissance*, trans. Fritz Hopman (London, 1924), 241–42; roughly corresponding to Huizinga, *The Autumn of the Middle Ages*, trans. Rodney J. Payton and Ulrich Mammitzsch (Chicago, 1996), 286.

4. The most trenchant critique is Howard Kaminsky, "From Lateness to Waning to Crisis: The Burden of the Later Middle Ages," *Journal of Early Modern History* 4 (2000): 85–125. On superstition, see Michael D. Bailey, "A Late-Medieval Crisis of Superstition?" *Speculum* 84 (2009): 633–61.

5. For Huizinga, see Wessel Krul, "In the Mirror of van Eyck: Johan Huizinga's *Autumn of the Middle Ages*," *Journal of Medieval and Early Modern Studies* 27 (1997): 353–84; more generally Erich Meuthen, "Gab es ein spätes Mittelalter?" in *Spätzeit: Studien zu den Problemen eines historischen Epochenbegriffs*, ed. Johannes Kunisch (Berlin, 1990), 91–135, at 108.

In this book, I have concentrated on the period from roughly 1300 to 1500 in order to highlight the complex developments attendant to debates about superstition and the particular contexts that shaped debate during a substantial but still relatively contained stretch of time. Already in the fifteenth century, the notion of diabolical, conspiratorial witchcraft began to alter these contexts, and in the sixteenth century the Reformation did so even more (although it did not utterly transform them). I also recognize, however, that a line drawn somewhere around the year 1500 does not represent any absolute watershed in the history of superstition.[6] Throughout the preceding chapters, I have referred to the two centuries on which I have mainly focused as "late medieval" not because I think some definable age of history declined to its end in those years, but simply because no other generally accepted designation yet exists for this era.

All periodizations and all sweeping characterizations of supposed historical epochs are of course artificial constructions, conveniences for historians and other scholars when they need to work in broad strokes. Grand periodizations, however, deeply set not just in academic but in more general intellectual and cultural frameworks, also exert their own force, and few if any periodic divides are as powerful, not just within European history but globally, as that of medieval/modern.[7] It is often meant to signify not just a passage of years but a supposedly wholesale transformation from a backward age mired in "irrational superstition" to a brave new world governed by scientific reason and characterized by endless horizons of technological and social progress. Western societies have used this construction to define their own development, frequently characterized by a sharp separation from (and sometimes a heroic overcoming of) the benighted past, and they have also used it as a tool to dominate non-Western societies and to justify that dominance.[8]

6. See Michael D. Bailey, *Magic and Superstition in Europe: A Concise History from Antiquity to the Present* (Lanham, Md., 2007), esp. 109; Bailey, "The Age of Magicians: Periodization in the History of European Magic," *MRW* 3 (2008): 1–28.

7. Margreta de Grazia, "The Modern Divide: From Either Side," *Journal of Medieval and Early Modern Studies* 37 (2007): 453–67, at 453; Kathleen Davis, *Periodization and Sovereignty: How Ideas of Feudalism and Secularization Govern the Politics of Time* (Philadelphia, 2008), 1.

8. Andrew Cole and D. Vance Smith, "Introduction: Outside Modernity," in *The Legitimacy of the Middle Ages: On the Unwritten History of Theory*, ed. Cole and Smith (Durham, N.C., 2010), 1–36, at 2; Kathleen Davis and Nadia Altschul, "The Idea of 'the Middle Ages' Outside Europe," in *Medievalisms in the Postcolonial World: The Idea of "the Middle Ages" Outside Europe*, ed. Davis and Altschul (Baltimore, 2009), 1–24, esp. 1–2.

In this final chapter, therefore, I want first to summarize the key developments related to superstition that I have traced in the fourteenth and fifteenth centuries, and then to carry the story of "medieval" superstition forward into the early modern era and ultimately into the realm of modernity itself. Of course this will not amount to a full study of superstition in these later periods, only an exploration of the peculiar afterlife of certain aspects of the discourse about superstition that this book has explored. In the sixteenth and seventeenth centuries, through all the religious and intellectual upheaval of the Reformation and Scientific Revolution, debates about superstition continued to address many of the same basic issues as in the fourteenth and fifteenth centuries. Even into the eighteenth-century Enlightenment, Europe never experienced any truly definitive moment of disenchantment that marked some absolute or dramatic shift in understandings of superstition or the superstitious. Nevertheless, disenchantment and a supposedly dramatic realignment of conceptions and concerns about superstition came to figure prominently in the notion of a major rupture between the "medieval" and the "modern" that eventually solidified in European history and became a key conceptual basis for European modernity.

This conclusion will therefore carry us quite far from the specific intricacies of fourteenth- and fifteenth-century debates about superstitious beliefs and practices. I will, however, venture to close the circle, at least in part, by suggesting how the complex history of medieval superstition sheds valuable light on supposedly disenchanted modernity and the processes of historical change that have led to it. This is a fairly standard gambit that I want to push in a somewhat new direction. Because no historian of Europe's Middle Ages can ever fully escape the power of the medieval/modern divide, we often succumb to it instead and seek to illustrate the significance of our work by positioning it in deliberate relation to the modern world. Either we strive to locate certain protomodern developments in medieval centuries (the "medieval origins of the modern state" is one famous example), or we stress the strange and therefore illuminating otherness—the alterity—of many medieval beliefs and practices.[9] The history of late medieval superstition could be cast in either mold. As theorists and critical thinkers increasingly undercut the basic conception of modernity that was established in the late nineteenth

---

9. See Paul Freedman and Gabrielle M. Speigel, "Medievalisms Old and New: The Rediscovery of Alterity in North American Medieval Studies," *AHR* 103 (1998): 677–704; also Paul Freedman, "The Medieval Other: The Middle Ages as Other," in *Marvels, Monsters, and Miracles: Studies in the Medieval and Early Modern Imaginations*, ed. Timothy S. Jones and David A. Sprunger (Kalamazoo, Mich., 2002), 1–24.

and early twentieth centuries, however, another means of relation, or at least of resonance, becomes possible. Insofar as a stilted and stylized idea of "medieval superstition" became a fundamental component of modernity, then the actual history of superstition in the late Middle Ages may allow us to better understand how the artifice of modernity developed, precisely because it reveals certain concepts and concerns supposedly critical to those later developments already under debate and undergoing important alteration in a period before they became weighted with any notions of radical newness or some epochal shift in European history.

Late Medieval Superstition in Sum

In one very meaningful sense, superstition never changes. It is always that which dominant elements within a society (or dominating elements from outside) categorize as illicit and beyond the bounds of proper belief, rational thought, or legitimate practice. The grounds for that judgment, and the intensity with which those boundaries are policed, can vary widely across space and time. Over the course of the fourteenth and fifteenth centuries in western Europe, concern about superstition grew more intense, although that intensification was hardly linear, and we must always keep in mind that, while some authorities were extremely preoccupied with the perceived dangers posed by superstitious practices, others remained largely indifferent. While Nicole Oresme and Heinrich of Langenstein were decrying astrological superstitions at the French royal court, for example, the future king Charles V was assembling the largest library of astrological texts in medieval Europe. And Oresme and Langenstein were themselves much more focused on "scientific" errors constituting superstition rather than the demonic threat that worried many of their contemporaries. One reason for such variances was the uncertain and often changing nature of what constituted superstition. Few people, if any, would have pursued actions that they themselves regarded as superstitious. Rather, these actions, as well as the beliefs that certain actions supposedly demonstrated or the basic understandings of natural and spiritual operations in which they were grounded, became superstitious in the eyes of others. Even authorities trained in the same schools of thought, however, sometimes came to very different conclusions about where the proper boundaries of superstition lay. Over these two centuries, conceptions of superstition and the dangers that it entailed shifted back and forth in some dramatic ways. And yet, for all the dynamism and important development in fourteenth- and fifteenth-century thought in this area, the theologians and other Christian authorities whose works lie at the heart of this book did not undertake any kind of intellectual revolution. Rather, they contributed to the sort of gradual change that characterizes most of history.

These men, all clerics educated in the scholastic tradition, built on what they regarded as firm bedrock, namely deeply rooted Christian opposition to *superstitio* and long-established conceptions of what superstition, in its essence, entailed. Like any bedrock, that tradition itself was at one time molten and mutable, but looking back from the fourteenth and fifteenth centuries, these men saw the writings of Augustine and Isidore, and even, for the most part, those of William of Auvergne and Thomas Aquinas, as stable and authoritative. In fact, of course, Augustine had written to impose order and stake out certain boundaries amid the vibrant interaction of Christianity and paganism in late antiquity. William and Thomas struggled to accommodate the new learning that had swept over Europe in the twelfth and thirteenth centuries, and to resolve some of the dilemmas to which it had given rise. As scholastic theology solidified and Aristotelian natural philosophy became almost universally accepted, demonic action and power, particularly as it supposedly manifested in acts of superstition and sorcery, had to be fit into these new systems, while at the same time an awkward space for potentially acceptable "natural magic" emerged. Also in the twelfth and thirteenth centuries, the church's ability and commitment to establish devotional control over the lay masses grew considerably. Especially after the Fourth Lateran Council in 1215, new and more stringent systems of preaching, confession, and ultimately inquisition spread across western Europe, imposing networks of instruction, observation, and discipline.

From these two great developments, the intellectual and the pastoral, grew the specific elements of concern and debate about superstition that manifested in the fourteenth and fifteenth centuries. At universities, clerical elites experimented with decidedly learned arts, some of which, such as astrological divination and astral magic, were grounded in natural philosophy, while others, like necromancy, boldly sought to control the powers of preternatural spirits. All of them tested the limits of superstition. Not surprisingly, critics arose, the ferocity of their opposition depending on their particular circumstances and often no doubt on their particular personalities. Popes and inquisitors decried necromancy. Worried courtiers attacked erroneous astrology, either as false science or as dangerous demonic idolatry, and warned princes against these perilous practices. Some of the most important figures to engage with superstition came, as one might expect, from the court and university of Paris, the preeminent intellectual center in northern Europe. There also, in the person of Jean Gerson, the growing concern within the church to define and control lay devotional practices in a broad and pervasive fashion merged with debates about elite necromantic conjuration and astral divination. Gerson's was not the only voice calling for an extension of concern about superstition to common beliefs and practices widespread among the laity, but his was certainly the most powerful. Even as he embodied the drive within the church to monitor lay piety more closely, however, he also exemplified the concomitant desire to foster and promote the devotional energies of the laity as much as possible, short of having them erupt into superstitious error.

In the early fifteenth century, these dual trends to regulate but also to promote lay piety manifested across Europe. Yet nowhere do the concerns they evoked appear to have been more intense than in the lands of the German Empire, where the writings of Jean Gerson exerted a particularly strong influence on the faculties of numerous new universities. The most vexing issue for these men was also the most basic: how to discern superstitious practices reliably from permissible ones. In the end, for all their efforts at categorization and explication, they never found a systematic solution to this problem. Their conviction that spiritual power, both demonic and divine, infused material creation precluded any kind of crisp "modern" separation between the physical and the spiritual realms, between the sacred and the profane, or between religion, science, and magic (not that modern divisions along these lines are, in reality, all that stable either). At the same time, their insistence on the terrible, almost insuperable power of demons, and of course on the absolute sovereignty of God, required them to deny that spiritual forces could be compelled by any mere human action or ritual performance. What mattered, certainly when supplicating the deity, was intention and internal conviction. Yet rites in themselves also remained important. Holy things could be debased by improper use even if one's convictions remained entirely pious. A garbled prayer could become a demonic invocation, whatever one's intent. In some accounts, demons seemed to crowd the air, hovering over humans in wait of any small error in ritual action that would allow them to swoop in and work their corruption. The idea of the tacit demonic pact, advocated by Augustine and reiterated by Aquinas, would appear to have given the lie to any insistence on the singular importance of pure faith and pious intent. One might believe, and believe, and yet still prove a villain, victim of an unintended but fundamentally damning performative slip.

Critics of superstition in the fourteenth and fifteenth centuries struggled with these problems and incompatibilities, and they hit upon some problematic but workable solutions, stressing the authority of the church to condemn actions based on their potential for superstition rather than their inherently superstitious nature, and above all focusing judgment on the person performing a rite rather than on the rite itself. They neither sought nor inadvertently achieved, however, any major reconceptualization of superstition or what it entailed, content always to ground themselves securely in past authority even as they faced the new conditions and challenges of their present. For all that they stressed demonic concerns, they could also express some surprising tolerance for many common rites and practices, either because they saw in them the expression of legitimate devotion, or just because they viewed them as less heinous than the horrors of diabolical witchcraft. They and the world they inhabited were complex and nuanced, always changing but by no means moving inevitably in a single clear direction. Such conclusions are fairly basic to history, but they are often forgotten in the history of superstition, especially when medieval superstition is set into standard schemes of the larger historical progress of the Western world.

Medieval Europe exists in an uneasy conceptual relationship with its modern progeny, conceived of being at once starkly different from but also foundational for the world that succeeded it.[10] These tensions lie as much in the realm of modern historical perceptions as in any past "reality," but they are no less real for that. Issues of superstition and disenchantment cast the complexities of this relationship in stark relief. On one hand, careful study of superstition elides any easy division between "late medieval" and "early modern," and the closer one looks, the more elusive seems the notion of disenchantment anywhere in the early modern centuries (and perhaps in the modern, as well). On the other hand, critics of superstition in the fourteenth and fifteenth centuries, certainly the eventual witch-hunters among them, can appear to epitomize a profoundly "other" medieval past, separated from modern Western rationalism not just by chronological distance but by a dramatic conceptual break. They have often been presented this way at least since the time of the Enlightenment. Crudely put, the modern world sees itself as disenchanted, and they were profoundly, at times viciously, not. To see how this situation came to be, we must trace the course of putative disenchantment, first in the early modern era and then amid the tangled thickets of modernity itself.

Superstition and Disenchantment in the Early Modern Era

In many ways, authorities continued to employ the category of superstition in the sixteenth, seventeenth, and even eighteenth centuries much as they had

---

10. Freedman, "Medieval Other," esp. 22–24.

during the fourteenth and fifteenth: as they revised or accommodated themselves to revisions of proper religious devotion and appropriate interaction between humanity and the divine; as they debated how spiritual power, both demonic and divine, might manifest in the physical world; as they fashioned new ways of knowing, understanding, and manipulating that world; and ultimately as they reconsidered and refashioned notions of rationality itself. Thus debates about the proper boundaries of superstition and condemnation of practices or modes of thought deemed to be superstitious remained complex and charged in the early modern era. Indeed, these matters became even more fraught as authorities deployed the concept of superstition to broach fundamental religious and intellectual issues ever more directly, and as they did so in contexts that were increasingly weighted with explicit invocations of newness and declarations that the benighted ideas of the past were at last being overcome. In all this, however, a specific moment of disenchantment is difficult to find.

At the juncture of the traditionally conceived Middle Ages and the early modern era, the period of the Renaissance occupies an ambivalent place. Already in the fifteenth century, Italian humanists considered that they and their society had broken with the immediate past, developing the very notion of a preceding "medieval" period of which they were no longer a part. Yet literally, of course, the Renaissance was not a novelty but a rebirth and a restoration, itself reiterating a characteristically medieval pattern of intellectual return to antiquity.[11] A long tradition of scholarship has effectively reframed many "Renaissance" developments as emerging from medieval trends rather than breaking decisively with them.[12] Also, and bearing more directly on its relative absence from my analysis here, the Renaissance has never been considered to have been a moment of disenchantment. Instead, Neoplatonically and hermetically inspired humanists developed new forms of occult philosophy and practice, creating what is often described as a distinctly Renaissance variety of magic. Debate now centers on whether that magic was in fact significantly different from medieval forms, but regardless the Renaissance has always been thought of, in part, as a magical age.[13]

Scholars now widely acknowledge that the origins of the Reformation and many of the basic reformist concerns that underlay the tumults of the

11. De Grazia, "Modern Divide," situates Renaissance notions of novelty within issues of periodization.

12. See William Caferro, *Contesting the Renaissance* (Oxford, 2011).

13. Frank Klaassen, "Medieval Ritual Magic in the Renaissance," *Aries* 3 (2003): 166–99; Richard Kieckhefer, "Did Magic Have a Renaissance? An Historiographic Question Revisited," in *Magic and the Classical Tradition*, ed. Charles Burnett and W. F. Ryan (London, 2006), 199–212.

sixteenth century also stretch far back into the Middle Ages. Unlike the Renaissance, however, the Reformation has not been so completely repositioned in terms of its medieval antecedent, and a tendency persists to treat it as marking a singular, decisive break with the medieval past. Constantin Fasolt has summarized this scholarship and subjected it to a powerful critique.[14] He does not build his case around the issue of superstition, but he could have. The history of magic and superstition represents an area of significant continuity between the fifteenth and sixteenth centuries. Basic concerns about superstition remained remarkably similar among both Protestants and Catholics, even as each group accused the other of succumbing to grave superstitious error. Likewise fear of witchcraft and methods of witch-hunting developed almost irrespective of confessional divides. The notion of a fully disenchanted Reformation, or a disenchanting one, has largely been put to rest in specialized scholarship.[15] Nevertheless, as Euan Cameron has argued in his sweeping study of superstition across the late medieval and early modern centuries, Reformation-era debates did introduce certain basic reconceptualizations of the meaning and efficacy of religious ritual that would eventually affect the understanding of superstition in important ways.[16] They also generated among both Protestant and Catholic authorities, although in different ways and to differing degrees, a rhetoric of "newness" and separation from the immediate past that deeply influenced later historical perceptions and periodizations.[17] The enduring association of the Reformation with the emergence of "modern" religion, resting in part on the period's rhetoric about superstition, is a major reason why it continues to be regarded as a point of such dramatic historical rupture.

In terms of continuities, superstition remained a significant concern, and opposition to superstition a central programmatic point, for reformers both Protestant and Catholic. In fact, while Cameron regards the entire period from the thirteenth through the eighteenth centuries as one of intense debate over superstition, other scholars have suggested that the absolute apogee of concern came in the 1500s, brought to a fever pitch by the intense religious strife of the Reformation itself.[18] In most ways, however, the intellectual

---

14. Constantin Fasolt, "Hegel's Ghost: Europe, the Reformation, and the Middle Ages," *Viator* 39 (2008): 345–86.

15. See Alexandra Walsham, "The Reformation and 'the Disenchantment of the World' Reassessed," *Historical Journal* 51 (2008): 497–528.

16. Cameron, *Enchanted Europe*, 156.

17. Fasolt, "Hegel's Ghost," 380–81.

18. Helen Parish and William G. Naphy, "Introduction," to *Religion and Superstition in Reformation Europe*, ed. Parish and Naphy (Manchester, 2002), 1–22, at 19.

foundations for these anxieties were no different from those that underlay the thought of the clerical authorities we have examined in the 1300s and 1400s. Most intellectuals continued to work within an essentially scholastic system in terms of both theology and natural philosophy, and they defined and delimited superstition based on these frameworks.[19] Neither did concern about witchcraft or the conduct of witch trials alter notably with the onset of the Reformation. Keith Thomas even put forward an influential argument that Protestantism, insofar as it enacted a certain measure of disenchantment by eliminating the protective "magic" provided by the medieval church, augmented fear of witchcraft and therefore promoted the need for witch hunts.[20] In fact, despite all their effort, ministers of the new faith met with little success stamping out the multitudinous rites by which people sought to protect themselves from harmful magical assault, or to restore health, or to perceive the future. While they did eliminate many practices bearing the clear stain of Catholicism—invocation of saints, veneration of relics, or use of consecrated sacramentals—they often saw new "Protestant" superstitions rise in place of these.[21]

In their designation of Catholic rites and Catholicism itself as superstitious, however, Protestant leaders did introduce an important new element into the discourse of superstition and its deployment to define the boundaries of proper religion.[22] At the heart of this opposition lay Protestantism's attack on the "magic" of the Catholic understanding of the sacraments, particularly the central sacrament of the Eucharist. While different forms of Protestantism each advanced their own interpretations, all stepped away, to varying degrees, from the medieval doctrine that the ritual consecration of the Host by a priest worked a real and complete transformation in the physical substance of the wafer. This move has been read by many scholars as a crucial element of disenchantment and of emerging modern religious

---

19. Cameron, *Enchanted Europe*, 175–76.

20. Keith Thomas, *Religion and the Decline of Magic: Studies in Popular Beliefs in Sixteenth and Seventeenth Century England* (1971; repr., New York, 1997), esp. 493–98; also R. W. Scribner, "The Reformation, Popular Magic, and the 'Disenchantment of the World,'" *Journal of Interdisciplinary History* 23 (1992–93): 475–94, at 487–88; reprinted in Scribner, *Religion and Culture in Germany (1400–1800)*, ed. Lyndal Roper (Leiden, 2001), 346–65.

21. See Scribner, "Reformation, Popular Magic, and the 'Disenchantment of the World,'" esp. 484; Scribner, "Magic and the Formation of Protestant Popular Culture in Germany," in Scribner, *Religion and Culture in Germany*, 323–45.

22. Jean Delumeau, "Les réformateurs et la superstition," in *Actes du colloque l'Amiral de Coligny et son temps* (Paris, 1974), 451–87, at 454–55; Cameron, *Enchanted Europe*, 171–72, and 196–99.

sensibilities.[23] At its core, it entailed a "revolution" of ritual theory, wherein rituals were now understood only as expressing symbolic meaning rather than producing any "real" effects.[24] Even at the heart of this great change, however, rituals remained deeply meaningful during the Reformation, and much of the concern among Protestant as well as Catholic authorities about magic and witchcraft continued to focus on defining proper ritual behavior and demarcating appropriate religious rites from illicit superstition.[25]

R. W. Scribner has identified many strands of development and debate in this regard. In 1529, for example, a bailiff in the small town of Urach in still-Catholic Württemberg was investigating a suspected witch. Unable to extract a confession, he went repeatedly to the local church to demand sacramental items, which he believed could help him test for witchcraft. The clergy resisted, in part objecting to the bailiff's assertion of control over them, but couching their complaint in concern that he would "abuse" the holy items by using them to probe for witchcraft.[26] Particularly telling on the other side of the confessional divide are the permutations that medieval Rogation Day ceremonies underwent in some Protestant lands. Originally priests processed with the consecrated Eucharist around fields in spring to protect the ripening crops. Protestants found this emphasis on the sacral power of the clergy and the sacramental item of the Eucharistic wafer inappropriate, so they initially substituted processions involving hymns and prayers, in order to refocus attention more clearly on pious supplication of divine protection. When even this rite seemed too "automatic," the preaching of a sermon was introduced instead.[27] Debated, contested, and changed over the years, ritual nevertheless remained an important component of society.

Nor was Protestantism's supposedly new conception of ritual action really so different from that of its Catholic counterpart or its medieval precedents, although the Reformation certainly expanded the debate in important ways. As we have seen, however, fourteenth- and fifteenth-century critics of superstition also stressed the absence of inherent power in ritual acts, which functioned only as a means of "signification" while other forces actually caused

---

23. Regina Mara Schwartz, *Sacramental Poetics at the Dawn of Secularism: When God Left the World* (Stanford, Calif., 2008), 18, and more broadly 3–35, highlighting connections to concepts of modernity.

24. Walsham, "Reformation and 'the Disenchantment of the World,'" 506; Edward Muir, *Ritual in Early Modern Europe* (Cambridge, 1997), 7–8, 147–81.

25. Muir, *Ritual*, 185–223.

26. R. W. Scribner, "Sorcery, Superstition and Society: The Witch of Urach, 1529," in Scribner, *Popular Culture and Popular Movements in Reformation Germany* (London, 1987), 257–75.

27. Scribner, "Magic and the Formation of Protestant Popular Culture," 327–28.

any effects associated with the performance of these rituals. They, too, worried incessantly that improper understandings of the true meaning of rituals lay at the root of most superstition. If the ritual revolution provides the basis for Protestantism's claim to have introduced some degree of disenchantment into European culture, then "medieval" critics of superstition were already becoming disenchanted as well.[28] In her insightful review of disenchantment in the Reformation, Alexandra Walsham has made the valuable proposal that, rather than looking for a singular moment of disenchantment, or even movement in a single direction along a spectrum, we should instead recognize cycles of disenchantment and reenchantment throughout this period.[29] This would surely allow us to see more clearly the real significance of the Reformation in terms of what came before and what came after.

Subsequent to the Reformation, the Scientific Revolution can appear to be a moment—or a movement—of radical disenchantment. In a straightforward narrative, a scientific mentality that utterly rejected magic or mysticism emerged largely in the course of the seventeenth century and created the modern world.[30] Weber himself first employed the phrase "disenchantment of the world" not in relation to religious developments as described in his *Protestant Ethic* but in a lecture on the place of science in, and as the basis of, the modern West.[31] In the twentieth and twenty-first centuries, science has often been held to be entirely separate from and even diametrically opposed to any spiritual or occult forms of knowledge or belief.[32] Historically, however, the situation has always been more complex. Scholarship on the history of early modern witchcraft, for example, has shown how the demonological ideas that supported the witch hunts were entirely compatible with much leading scientific thought at that time.[33] Historians of early modern science

---

28. More fully on this point, see also Michael D. Bailey, "The Disenchantment of Magic: Spells, Charms, and Superstition in Early European Witchcraft Literature," *AHR* 111 (2006): 383–404.

29. Walsham, "Reformation and 'the Disenchantment of the World,'" 527.

30. Morris Berman, *The Reenchantment of the World* (Ithaca, N.Y., 1981), 15–24. On the complicated place of science in modernity, see Steven Shapin, *Never Pure: Historical Studies of Science as If It Was Produced by People with Bodies, Situated in Time, Space, Culture, and Society, and Struggling for Credibility and Authority* (Baltimore, 2010), 377–91.

31. Weber, "Science as a Vocation" (as n. 2 above). Weber first delivered this lecture in Munich in 1917. He then included the phrase "Entzauberung der Welt" in the revised edition of his *Protestant Ethic* published in 1920–21.

32. As the physicist Robert L. Park writes at the conclusion to his *Superstition: Belief in the Age of Science* (Princeton, N.J., 2008), 215: "Science is the only way of knowing—everything else is just superstition."

33. Stuart Clark, *Thinking with Demons: The Idea of Witchcraft in Early Modern Europe* (Oxford, 1997), 155–56, 294–311.

have likewise long recognized important connections between their field and that of early modern magic and "occult philosophies."[34] Rather than a strict dialectic between magic and science, many scholars now see a three-way debate between the traditional scholastic system of Aristotelian thought, which supported a particular understanding of magic and the occult, newer "Renaissance" cosmologies that allowed a different space for spiritual and occult forces in the universe, and the strictly physical mechanical philosophy of the seventeenth century.[35] Studies of "secrets" and "wonders," closely related to magical and occult mentalities in early modern Europe, have also revealed a complex ebb and flow through this period rather than any simple linear movement toward a discernibly "modern" mode of thought that might characterize a distinct new era.[36] As sharp boundaries between early modern science and magic erode, yet another of the supposedly great divides between the medieval and the modern eras begins to evaporate as well.

As we have seen, debates about superstition in the fourteenth and fifteenth centuries, especially those regarding issues of elite astrology or astral magic, inevitably involved debates about the natural properties of the physical universe, the extent to which human beings could understand those properties, and how they might harness and manipulate them. In attempting to define the boundaries of superstition, authorities working in these areas had to consider what separation, if any, existed between the natural and the supernatural realms, and between engagement with purely physical forces versus the invocation of spiritual powers. In doing so, they sometimes imposed distinctions that can appear quite modern. Nicole Oresme, in particular, eventually came to a position that removed almost all spiritual forces from the physical universe. Many later scholars, including many historians of science, have therefore categorized him as a protomodern figure, a harbinger of things to come.[37] I am not opposed to that view, which in a sense is clearly true, but I also want to stress that he was not an aberrant genius unconnected to his time. If his views did not attain much contemporary support in their

---

34. E.g., essays collected in Brian Vickers, ed., *Occult and Scientific Mentalities in the Renaissance* (Cambridge, 1984). Although Vickers himself maintains a distinction between science and magic, he admits to a "continuum" of overlapping development ("Introduction," 29).

35. Brian Easlea, *Witch Hunting, Magic and the New Philosophy: An Introduction to the Debates of the Scientific Revolution 1450–1750* (Brighton, U.K., 1980), 89–90.

36. William Eamon, *Science and the Secrets of Nature: Books of Secrets in Medieval and Early Modern Culture* (Princeton, N.J., 1994); Lorraine Daston and Katharine Park, *Wonders and the Order of Nature 1150–1750* (New York, 1998).

37. See chap. 2, n. 83.

full extremity, they were nevertheless extreme expressions of eminently "medieval" positions.

In the course of the seventeenth century, Oresme's level of skepticism about the reality of virtually all spiritual activity in the physical world began to become more common among "enlightened" thinkers. Thomas Hobbes and Baruch Spinoza, for example, both denied that powerful demonic spirits actively interfered in the world, and also that God tinkered with his creation through continual miracles. At the end of the century, the Dutch clergyman Balthasar Bekker published *The Enchanted World* (*De Betoverde Weereld*), an extremely influential skeptical work directed against belief in witchcraft and other superstitions.[38] The removal of direct demonic (and divine) action from the world was a major feature of the Enlightenment, or at least an important aspect of the thought of many major Enlightenment figures, and gives this period a real claim to being one of significant disenchantment.[39] Of course, the skepticism that manifested in the Enlightenment was not altogether new. The extent of demonic power and its physical as opposed to purely spiritual or illusory nature had figured in debates about superstition for centuries. In addition to having encountered it, at its most extreme, in the thought of Nicole Oresme, we have also seen it, in a perhaps more "typically medieval" form, in the debates that surrounded the canon *Episcopi*. The canon's skepticism was ultimately not that of Enlightenment thinkers, and one can fairly assert that the degree of skepticism that developed during the Enlightenment was of a different order from any that had come before. Yet connections and continuities did exist.

Moreover, one cannot argue simply that enlightened intellectuals stopped "thinking with demons" altogether. Scholarship has increasingly focused on how the spiritual and the supernatural remained very important to many of them.[40] Most of the intellectuals of the later seventeenth and the eighteenth centuries remained clergymen of a fairly conventional sort, and their

---

38. Cameron, *Enchanted Europe*, 247–69; also Andrew Fix, *Fallen Angels: Balthasar Bekker, Spirit Belief, and Confessionalism in the Seventeenth-Century Dutch Republic* (Dordrecht, Neth., 1999); Jonathan Israel, *Radical Enlightenment: Philosophy and the Making of Modernity, 1650–1750* (Oxford, 2001), 218–29, 378–85.

39. S. J. Barnett, *The Enlightenment and Religion: The Myths of Modernity* (Manchester, 2003), makes the point that the Enlightenment should not be defined purely in terms of a few elite thinkers but as a broad societal movement. Nevertheless, later European intellectuals focused mainly on those major thinkers when they looked back at the Enlightenment to construct notions of modernity.

40. Walsham, "Reformation and 'the Disenchantment of the World,'" 525. See generally Barnett, *Enlightenment and Religion*; David Sorkin, *The Religious Enlightenment: Protestants, Jews, and Catholics from London to Vienna* (Princeton, N.J., 2008). My phrase comes from Clark, *Thinking with Demons*, although he does not deal extensively with the Enlightenment himself.

concerns about superstition were not so radically different from those of earlier authorities. Many continued to think of superstition primarily in terms of demonic error.[41] Even if they largely denied physical consequences to demonic action, they remained deeply worried about the equally real spiritual effects that demons might produce, as indicated by enduring concerns about the reality of demonic possession. In the late eighteenth century, for example, the German priest Johann Joseph Gassner performed an incredible series of exorcisms and spiritual healings, sparking a mass furor (supposedly in less than a year between 1775 and 1776 he treated some twenty thousand patients). Reports of his exploits circulated far and wide and drew intense criticism but also, remarkably, some support from both Catholic and Protestant intellectuals.[42] Indeed, it is now possible to argue, in the words of one expert, that the Enlightenment "actually served to foster a resurgence of interest in, and discussion of, the supernatural."[43] Certainly the expansion of education and literacy, and the associated growth of print culture, allowed for an unprecedented surge in publications on and about magic, superstition, and the occult, intended not just as fodder for skeptical elites but as entertainment and sometimes even instruction for the newly literate masses.[44]

Of course, a number of Enlightenment thinkers advanced powerful arguments against superstitious beliefs and practices, which they saw as a key impediment blocking social and political progress. Voltaire and other *philosophes* used the label of superstition to brand much official religion as irrational, although really they targeted the power of established churches as political institutions, which they saw as promoting sectarian discord and stifling education in order to prop up the existing ruling structure.[45] Entries in the *Encyclopédie* stressed the political and social dangers of superstition rather than purely intellectual or spiritual ones, and the French Revolution emphatically turned the Enlightenment cry to eradicate superstition into

---

41. Martin Pott, *Aufklärung und Aberglaube: Die deutsche Frühaufklärung im Spiegel ihrer Aberglaubenskritik* (Tübingen, 1992), 135–36 (on German Protestants); Bernard Dompnier, "Les Hommes d'Église et la superstition entre XVIIe et XVIIIe siècles," in *La superstition à l'âge des Lumières*, ed. Dompnier (Paris, 1998), 13–47 (on French Catholics).

42. H. C. Erik Midelfort, *Exorcism and Enlightenment: Johann Joseph Gassner and the Demons of Eighteenth-Century Germany* (New Haven, Conn., 2005).

43. Walsham, "Reformation and 'the Disenchantment of the World,'" 526.

44. Sabine Doering-Manteuffel, "The Dissemination of Magical Knowledge in Enlightenment Germany: The Supernatural and the Development of Print Culture," in *Beyond the Witch Trials: Witchcraft and Magic in Enlightenment Europe*, ed. Owen Davies and Willem de Blécourt (Manchester, 2004), 187–206; Owen Davies, *Grimoires: A History of Magic Books* (Oxford, 2009), 98–101.

45. Cameron, *Enchanted Europe*, 305–9.

a political tool, targeting anything deemed to be counterrevolutionary as superstitious.[46]

An often employed formulation holds that during the Enlightenment the meaning of superstition shifted from a "perversion of religion" to a "perversion of reason."[47] A better construction would be that secular, scientific reason largely displaced religious authority as the main arbiter of what constituted superstition. Opponents of superstitious error no longer grounded their concern or their arguments in theology because theology itself no longer occupied an absolutely central place in Europe's intellectual culture. Nevertheless, superstition in the eighteenth century and thereafter was clearly still connected in basic ways to notions of improper religion. As for the invocation of "reason," what is rational changes over time and across cultures. Enlightened *philosophes* regarded practices they considered to be superstitious as irrational, but so did the scholastic theologians of earlier centuries. The anonymous author of one fifteenth-century treatise *On Superstitions* specifically condemned superstition as a "defect of reason in relation to religion."[48] This is not to contest the fact that the period of the Enlightenment witnessed major changes in conceptualizations and deployments of the category of superstition, but to stress that, just as with the Reformation and the Scientific Revolution, these changes represented a development of earlier thought, not a completely radical break from it.

Perhaps the most significant change regarding superstition associated with the Enlightenment had to do not with basic conceptions about the category, but with the degree of serious concern that it now evoked. Intellectual authorities had always considered some superstitions to be basically harmless folly. As belief in the active presence and physical menace of demonic spirits declined, many came to view more and more areas of superstition this way. Regarded collectively, superstitious errors might still create serious societal problems, but taken as individual practices, they imperiled no souls and injured no bodies. They could therefore increasingly be dismissed as quaint

---

46. Lucette Perol, "La notation de superstition de Furetière au *Dictionnaire de trévoux* et à l'*Encyclopédie*," in *Superstition à l'âge des Lumières*, 67–92, at 70–73; Philippe Bourdin, "Révolution et superstition: L'exemple du Puy-de-Dôme," in *Superstition à l'âge des Lumières*, 213–37.

47. Dieter Harmening, *Superstitio: Überlieferungs- und theoriegeschichtliche Untersuchungen zur kirchlich-theologischen Aberglaubensliteratur des Mittelalters* (Berlin, 1979), 5; Pott, *Aufklärung und Aberglaube*, 124, takes up the formulation, but problematizes it. See also Cameron, *Enchanted Europe*, 244; and S. A. Smith, "Introduction," in *The Religion of Fools? Superstition Past and Present*, ed. S. A. Smith and Alan Knight (Oxford, 2008), 7–55, at 9, 48.

48. Anonymous, *De superstitionibus* (M), 16v: "Notandum quod vicium opponitum religioni consistit in hoc quod inclinat ad actus deformes recte rationi circa diuinum cultum."

curiosities.[49] A telling indication of this shift was that in the nineteenth century the investigation of superstition became solidly the purview not of church inquisitors and civic magistrates but of folklorists, whose discipline essentially emerged at this time.[50] An attitude of bemused curiosity combined with a certain degree of frustration that "irrational" practices do not simply evaporate in the light of scientific "truth" continues to characterize many modern authorities when confronting superstition.[51]

Yet the modern West is hardly disenchanted. In a valuable historiographical overview, Michael Saler has identified three distinct ways in which the modern period experiences enchantment.[52] The relationship between modernity and enchantment can be strictly "binary," in which traditional magical practices from earlier periods endure into the modern era but are treated as anachronisms within modern society. Equally oppositional is the "dialectic" relationship, in which modernity is seen to have overcome traditional modes of enchantment, but the means by which it has disenchanted the world—assertions of scientific rationality and universalist conceptions of human values and progress—themselves assume irrational, "mythic" dimensions. This reenchantment can carry very dark overtones, and some cultural theorists assert that excessive faith in the absolute value of these modern myths has produced some of the most violent horrors of the nineteenth and twentieth centuries.[53] A third relationship, however, is "antinomial," focusing again on actual magical beliefs and practices, here regarded not merely as the residue of an earlier age or inherently antithetical to other aspects of the modern world but as fully integrated products of that world.

A number of historians have begun to investigate magic in the modern period along the lines of this third approach. They have paid much attention to movements of nineteenth- and early twentieth-century occultism, which thrived among the thoroughly modern bourgeoisie of western Europe and North America.[54] The Wiccan movement, too, for all its original claims to

---

49. Cameron, *Enchanted Europe*, 248, 299.

50. Ibid., 311–12; Alexandra Walsham, "Recording Superstition in Early Modern Britain: The Origins of Folklore," in *Religion of Fools*, 178–206.

51. Gustav Jahoda, *The Psychology of Superstition* (London, 1969), 141.

52. Michael Saler, "Modernity and Enchantment: A Historiographic Review," *AHR* 111 (2006): 692–716.

53. Famously in Horkheimer and Adorno, *Dialectic of Enlightenment* (see n. 64 below). Saler, "Modernity and Enchantment," esp. 698–99, notes critiques by Nietzsche, Marx, Freud, and Weber himself.

54. Saler, "Modernity and Enchantment," focuses mainly on this scholarship. See especially Alex Owen, *The Place of Enchantment: British Occultism and the Culture of the Modern* (Chicago, 2004); Corinna Treitel, *A Science for the Soul: Occultism and the Genesis of the German Modern* (Baltimore,

be a tradition rooted in deep antiquity, has now been positioned fully in modern history, and in fact Wiccans' conscious appropriation and deployment of their own pseudohistory has been recognized not just as eminently modern but indeed postmodern.[55] Of course, even "traditional" magical practices are never static; they too change and take on distinctly modern forms. And scholars have also begun to explore how narratives about magic and the occult constitute a real instantiation of enchantment in the modern world, leading to compelling studies of the complex relationship between "real" magic and stage magic, performative conjuring (which itself has a long historical tradition), and evocations of magical wonder in modern film and literature.[56] Outside the West, meanwhile, magical and superstitious practices both traditional and newly developed exist as an essential although often powerfully contested aspect of various "modernities" around the world.[57] In some places, concern over such practices has reached terrifying levels, erupting into mob violence and occasionally even officially sanctioned witch trials.[58] While overtly violent responses to perceived magical assault are kept to a minimum in the West, owing to social and legal systems that refuse to tolerate them, surveys show that perhaps 10 to 15 percent of people in modern Europe continue to profess a belief in the reality of witchcraft in some fashion.[59]

If the modern world remains evidently enchanted, however, and if modern conceptions of magic and superstition relate to earlier ones along a continuum of often nonlinear development, nevertheless modernity as a theoretical construct rather than just a periodization has long been conceived in terms of radical disenchantment. Moreover, it has often been characterized specifically by the sharp opposition of modern, scientific rationality to "medieval"

2004); David Allen Harvey, *Beyond Enlightenment: Occultism and Politics in Modern France* (DeKalb, Ill., 2005); John Warne Monroe, *Laboratories of Faith: Mesmerism, Spiritism, and Occultism in Modern France* (Ithaca, N.Y., 2008); Alison Butler, *Victorian Occultism and the Making of Modern Magic: Invoking Tradition* (Basingstoke, U.K., 2011).

55. On Wicca's history, see Ronald Hutton, *The Triumph of the Moon: A History of Modern Pagan Witchcraft* (Oxford, 1999). On Wicca's postmodernism, see Jo Pearson, "Writing Witchcraft: The Historians' History, the Practitioners' Past," in *Witchcraft Historiography*, ed. Jonathan Barry and Owen Davies (Basingstoke, U.K., 2007), 225–41.

56. Simon During, *Modern Enchantments: The Cultural Power of Secular Magic* (Cambridge, Mass., 2002); Michael Mangan, *Performing Dark Arts: A Cultural History of Conjuring* (Chicago, 2007).

57. For some coverage of various regions, see essays in Birgit Meyer and Peter Pels, eds., *Magic and Modernity: Interfaces of Revelation and Concealment* (Stanford, Calif., 2003); and *Religion of Fools?* (as n. 47 above), 229–335.

58. Wolfgang Behringer, *Witches and Witch-Hunts: A Global History* (Cambridge, 2004), 1–2, 223, 227–28.

59. Ibid., 21.

superstition. Some theorists have now also begun to formulate powerful critiques of this paradigm, and because theoretical modernity is inextricably entangled with issues of chronological periodization, they all to varying degrees draw from and speak to history. Ironically, historians themselves can be quite inattentive to grand constructs like modernity. Immersed in the infinite particularities of specific historical developments, we may use such concepts as broad frames, but we often don't engage very deeply with the conceptual or theoretical issues they may raise.[60] For most of this book, I have kept my focus firmly on the particular complexities of the history of late medieval superstition. Having in this chapter challenged some of the standard periodizations in which that history is embedded, however, I want to close with the issue of modernity and suggest a new way in which the history of late medieval superstition can be set in relation to it.

Disenchantment, Modernity, and Medieval Superstition

If disenchantment is at once an encompassing and uncertain concept, modernity is even more so.[61] Yet their relationship to one another is undeniable. Many theorists regard disenchantment as central not just to modern sensibilities regarding magic, but to the formulation of modern science; to issues in philosophy, art, literature, and culture; certainly to religion and ritual; and to notions of Western secularism.[62] Not surprisingly given the sociologist Weber's important formulation of disenchantment, it has served as a central focus of debate in social and political theory throughout the twentieth century.[63] In every field to which it has been applied, disenchantment has always generated some discontent, and its putative effects, like those of modernity itself, have often been seen as ambivalent (a view held by Weber himself) or even terribly destructive. An

---

60. Lynn Hunt, *Measuring Time, Making History* (Budapest, 2008), 22; also the editors' introduction to the special roundtable section "Historians and the Question of 'Modernity,'" *AHR* 116 (2011): 631–751, at 631.

61. For broad reconsiderations, see Susan Stanford Friedman, "Definitional Excursions: The Meanings of *Modern/Modernity/Modernism*," *Modernism/Modernity* 8 (2001): 493–513; Friedman, "Planetarity: Musing Modernist Studies," *Modernism/Modernity* 17 (2010): 471–99. My discussion here, however, should be understood to refer to the historical conception of modernity as developed in western Europe.

62. E.g., Peter Pels, "Introduction: Magic and Modernity," in *Magic and Modernity*, 1–38, at 26–29; Randall Styers, *Making Magic: Religion, Magic, and Science in the Modern World* (Oxford, 2004), 12–13; Joshua Landy and Michael Saler, "Introduction: The Varieties of Modern Enchantment," in *The Re-Enchantment of the World: Secular Magic in a Rational Age*, ed. Landy and Saler (Stanford, Calif., 2009), 1–14, at 3–7.

63. A useful overview is Gilbert G. Germain, *A Discourse on Disenchantment: Reflections on Politics and Technology* (Albany, N.Y., 1993).

extremely influential formulation of the latter view came in the mid-twentieth century from Max Horkheimer and Theodor Adorno, writing in response to the horrors of Nazism and the Second World War.[64] They argued that the Enlightenment's central aim was disenchantment, which they defined broadly as the drive to "dispel myths, [and] to overthrow fantasy with knowledge." Yet the society that had grown out of that effort had, in their view, become caught in a web of its own mythologies that now "permeated the sphere of the profane": self-justifying discourses of scientific rationality, progress, and so forth. In light of these developments, "existence, thoroughly cleansed of demons and their conceptual descendants, takes on, in its gleaming naturalness, the numinous character which former ages attributed to demons."[65]

Disenchantment in this expansive sense entails far more than just a rejection of magic and a critique of superstition. Likewise scholars focusing on continuing "enchantment" or modes of "reenchantment" in the modern world need not address "the magical" in any narrow or literal sense. Yet nonmetaphorical magic and superstition have certainly played an important role in the definition and functioning of modernity, especially in terms of conceptions about modern religion as well as its supposed great opposites, science and secular rationalism.[66]

Both scientific rationality and the modern Western conception of religion make claims to universal applicability. They position themselves as natural categories—"gleamingly natural" as Horkheimer and Adorno would have it—available to all human beings, but only after extraneous beliefs and practices frequently categorized as magical or superstitious that obscure their putative core essence have been removed. In fact, however, both "science" and "religion" are historically and culturally specific categories, developing as a series of negotiations and constructions particular to western Europe. The same could be said of modern secularism.[67] Once these historical specificities are recognized, then both secular scientific rationality and "real" or "authentic" religion, as it is sometimes designated, appear not

---

64. Max Horkheimer and Theodor W. Adorno, *Dialectic of Enlightenment: Philosophical Fragments*, ed. Gunzelin Schmid Noerr, trans. Edmund Jephcott (Stanford, Calif., 2002), with a discussion by the editor of the work's influence on later critical theory at 217–47.

65. Ibid., 21.

66. Styers, *Making Magic*; Stanley Jeyaraja Tambiah, *Magic, Science, Religion, and the Scope of Rationality* (Cambridge, 1990), esp. 1–31.

67. On science, see e.g. Shapin, *Never Pure*; on religion, Talal Asad, *Genealogies of Religion: Discipline and Reasons of Power in Christianity and Islam* (Baltimore, 1993), esp. 27–54; also Tomoko Masuzawa, *The Invention of World Religions: Or, How European Universalism Was Preserved in the Language of Pluralism* (Chicago, 2005); on secularism, Talal Asad, *Formations of the Secular: Christianity, Islam, Modernity* (Stanford, Calif., 2003), esp. 1–66.

As inherently natural categories that require only the removal of superfluous elements to make them manifest, but as constructions that are, and need to be, continually fashioned and reinforced by authorities drawing boundaries to separate aspects they deem appropriate from those they exclude, often by labeling them superstitious.

Gyan Prakash, a historian of science and technology in India, has provided astute analysis of how the category of superstition has functioned in the development and to some extent the imposition of modernity. I qualify "imposition" because, although he deals with colonial India, his is not a simple story of European powers using modern science and technology to dominate non-European peoples. That domination inescapably underlies his accounts, but he also brings to light how India's own colonial elite, drawn to Western science and the progress (and power) promised by technology, attempted to "purify" Hinduism, identifying and removing what they determined to be superstitious elements in order to make it more compatible with Western scientific rationalism.[68] This process also worked to reshape "real" Hinduism into a religion more understandable in terms of Western models. In a similar vein, some native elites responded to European science by arguing for the existence of an original "Hindu science" contained in the ancient Vedas that could stand on par with the supposed rationality (in modern terms) of the ancient Greeks, but which had been corrupted by centuries of superstitious accretions, that is, magical rites and rituals, and a profusion of gods, temples, and holy men. By indentifying and condemning as superstitious those aspects of Hinduism that obscured a core of perceived rational scientific knowledge, these elites could then at least in part come to terms with the spread of Western science and technology throughout British India not as an imperial imposition but as the restoration of an indigenous inheritance.[69]

In many ways the history of late medieval superstition and the debates that surrounded perceived superstitious practices merge easily with this analysis of how discourses about superstition and disenchantment have been deployed in the modern world and in the construction of modernity.[70] In the

---

68. Gyan Prakash, "Between Science and Superstition: Religion and the Modern Subject of the Nation in Colonial India," in *Magic and Modernity*, 39–59.

69. Gyan Prakash, *Another Reason: Science and the Imagination of Modern India* (Princeton, N.J., 1999), esp. 86–120.

70. Similarities between medieval studies and postcolonial studies vis-à-vis their relation to modernity have been recognized by scholars on both sides: e.g., Dipesh Chakrabarty, "Historicism and Its Supplements: A Note on a Predicament Shared by Medieval and Postcolonial Studies," in *Medievalisms in the Postcolonial World* (as n. 8 above), 109–19; Carol Symes, "When We Talk about Modernity," *AHR* 116 (2011): 715–26.

fourteenth and fifteenth centuries, too, dominant elites sought to define and defend the boundaries of what they deemed to be legitimate religion and science (natural philosophy) by seeking to identify systematically those elements they regarded as corruptions or improper accretions. In this sense, one might say that essential processes of modernity were under way well before the modern or even early modern period as generally defined. Such an assertion produces an immediate shock, however, and not unjustly so, because the men who appear in this analysis so surprisingly modern in their use of superstition to form and reinforce other categories of belief, knowledge, and practice were themselves, when seen from the more typical perspective assumed by modernity, hopelessly superstitious. The figure of the credulous witch-hunter, willing to sentence other human beings to burn at the stake because he believed them to be in league with dark spiritual forces through which they worked terribly real and destructive magic, provided the literal embodiment of irrational, repressive, "medieval" superstition from which Enlightenment *philosophes* so earnestly sought to liberate European society.

One way to understand this paradox, certainly, is to regard these men, and this period, as hopelessly confused, groping toward certain seemingly inherent "truths" that only future periods would fully and correctly comprehend. This view fits well with the idea of a distinctly "late" and "waning" Middle Ages when decaying modes of medieval thought supposedly groaned under the weight of their own incongruence before finally giving way to vibrant (and "correct") new forms. It also readily supports notions of singular disenchantment: that at some particular historical juncture, paradigmatically "medieval" confusion and irrationality had to be overthrown before European society could progress into the clear light of modernity. These are all positions that historians now tend to dismiss, and certainly that the actual history of superstition tends to complicate or even efface. Nevertheless, they retain a good deal of their conceptual power.

As the historian Jonathan Sheehan has noted regarding one major effort to distinguish a discrete modern, secular age from what went before, the enduring need to posit a clear "before" and "after" is wholly "*internal* to this secular age and disconnected to the *external* flow of time, events, and peoples."[71] In other words, it is disconnected from actual history. Thus, despite all the historical critiques directed against the traditional medieval/modern

---

71. Jonathan Sheehan, "When Was Disenchantment? History and the Secular Age," in *Varieties of Secularism in a Secular Age*, ed. Michael Warner, Jonathan VanAntwerpen, and Craig Calhoun (Cambridge, Mass., 2010), 217–42, at 229 (emphases in the original). His focus is on Charles Taylor, *A Secular Age* (Cambridge, Mass., 2007).

divide, aspects of that divide persist, whether in notions of a feudal society transformed into a capitalist one, or an age of faith giving way to secularism, or a culture locked in the bonds of primitive superstition finally liberated by disenchanted scientific rationality.[72] Similarly, despite all the scholarship suggesting that disenchantment itself has only ever been gradual, incomplete, and cyclical rather than linear, the idea that some kind of distinct threshold exists somewhere in the sixteenth, seventeenth, or eighteenth centuries remains deeply ingrained. The forces or factors precipitating that imagined moment of disenchantment are, moreover, almost never presented as emerging from prior modes of thinking about magic and superstition, and certainly not from any "medieval" conceptions of religion or science. Instead, some external factor is posited as having imposed itself, fundamentally altering how superstition was conceived. The critical catalyst might be the new ideas of ritual and religion constituted in the Reformation, or a "revolution" in scientific thought and method, or the paradigmatically modern rationality propounded by a radical Enlightenment. Of course important developments occurred in each of these periods that can sensibly and usefully be categorized under these broad rubrics. But the rhetoric of dramatic newness and rupture with the past that has traditionally accompanied these landmarks of Europe's early modern era has also obscured much of the real nature of the historical change that occurred in the several centuries that they span.[73]

In the continuing power of these categorical periodizations, we can see something of modernity's drive toward strict dichotomization, most evident in the sharp separation imposed between "the modern" and everything that has come before it or continues to exist outside of it: the premodern, the primitive, the traditional, the "medieval." We can also see modernity's obsession with conceptual purity, and its conviction that it has finally achieved a true, unmediated, and natural conception of the world. These characteristics apply, of course, to modernity not simply as a chronological period succeeding others but as a distinct ideological project, one that theorists have been subjecting to trenchant reappraisal for many years. Of all the critics of post-Enlightenment modernity, the one who I find speaks most effectively to basic dynamics related to the history of superstition and disenchantment (ironically enough, since he engages only slightly with issues of disenchantment and not at all with superstition) is Bruno Latour. Not only does he

---

72. Davis, *Periodization* (as n. 7 above).

73. De Grazia, "Modern Divide"; Fasolt, "Hegel's Ghost"; Hunt, *Measuring Time*, 48–72; Moshe Sluhovsky, "Discernment of Difference, the Introspective Subject, and the Birth of Modernity," *Journal of Medieval and Early Modern Studies* 36 (2006): 169–99.

provide a useful framework in which to position and explicate modernity's continuing perception of "medieval superstition," but more important, from my perspective, his critique of modernity lends a particular relevance to the complex and at times confusing thought of the fourteenth- and fifteenth-century authorities I have focused on in this book.

As a theorist of modern science and science studies, Latour sees modernity constructing two distinct ontological zones. For him, these are not the spiritual and physical or the sacred and profane but rather the human and the nonhuman, which essentially translate to the sociopolitical and the natural-scientific. Spiritual forces, while not denied entirely, are for all intents and purposes removed from consideration as active components in either zone.[74] His main argument is that the maintenance of absolute boundaries between these spheres is essential to modernity's conception of itself. That is, modern social and political structures are perceived as entirely independent of the natural world, and this separation is what makes them modern. Of course, modern people exist within nature, but they and the societies they create stand aloof from it. Unlike premodern people, whose cultures are thoroughly infused with and subject to natural forces that they often personify as gods or demons, modern people construct their societies based on rationalized principles of their own determining. Likewise, while humans and human society obviously interact with and affect the natural world in countless ways, what are defined as purely human concerns (politics, economics, law, morality) do not impinge on or alter nature itself, which exists entirely independent of them. For example, while some scientists may allow politics, or religious belief, or other human elements to shape their research or the conclusions they draw in certain ways, the essential modern scientific conception remains that nature exists objectively, not as an aspect or reflection of any human construction, and ideally should be investigated as such.

Latour insists that this system of sharp dichotomization is untrue, merely a screen that modernity has laid over reality. In fact, elements of these two zones mix constantly to form intricate and interconnected networks of "hybrids" that actually constitute the unitary fabric of the world and human existence in it. But modernity refuses to see this. Instead, the "modern critical stance" engages in a perpetual process of "purification," taking undifferentiated reality and dividing it into predetermined, distinct categories. Behind this facade, however, a process of "translation" occurs as new hybrid forms

---

74. Bruno Latour, *We Have Never Been Modern*, trans. Catherine Porter (Cambridge, Mass., 1993), 10–11, 32–33.

continually emerge from older ones. Precisely because he is attempting to undermine modern categories, Latour diligently avoids categorical terminology aside from that of his own devising. He does not want to separate the artificial from the natural or even the mental from the physical. Instead, everything interconnects and proceeds by "networks."[75]

For Latour, recognizing these dynamics leads to a critique of modernity itself. For the historian, it offers a way to understand the deeply ingrained compulsion to reshape complex, gradual historical developments into discrete moments of sudden, revolutionary change that break completely with the past. Latour himself asserts that the modern notion of history, and indeed of time, fits his theories. That is, while actual historical change is messy, complex, and hybrid, the modern critical stance wants to see the past in terms of clear, distinct, and orderly forms. The process of change itself is purified, but in that purification the true nature of historical developments is masked, even denied. Major change is held to be induced not by interactions within the system itself, but by "radical revolution," the "miraculous emergence of new things that have always already been there."[76] Latour is thinking very much of the history of the Scientific Revolution, and he extends his analysis forward to the French Revolution, but one could easily apply the same basic structure to the Renaissance or Reformation as well.

Limiting our focus to the history of magic and superstition, this theory very effectively explains how the process of disenchantment in the early modern period has so often been perceived. Precisely because being disenchanted is (theoretically) so essential to being modern, it resists being seen as a gradual, complex, incomplete process. Instead, we find the enduring tendency, despite all accrued evidence, to present disenchantment as a radically new mode of thought and perception, unattached to earlier "superstitious" mentalities and contingent instead on equally revolutionary new forms of religion, science, or rationality itself. Indeed, if the deliberate rhetoric of newness that took powerful form in the Renaissance and Reformation represents the first glimmer of the "modern critical stance" as Latour conceives it, this goes a long way toward suggesting how a full and nuanced understanding of shifting debates and modulating concerns about superstition came to be obscured through much of early modern history. Not just later scholars looking back but the very intellectuals who at the time conceptualized and

---

75. In addition to Latour's own work, see the useful overview of his main ideas in Graham Harman, *Prince of Networks: Bruno Latour and Metaphysics* (Melbourne, 2009), esp. 11–95.

76. Latour, *We Have Never Been Modern*, 70.

conducted those debates were starting to see the issues with which they grappled in a somewhat "modern" light.

All this brings us back to late medieval debates about superstition and the men who tried to draw reliable and (in their minds, certainly) rational boundaries around an often ambiguous category of superstitious beliefs and practices. In their efforts, they faced a number of intellectual dilemmas, and they were sometimes clearly troubled by their own conclusions or lack thereof, as well as by the conclusions presented by other authorities, both past and present. But we would do them a profound disservice if we saw them as somehow innately confused or fundamentally muddled in their thinking. Nor should we interpret them merely in terms of enduring enchantment or emerging disenchantment, as bulwarks of a curious medieval alterity or as harbingers of some kind of protomodernity. They were not any of these things for the simple reason that they lived and wrote before the modern impetus to divide history in these ways began to develop.

These men insisted that the only power of ritual actions lay in signification, not in direct effects. They stressed, to a degree, the devotional importance of interior belief and intention over that of external action. And they carefully delimited the potential action of most spiritual forces within the natural world, opening the possibility, albeit one seized only in the rarest cases during this period, of constructing a fairly substantial divide between the spiritual realm and the material world. At the same time, within the boundaries that they posited, most of these authorities attributed a broad scope and terrifyingly physical reality to spiritual presence and power. They remained committed to maintaining a real meaning and importance in ritual that extended beyond its symbolic function. And in the realm of natural philosophy, they accepted that spiritual powers often and easily involved themselves in otherwise purely natural operations. Diligent theorists of superstition, often employing the term and the concept in what can appear to be evidently "modern" ways to construct or reinforce categories of proper religion and natural science, they were also deeply superstitious themselves, from the perspective of modernity, because they transgressed so many boundaries of the modern categories of religion, science, and rationality that have been imposed back on them. In Latour's language, they were hybrid.

If Latour is right, however, and strict modern categorizations obscure much about the world as it actually is, including historical processes by which the modern world came into being, then the seemingly incongruent, hybrid nature of fourteenth- and fifteenth-century authorities' understanding of and approach to superstition becomes especially edifying. Their debates, understood as fully as possible in their own terms, not only illuminate an important aspect of that era but also allow us to see more directly the complex and often subtle dynamics by which ideas of superstition and the profound concerns that they encoded actually shifted over time. In their writings, still unencumbered by a consciousness of newness that becomes increasingly prevalent from the sixteenth through the eighteenth centuries—still so "medieval," to reappropriate the term with some positive spin, rather than (early) modern—we find not so much even distinct "cycles of desacralization and resacralization, disenchantment and re-enchantment" as the complete blurring of these categories (again, from the modern perspective).[77] And yet it was medieval authorities' efforts to establish boundaries and create clear, meaningful categories that produced some very real historical change. The sort of change we see taking place in the 1300s and 1400s clearly continued through the early modern centuries as well, but the further we move forward in time the more it becomes subsumed within, and so to some extent inevitably obscured by, the gradual advent of "modernity."

Latour proclaims that "we have never been modern." By this he means that the hybridization that modernity denies has never ceased. It remains essential to the development and "progress" that characterizes the modern era. Particularly as that progress speeds up, as science reveals how fully humanity is still a part of nature, not just subject to but indelibly shaped by natural forces, while at the same time technology imposes itself everywhere and refashions the very nature of the world in which we live, the clear and orderly divisions on which modernity is founded start to fray. If we accept this, then we may find that the writings of medieval authorities who addressed and debated the issue of superstition prove interesting and informative not just because they illuminate a historical period or processes of historical change, but also because we are now somewhat escaping the conceptual strictures of a modernity that they entirely predate.

A complete demolition of all the discourses of modernity as they relate to the history of superstition is probably not possible, and perhaps not even desirable. Dipesh Chakrabarty, a historical theorist who is also deeply concerned about modernity's obscuring effects, nevertheless argues strongly against discarding notions of modernity or disenchantment as heuristic tools. We must, however, remain aware of the problems they entail and the complexities they can mask. All historians inevitably engage in a process of translation,

---

77. Walsham, "Reformation and 'the Disenchantment of the World,'" 527 (as above, n. 29, or introduction, n. 12).

endeavoring to describe the past in terms that are meaningful to the present while still remaining essentially faithful to the past itself.[78] This task is all the trickier when such a historically contested term as "superstition" is the very object of our study. Moreover, we must acknowledge that, whatever our stated desire to approach the past on its own terms, the importance and in some cases basic meaning of certain aspects of the past change in light of future developments. I do not mean simply that how we see a particular moment in time changes over time, but that any particular moment as a part of history is fundamentally different from that same moment as it was being lived out by human actors.[79] History is a way of seeing the past from the present. It is not, in the final analysis, purely about objectivity, authenticity, or absolute fidelity to how people in the past actually viewed their world.[80] The history of a concept, especially, even if focused on the development it underwent at a particular time, must therefore also take into account at least somewhat how it later came to be construed.

Whether or not we have ever been modern, and whether or not we are now—in the West, and only partially—disenchanted, we are not like the popes, preachers, and theologians who constructed and contested notions of superstition in the fourteenth and fifteenth centuries. Momentous developments stand between them and us, and if we do not acknowledge that, then we abandon history. Neither, however, are we utterly disconnected from them. Their notions of superstition lead to ours, and they help elucidate the dynamics of that change. These connections explain why the history of "medieval" superstition worms its way through the early modern period and even into the heart of modernity itself.

---

78. Dipesh Chakrabarty, *Provincializing Europe: Postcolonial Thought and Historical Difference*, rev. ed. (Princeton, N.J., 2007), 72–96; see also Chakrabarty, *Habitations of Modernity: Essays in the Wake of Subaltern Studies* (Chicago, 2002), xx; and Chakrabarty, "Historicism and Its Supplements," esp. 117–19.

79. My thinking somewhat follows Bruno Latour, "The Historicity of Things," in Latour, *Pandora's Hope: Essays on the Reality of Science Studies* (Cambridge, Mass., 1999), 145–73; discussed in Harman, *Prince of Networks*, 84–85; see also Chakrabarty's discussion of historical perspective and anachronism in *Provincializing Europe*, 243.

80. See Constantin Fasolt's important rumination on *The Limits of History* (Chicago, 2004), esp. 3–45.

Epilogue

> The past is never dead. It's not even past.
> —William Faulkner, *Requiem for a Nun*
>
> All history is modern history.
> —Wallace Stevens, "Adagia"

Superstition is a perennial issue, not just in histories of religion, but also in science, philosophy, politics, and culture. The word *superstitio* originated with the Romans perhaps a century before the time of Christ, only to be adopted and refashioned by Christian writers in late antiquity. The concept of certain beliefs and behaviors being "superstitious" (*superstitiosus*) was even older. These terms, along with their vernacular cognates and direct translations, have proved enormously enduring, and that stability of language can contribute to a sense that the issues encompassed under the label of superstition may be not just perennial but essentially static. As we have seen, Christian authorities writing in the fourteenth and fifteenth centuries readily drew descriptive terminology and definitions across a full millennium from the early church fathers and even from some ancient Roman sources. Then there is the abiding modern prejudice to view both the "medieval" and the "superstitious" as indicative of fundamentally immutable premodern irrationality. Clearly, however, superstition has a dynamic history. The kinds of beliefs and practices censured as superstitious have changed over time, as have the manner, intensity, and focus with which authorities have defined and deployed the word.

Western Europe in the fourteenth and fifteenth centuries witnessed significant growth in concern on the part of many religious and intellectual authorities over the various beliefs and practices that they condemned as superstitious, as well as some important changes in how they conceived of the category of superstition itself. This was a period of notable tensions and transitions, although not of any absolute transformation or reconfiguration. In the writings of the men who attempted to delineate the boundaries of superstition in these two hundred years we can see how some of the major intellectual, political, and pastoral developments of preceding centuries worked themselves out both in elite, courtly contexts and in common society. We can also examine lines of thought that would feed into coming concerns about supposed sects of diabolical witches, and more broadly still into major aspects of Reformation-era theology, religiosity, and ritual practice. Focusing on debate about superstition before the Reformation or indeed any of the other putative watersheds of modernity, we find a society, or more accurately a small but powerful elite within that society, still comfortably reliant on traditional definitions and ancient authorities, with little thought of advancing any profoundly new systems of thought. And yet they were engaged in constructing and negotiating boundaries that would continue to resonate powerfully through subsequent Western and also world history: between the physical and the spiritual, between the rational and the fantastic, and between directly effective action and merely symbolic signification.

We inevitably also confront in the texts examined here some of the varied manifestations in practice of powerful ideas and beliefs diffused multifariously throughout a society, and the problems these might generate for authorities seeking to exert power and impose structures of control. It is not just agents of modernity who endeavor to "purify" densely interwoven experiences into clear and distinct conceptual categories. The boundaries that theologians and other authorities drew in the fourteenth and fifteenth centuries and the categories within which they comfortably or at times uncomfortably operated can be quite different from those on which modernity has been thought to depend. But, while that indicates a considerable distance between then and now, it does not demonstrate an absolute separation. We need to keep the structures of modernity in mind as we examine "medieval" superstition both to perceive real difference and also to avoid imposing too extreme an "otherness" on the distant past. Particularly as we become increasingly skeptical about such absolute abstractions as disenchantment and modernity itself, the supposed alterities of the medieval era become interesting not just in their own right but as valuable lenses through which to refract the present.

Superstition is clearly not anymore (at least in the modern West) the deadly serious issue it could be in the fourteenth and fifteenth centuries. I tend to smile and even chuckle just a bit as I hold my mass-produced plastic

Saint Joseph in my hand. So, I imagine, do many who might nonetheless actually choose to bury him in their yards while trying to sell their houses. Whether or not they fervently believe that this action will help draw some supernatural power to aid them, they almost certainly do not believe that it could cause any harm. Similarly the students at my university who so diligently divert their course around the zodiac seal embedded in our Memorial Union foyer floor are not gripped by any terrible fear of threatening occult forces. They do so because it is tradition, or, rather less augustly phrased, because it is simply what is done in that space and in relation to that symbol, just one among countless mostly unreflective practices that make up the course of a day. If someone accused them of behaving superstitiously, they might or might not be mildly offended, but they would have little reason to care and no cause to worry that they might incur any punishment or penalty, either human or divine, because of this. Of course, some charges of superstition can still carry serious implications in the modern world—imagine a scientist accused of believing in astrology or a politician suspected of practicing witchcraft—but there can be no doubt that harsh repercussions followed accusations of superstition far more frequently in the past. Nevertheless, we should also not forget that even earnest late medieval authorities included a few outright jokes in their mostly stolid writing about superstition, and I am confident that they too smiled at the thought of at least some of the beliefs and practices they surveyed far more often than their serious theological treatises, legal injunctions, and moralizing sermons will ever indicate.

To an extent, this book has pursued a phantom. There was never a single, clear, coherent category of superstition in the late medieval period, a legalistically precise allegation that always carried exactly the same connotation and consequences. Rather, various authorities, backed by and wielding various forms of social and intellectual power, sought to fashion such a category, in order to give greater order to their world and to exert greater control over it. They neither succeeded nor failed, because they were engaged in a process, not a discrete act. Superstition is always a charge, and hence it is an inherently charged word, then and now. My concern in this book has been to chart the changing nature and intensity of that charge in a particular place and time. Positioning superstition in history means thinking about how different societies define proper belief, legitimate knowledge, and acceptable behavior. It also means considering how much importance societies place on conforming to those strictures, and what sort of penalties they may impose on transgressors. This is not a medieval story, or a modern one. For better or worse, it is a human story, one of rectitude and fear, of judgment and power.

❦ Appendix

Bibliographical and Dating Information on Major Late Medieval Sources Addressing Superstition

Some fourteenth- and fifteenth-century texts addressing superstition exist in modern editions, but many are found only in early modern printings or in medieval manuscripts. Rather than burden footnotes with extensive source descriptions, I present essential information here. For each work, I list the principal copy on which I have relied, whether manuscript, early printing, or modern edition. Unless otherwise indicated, all citations throughout the book refer to that version. When I have consulted additional copies of a text, they are listed subsequently. Finally, I provide the source of the dating that I have followed for each work.

Anonymous, *De divinacionibus* (ca. 1415)

- Principal copy used: Trier, Stadtbibliothek, MS 265, 164r–183r.
- Additional copy consulted: partial edition (as *Tractatus de daemonibus*) in *Quellen*, 82–86.
- Dating: *Quellen*, 82.

Anonymous, *De superstitionibus* (before ca. 1445) (= *De superstitionibus* [E])

- Principal copy used: Erlangen, Universitätsbibliothek, MS 585, 175v–176v.
- Dating: Erlangen catalog.

Anonymous, *De superstitionibus* (before 1459) (= De superstitionibus [M])

- Principal copy used: Munich, BSB, Clm 4727, 1r–78v.
- Additional copies consulted: Munich, BSB, Clm 4707, 1r–70v; Clm 18257, 5r–52v; Clm 26923, 1r–67r.
- Also found in: Olomouc, Vědecká knihovna, M.II.108, 95r–142r.[1]
- Dating: internal evidence at Clm 4727, 141r.

Anonymous, *De superstitionibus, magia, sortilegiis, etc.* (fifteenth century)

- Principal copy used: Munich, BSB, Clm 8345, 294v–297r.
- Dating: Munich catalog.

Anonymous, *Les Évangiles des quenouilles* (ca. mid-fifteenth century, before 1474)

- Principal copy used: Madeleine Jeay and Kathleen Garay, eds. and trans., *The Distaff Gospels: A First Modern English Edition of "Les Évangiles des Quenouilles"* (Peterborough, Ont.: Broadview Press, 2006).
- Additional copy consulted: Madeleine Jeay, ed., *Les Évangiles des quenouilles* (Montreal: Presses de l'Université de Montréal, 1985).
- Dating: Jeay and Garay, *Distaff Gospels*, 26; Jeay, *Évangiles*, 35.

Carpenter, Alexander, *Destructorium viciorum* (ca. 1429)

- Principal copy used: Carpenter, *Destructorium viciorum* (Paris, 1521).
- Dating: G. R. Owst, *The Destructorium Viciorum of Alexander Carpenter: A Fifteenth-Century Sequel to "Literature and Pulpit in Medieval England"* (London: S. P.C.K., 1952), 5–6.

D'Ailly, Pierre, *Apologetica defensio astronomice veritatis* (1414)

- Principal copy used: Pierre d'Ailly, *Imago mundi et varia eiusdem auctoris et Joannis Gerson opuscula* (Louvain, ca. 1483), 138r–140v.
- Dating: Laura Smoller, *History, Prophecy, and the Stars: The Christian Astrology of Pierre d'Ailly, 1350–1420* (Princeton, N.J.: Princeton University Press, 1994), 136–37.

---

1. Not consulted directly, but see Zdeněk Uhlíř, "Texte über den Aberglauben in den tschechischen Handschriftensammlungen des Mittelalters," in *Religion und Magie in Ostmitteleuropa: Spielräume theologischer Normierungsprozesse in Spätmittelalter und Früher Neuzeit*, ed. Thomas Wünsch (Berlin, 2006), 101.

D'Ailly, Pierre, *Alia secunda apologetica defensio eiusdem* (1414)

- Principal copy used: d'Ailly, *Imago mundi* . . . , 140v–143r.
- Dating: Smoller, *History, Prophecy, and the Stars*, 136–37.

D'Ailly, Pierre, *Apologia astrologie defensiva* (1419)

- Principal copy used: *OC*, 2:218–21.
- Dating: *OC*, 2:218; Smoller, *History, Prophecy, and the Stars*, 136–37.

D'Ailly, Pierre, *Concordantia astronomie cum hystorica narratione* (1414)

- Principal copy used: d'Ailly, *Concordantia astronomie cum theologia, Concordantia astronomie cum hystorica narratione, et Elucidarium duorum precedentium* (Augsburg, 1490) (no foliation).
- Additional copy consulted: d'Ailly, *Imago mundi* . . . , 97v–115r.
- Dating: Smoller, *History, Prophecy, and the Stars*, 136–37.

D'Ailly, Pierre, *De concordia discordantium astronomorum* (1415)

- Principal copy used: d'Ailly, *Imago mundi* . . . , 143r–152v.
- Dating: Smoller, *History, Prophecy, and the Stars*, 136–37.

D'Ailly, Pierre, *De legibus et sectis contra superstitiosos astronomos* (1410)

- Principal copy used: d'Ailly, *Imago mundi* . . . , 38r–51v.
- Additional copy consulted: d'Ailly, *Tractatus de legibus et sectis contra superstitiosos astronomos* (Rouen, 1489/91).
- Dating: Smoller, *History, Prophecy, and the Stars*, 136–37.

D'Ailly, Pierre, *Elucidarium astronomice concordie cum theologica et historica veritate* (1414)

- Principal copy used: d'Ailly, *Concordantia* . . . (no foliation).
- Additional copy consulted: d'Ailly, *Imago mundi* . . . , 115r–138r.
- Dating: Smoller, *History, Prophecy, and the Stars*, 136–37.

D'Ailly, Pierre, *Vigintiloquium de concordantia astronomice veritatis cum theologia* (1414)

- Principal copy used: d'Ailly, *Concordantia* . . . (no foliation).
- Additional copy consulted: d'Ailly, *Imago mundi* . . . , 84r–97r.
- Dating: Smoller, *History, Prophecy, and the Stars*, 136–37.

Denys the Carthusian, *Contra vitia superstitionum* (ca. 1450?)

- Principal copy used: Denys the Carthusian, *Contra Alchoranum et sectam Machometicam libri quinque, De instituendo bello adversus Turcas et de generali celebrando Concilio, Contra vitia superstitionum* (Cologne, 1533), 598–628.

- Dating: Lynn Thorndike, *A History of Magic and Experimental Science*, 8 vols. (New York: Macmillan and Columbia University Press, 1923–58), 4:291.[2]

Ebendorfer, Thomas, *De decem praeceptis* (1438/39)

- Principal copy used: partial edition in Anton E. Schönbach, "Zeugnisse zur deutschen Volkskunde des Mittelalters," *Zeitschrift des Vereins für Volkskunde* 12 (1902): 1–14.
- Dating: Alphons Lhotsky, *Thomas Ebendorfer: Ein österreichischer Geschichtschreiber, Theologe und Diplomat des 15. Jahrhunderts*, MGH Schriften 15 (Stuttgart: Hiersemann, 1957), 81.

Eymerich, Nicolau, *Contra alchimistas* (1396)

- Principal copy used: edition in Sylvain Matton, "Le traité *Contra les alchimistes* de Nicolas Eymerich," *Chrysopoeia* 1 (1987): 93–136.
- Dating: internal evidence at *Contra alchimistas*, 134.

Eymerich, Nicolau, *Contra astrologos imperitos atque nigromanticos* (1395/96)

- Principal copy used: Paris, Bibliothèque nationale de France, Lat. 3171, 75r–89v.
- Additional copy consulted: partial edition in Julien Véronèse, "Le *Contra astrologos imperitos atque nigromanticos* (1395–96) de Nicolas Eymerich (O. P.): Contexte de rédaction, classification des arts magiques et divinatoires, édition critique partielle," in *Chasse aux sorcières et démonologie: Entre discours et pratiques (XIVe–XVIIe siècles)*, ed. Martine Ostorero, Georg Modestin, and Kathrin Utz Tremp, ML 36 (Florence: SISMEL, 2010), 271–329.
- Dating: Véronèse, "Le *Contra astrologos*," 272.

Eymerich, Nicolau, *Contra demonum invocatores* (1359)

- Principal copy used: Paris, Bibliothèque nationale de France, Lat. 1464, 100r–161r.
- Dating: Claudia Heimann, *Nicolaus Eymerich (vor 1320–1399)— praedicator veridicus, inquisitor intrepidus, doctor egregious: Leben und Werk*

---

2. On general difficulties dating many of Denys's works, see Dirk Wasserman, *Dionysius der Kartäuser: Einführung in Werk und Gedankenwelt* (Salzburg, 1996), 14–15.

eines Inquisitors, Spanische Forschungen der Görresgesellschaft n.s. 37 (Münster: Aschendorff, 2001), 27.

Eymerich, Nicolau, *Directorium inquisitorum* (1376)

- Principal copy used: Eymerich, *Directorium inquisitorum*, ed. F. Peña (Rome, 1587).
- Dating: Heimann, *Nicolaus Eymerich*, 50.

Gerson, Jean, *Adversus superstitionem in audiendo missam* (1429)

- Principal copy used: *OC*, 10:141–43.
- Dating: *OC*, 10:75.

Gerson, Jean, *Contra superstitionem sculpturae leonis* (1428)

- Principal copy used: *OC*, 10:131–34.
- Dating: *OC*, 10:75.

Gerson, Jean, *Contra superstitiosam dierum observantiam* (1421)

- Principal copy used: *OC*, 10:116–21.
- Dating: *OC*, 10:74.

Gerson, Jean, *De erroribus circa artem magicam* (1402)

- Principal copy used: *OC*, 10:77–90.
- Dating: *OC*, 10:73.

Gerson, Jean, *De observatione dierum quantum ad opera* (1425)

- Principal copy used: *OC*, 10:128–30.
- Dating: *OC*, 10:75.

Gerson, Jean, *De respectu coelestium siderum* (1419)

- Principal copy used: *OC*, 10:109–16.
- Dating: *OC*, 10:74.

Gerson, Jean, *Trilogium astrologiae theologizatae* (1419)

- Principal copy used: *OC*, 10:90–109.
- Dating: *OC*, 10:74.

Hartlieb, Johannes, *Das Buch aller verbotenen Künste* (1456 or thereafter, no later than 1464)

- Principal copy used: Hartlieb, *Das Buch aller verbotenen Künste, des Aberglaubens und der Zauberei*, ed. and trans. Falk Eisermann and

Eckhard Graf, *Esoterik des Abendlandes 4* (Ahlerstedt, Ger.: Param, 1989).

* Dating: Frank Furbeth, *Johannes Hartlieb: Untersuchung zu Leben und Werk*, Hermaea: Germanistische Forschungen n.s. 64 (Tübingen: Max Niemeyer, 1992), 76–77.

Heinrich of Gorkum, *De superstitiosis quibusdam casibus* (ca. 1425)

* Principal copy used: Heinrich of Gorkum, *Tractatus de superstitiosis quibusdam casibus, Tractatus de celebratione festorum, Omelia beati Johannis Crisostomi de cruce et latrine* (Blaubeuren, ca. 1477), 1r–6v.
* Additional copies consulted: Munich, BSB, Clm 7644, 78r–83v; Heinrich of Gorkum, *Tractatus de superstitiosis quibusdam casibus, Tractatus de celebratione festorum* (Esslingen, before 1474), 1r–9v; partial edition in *Quellen*, 87–88.
* Dating: *Quellen*, 87.

Heinrich of Langenstein, *Contra astrologos coniunctionistas de eventibus futurorum* (1373)

* Principal copy used: edition in Hubert Pruckner, *Studien zu den astrologischen Schriften des Heinrich von Langenstein*, Studien der Bibliothek Warburg 14 (Leipzig: Teubner, 1933), 139–206.
* Dating: Pruckner, *Studien*, 20.

Heinrich of Langenstein, *Questio de cometa* (1368/69)

* Principal copy used: edition in Pruckner, *Studien*, 89–138.
* Dating: Pruckner, *Studien*, 9.

Hemmerli, Felix, *De benedictionibus aure cum sacramento faciendis* (ca. 1451/52)

* Principal copy used: Hemmerli, *Varie oblectationis opuscula et tractatus* (Strassburg, 1497 or after), 100r–103r.
* Dating: Balthasar Reber, ed., *Felix Hemmerlin von Zürich, neu nach den Quellen bearbeitet* (Zurich: Mener & Zeller, 1846), 336.

Hemmerli, Felix, *De credulitate demonibus adhibenda* (after 1455)

* Principal copy used: Hemmerli, *Opuscula et tractatus*, 111r–115v.
* Dating: internal evidence at *De credulitate*, 111r.

Hemmerli, Felix, *De exorcismis* (1456/57)

* Principal copy used: Hemmerli, *Opuscula et tractatus*, 103v–106r.

- Dating: Catherine Chène, *Juger les vers: Exorcismes et procès d'animaux dans le diocese de Lausanne (XVe–XVIe s.)*, CLHM 14 (Lausanne: Université de Lausanne, 1995), 24–25.

Hemmerli, Felix, *Tractatus exorcismorum seu adiurationum* (1451/52)

- Principal copy used: Hemmerli, *Opuscula et tractatus*, 106r–110v.
- Dating: Reber, *Felix Hemmerlin*, 336.

Jacquier, Nicolas, *Flagellum haereticorum fascinariorum* (1458)

- Principal copy used: Jacquier, *Flagellum haereticorum fascinariorum* (Frankfurt, 1581).
- Dating: Martine Ostorero, *Le diable au sabbat: Littérature démonologique et sorcellerie (1440–1460)*, ML 38 (Florence: SISMEL, 2010), 129–31.

Jakob of Paradise, *De potestate demonum* (1452)

- Principal copy used: Munich, BSB, Clm 18378, 245r–272r.
- Additional copies consulted: Augsburg, Staats- und Stadtbibliothek, 2° Cod 338, 177r–198v; Berlin, Staatsbibliothek, Cod. Lat. Qu. 919, 1r–30r; Berlin, Staatsbibliothek, Cod. Theol. Fol. 668, 298r–320r; Munich, BSB, Clm 9105, 167r–211r.
- Dating: Dieter Mertens, *Iacobus Carthusiensis: Untersuchungen zur Rezeption der Werke des Kartäusers Jakob von Paradies (1381–1465)*, Veröffentlichungen des Max-Planck-Instituts für Geschichte 50, Studien zur Germania Sacra 13 (Göttingen: Vandenhoeck & Ruprecht, 1976), 40.

Johannes of Frankfurt, *Quaestio utrum potestas cohercendi demones fieri possit per caracteres, figuras atque verborum prolationes* (1405)

- Principal copy used: edition in *Quellen*, 71–82.
- Additional copies consulted: Munich, BSB, Clm 3417, 43v–48v; Clm 15320, 150r–155r; Clm 18142, 330r–336r (labeled as *Questio bona de sortilegii*).
- Dating: Dorothea Walz et al., eds., *Zwölf Werke des Heidelberger Theologen und Inquisitors*, Editiones Heidelbergenses 29 (Heidelberg: Universitätsverlag C. Winter, 2000), 227–30.

Johannes of Wünschelburg, *De superstitionibus* (ca. 1440)

- Principal copy used: Wrocław, Biblioteka Uniwersytecka, 239 (I F 212), 228r–258v.

- Additional copies consulted: Dresden, Sächsische Landesbibliothek—
  Staats- und Universitätsbibliothek, Cod. P. 104, 1r–38v; Wrocław,
  Biblioteka Uniwersytecka, 6098 (Mil. II 46), 419r–446r.
- Dating: *Quellen*, 104.

Kramer, Heinrich, *Malleus maleficarum* (1486)

- Principal copy used: Henricus Institoris, O. P., and Jacobus Sprenger,
  O. P., *Malleus Maleficarum*, ed. and trans. Christopher Mackay, 2 vols.
  (Cambridge: Cambridge University Press, 2006).
- Dating: Mackay, "Introduction," in *Malleus maleficarum*, 1:136.

Martin of Arles, *De superstitionibus* (ca. 1500)

- Principal copy used: Martin of Arles, *De superstitionibus* (Rome,
  1559).
- Additional copy consulted: edition in José Goñi Gaztambide, "El
  tratado 'De superstitionibus' de Martín de Andosilla," *Cuadernos de
  Etnología y Etnografía de Navarre* 3 (1971): 249–322 (based on the
  edition printed in Lyon, 1510).
- Dating: Gaztambide, "El tratado 'De superstitionibus,'" 262.[3]

Nider, Johannes, *Formicarius* (1436–38)

- Principal copy used: Nider, *Formicarius*, ed. G. Colvener (Douai,
  1602).
- Additional copies consulted: Basel, Öffentliche Bibliothek der
  Universität, B III 15, 81r–186r; partial edition by Catherine Chène
  in *L'imaginaire du sabbat: Edition critique des textes les plus anciens
  (1430 c.–1440 c.)*, ed. Martine Ostorero, Agostino Paravicini Bagliani,
  and Kathrin Utz Tremp, in collaboration with Catherine Chène,
  CLHM 26 (Lausanne: Université de Lausanne, 1999), 122–99.
- Dating: Michael D. Bailey, *Battling Demons: Witchcraft, Heresy, and
  Reform in the Late Middle Ages* (University Park: Pennsylvania State
  University Press, 2003), 153.

---

3. There has, however, been much speculation and debate. Henry Charles Lea, *Materials toward a
History of Witchcraft*, ed. Arthur C. Howland, 3 vols. (Philadelphia, 1939), 1:297, suggests sometime
in the middle third of the fifteenth century, mainly because Martin quotes extensively from Johannes
Nider, who wrote in the 1430s, but fails to mention the *Malleus maleficarum* of 1486. For the same
reason, Julio Caro Baroja, *The World of the Witches*, trans. O. N. V. Glendinning (Chicago, 1964), 145,
suggests sometime after 1466. Fabián Alejandro Campagne, *Homo Catholicus, Homo Superstitiosus:
El discurso antisupersticioso en la España de los siglos XV a XVIII* (Madrid, 2002), 90, states without
elaboration that the work was probably written in the last decades of the fifteenth century.

Nider, Johannes, *Preceptorium divine legis* (1438)

- Principal copy used: Nider, *Preceptorium divine legis* (Milan, 1489).
- Dating: Bailey, *Battling Demons*, 153.

Nikolaus of Dinkelsbühl, *De preceptis decalogi* (1423)

- Principal copy used: Nikolaus of Dinkelsbühl, *De dilectione dei et proximi, De preceptis decalogi, De oratione dominica* . . . (Strassburg, 1516), 22v–49r.
- Additional copies consulted: Munich, BSB, Clm 3024, 91r–133r; Clm 3417, 179r–225v.
- Dating: Alois Madre, *Nikolaus von Dinkelsbühl Leben und Schriften: Ein Beitrag zur theologischen Literaturgeschichte*, Beiträge zur Geschichte der Philosophie und Theologie des Mittelalters 40.4 (Münster: Aschendorffsche Verlagsbuchhandlung, 1965), 171.

Nikolaus of Jauer, *De superstitionibus* (1405)

- Principal copy used: Philadelphia, University of Pennsylvania, MS Codex 78, 35r–63v.
- Additional copies consulted: Munich, BSB, Clm 3024, 184r–210r; Clm 3041, 188r–219r; Clm 4721, 202r–220r; Vatican City, Biblioteca Apostolica Vaticana, Pal. Lat. 679, 164r–205r; Pal. Lat. 719, 64r–77v.
- Dating: Adolph Franz, *Der Magister Nikolaus Magni de Jawor: Ein Beitrag zur Literatur- und Gelehrtengeschichte des 14. und 15. Jahrhunderts* (Freiburg im/Br.: Herder, 1898), 161.

Nikolaus of Jauer, *Refutatio* (of errors of Werner of Friedberg) (1405)

- Principal copy used: Munich, BSB, Clm 4721, 199r–202r.
- Additional copy consulted: Munich, BSB, Clm 3041, 183v–188r.
- Dating: Franz, *Magister Nikolaus Magni*, 154.

Oresme, Nicole, *Contra judiciarios astronomos* (before 1361?)

- Principal copy used: edition in G. W. Coopland, *Nicole Oresme and the Astrologers: A Study of His Livre de Divinacions* (Cambridge, Mass.: Harvard University Press, 1952), 123–41.
- Additional copy consulted: edition in Pruckner, *Studien*, 227–45.
- Dating: Coopland, *Nicole Oresme*, 20.

Oresme, Nicole, *De causis mirabilium (Quodlibeta)* (1370?)

- Principal copy used: edition in Bert Hansen, *Nicole Oresme and the Marvels of Nature: A Study of His "De causis mirabilium" with Critical*

Edition, Translation, and Commentary, Studies and Texts 68 (Toronto: Pontifical Institute of Medieval Studies, 1985), 135–363.

• Dating: Hansen, *Nicole Oresme*, 43–48.[4]

Oresme, Nicole, *De commensurabilitate vel incommensurabilitate motuum celi* (between 1351 and 1377, likely before 1362)

• Principal copy used: edition in Edward Grant, *Nicole Oresme and the Kinematics of Circular Motion: Tractatus de commensurabilitate vel incommensurabilitate motuum celi*, University of Wisconsin Publications in Medieval Science 15 (Madison: University of Wisconsin Press, 1971), 171–323.
• Dating: Grant, *Nicole Oresme*, 4–5.

Oresme, Nicole, *De configurationibus qualitatum et motuum* (likely 1350s)

• Principal copy used: edition in Marshall Clagett, *Nicole Oresme and the Medieval Geometry of Qualities and Motions: A Treatise on the Uniformity and Difformity of Intensities Known as* Tractatus de configurationibus qualitatum et motuum, University of Wisconsin Publications in Medieval Science 12 (Madison: University of Wisconsin Press, 1968), 157–435.
• Dating: Clagett, *Nicole Oresme*, 14.

Oresme, Nicole, *Livre de divinacions* (1361/65)

• Principal copy used: edition in Coopland, *Nicole Oresme*, 50–121.
• Dating: Coopland, *Nicole Oresme*, 1.

Oresme, Nicole, *Quaestio contra divinatores horoscopios* (1370?)

• Principal copy used: edition in Stefano Caroti, "Nicole Oresme: Quaestio contra divinatores horoscopios," *Archives d'histoire doctinale et littéraire du moyen âge* 43 (1976): 201–310.
• Dating: Hansen, *Nicole Oresme*, 17.[5]

Pignon, Laurens, *Contre les devineurs* (1411)

• Principal copy used: edition in Jan R. Veentra, *Magic and Divination at the Courts of Burgundy and France: Text and Context of Laurens Pignon's*

4. Joel Kaye, "Law, Magic, and Science: Constructing a Border between Licit and Illicit Knowledge in the Writings of Nicole Oresme," in *Law and the Illicit in Medieval Europe*, ed. Ruth Mazo Karras, Joel Kaye, and E. Ann Matter (Philadelphia, 2008), 225–37 and 298–303, at 229 and 300 n. 21, notes the work could also be dated to 1350/55.

5. Clagett, *Nicole Oresme*, 129–31, suggests redating to the 1350s.

"Contre les devineurs" (1411), Brill's Studies in Intellectual History 83 (Leiden: Brill, 1998), 223–339.
- Dating: Veentra, *Magic and Divination*, 1.

Schwarz (Nigri), Johannes, *De divinacionibus* (1466)

- Principal copy used: Munich, BSB, Clm 26825, 297v–325r.
- Dating: internal evidence at Clm 26825, 325v.

Ulrich of Pottenstein, *Dekalog-Auslegung* (1390s–1411/12)

- Principal copy used: Ulrich of Pottenstein, *Dekalog-Auslegung: Das erste Gebot, Text und Quellen*, ed. Gabriele Baptist-Hlawatsch, Texte und Textgeschichte 43 (Tübingen: Max Niemeyer, 1995).
- Dating: Baptist-Hlawatsch, introduction to *Dekalog-Auslegung*, 20–22.

Werner of Friedberg, *Responsiones* (1405)

- Principal copy used: edition in Robert E. Lerner, "Werner di Friedberg intrappolato dalla legge," in *La parola all'accusato*, ed. Jean-Claude Maire Vigueur and Agostino Paravicini Bagliani (Palermo: Sellerio, 1991), 268–81.
- Dating: Lerner, "Werner di Friedberg," 279.

Werner of Friedberg, *Revocatio errorum* (1405)

- Principal copy used: Munich, BSB, Clm 4721, 198r–v.
- Additional copies consulted: Munich, BSB, Clm 3041, 182r–183r.
- Dating: Franz, *Magister Nikolaus Magni*, 151.

🐚 BIBLIOGRAPHY

Major Late Medieval Sources on Superstition

See appendix.

Other Primary Sources

Aquinas, Thomas. *The "De Malo" of Thomas Aquinas*. Edited by Brian Davies. Translated by Richard Regan. Oxford: Oxford University Press, 2001.

———. *Summa contra gentiles*. In Aquinas, *Opera omnia iussu Leonis XIII P.M. edita*, vols. 13–15. Rome: Typis Riccardi Garroni, 1918–30.

———. *Summa theologiae: Latin Text and English Translation*. 60 vols. New York: Blackfriars and McGraw-Hill, 1964–81.

Augustine. *Confessionum libri XIII*. Edited by Lucas Verheijen. CCSL 27. Turnhout: Brepols, 1981.

———. *Contra academicos*. Edited by W. M. Green. CCSL 29. Turnhout: Brepols, 1970.

———. *De civitate dei*. Edited by Bernard Dombart and Alphonse Kalb. CCSL 47–48. Turnhout: Brepols, 1955.

———. *De divinatione daemonum*. Edited by Iosephus Zycha. CSEL 41, pp. 599–618. Vienna: Tempsky, 1900.

———. *De doctrina Christiana*. Edited by Joseph Martin. CCSL 32. Turnhout: Brepols, 1962.

———. *De vera religione*. Edited by K.-D. Daur. CCSL 32. Turnhout: Brepols, 1962.

Bodin, Jean. *De la démonomanie des sorciers*. Paris, 1581.

Boretius, Alfred, ed. *MGH, Leges 2, Capitularia regum Francorum 1*. Hannover: Impensis Bibliopolii Hahniani, 1883.

Boureau, Alain. *Le pape et les sorciers: Une consultation de Jean XXII sur la magie en 1320 (Manuscrit B.A.V. Borghese 348)*. Sources et documents d'histoire de Moyen Âge 6. Rome: École Française de Rome, 2004.

Burchard of Worms. *Decretorum libri viginti*. PL 140, cols. 537–1058. Paris: Garnier Fratres, 1880.

Caesarius of Arles. *Sancti Caesarii Arelatensis sermones*. Edited by Germain Morin. CCSL 103-104. Turnhout: Brepols, 1953.

Caesarius of Heisterbach. *Dialogus miraculorum*. Edited by Joseph Strange. 2 vols. 1851. Reprint, Ridgewood, N.J.: Gregg Press, 1966.

Cicero. *De natura deorum*. Edited by Arthur Stanley Pease. 2 vols. Cambridge, Mass.: Harvard University Press, 1955–58.

Coste, Jean, ed. *Boniface VIII en procès: Articles d'accusation et dépositions des témoins (1303–1311)*. Pubblicazioni della Fondazione Camillo Caetani, Studi e documenti d'archivio 5. Rome: L'Erma di Bretschneider, 1995.

Davidson, L. S., and J. O. Ward, eds. and trans. *The Sorcery Trial of Alice Kyteler: A Contemporary Account (1324) Together with Related Documents in English Translation, with Introduction and Notes.* Binghamton, N.Y.: Medieval and Renaissance Texts and Studies, 1993.

Denifle, Heinrich, ed. *Chartularium Universitatis Parisiensis.* 4 vols. 1889–97. Reprint, Brussels: Culture et Civilisation, 1964.

Dives and Pauper. Edited by Priscilla Heath Barnum. 3 vols. EETS 275, 280, 323. London: Oxford University Press, 1976–2004.

Emery, Kent, ed. *Dionysii Cartusiensis Opera Selecta.* CCCM 121–121a. Turnhout: Brepols, 1991.

Friedberg, Emil, ed. *Corpus Iuris Canonici.* 2 vols. 1879–81. Reprint, Graz: Akademische Druck- und Verlagsanstalt, 1955.

Friedlander, Alan, ed. *Processus Bernardi Delitiosi: The Trial of Fr. Bernard Délicieux, 3 September–8 December 1319.* Transactions of the American Philosophical Society 86.1. Philadelphia: American Philosophical Society, 1996.

Gerson, Jean. *Oeuvres complètes.* Edited by P. Glorieux. 10 vols. Paris: Desclée, 1960–73.

Hansen, Joseph, ed. *Quellen und Untersuchungen zur Geschichte des Hexenwahns und der Hexenverfolgung im Mittelalter.* 1901. Reprint, Hildesheim: Georg Olms, 1963.

Horrox, Rosemary, ed. and trans. *The Black Death.* Manchester: Manchester University Press, 1994.

Isidore of Seville. *Etymologiarum sive originum libri XX.* Edited by W. M. Lindsay. 2 vols. 1911. Reprint, Oxford: Clarendon, 1971.

John of Salisbury. *Policraticus I–IV.* Edited by K. S. B. Keats-Rohan. CCCM 118. Turnhout: Brepols, 1993.

Justin Martyr. *The First and Second Apologies.* Edited and translated by Leslie William Barnard. Ancient Christian Writers 56. Mahwah, N.J.: Paulist Press, 1997.

Lea, Henry Charles. *Materials toward a History of Witchcraft.* Edited by Arthur C. Howland. 3 vols. Philadelphia: University of Pennsylvania Press, 1939.

Martin of Braga. *Martini episcopi Bracarensis opera omnia.* Edited by Claude W. Barlow. Papers and Monographs of the American Academy in Rome 12. New Haven, Conn.: Yale University Press, 1950.

———. *Pro castigatione rusticorum.* Edited and translated by Gennaro Lopez. Biblioteca di Cultura Romanobarbarica 3. Rome: Herder, 1998.

Mézières, Philippe. *Le songe du vieil pelerin.* Edited by G. W. Coopland. 2 vols. Cambridge: Cambridge University Press, 1969.

Mommsen, Theodor, and Paul M. Meyer, eds. *Theodosiani libri XVI cum Constitutionibus Sirmondianis et Leges novellae ad Theodosianum pertinentes.* 2 vols. Berlin: Weidemann, 1905.

Nikolaus of Dinkelsbühl. *Der Herrengebetskommentar des Nikolaus von Dinkelsbühl: Deutsche Übersetzung nach der textkritischen lateinischen Ausgabe.* Translated by Rudolf Damerau. Studien zu den Grundlagen der Reformation 11. Giessen: Wilhelm Schmitz, 1972.

Oresme, Nicole. *De visione stellarum.* In Dan Burton, *Nicole Oresme's "De visione stellarum" (On Seeing the Stars): A Critical Edition of Oresme's Treatise on Optics and Atmospheric Refraction, with an Introduction, Commentary, and English Translation.* Medieval and Early Modern Science 7. Leiden: Brill, 2007.

Ostorero, Martine, Agostino Paravicini Bagliani, and Kathrin Utz Tremp, eds. *L'imaginaire du sabbat: Edition critique des texts les plus anciens (1430 c.–1440 c.)*. With Catherine Chène. CLHM 26. Lausanne: Université de Lausanne, 1999.

Piché, David, ed. and trans. *La condamnation parisienne de 1277: Nouvelle edition du texte latin, traduction, introduction et commentaire*. Paris: Vrin, 1999.

Schmitz, Hermann Joseph. *Die Bussbücher und das kanonische Bussverfahren: Nach handschriftlichen Quellen dargestellt*. 2 vols. 1898. Reprint, Graz: Akademische Druck- und Verlagsanstalt, 1958.

Tinctor, Jean. *Invectives contre la secte de vauderie*. Edited by Émile Van Balberghe and Frédéric Duval. Tournai—Art et Histoire 14. Tournai: Archives du Chapitre cathédral, 1999.

Vidal, J.-M., ed. *Bullaire de l'inquisition française au XIVe siècle et jusqu'à la fin du grand schism*. Paris: Librairie Letouzey et Ané, 1913.

Vives, José, ed. *Concilios Visigóticos e Hispano-Romanos*. With Tomás Marín Martínez and Gonzalo Martínez Díez. Barcelona: Consejo Superior de Investigaciones Científicas, Instituto Enrique Flórez, 1963.

William of Auvergne. *Opera omnia*. Venice, 1591.

Secondary Sources

Agrimi, Jole, and Chiara Crisciani. "Savoir médical et anthropologie religieuse: Les représentations et les fonctions de la vetula (XIIIe–XVe siècle)." *Annales ESC* 48.5 (1993): 1281–1308.

Ahnert, Thomas. *Religion and the Origins of the German Enlightenment: Faith and the Reform of Learning in the Thought of Christian Thomasius*. Rochester, N.Y.: University of Rochester Press, 2006.

Anderson, Wendy Love. "Gerson's Stance on Women." In McGuire, *Companion to Jean Gerson*, 293–315.

Asad, Talal. *Formations of the Secular: Christianity, Islam, Modernity*. Stanford, Calif.: Stanford University Press, 2003.

———. *Genealogies of Religion: Discipline and Reasons of Power in Christianity and Islam*. Baltimore: Johns Hopkins University Press, 1993.

Austin, Greta. *Shaping Church Law around the Year 1000: The "Decretum" of Burchard of Worms*. Farnham, U.K.: Ashgate, 2009.

Bächtold-Stäubli, Hans, ed. *Handwörterbuch des deutschen Aberglaubens*. With Eduard Hoffmann-Krayer. 10 vols. 1929–42. Reprint, Berlin: Walter de Gruyter, 2000.

Bailey, Michael D. "The Age of Magicians: Periodization in the History of European Magic." *MRW* 3 (2008): 1–28.

———. *Battling Demons: Witchcraft, Heresy, and Reform in the Late Middle Ages*. University Park: Pennsylvania State University Press, 2003.

———. "Concern over Superstition in Late Medieval Europe." In Smith and Knight, *Religion of Fools?* 115–33.

———. "The Disenchantment of Magic: Spells, Charms, and Superstition in Early European Witchcraft Literature." *AHR* 111 (2006): 383–404.

———. "The Feminization of Magic and the Emerging Idea of the Female Witch in the Late Middle Ages." *Essays in Medieval Studies* 19 (2002): 120–34.

——. "From Sorcery to Witchcraft: Clerical Conceptions of Magic in the Later Middle Ages." *Speculum* 76 (2001): 960–90.

——. "A Late-Medieval Crisis of Superstition?" *Speculum* 84 (2009): 633–61.

——. *Magic and Superstition in Europe: A Concise History from Antiquity to the Present.* Lanham, Md.: Rowman and Littlefield, 2007.

——. "The Meanings of Magic." *MRW* 1 (2006): 1–23.

——. "Reformers on Sorcery and Superstition." In Mixson and Roest, *A Companion to Observant Reform* (forthcoming).

Baptist-Hlawatsch, Gabriele. *Das katechetische Werk Ulrichs von Pottenstein: Sprachliche und rezeptionsgeschichtliche Untersuchungen.* Texte und Textgeschichte 4. Tübingen: Max Niemeyer, 1980.

Barber, Malcolm. *The Trial of the Templars.* 2nd ed. Cambridge: Cambridge University Press, 2006.

Barnett, S. J. *The Enlightenment and Religion: The Myths of Modernity.* Manchester: Manchester University Press, 2003.

Barry, Jonathan, and Owen Davies, eds. *Witchcraft Historiography.* Basingstoke, U.K.: Palgrave Macmillan, 2007.

Baumann, Karin. *Aberglaube für Laien: Zur Programmatik und Überlieferung spätmittelalterlicher Superstitionenkritik.* 2 vols. Quellen und Forschungen zur europäischen Ethnologie 6.1–6.2. Würzburg: Königshausen & Neumann, 1989.

Behringer, Wolfgang. "How Waldensians Became Witches: Heretics and Their Journey to the Other World." In *Communicating with the Spirits*, edited by Gábor Klaniczay and Éva Pócs, in collaboration with Eszter Csonka-Takács, 155–92. Demons, Spirits, Witches 1. Budapest: Central European University Press, 2005.

——. *Witches and Witch-Hunts: A Global History.* Cambridge: Polity Press, 2004.

Behringer, Wolfgang, and Günter Jerouschek. "'Das unheilvollste Buch der Weltliteratur'? Zur Entstehung- und Wirkungsgeschichte des Malleus Maleficarum und zu den Anfängen der Hexenverfolgung." In *Der Hexenhammer*, edited and translated by Behringer, Jerouschek, and Werner Tschacher, 9–98. Munich: Taschenbuch Verlag, 2000.

Bennett, Beth S. "The Significance of the *Rhetorimachia* of Anselm de Besate in the History of Rhetoric." *Rhetorica* 5.3 (1987): 231–50.

Berman, Morris. *The Reenchantment of the World.* Ithaca, N.Y.: Cornell University Press, 1981.

Blumenfeld-Kosinski, Renate. *Poets, Saints, and Visionaries of the Great Schism, 1378–1417.* University Park: Pennsylvania State University Press, 2006.

Bonney, Françoise. "Autour de Jean Gerson: Opinions de théologiens sur les superstitions et la sorcellerie au début du XVe siècle." *Moyen Âge* 77 (1971): 85–98.

Boudet, Jean-Patrice. "A 'College of Astrology and Medicine'? Charles V, Gervais Chrétien, and the Scientific Manuscripts of Maître Gervais's College." *Studies in History and Philosophy of Biological and Biomedical Sciences* 41 (2010): 99–108.

——. "Les condamnations de la magie à Paris en 1398." *Revue Mabillon* 12 (2001): 121–57.

———. *Entre science et* nigromance: *Astrologie, divination et magie dans l'Occident médiévale (XIIe–XVe siècle)*. Histoire ancienne et médiéval 83. Paris: Publications de la Sorbonne, 2006.

———. "La papauté d'Avignon et l'astrologie." In *Fin du monde et signes des temps: Visionnaires et prophètes en France méridionale (fin XIIIe–début XVe siècle)*, 257–93. Cahiers de Fanjeaux: Collection d'histoire religieuse du Languedoc aux XIIIe et XIVe siècles 27. Toulouse: Éditions Privat, 1992.

Bourdin, Philippe. "Révolution et superstition: L'exemple du Puy-de-Dôme." In Dompnier, *Superstition à l'âge des Lumières*, 213–37.

Boureau, Alain. *Satan the Heretic: The Birth of Demonology in the Medieval West*. Translated by Teresa Lavender Fagan. Chicago: University of Chicago Press, 2006.

Bracha, Krzysztof. "Between Learned and Popular Culture: The Example of Preaching in Poland during the Late Middle Ages: *Sermones dominicales et festivales* from the Collection Ascribed to Piotr of Miłosław." *Quaestiones Medii Aevi Novae* 8 (2003): 105–31.

———. "Der Einfluß der neuen Frömmigkeit auf die spätmittelalterliche Kritik am Aberglauben im Reformschrifttum Mitteleuropas." In *Die "Neue Frömmigkeit" in Europa im Spätmittelalter*, edited by Marek Derwich and Martial Staub, 225–48. Veröffentlichungen des Max-Planck-Instituts für Geschichte 205. Göttingen: Vandenhoeck & Ruprecht, 2004.

———. "Kritik an den Glaubens- und Verhaltensformen und an der Aberglaubenspraxis im kirchlichen reformatorischen Schrifttum des Spätmittelalters." In *Christianity in East Central Europe: Late Middle Ages*, edited by Paweł Kras and Wojciech Polak, 271–82. Lublin, Poland: Instytut Europy Środkowo Wschodniej, 1999.

———. "Die Kritik des Aberglaubens, der Irrtümer und Mißbräuche im Kult bei Jacobus Cartusiensis." In *Bücher, Bibliotheken und Schriftkultur der Kartäuser: Festgabe zum 65. Geburtstag von Edward Potkowski*, edited by Sönke Lorenz, 151–63. Stuttgart: Steiner, 2002.

———. "Magie und Aberglaubenskritik in der Predigten des Spätmittelalters in Polen." In Wünsch, *Religion und Magie in Ostmitteleuropa*, 197–215.

———. *Teolog, diabeł i zabobony: Świadectwo traktatu Mikołaja Magni z Jawora 'De superstitionibus' (1405 r.)*. Warsaw: Neriton, 1999.

Broedel, Hans Peter. *The Malleus Maleficarum and the Construction of Witchcraft: Theology and Popular Belief*. Manchester: Manchester University Press, 2003.

Browe, Peter. "Die Eucharistie als Zaubermittel im Mittelalter." *Archiv für Kulturgeschichte* 20 (1930): 134–54.

Brown, D. Catherine. *Pastor and Laity in the Theology of Jean Gerson*. Cambridge: Cambridge University Press, 1987.

Burnett, Charles. "Talismans: Magic as Science? Necromancy among the Seven Liberal Arts." In Burnett, *Magic and Divination in the Middle Ages: Texts and Techniques in the Islamic and Christian Worlds*, 1–15. Aldershot, U.K.: Ashgate, 1996.

Butler, Alison. *Victorian Occultism and the Making of Modern Magic: Invoking Tradition*. Basingstoke, U.K.: Palgrave Macmillan, 2011.

Bynum, Caroline Walker. *Christian Materiality: An Essay on Religion in Late Medieval Europe*. New York: Zone Books, 2011.

——. *Wonderful Blood: Theology and Practice in Northern Germany and Beyond.* Philadelphia: University of Pennsylvania Press, 2007.

Caciola, Nancy. *Discerning Spirits: Divine and Demonic Possession in the Middle Ages.* Ithaca, N.Y.: Cornell University Press, 2003.

Caferro, William. *Contesting the Renaissance.* Oxford: Wiley-Blackwell, 2011.

Callan, Maeve B. "'No Such Art in This Land': Heresy and Witchcraft in Ireland, 1310–1360." PhD diss., Northwestern University, 2002.

Cameron, Euan. *Enchanted Europe: Superstition, Reason, and Religion 1250–1750.* Oxford: Oxford University Press, 2010.

Camille, Michael. "Visual Art in Two Manuscripts of the Ars Notoria." In Fanger, *Conjuring Spirits,* 110–39.

Campagne, Fabián Alejandro. *Homo Catholicus, Homo Superstitiosus: El discurso antisupersticioso en la España de los siglos XV a XVIII.* Madrid: Miño y Dávila, 2002.

Carey, Hilary. *Courting Disaster: Astrology at the English Court and University in the Later Middle Ages.* London: Macmillan, 1992.

——. "Judicial Astrology in Theory and Practice in Later Medieval Europe." *Studies in History and Philosophy of Biological and Biomedical Sciences* 41 (2010): 90–98.

Caro Baroja, Julio. *The World of the Witches.* Translated by O. N. V. Glendinning. Chicago: University of Chicago Press, 1964.

Caroti, Stefano. "La critica contro l'astrologia di Nicole Oresme e la sua influenza nel Medioevo e nel Rinascimento." *Atti della Accademia Nazionale dei Lincei: Memorie, Classe di Scienze morali, storiche e filologiche,* ser. 8, vol. 23 (1979): 545–685.

——. "Nicole Oresme's Polemic against Astrology in his 'Quodlibeta.'" In *Astrology, Science and Society: Historical Essays,* edited by Patrick Curry, 75–93. Woodbridge, U.K.: Boydell, 1987.

Chakrabarty, Dipesh. *Habitations of Modernity: Essays in the Wake of Subaltern Studies.* Chicago: University of Chicago Press, 2002.

——. "Historicism and Its Supplements: A Note on a Predicament Shared by Medieval and Postcolonial Studies." In *Medievalisms in the Postcolonial World: The Idea of "the Middle Ages" outside Europe,* edited by Kathleen Davis and Nadia Altschul, 109–19. Baltimore: Johns Hopkins University Press, 2009.

——. *Provincializing Europe: Postcolonial Thought and Historical Difference.* Rev. ed. Princeton, N.J.: Princeton University Press, 2007.

Champion, Matthew. "Crushing the Canon: Nicolas Jacquier's Response to the Canon *Episcopi* in the *Flagellum haereticorum fascinariorum.*" *MRW* 6 (2011): 183–211.

Chène, Catherine. *Juger les vers: Exorcismes et procès d'animaux dans le diocese de Lausanne (XVe–XVIe s.).* CLHM 14. Lausanne: Université de Lausanne, 1995.

Chène, Catherine, and Martine Ostorero. "Démonologie et misogynie: L'émergence d'un discours spécifique sur la femme dans l'élaboration doctrinale du sabbat au XVe siècle." In *Les femmes dans la société européenne/die Frauen in der europäischen Gesellschaft: 8e Congrès des Historiennes suisses/8. Schweizerische Historikerinnentagung,* edited by Anne-Lisa Head-König and Liliane Mottu-Weber, 171–96. Geneva: Droz, 2000.

Clagett, Marshall. *Nicole Oresme and the Medieval Geometry of Qualities and Motions: A Treatise on the Uniformity and Difformity of Intensities Known as* Tractatus de configurationibus qualitatum et motuum. University of Wisconsin Publications in Medieval Science 12. Madison: University of Wisconsin Press, 1968.

Clark, Stuart. *Thinking with Demons: The Idea of Witchcraft in Early Modern Europe.* Oxford: Oxford University Press, 1997.

Cobban, A. B. *The Medieval Universities: Their Development and Organization.* London: Methuen, 1975.

Cohn, Norman. *Europe's Inner Demons: The Demonization of Christians in Medieval Christendom.* 2nd ed. Chicago: University of Chicago Press, 2000.

Cole, Andrew, and D. Vance Smith. "Introduction: Outside Modernity." In *The Legitimacy of the Middle Ages: On the Unwritten History of Theory,* edited by Andrew Cole and D. Vance Smith, 1–36. Durham, N.C.: Duke University Press, 2010.

Collins, David J. "Albertus, Magnus or Magus? Magic, Natural Philosophy, and Religious Reform in the Late Middle Ages." *Renaissance Quarterly* 63 (2010): 1–44.

Conti, Fabrizio. "Preachers and Confessors against 'Superstitions': Bernardino Busti and Sermon 16 of his *Rosarium Sermonum.*" *MRW* 6 (2011): 62–91.

Coopland, G. W. *Nicole Oresme and the Astrologers: A Study of his Livre de Divinacions.* Cambridge, Mass.: Harvard University Press, 1952.

Daston, Lorraine, and Katharine Park. *Wonders and the Order of Nature 1150–1750.* New York: Zone Books, 1998.

Davies, Owen. *Cunning-Folk: Popular Magic in English History.* London: Hambledon, 2003.

———. *Grimoires: A History of Magic Books.* Oxford: Oxford University Press, 2009.

Davis, Kathleen. *Periodization and Sovereignty: How Ideas of Feudalism and Secularization Govern the Politics of Time.* Philadelphia: University of Pennsylvania Press, 2008.

Davis, Kathleen, and Nadia Altschul. "The Idea of 'the Middle Ages' outside Europe." In *Medievalisms in the Postcolonial World: The Idea of "the Middle Ages" outside Europe,* edited by Davis and Altschul, 1–24. Baltimore: Johns Hopkins University Press, 2009.

Decker, Rainer. *Witchcraft and the Papacy: An Account Drawing from the Formerly Secret Records of the Roman Inquisition.* Translated by H. C. Erik Midelfort. Charlottesville: University of Virginia Press, 2008.

De Grazia, Margreta. "The Modern Divide: From Either Side." *Journal of Medieval and Early Modern Studies* 37 (2007): 453–67.

Delaurenti, Béatrice. *La puissance des mots—"Virtus verborum": Débats doctrinaux sur le pouvoir des incantations au Moyen Âge.* Paris: Cerf, 2007.

Delumeau, Jean. "Les réformateurs et la superstition." In *Actes du colloque l'Amiral de Coligny et son temps,* 451–87. Paris: Société de l'Histoire du Protestantisme Français, 1974.

De Mayo, Thomas B. *The Demonology of William of Auvergne: By Fire and Sword.* Lewiston, N.Y.: Edwin Mellen Press, 2007.

Dinzelbacher, Peter. *Angst im Mittelalter: Teufels-, Todes- und Gotteserfahrung: Mentalitätsgeschichte und Ikonographie.* Paderborn: Schöningh, 1996.

Doering-Manteuffel, Sabine. "The Dissemination of Magical Knowledge in Enlightenment Germany: The Supernatural and the Development of Print Culture." In *Beyond the Witch Trials: Witchcraft and Magic in Enlightenment Europe*, edited by Owen Davies and Willem de Blécourt, 187–206. Manchester: Manchester University Press, 2004.

Dompnier, Bernard. "Les Hommes d'Église et la superstition entre XVIIe et XVIIIe siècles." In Dompnier, *Superstition à l'âge des Lumières*, 13–47.

———, ed. *La superstition à l'âge des Lumières*. Champion-Varia 25. Paris: Honoré Champion, 1998.

Duffy, Eamon. *Marking the Hours: English People and Their Prayers 1240–1570*. New Haven, Conn.: Yale University Press, 2004.

———. *The Stripping of the Altars: Traditional Religion in England, 1400–1580*. New Haven, Conn.: Yale University Press, 1992.

During, Simon. *Modern Enchantments: The Cultural Power of Secular Magic*. Cambridge, Mass.: Harvard University Press, 2002.

Eamon, William. *Science and the Secrets of Nature: Books of Secrets in Medieval and Early Modern Culture*. Princeton, N.J.: Princeton University Press, 1994.

Easlea, Brian. *Witch Hunting, Magic and the New Philosophy: An Introduction to the Debates of the Scientific Revolution 1450–1750*. Brighton, U.K.: Harvester, 1980.

Elliott, Dyan. *The Bride of Christ Goes to Hell: Metaphor and Embodiment in the Lives of Pious Women, 200–1500*. Philadelphia: University of Pennsylvania Press, 2012.

———. *Proving Woman: Female Spirituality and Inquisitional Culture in the Later Middle Ages*. Princeton, N.J.: Princeton University Press, 2004.

Elm, Kaspar, ed. *Reformbemühungen und Observanzbestrebungen im spätmittelalterlichen Ordenswesen*. Berliner Historische Studien 14, Ordensstudien 6. Berlin: Dunker & Humblot, 1989.

Fanger, Claire, ed. *Conjuring Spirits: Texts and Traditions of Ritual Magic*. University Park: Pennsylvania State University Press, 1998.

———, ed. *Invoking Angels: Theurgic Ideas and Practices, Thirteenth to Sixteenth Centuries*. University Park: Pennsylvania State University Press, 2012.

———. "Plundering the Egyptian Treasure: John the Monk's *Book of Visions* and Its Relation to the Ars Notoria of Solomon." In Fanger, *Conjuring Spirits*, 216–49.

Fasolt, Constantin. "Hegel's Ghost: Europe, the Reformation, and the Middle Ages." *Viator* 39 (2008): 345–86.

———. *The Limits of History*. Chicago: University of Chicago Press, 2004.

Filotas, Bernadette. *Pagan Survivals, Superstitions and Popular Cultures in Early Medieval Pastoral Literature*. Studies and Texts 151. Toronto: Pontifical Institute of Medieval Studies, 2005.

Finke, Heinrich. *Aus den Tagen Bonifaz VIII: Funde und Forschungen*. Vorreformationsgeschichtliche Forschungen 2. Münster: Aschendorffschen Buchhandlung, 1902.

Fix, Andrew. *Fallen Angels: Balthasar Bekker, Spirit Belief, and Confessionalism in the Seventeenth-Century Dutch Republic*. International Archives of the History of Ideas 165. Dordrecht, Neth.: Kluwer, 1999.

Flint, Valerie I. J. "The Demonisation of Magic and Sorcery in Late Antiquity: Christian Redefinitions of Pagan Religions." In *Witchcraft and Magic in Europe: Ancient Greece and Rome*, edited by Bengt Ankarloo and Stuart Clark, 277–348. Philadelphia: University of Pennsylvania Press, 1999.

———. *The Rise of Magic in Early Medieval Europe*. Princeton, N.J.: Princeton University Press, 1991.

Franz, Adolph. *Der Magister Nikolaus Magni de Jawor: Ein Beitrag zur Literatur- und Gelehrtengeschichte des 14. und 15. Jahrhunderts*. Freiburg im/Br: Herder, 1898.

Fraser, Kyle A. "The Contested Boundaries of 'Magic' and 'Religion' in Late Pagan Monotheism." *MRW* 4 (2009): 131–51.

Freedman, Paul. "The Medieval Other: The Middle Ages as Other." In *Marvels, Monsters, and Miracles: Studies in the Medieval and Early Modern Imaginations*, edited by Timothy S. Jones and David A. Sprunger, 1–24. Studies in Medieval Culture 42. Kalamazoo, Mich.: Medieval Institute Publications, 2002.

Freedman, Paul, and Gabrielle M. Spiegel. "Medievalisms Old and New: The Rediscovery of Alterity in North American Medieval Studies." *AHR* 103 (1998): 677–704.

Friedlander, Alan. *The Hammer of the Inquisitors: Brother Bernard Délicieux and the Struggle against the Inquisition in Fourteenth-Century France*. Cultures, Beliefs, and Traditions 9. Leiden: Brill, 2000.

Friedman, Susan Stanford. "Definitional Excursions: The Meanings of *Modern/Modernity/Modernism*." *Modernism/Modernity* 8 (2001): 493–513.

———. "Planetarity: Musing Modernist Studies." *Modernism/Modernity* 17 (2010): 471–99.

Fürbeth, Frank. *Heilquellen in der deutschen Wissensliteratur des Spätmittelalters: Zur Genese und Funktion eines Paradigmas der Wissensvermittlung am Beispiel des "Tractatus de balneis naturalibus" von Felix Hemmerli und seiner Rezeption, mit einer Edition des Textes und seiner frühneuhochdeutschen Übersetzung*. Wissensliteratur im Mittelalter 42. Wiesbaden: Ludwig Reichert, 2004.

———. *Johannes Hartlieb: Untersuchung zu Leben und Werk*. Hermaea: Germanistische Forschungen n.s. 64. Tübingen: Max Niemeyer, 1992.

Gautier-Dalché, J. "Oresme et son temps." In *Nicolas Oresme: Tradition et innovation chez un intellectuel du XIVe siècle*, edited by P. Souffrin and A. P. Segonds, 7–11. Paris: Société d'Édition "Les Belles Lettres," 1988.

Gentilcore, David. *From Bishop to Witch: The System of the Sacred in Early Modern Terra d'Otranto*. Manchester: Manchester University Press, 1992.

Germain, Gilbert G. *A Discourse on Disenchantment: Reflections on Politics and Technology*. Albany, N.Y.: State University of New York Press, 1993.

Ginzburg, Carlo. "The Inquisitor as Anthropologist." In Ginzburg, *Clues, Myths, and the Historical Method*, translated by John Tedeschi and Anne Tedeschi, 156–64. Baltimore: Johns Hopkins University Press, 1989.

Gmelch, George, and Richard Felson. "Can a Lucky Charm Get You through Organic Chemistry?" *Psychology Today*, December 1980, 75–78.

Graf, Fritz. "Augustine and Magic." In *The Metamorphosis of Magic from Late Antiquity to the Early Modern Period*, edited by Jan N. Bremmer and Jan R. Veenstra, 87–103. Groningen Studies in Cultural Change 1. Leuven: Peeters, 2002.

Grant, Edward. *Nicole Oresme and the Kinematics of Circular Motion: Tractatus de commensurabilitate vel incommensurabilitate motuum celi.* University of Wisconsin Publications in Medieval Science 15. Madison: University of Wisconsin Press, 1971.

Grimm, Jacob. *Teutonic Mythology.* Translated by James Stevens Stalleybrass. 4 vols. London: George Bell, 1882–88.

Guenée, Bernard. *Between Church and State: The Lives of Four French Prelates in the Late Middle Ages.* Translated by Arthur Goldhammer. Chicago: University of Chicago Press, 1991.

Hackett, Jeremiah. "Roger Bacon on Astronomy-Astrology: The Sources of the *Scientia Experimentalis.*" In *Roger Bacon and the Sciences: Commemorative Essays,* edited by Jeremiah Hackett, 174–98. Studien und Texte zur Geistesgeschichte des Mittelalters 57. Leiden: Brill, 1997.

Hansen, Bert. *Nicole Oresme and the Marvels of Nature: A Study of his "De causis mirabilium" with Critical Edition, Translation, and Commentary.* Studies and Texts 68. Toronto: Pontifical Institute of Medieval Studies, 1985.

Harman, Graham. *Prince of Networks: Bruno Latour and Metaphysics.* Melbourne: re.press, 2009.

Harmening, Dieter. "'Magische Volkskultur': Ethnographischer Befund oder literarisches Konstrukt? Quellenkritische Probleme zwischen historischer Anthropologie und Volkskunde." *Mediaevalia Historica Bohemica* 7 (2000): 55–90.

———. "Spätmittelalterliche Aberglaubenskritik in Dekalog- und Beichtliteratur." In *Volksreligion im hohen und späten Mittelalter,* edited by Peter Dinzelbacher and Dieter R. Bauer, 243–51. Quellen und Forschungen aus dem Gebiet der Geschichte n.s. 13. Paderborn: Schöningh, 1990.

———. *Superstitio: Überlieferungs- und theoriegeschichtliche Untersuchungen zur kirchlich-theologischen Aberglaubensliteratur des Mittelalters.* Berlin: Erich Schmidt Verlag, 1979.

Harvey, David Allen. *Beyond Enlightenment: Occultism and Politics in Modern France.* DeKalb: Northern Illinois University Press, 2005.

Heimann, Claudia. *Nicolaus Eymerich (vor 1320–1399)—praedicator veridicus, inquisitor intrepidus, doctor egregius: Leben und Werk eines Inquisitors.* Spanische Forschungen der Görresgesellschaft n.s. 37. Münster: Aschendorff, 2001.

———. "*Quis proprie hereticus est*? Nicolaus Eymerichs Häresiebegriff und dessen Anwendung auf die Juden." In *Praedicatores Inquisitores I: The Dominicans and the Medieval Inquisition, Acts of the 1st International Seminar on the Dominicans and the Inquisition, 23–25 February 2002,* edited by Wolfram Hoyer, 595–624. Dissertationes Historiciae 29. Rome: Istituto storico Domenicano, 2004.

Hen, Yitzhak. *Culture and Religion in Merovingian Gaul A.D. 481–751.* Cultures, Beliefs, and Traditions 1. Leiden: Brill, 1995.

Hendrix, Scott E. *How Albert the Great's "Speculum Astronomiae" Was Interpreted and Used by Four Centuries of Readers: A Study in Late Medieval Medicine, Astronomy, and Astrology.* Lewiston, N.Y.: Edwin Mellen Press, 2010.

Hersperger, Patrick. *Kirche, Magie, und "Aberglaube": Superstitio in der Kanonistik des 12. und 13. Jahrhunderts.* Cologne: Böhlau, 2010.

Hertel, G. "Abergläubische Gebräuche aus dem Mittelalter." *Zeitschrift des Vereins für Volkskunde* 11 (1901): 272–79.

Herzig, Tamar. "Flies, Heretics, and the Gendering of Witchcraft." *MRW* 5 (2010): 51–80.

———. "Witches, Saints, and Heretics: Heinrich Kramer's Ties with Italian Women Mystics." *MRW* 1 (2006): 24–55.

Hlaváček, Ivan, and Alexander Patschovsky, eds. *Reform von Kirche und Reich zur Zeit der Konzilien von Konstanz (1414–1418) und Basel (1431–1449)*. Constance: Universitätsverlag Konstanz, 1996.

Hobbins, Daniel. *Authorship and Publicity before Print: Jean Gerson and the Transformation of Late Medieval Learning*. Philadelphia: University of Pennsylvania Press, 2009.

———. "Gerson on Lay Devotion." In McGuire, *Companion to Jean Gerson*, 41–78.

———. "Jean Gerson's Authentic Tract on Joan of Arc: *Supra facto puellae et credulitate sibi praestanda* (14 May 1429)." *Mediaeval Studies* 67 (2005): 99–155.

———. "The Schoolman as Public Intellectual: Jean Gerson and the Late Medieval Tract." *AHR* 108 (2003): 1308–37.

Hoggard, Brian. "The Archeology of Counter-Witchcraft and Popular Magic." In *Beyond the Witch Trials: Witchcraft and Magic in Enlightenment Europe*, edited by Owen Davies and Willem de Blécourt, 167–86. Manchester: Manchester University Press, 2004.

Horkheimer, Max, and Theodor W. Adorno. *Dialectic of Enlightenment: Philosophical Fragments*. Edited by Gunzelin Schmid Noerr. Translated by Edmund Jephcott. Stanford, Calif.: Stanford University Press, 2002.

Huizinga, Johan. *The Autumn of the Middle Ages*. Translated by Rodney J. Payton and Ulrich Mammitzsch. Chicago: University of Chicago Press, 1996.

———. *The Waning of the Middle Ages: A Study of the Forms of Life, Thought, and Art in France and the Netherlands in the Dawn of the Renaissance*. Translated by Fritz Hopman. London: Edward Arnold, 1924.

Hunt, Lynn. *Measuring Time, Making History*. Budapest: Central European University Press, 2008.

Hutton, Ronald. *The Triumph of the Moon: A History of Modern Pagan Witchcraft*. Oxford: Oxford University Press, 1999.

Iribarren, Isabel. "From Black Magic to Heresy: A Doctrinal Leap in the Pontificate of John XXII." *Church History* 76 (2007): 32–60.

Israel, Jonathan. *Radical Enlightenment: Philosophy and the Making of Modernity, 1650–1750*. Oxford: Oxford University Press, 2001.

Jahoda, Gustav. *The Psychology of Superstition*. London: Allen Lane, 1969.

Janssen, L. F. "'Superstitio' and the Persecution of the Christians." *Vigiliae Christianae* 33 (1979): 131–59.

Jeay, Madeleine. *Savoir faire: Une analyse des croyances des "Évangiles des quenouilles" (XVe siècle)*. Montreal: Editions Ceres, 1982.

Jones, William R. "Political Uses of Sorcery in Medieval Europe." *Historian* 34 (1972): 670–87.

Kaeppeli, Thomas. *Scriptores Ordinis Praedicatorum Medii Aevi*. 4 vols. Rome: Istituto Storico Domenicano, 1970–93.

Kamerick, Kathleen. "Shaping Superstition in Late Medieval England." *MRW* 3 (2008): 29–53.

Kaminsky, Howard. "From Lateness to Waning to Crisis: The Burden of the Later Middle Ages." *Journal of Early Modern History* 4 (2000): 85–125.

Kaye, Joel. "Law, Magic, and Science: Constructing a Border between Licit and Illicit Knowledge in the Writings of Nicole Oresme." In *Law and the Illicit in Medieval Europe,* edited by Ruth Mazo Karras, Joel Kaye, and E. Ann Matter, 225–37. Philadelphia: University of Pennsylvania Press, 2008.

Kieckhefer, Richard. "Did Magic Have a Renaissance? An Historiographic Question Revisited." In *Magic and the Classical Tradition,* edited by Charles Burnett and W. F. Ryan, 199–212. Warburg Institute Colloquia 7. London: Warburg Institute and Nino Aragno, 2006.

——. *European Witch Trials: Their Foundations in Popular and Learned Culture, 1300–1500.* Berkeley: University of California Press, 1976.

——. *Forbidden Rites: A Necromancer's Manual of the Fifteenth Century.* University Park: Pennsylvania State University Press, 1998.

——. "Magic at Innsbruck: The Case of 1485 Reexamined." In Wünsch, *Religion und Magie in Ostmitteleuropa,* 11–29.

——. *Magic in the Middle Ages.* Cambridge: Cambridge University Press, 1989.

——. "Mythologies of Witchcraft in the Fifteenth Century." *MRW* 1 (2006): 79–108.

——. "The Specific Rationality of Medieval Magic." *AHR* 99 (1994): 813–36.

——. "Witchcraft, Necromancy and Sorcery as Heresy." In *Chasse aux sorcières et démonologie: Entre discours et pratiques (XIVe–XVIIe siècles),* edited by Martine Ostorero, Georg Modestin, and Kathrin Utz Tremp, 133–53. ML 36. Florence: SISMEL, 2010.

Klaassen, Frank. "English Manuscripts of Magic, 1300–1500: A Preliminary Survey." In Fanger, *Conjuring Spirits,* 3–31.

——. "Medieval Ritual Magic in the Renaissance." *Aries* 3 (2003): 166–99.

Klaniczay, Gábor. "The Process of Trance: Heavenly and Diabolic Apparitions in Johannes Nider's *Formicarius.*" In *Procession, Performance, Liturgy, and Ritual: Essays in Honor of Bryan R. Gillingham,* edited by Nancy Van Deusen, 203–58. Ottawa: Institute of Medieval Music, 2007.

Klingshirn, William E. *Caesarius of Arles: The Making of a Christian Community in Late Antique Gaul.* Cambridge: Cambridge University Press, 1994.

Konda, Guillaume, *Le discernement et la malice des pratiques superstitieuses d'après les sermons de S. Césaire d'Arles.* Rome: Officium Libri Catholici, 1970.

Koopmans, Jelle. "Archéologies des *Évangiles des quenouilles.*" In *Autour des quenouilles: La parole des femmes (1450–1600),* edited by Jean-François Courouau, Philippe Gardy, and Jelle Koopmans, 13–29. Texte, Codex & Contexte 10. Turnhout: Brepols, 2010.

Kreuzer, Georg. *Heinrich von Langenstein: Studien zur Biographie und zu den Schismatraktaten unter besonderer Berücksichtigung der Epistola pacis und der Epistola concilii pacis.* Quellen und Forschungen aus dem Gebiet der Geschichte n.s. 6. Paderborn: Schöningh, 1987.

Krul, Wessel. "In the Mirror of van Eyck: Johan Huizinga's *Autumn of the Middle Ages.*" *Journal of Medieval and Early Modern Studies* 27 (1997): 353–84.

Landy, Joshua, and Michael Saler. "Introduction: The Varieties of Modern Enchantment." In *The Re-Enchantment of the World: Secular Magic in a Rational Age*, edited by Joshua Landy and Michael Saler, 1–14. Stanford, Calif.: Stanford University Press, 2009.

Láng, Benedek. *Unlocked Books: Manuscripts of Learned Magic in the Medieval Libraries of Central Europe*. University Park: Pennsylvania State University Press, 2008.

Lasson, Emilie. *Superstitions médiévales: Une analyse d'après l'exégèse du premier commandement d'Ulrich de Pottenstein*. Nouvelle Bibliothèque du Moyen Âge 102. Paris: Honoré Champion, 2010.

Latour, Bruno. *Pandora's Hope: Essays on the Reality of Science Studies*. Cambridge, Mass.: Harvard University Press, 1999.

———. *We Have Never Been Modern*. Translated by Catherine Porter. Cambridge, Mass.: Harvard University Press, 1993.

Lea, Henry Charles. *A History of the Inquisition of the Middle Ages*. 3 vols. New York: Macmillan, 1888.

———. *Materials toward a History of Witchcraft*. Edited by Arthur C. Howland. 3 vols. Philadelphia: University of Pennsylvania Press, 1939.

Lejbowicz, Max. "Chronologie des écrits anti-astrologiques de Nicole Oresme: Étude sur un cas de scepticisme dans la deuxième moitié du XIVe siècle." In *Autour de Nicole Oresme: Actes du Colloque Oresme organisé à l'Université de Paris XII*, edited by Jeannine Quillet, 119–76. Paris: J. Vrin, 1990.

Lerner, Robert E. "The Pope and the Doctor." *Yale Review* 78, no. 1 (1988/89): 62–79.

———. "Werner di Friedberg intrappolato dalla legge." In *La parola all'accusato*, edited by Jean-Claude Maire Vigeur and Agostino Paravicini Bagliani, 268–81. Palermo: Sellerio, 1991.

Levack, Brian P. *The Witch-Hunt in Early Modern Europe*. 3rd ed. London: Pearson Longman, 2006.

Lewis, Jerry M., and Timothy J. Gallagher. "The Salience of Friday the 13th for College Students." *College Student Journal* 32 (2001): 216–22.

Lhotsky, Alphons. *Thomas Ebendorfer: Ein österreichischer Geschichtschreiber, Theologe und Diplomat des 15. Jahrhunderts*. MGH Schriften 15. Stuttgart: Hiersemann, 1957.

Linsenmann, Thomas. *Die Magie bei Thomas von Aquin*. Veröffentlichungen des Grabmann-Institutes zur Erforschung der mittelalterlichen Theologie und Philosophie 44. Berlin: Akademie Verlag, 2000.

Madre, Alois. *Nikolaus von Dinkelsbühl Leben und Schriften: Ein Beitrag zur theologischen Literaturgeschichte*. Beiträge zur Geschichte der Philosophie und Theologie des Mittelalters 40.4. Münster: Aschendorffsche Verlagsbuchhandlung, 1965.

Maier, Anneliese. "Eine Verfügung Johannes XXII. über die Züstandigkeit der Inquisition für Zaubereiprozesse." *Archivum Fratrum Praedicatorum* 22 (1952): 226–46.

Mangan, Michael. *Performing Dark Arts: A Cultural History of Conjuring*. Chicago: Intellect Books, 2007.

Manitius, Karl. "Magie und Rhetorik bei Anselm von Besate." *Deutsches Archiv für Erforschung des Mittelalters* 12 (1956): 52–72.

Martin, Dale B. *Inventing Superstition: From the Hippocratics to the Christians.* Cambridge, Mass.: Harvard University Press, 2004.

Masuzawa, Tomoko. *The Invention of World Religions: Or, How European Universalism Was Preserved in the Language of Pluralism.* Chicago: University of Chicago Press, 2005.

Mazour-Matusevich, Yelena. "Gerson's Legacy." In McGuire, *Companion to Jean Gerson*, 357–99.

McGuire, Brian Patrick, ed. *A Companion to Jean Gerson.* Brill's Companions to the Christian Tradition 3. Leiden: Brill, 2006.

——. "In Search of Jean Gerson: Chronology of His Life and Works." In McGuire, *Companion to Jean Gerson*, 1–39.

——. *Jean Gerson and the Last Medieval Reformation.* University Park: Pennsylvania State University Press, 2005.

Meier, Ludger. *Die Werke des Erfurter Kartäusers Jakob von Jüterbog in ihrer handschriftlichen Überlieferung.* Beiträge zur Geschichte der Philosophie und Theologie des Mittelalters 37.5. Münster: Aschendorffsche Verlagsbuchhandlung, 1955.

Mercier, Franck. *La Vauderie d'Arras: Une chasse aux sorcières à l'Automne du Moyen Âge.* Rennes: Presses Universitaires de Rennes, 2006.

Mertens, Dieter. *Iacobus Carthusiensis: Untersuchungen zur Rezeption der Werke des Kartäusers Jakob von Paradies (1381–1465).* Veröffentlichungen des Max-Planck-Instituts für Geschichte 50, Studien zur Germania Sacra 13. Göttingen: Vandenhoeck & Ruprecht, 1976.

Meuthen, Erich. "Gab es ein spätes Mittelalter?" In *Spätzeit: Studien zu den Problemen eines historischen Epochenbegriffs*, ed. Johannes Kunisch, 91–135. Historische Forschungen 42. Berlin: Duncker & Humblot, 1990.

Meyer, Birgit, and Peter Pels, eds. *Magic and Modernity: Interfaces of Revelation and Concealment.* Stanford, Calif: Stanford University Press, 2003.

Midelfort, H. C. Erik. *Exorcism and Enlightenment: Johann Joseph Gassner and the Demons of Eighteenth-Century Germany.* New Haven, Conn.: Yale University Press, 2005.

Mixson, James, and Bert Roest, eds. *A Companion to Observant Reform in the Later Middle Ages and Beyond.* Leiden: Brill, forthcoming.

Moeller, Bernd. "Frömmigkeit in Deutschland um 1500." *Archiv für Reformationsgeschichte* 56 (1965): 3–31.

Monroe, John Warne. *Laboratories of Faith: Mesmerism, Spiritism, and Occultism in Modern France.* Ithaca, N.Y.: Cornell University Press, 2008.

Montesano, Marina. *"Supra acqua et supra ad vento": "Superstizioni," maleficia e incantamenta nei predicatori Francescani osservanti (Italia, sec. XV).* Nuovi Studi Storici 46. Rome: Istituto Storico Italiano per il Medio Evo, 1999.

Mormando, Franco. *The Preacher's Demons: Bernardino of Siena and the Social Underworld of Early Renaissance Italy.* Chicago: University of Chicago Press, 1999.

Morton, Peter A. "Lutheran Naturalism, Popular Magic, and the Devil." In *The Devil in Society in Premodern Europe*, edited by Richard Raiswell and Peter Dendle, 409–35. Essays and Studies 28. Toronto: Center for Renaissance and Reformation Studies, 2012.

Mourin, Louis. *Jean Gerson: Prédicateur français.* Bruges: De Tempel, 1952.

Muchembled, Robert. *A History of the Devil from the Middle Ages to the Present.* Translated by Jean Birrell. Cambridge: Cambridge University Press, 2003.

Muir, Edward. *Ritual in Early Modern Europe.* Cambridge: Cambridge University Press, 1997.

Nederman, Cary J. *John of Salisbury.* Medieval and Renaissance Texts and Studies 288. Tempe: Arizona Center for Medieval and Renaissance Studies, 2005.

Newman, Barbara. *From Virile Woman to WomanChrist: Studies in Medieval Religion and Literature.* Philadelphia: University of Pennsylvania Press, 1995.

Nold, Patrick. "Thomas of Braunceston O.M./O.P." In *Kirchenbild und Spiritualität: Dominikanische Beiträge zur Ekklesiologie und zum kirchlichen Leben in Mittelalter; Festschrift für Ulrich Horst O.P.,* edited by Thomas Prügl and Marianne Schlosser, 179–95. Paderborn: Schöningh, 2007.

Oakley, Francis. *The Political Thought of Pierre d'Ailly: The Voluntarist Tradition.* New Haven, Conn.: Yale University Press, 1964.

Ostorero, Martine. *Le diable au sabbat: Littérature démonologique et sorcellerie (1440–1460).* ML 38. Florence: SISMEL, 2011.

Owen, Alex. *The Place of Enchantment: British Occultism and the Culture of the Modern.* Chicago: University of Chicago Press, 2004.

Owst, G. R. *The Destructorium viciorum of Alexander Carpenter: A Fifteenth-Century Sequel to "Literature and the Pulpit in Medieval England."* London: S. P.C.K., 1952.

Paravicini Bagliani, Agostino. *Boniface VIII: Un pape hérétique?* Paris: Payot, 2003.

Paravy, Pierrette. *De la chrétienté romaine à la Réforme en Dauphiné: Évêques, fidèles et déviants (vers 1340–vers 1530).* 2 vols. Rome: École française de Rome, 1993.

Parish, Helen, and William G. Naphy. "Introduction." In *Religion and Superstition in Reformation Europe,* edited by Parish and Naphy, 1–22. Manchester: Manchester University Press, 2002.

Park, Robert L. *Superstition: Belief in the Age of Science.* Princeton, N.J.: Princeton University Press, 2008.

Pascoe, Louis B. *Jean Gerson: Principles of Church Reform.* Studies in Medieval and Reformation Thought 7. Leiden: Brill, 1973.

Pearson, Jo. "Writing Witchcraft: The Historians' History, the Practitioners' Past." In Barry and Davies, *Witchcraft Historiography,* 225–41.

Pels, Peter. "Introduction: Magic and Modernity." In Meyer and Pels, *Magic and Modernity,* 1–38.

Perol, Lucette. "La notation de superstition de Furetière au *Dictionnaire de trévoux* et à l'*Encyclopédie.*" In Dompnier, *Superstition à l'âge des Lumières,* 67–92.

Peters, Edward. *The Magician, the Witch, and the Law.* Philadelphia: University of Pennsylvania Press, 1978.

———. "The Medieval Church and State on Superstition, Magic and Witchcraft: From Augustine to the Sixteenth Century." In *Witchcraft and Magic in Europe: The Middle Ages,* edited by Bengt Ankarloo and Stuart Clark, 173–245. Philadelphia: University of Pennsylvania Press, 2002.

Pott, Martin. *Aufklärung und Aberglaube: Die deutsche Frühaufklärung im Spiegel ihrer Aberglaubenskritik.* Studien zur deutschen Literatur 119. Tübingen: Max Niemeyer, 1992.

Prakash, Gyan. *Another Reason: Science and the Imagination of Modern India*. Princeton, N.J.: Princeton University Press, 1999.

——. "Between Science and Superstition: Religion and the Modern Subject of the Nation in Colonial India." In Meyer and Pels, *Magic and Modernity*, 39–59.

Provost, Alain. "On the Margins of the Templars' Trial: The Case of Bishop Guichard of Troyes." In *The Debate on the Trial of the Templars (1307–1314)*, edited by Jochen Burgtorf, Paul F. Crawford, and Helen J. Nicholson, 117–27. Farnham, U.K.: Ashgate, 2010.

Pruckner, Hubert. *Studien zu den astrologischen Schriften des Heinrich von Langenstein*. Studien der Bibliothek Warburg 14. Leipzig: Teubner, 1933.

Quillet, Jeannine. "Enchantements et désenchantement de la nature selon Nicole Oresme." In *Mensch und Natur im Mittelalter*, edited by Albert Zimmermann and Andreas Speer, 321–29. Miscellanea Mediaevalia: Veröffentlichungen des Thomas-Instituts der Universität zu Köln 21. Berlin: Walter de Gruyter, 1991.

Rampton, Martha. "Burchard of Worms and Female Magical Ritual." In *Medieval and Early Modern Ritual: Formalized Behavior in Europe, China and Japan*, edited by Joëlle Rollo-Koster, 7–34. Cultures, Beliefs, and Traditions 13. Leiden: Brill, 2002.

Reber, Balthasar, ed. *Felix Hemmerlin von Zürich, neu nach den Quellen bearbeitet*. Zurich: Mener & Zeller, 1846.

Rivard, Derek A. *Blessing the World: Ritual and Lay Piety in Medieval Religion*. Washington, D.C.: Catholic University of America Press, 2009.

Roper, Jonathan, ed. *Charms and Charming in Europe*. Basingstoke, U.K.: Palgrave Macmillan, 2004.

Rosier-Catach, Irène. "Signes sacramentels et signes magiques: Guillaume d'Auvergne et la théorie du pacte." In *Autour de Guillaume d'Auvergne († 1249)*, edited by Franco Morenzoni and Jean-Yves Tilliette, 93–116. Bibliothèque d'histoire culturelle du Moyen Âge 2. Turnhout: Brepols, 2005.

Ruh, Kurt, ed. *Die deutsche Literatur des Mittelalters: Verfasserlexikon*. 2nd ed. 14 vols. Berlin: Walter de Gruyter, 1978–2008.

Russell, Jeffrey Burton. *Lucifer: The Devil in the Middle Ages*. Ithaca, N.Y.: Cornell University Press, 1984.

——. *Witchcraft in the Middle Ages*. Ithaca, N.Y.: Cornell University Press, 1972.

Ryan, Michael A. *A Kingdom of Stargazers: Astrology and Authority in the Late Medieval Crown of Aragon*. Ithaca, N.Y.: Cornell University Press, 2011.

Saler, Michael. "Modernity and Enchantment: A Historiographic Review." *AHR* 111 (2006): 692–716.

Salzman, Michele R. "'Superstitio' in the Codex Theodosianus and the Persecution of the Pagans." *Vigiliae Christianae* 41 (1987): 172–88.

Schmitt, Jean-Claude. *The Holy Greyhound: Guinefort, Healer of Children since the Thirteenth Century*. Translated by Martin Thom. Cambridge Studies in Oral and Literate Culture 6. Cambridge: Cambridge University Press, 1983.

——. "Les 'superstitions.'" In *Histoire de la France religieuse*, vol. 1, *Des dieux de la Gaule à la papauté d'Avignon*, edited by Jacques Le Goff, 417–551. Paris: Seuil, 1988.

Schnyder, André. *Malleus Maleficarum von Heinrich Institoris (alias Kramer) unter Mithilfe Jakob Sprengers aufgrund der dämonologischen Tradition zusammengestellt: Kommentar zur Wiedergabe des Erstdrucks von 1487 (Hain 9238)*. Litterae 116. Göppingen: Kümmerle, 1993.

Schwartz, Regina Mara. *Sacramental Poetics at the Dawn of Secularism: When God Left the World*. Stanford, Calif.: Stanford University Press, 2008.

Scribner, R. W. "'Incombustible Luther': The Image of the Reformer in Early Modern Germany." *Past and Present* 110 (1986): 38–68.

———. "Magic and the Formation of Protestant Popular Culture in Germany." In R. W. Scribner, *Religion and Culture in Germany (1400–1800)*, edited by Lyndal Roper, 323–45. Studies in Medieval and Reformation Thought 81. Leiden: Brill, 2001.

———. "The Reformation, Popular Magic, and the 'Disenchantment of the World.'" *Journal of Interdisciplinary History* 23 (1992–93): 475–94. Reprinted in Scribner, *Religion and Culture in Germany (1400–1800)*, edited by Lyndal Roper, 346–65. Studies in Medieval and Reformation Thought 81. Leiden: Brill, 2001.

———. "Ritual and Popular Religion in Catholic Germany at the Time of the Reformation." *Journal of Ecclesiastical History* 35 (1984): 47–77. Reprinted in Scribner, *Popular Culture and Popular Movements in Reformation Germany*, 17–47. London: Hambledon, 1987.

———. "Sorcery, Superstition, and Society: The Witch of Urach, 1529." In R. W. Scribner, *Popular Culture and Popular Movements in Reformation Germany*, 257–75. London: Hambledon, 1987.

Segl, Peter. "Heinrich Institoris: Persönlichkeit und literarisches Werk." In *Der Hexenhammer: Entstehung und Umfeld des Malleus maleficarum von 1487*, edited by Peter Segl, 103–26. Cologne: Bohlau, 1988.

Shank, Michael H. "Academic Consulting in Fifteenth-Century Vienna: The Case of Astrology." In *Texts and Contexts in Ancient and Medieval Science: Studies on the Occasion of John E. Murdoch's Seventieth Birthday*, edited by Edith Sylla and Michael McVaugh, 245–70. Brill's Studies in Intellectual History 78. Leiden: Brill, 1997.

———. *"Unless You Believe, You Shall Not Understand": Logic, University, and Society in Late Medieval Vienna*. Princeton, N.J.: Princeton University Press, 1988.

Shapin, Steven. *Never Pure: Historical Studies of Science as If It Was Produced by People with Bodies, Situated in Time, Space, Culture, and Society, and Struggling for Credibility and Authority*. Baltimore: Johns Hopkins University Press, 2010.

Sheehan, Jonathan. "When Was Disenchantment? History and the Secular Age." In *Varieties of Secularism in a Secular Age*, edited by Michael Warner, Jonathan VanAntwerpen, and Craig Calhoun, 217–42. Cambridge, Mass.: Harvard University Press, 2010.

Skemer, Don C. *Binding Words: Textual Amulets in the Middle Ages*. University Park: Pennsylvania State University Press, 2006.

Sluhovsky, Moshe. "Discernment of Difference, the Introspective Subject, and the Birth of Modernity." *Journal of Medieval and Early Modern Studies* 36 (2006): 169–99.

Šmahel, František. "Stärker als der Glaube: Magie, Aberglaube und Zauber in der Epoche des Hussitismus." *Bohemia: Zeitschrift für Geschichte und Kultur der bömischen Länder/A Journal of History and Civilization in East Central Europe* 32 (1991): 316–37.

Smith, Jonathan Z. "Religion, Religions, Religious." In *Critical Terms for Religious Studies*, edited by Mark C. Taylor, 269–84. Chicago: University of Chicago Press, 1998.

Smith, S. A. Introduction. In Smith and Knight, *Religion of Fools?* 7–55.

Smith, S. A., and Alan Knight, eds. *The Religion of Fools? Superstition Past and Present.* Past and Present Supplement 3. Oxford: Oxford University Press, 2008.

Smoller, Laura Ackerman. *History, Prophecy, and the Stars: The Christian Astrology of Pierre d'Ailly, 1350–1420.* Princeton, N.J.: Princeton University Press, 1994.

Sorkin, David. *The Religious Enlightenment: Protestants, Jews, and Catholics from London to Vienna.* Princeton, N.J.: Princeton University Press, 2008.

Steneck, Nicholas H. *Science and Creation in the Middle Ages: Henry of Langenstein (d. 1397) on Genesis.* Notre Dame, Ind.: University of Notre Dame Press, 1976.

Stephens, Walter. *Demon Lovers: Witchcraft, Sex, and the Crisis of Belief.* Chicago: University of Chicago Press, 2002.

Styers, Randall. *Making Magic: Religion, Magic, and Science in the Modern World.* Oxford: Oxford University Press, 2004.

Symes, Carol. "When We Talk about Modernity." *AHR* 116 (2011): 715–26.

Tambiah, Stanley Jeyaraja. *Magic, Science, Religion, and the Scope of Rationality.* Cambridge: Cambridge University Press, 1990.

Taylor, Charles. *A Secular Age.* Cambridge, Mass.: Harvard University Press, 2007.

Taylor, Larissa. *Soldiers of Christ: Preaching in Late Medieval and Reformation France.* New York: Oxford University Press, 1992.

Thomas, Keith. *Religion and the Decline of Magic: Studies in Popular Beliefs in Sixteenth and Seventeenth Century England.* 1971. Reprint, New York: Oxford University Press, 1997.

Thorndike, Lynn. *A History of Magic and Experimental Science.* 8 vols. New York: Macmillan and Columbia University Press, 1923–58.

Treitel, Corinna. *A Science for the Soul: Occultism and the Genesis of the German Modern.* Baltimore: Johns Hopkins University Press, 2004.

Tschacher, Werner. "Der Flug durch die Luft zwischen Illusionstheorie und Realitätsbeweis: Studien zum sog. Kanon Episcopi und zum Hexenflug." *Zeitschrift der Savigny-Stiftung für Rechtsgeschichte* 116, Kan. Abt. 85 (1999): 225–76.

———. *Der Formicarius des Johannes Nider von 1437/38: Studien zu den Anfängen der europäischen Hexenverfolgungen im Spätmittelalter.* Aachen: Shaker Verlag, 2000.

Uhlíř, Zdeněk. "Texte über den Aberglauben in den tschechischen Handschriftensammlungen des Mittelalters." In Wünsch, *Religion und Magie in Ostmitteleuropa,* 85–120.

Utz Tremp, Kathrin. "Predigt und Inquisition: Der Kampf gegen die Häresie in der Stadt Freiburg (erste Hälfte des 15. Jahrhunderts)." In *Mirificus Praedicator: À l'occasion du sixième centenaire du passage de Saint Vincent Ferrier en pays romand,* edited by Paul-Bernard Hodel and Franco Morenzoni, 205–32. Dissertationes Historicae 32. Rome: Istituto Storico Domenicano, 2006.

———. *Von der Häresie zur Hexerei: "Wirkliche" und imaginäre Sekten im Spätmittelalter.* MGH Schriften 59. Hannover: Hahnsche Buchhandlung, 2008.

———. "Witches' Brooms and Magic Ointments: Twenty Years of Witchcraft Research at the University of Lausanne (1989–2009)." *MRW* 5 (2010): 173–87.

Van Balberghe, Émile, and Jean-François Gilmont. "Les théologiens et la 'vauderie' au XVe siècle: À propos des oeuvres de Jean Tinctor à la bibliothèque de l'abbaye de Parc." In *Miscellanea codicologica F. Masai dicata*, edited by Pierre Cockshaw, Monique-Cécile Garand, and Pierre Jodogne, 393–411. Ghent: Story-Scientia, 1979.

Van Engen, John. "The Future of Medieval Church History." *Church History* 71 (2002): 492–522.

———. "Multiple Options: The World of the Fifteenth-Century Church." *Church History* 77 (2008): 257–84.

———. *Sisters and Brothers of the Common Life: The Devotio Moderna and the World of the Later Middle Ages.* Philadelphia: University of Pennsylvania Press, 2008.

Van Liere, Frans. "Witchcraft as Political Tool? John XXII, Hugues Géraud, and Matteo Visconti." *Medieval Perspectives* 16 (2001): 165–73.

Vansteenberghe, E. "Le traité contra Nicolas Colne." *Revue des sciences religieuses* 15 (1935): 532–39.

Veenstra, Jan R. "Cataloguing Superstition: A Paradigmatic Shift in the Art of Knowing the Future." In *Pre-Modern Encyclopaedic Texts: Proceedings of the Second COMERS Congress, Groningen, 1–4 July 1996*, edited by Peter Binkley, 169–80. Brill's Studies in Intellectual History 79. Leiden: Brill, 1997.

———. *Magic and Divination at the Courts of Burgundy and France: Text and Context of Laurens Pignon's "Contre les devineurs" (1411).* Brill's Studies in Intellectual History 83. Leiden: Brill, 1998.

Verdon, Jean. *Les superstitions au Moyen Âge.* Paris: Perrin, 2008.

Verger, Jacques. *Les universités au Moyen Âge.* Paris: Presses Universitaires de France, 1973.

Véronèse, Julien. *L'Ars notoria au Moyen Âge: Introduction et édition critique.* ML 21, Salomon Latinus 1. Florence: SISMEL, 2007.

———. "Le *Contra astrologos imperitos atque nigromanticos* (1395–1396) de Nicolas Eymerich (O. P.): Contexte de rédaction, classification des arts magiques et divinatoires, édition critique partielle." In *Chasses aux sorcières et démonologie: Entre discours et pratiques (XIVe–XVIIe siècles)*, edited by Martine Ostorero, Georg Modestin, and Kathrin Utz Tremp, 271–329. ML 36. Florence: SISMEL, 2010.

———. "Contre la divination et la magie à la cour: Trois traités addressés à des grands aux XIVe et XVe siècles." *Micrologus: Natura, Scienze e Società Medievali—Nature, Sciences and Medieval Societies* 16 (2008): 405–31.

———. "Jean sans Peur et la 'foie secte' des devins: Enjeux et circonstances de la rédaction du traité *Contre les devineurs* (1411) de Laurent Pignon." *Médiévales* 40 (2001): 113–32.

———. "Magic, Theurgy, and Spirituality in the Medieval Ritual of the *Ars notoria*." In Fanger, *Invoking Angels*, 37–78.

Vickers, Brian, ed. *Occult and Scientific Mentalities in the Renaissance.* Cambridge: Cambridge University Press, 1984.

Voltmer, Rita. *Wie der Wächter auf dem Turm: Ein Prediger und seine Stadt; Johannes Geiler von Kaysersberg (1445–1510) und Straßburg.* Beiträge zur Landes- und Kulturgeschichte 4. Trier: Porta Alba, 2005.

Vyse, Stuart A. *Believing in Magic: The Psychology of Superstition.* New York: Oxford University Press, 1997.

Wade, Elizabeth I. "Magic and Superstition in a Fifteenth-Century Student Notebook." *Fifteenth-Century Studies* 28 (2003): 224–41.

Wade-Sirabian, Elizabeth I. "Fifteenth-Century Medicine and Magic at the University of Heidelberg." *Fifteenth-Century Studies* 32 (2007): 191–208.

Walsham, Alexandra. "Recording Superstition in Early Modern Britain: The Origins of Folklore." In Smith and Knight, *Religion of Fools?* 178–206.

———. "The Reformation and 'the Disenchantment of the World' Reassessed." *Historical Journal* 51 (2008): 497–528.

Walz, Dorothea et al., eds. *Zwölf Werke des Heidelberger Theologen und Inquisitors.* Editiones Heidelbergenses 29. Heidelberg: Universitätsverlag C. Winter, 2000.

Wassermann, Dirk. *Dionysius der Kartäuser: Einführung in Werk und Gedankenwelt.* Analecta Cartusiana 133. Salzburg: Institute für Anglistik und Amerikanistik, 1996.

Watkins, C. S. *History and the Supernatural in Medieval England.* Cambridge: Cambridge University Press, 2007.

Weber, Max. *The Protestant Ethic and the Spirit of Capitalism.* Translated by Talcott Parsons. New York: Scribner's, 1958.

———. "Science as a Vocation." In *From Max Weber: Essays in Sociology,* edited and translated by H. H. Gerth and C. Wright Mills, 129–56. New York: Oxford University Press, 1946.

Weiler, A. G. *Heinrich von Gorkum († 1431): Seine Stellung in der Philosophie und der Theologie des Spätmittelalters.* Hilversum, Neth.: P. Brand, 1962.

Weill-Parot, Nicolas. "Astrologie, médecine et art talismanique à Montpellier: Les sceaux astrologiques pseudo-Arnaldiens." In *L'Université de Médecine de Montpellier et son rayonnement (XIIIe–XVe siècles),* edited by Daniel Le Blévec, 157–74. Turnhout: Brepols, 2004.

———. *Les "images astrologiques" au Moyen Âge et à la Renaissance: Spéculations intellectuelles et pratiques magiques (XIIe–XVe siècle).* Sciences, techniques et civilisations du Moyen Âge à l'aube des Lumières 6. Paris: Honoré Champion, 2002.

Wiesner, Merry E. *Working Women in Renaissance Germany.* New Brunswick, N.J.: Rutgers University Press, 1986.

Wilson, Stephen. *The Magical Universe: Everyday Ritual and Magic in Pre-Modern Europe.* London: Hambledon, 2000.

Winroth, Anders. *The Making of Gratian's Decretum.* Cambridge: Cambridge University Press, 2000.

Wood, Ian N. "Pagan Religions and Superstitions East of the Rhine from the Fifth to the Ninth Century." In *After Empire: Towards an Ethnology of Europe's Barbarians,* edited by G. Ausenda, 253–68. Woodbridge, U.K.: Boydell and Brewer, 1995.

Wünsch, Thomas, ed. *Religion und Magie in Ostmitteleuropa: Spielräume theologischer Normierungsprozesse in Spätmittelalter und Früher Neuzeit.* Religions- und Kulturgeschichte in Ostmittel- und Südosteuropa 8. Berlin: LIT Verlag, 2006.

Ziegler, Joseph. *Medicine and Religion c. 1300: The Case of Arnau de Vilanova.* Oxford: Clarendon, 1998.

❧ INDEX